DECISION-MAKING IN INTERNATIONAL CONSTRUCTION ARBITRATION

This book contributes to the empirical understanding of how arbitrators make their decisions on the substance of commercial disputes arising from international construction projects. It is based on in-depth interviews with 28 international construction arbitrators and on the analysis of dozens of international construction arbitration awards. The combined experience of those who participated in the author's research amounted to hundreds of international construction arbitrations (~ 300 cases) in addition to several hundred international commercial arbitrations.

It presents the results of the first and largest research to be undertaken in this area, and it will be useful to arbitration practitioners and scholars and to the wider audience of dispute resolution students, practitioners, and theorists. In turn, the book examines to what extent international arbitrators apply the law as the substantive norm, providing an explanation for that, and then offers insights into whether arbitrators, in fact, lean towards commercial and transnational norms to construe the parties' contract before discussing to what extent international arbitrators take into account fairness considerations to reach their decisions on the merits of the parties' claims. The book also examines to what extent international arbitrators apply mandatory rules of foreign law. Lastly, it provides insight into the effect of arbitrators' background characteristics on their decisions.

Written for arbitration practitioners (arbitrators and legal counsel) and scholars, the book will be useful for both experienced arbitrators and those starting their arbitration career or studying for their arbitration qualification. It will also be useful for project professionals involved in contract management and dispute resolution.

Dr Haytham Besaiso is a senior lecturer in project management at the Cardiff School of Management. He teaches commercial project management, strategic project management, and project finance modules in the MSc Project Management programme. Haytham's research interests focus on the commercial aspects of project-based work, such as project procurement management, contract management, and alternative dispute resolution. He aims to develop a niche specialism in the area of contracting and how commercial contract law relates to the project work in a commercial context.

PRACTICAL LEGAL GUIDES FOR CONSTRUCTION
AND TECHNOLOGY PROJECTS

Series Editor: Donald Charrett

The books in this series provide lawyers and construction professionals with the relevant knowledge, resources and practical guidance to understand the contemporary construction industry and the law necessary to achieve successful outcomes for construction projects. The topics covered include front-end issues such as project procurement, the production, negotiation and administration of contracts, and the avoidance of disputes, as well as backend issues such as taking part in, managing or resolving disputes. The series aims to keep abreast of the technologies that have increasing impact in changing traditional ways of working, contracting and resolving disputes.

FIDIC CONTRACTS IN ASIA PACIFIC
A Practical Guide to Application
Donald Charrett

CONTRACTS FOR CONSTRUCTION AND ENGINEERING PROJECTS
Second Edition
Donald Charrett

CONTRACTS FOR INFRASTRUCTURE PROJECTS
An International Guide to Application
Donald Charrett

FIDIC CONTRACTS IN EUROPE
A Practical Guide to Application
Donald Charrett

FIDIC CONTRACTS IN THE AMERICAS
A Practical Guide to Application
Donald Charrett

FIDIC CONTRACTS IN AFRICA AND THE MIDDLE EAST
A Practical Guide to Application
Donald Charrett

DECISION-MAKING IN INTERNATIONAL CONSTRUCTION ARBITRATION
Haytham Besaiso

For more information, please visit: www.routledge.com/Practical-Legal-Guides-for-Construction-and-Technology-Projects/book-series/PLGCTP

DECISION-MAKING IN INTERNATIONAL CONSTRUCTION ARBITRATION

HAYTHAM BESAISO

informa law
from Routledge

Designed cover image: Getty

First published 2024
by Informa Law from Routledge
4 Park Square, Milton Park, Abingdon, Oxon OX14 4RN

and by Informa Law from Routledge
605 Third Avenue, New York, NY 10158

Informa Law from Routledge is an imprint of the Taylor & Francis Group, an informa business

British Library Cataloguing-in-Publication Data
A catalogue record for this book is available from the British Library

ISBN: 9781032299204 (hbk)
ISBN: 9781032299228 (pbk)
ISBN: 9781003302728 (ebk)

DOI: 10.4324/b22975

Typeset in Times New Roman
by Deanta Global Publishing Services, Chennai, India

To Aishe, Maryam and Odai

CONTENTS

PREFACE

Much has been written and said about international commercial arbitration. These publications usually focus on conceptual or procedural aspects. There is a paucity of literature on international construction arbitration, a subset of international commercial arbitration that is worth special treatment, and how international arbitrators make their substantive decisions.

International construction arbitration has the largest representation in the growing field of international commercial arbitration. Nowadays, arbitration is the default dispute resolution method in the international construction sector. The significance of arbitration to the growth or even to the existence of cross-border construction activities cannot be overstated. The key role arbitration plays has given rise to a pressing need to understand how arbitrators make their decisions on these multi-billion international construction disputes. Several leading arbitration scholars and practitioners voiced their concerns about this lack of knowledge and demanded more attention to this area of enquiry. Nevertheless, this vital area of intellect has received scant attention in the literature.

This book fills the gap in knowledge concerning this area. This book aims to answer a question that many entrants to the field, as well as veterans of international arbitration, ask during the course of their arbitration career: how do arbitrators decide on the substance of disputes arising from international construction contracts? In fact, this was a question that lingered in my mind for years as a project manager and a contract manager in charge of claims and dispute resolution. In the instances when disputes were heading to arbitration, I kept wondering how arbitrators would decide. In particular, I was intrigued by several questions concerning the extent to which arbitrators adhere to the terms of the parties' contract, the impact of the governing law, and arbitrators' backgrounds and personal views on the construction of the contract. Also, as most construction contracts I dealt with used FIDIC or FIDIC-derived conditions of contract, I found myself on certain occasions referring to commentaries and courts' decisions related to FIDIC conditions that were produced in different parts of the world. On those occasions, it was unclear how receptive arbitrators would be to such arguments that were based on foreign law. My curiosity and the lack of answers to my questions motivated me to do research and pursue a doctoral journey to find the answers. This book builds on the research I did as part of my doctorate at the University of Manchester and the follow-up work to expand its coverage of the subject.

This book provides empirical insight into the black box of arbitral decision-making on the substance of international construction disputes. In particular, it examines 'how' arbitrators apply certain substantive norms, which are sometimes incompatible, to the parties' dispute in order to reach their decision, and 'why' they do so. This book follows an inductive theory-building sociological approach. It adopts the guidelines of the constructivist-grounded theory. To gather the data necessary for theory-building, the author undertook

28 semi-structured interviews with international construction arbitrators. The interviews were undertaken face to face in London, Toronto, and Dubai, and via Skype or telephone conference. The interview data are supplemented with international construction arbitration awards.

This book is presented in nine chapters. Chapter 1 introduces the reader to the book. It reviews scholarly and professional literature that is relevant to the inquiry and establishes that the knowledge of arbitral decision-making is truly lacking. Chapter 2 provides a background to international construction arbitration and steers the conversation towards arbitral decision-making. The following six chapters discuss specific concepts or substantive norms that are relevant to the arbitral decision-making process, such as the effect of the substantive law, trade usages and customs, transnational legal norms, fairness considerations, mandatory rules of foreign law, and the arbitrator's background.

This book is relevant to new entrants to the field of international construction arbitration as well as practitioners, whether in-house counsel or arbitrators. The problem with arbitration is that it is private and confidential. Hence, arbitrators' knowledge of how their fellow arbitrators make their decisions is limited. It is also relevant to the wide range of participants in international construction projects, such as financiers, owners, engineers, project leaders, project managers, contracts managers, and dispute resolvers (e.g., mediators and adjudicators).

I hope you enjoy reading this book.

Haytham Besaiso
Cardiff, UK

ACKNOWLEDGEMENT

This work could not have been accomplished without the help and support of many people to whom I am thankful and appreciative.

This book is based on my doctoral thesis, and, hence, it would not be possible without the kind and generous support I received from many people during my doctorate journey. I wish to express sincere gratitude to my former doctoral supervisor, Peter Fenn, for his great guidance and support. I am thankful to the School of Mechanical Aerospace and Civil Engineering at the University of Manchester for awarding me the first 'Management of Projects Studentship', which enabled me to do the main research underpinning this book. I am grateful for the recognition I received for my work from a number of institutions during my doctorate. In particular, I am honoured to have received the Society of Construction Arbitrators' Norman Royce Prize in 2017 and the Worshipful Company of Arbitrators' Travelling Scholarship in 2017. I am also grateful for the recognition I received from the University of Manchester as 'being an exceptional and dedicated' researcher in 2018.

I am immensely conscious of, and thankful for, the 28 international construction arbitrators who so graciously agreed to participate in my research. It is a pity that I cannot mention the names of those great men and women who were kind and generous to give me some of their time despite their extremely busy schedules. Without them, the completion of this work would not have been possible.

From the depths of my heart, I am grateful to my wife for her immense patience with my disturbed work–life balance.

ABBREVIATIONS

AAA	American Arbitration Association
ADR	Alternative Dispute Resolution
CRCICA	The Cairo Regional Centre for International Commercial Arbitration
DIAC	Dubai International Arbitration Centre
EOT	Extension of Time
FIDIC	Fédération Internationale des Ingénieurs-Conseils (International Federation of Consulting Engineers)
HKIAC	Hong Kong International Arbitration Centre
IBA	International Bar Association
ICC	International Chamber of Commerce
ICDR	International Center for Dispute Resolution (the international division of the AAA)
ICE	Institution of Civil Engineers
ICL	International Construction Law
ICLR	International Construction Law Review
JCT	Joint Contracts Tribunal
LAD	Liquidated Damages
LCIA	London Court of International Arbitration
NEW YORK CONVENTION	United Nations Convention on the Recognition and Enforcement of Foreign Arbitral Awards (1958)
RIBA	Royal Institute of British Architects
SIAC	Singapore International Arbitration Centre
UNCITRAL	UN Commission on International Trade Law
UNCITRAL MODEL LAW	The UNCITRAL Model Law on International Commercial Arbitration (1985, with amendments adopted in 2006)
UNIDROIT	The International Institute for the Unification of Private Law
UNIDROIT PRINCIPLES	UNIDROIT Principles of International Commercial Contracts (2006)

CHAPTER 1

Introduction

1.1 Introduction

This chapter sets the scene and explains the need for this book. It highlights its importance and how it contributes to our empirical knowledge of how international construction arbitrators make their decisions on the substance of disputes arising from international construction projects. It demarcates the book's focus and scope. Then, this chapter discusses the methodology of the research underpinning this book. Finally, it introduces the overall structure of the book.

1.2 Background

The impact of globalisation on modern-day commerce is enormous. It has led to significant growth in cross-border commercial activities, including construction works. Construction works have been transformed from being a national commercial undertaking to also being a transnational commercial enterprise (Molineaux, 1997). Cross-border construction projects help in building modern infrastructure (transport, water supply, sewerage, electricity, etc.) in less developed countries lacking the technological resources and sometimes the financial resources (Hernandez-Garcia, 2009). In today's globalised world, international construction is an important contributor to the world's trade and commerce (Charrett, 2012).

This important cross-border commercial activity, which involves tremendous amounts of money at stake, could not function without enforceable contracts. Commercial contracts that will be honoured and enforced are fundamental for international trade, including international construction (Charrett, 2012).

However, the world lacks transnational commercial courts or technology and construction courts of mandatory jurisdiction. Also, each party will typically resist provisions providing for litigation in the other party's national courts because of fear of bias (Nazzini, 2018). Further, state entities, which are often party to an international construction contract, do not accept to subject themselves to the jurisdiction of a foreign national court due to sovereignty issues (Thompson, 1977).

International arbitration provides the solution to these problems and provides indispensable assurance for the contracting parties that their contracts will be enforced (Park, 2009). In this respect, the importance of arbitration to international construction cannot be overstated. It can be argued that if this international private justice system had not existed, international construction contracts would have been concluded at significantly higher prices to reflect the higher risks (Park, 2009; Charrett, 2012) or even would have been a rare occurrence. The real effect, however, seems to be that international arbitration has fuelled the growth of international construction (Charrett, 2012).

DOI: 10.4324/b22975-1

The relationship between international arbitration and international construction seems to be far from a one-way causal relationship. The boom in international construction projects (Hernandez-Garcia, 2009) and the rise of international construction arbitrations in the second half of the 20th century (Hoffmann, 1989) appear to have a causal loop relationship. The large-scale petrodollar international construction projects of the 1970s and 1980s in the Arab world led to a series of high-profile arbitrations. After years of suspicion and mistrust, the success of these gigantic arbitrations laid the foundation for the acceptance of international commercial arbitration as an international private justice system (Dezalay and Garth, 1998). Since then, arbitration has been fuelling the growth of international construction projects. This growth is, in part, a result of the assurance arbitration offers to multinational construction companies that their disputes will be decided in a neutral forum that delivers an enforceable award (Hernandez-Garcia, 2009). The neutrality of the forum for dispute resolution and the enforceability of the award make arbitration the fundamental and preferred dispute resolution technique for cross-border disputes in the construction industry (Friedland and Mistelis, 2015). A study undertaken by the School of International Arbitration at the Queen Mary University of London and sponsored by PricewaterhouseCoopers found that arbitration's popularity varies across industries. In the construction industry, international arbitration was overwhelmingly selected as the preferred dispute resolution method (Lagerberg and Mistelis, 2013).

The importance of arbitration to the construction sector, or vice versa, is also evident from the largest representation the construction industry has in international commercial arbitration in terms of both the number and the size of disputes submitted to arbitration. The caseload statistics of the world's main arbitration institutions show that the number of commercial disputes being referred to international arbitration is rising (Drahozal and Naimark, 2005; Franck et al., 2017). The statistical evidence shows that thousands of commercial disputes are submitted annually to some of the major international arbitral institutions (Drahozal and Naimark, 2005; Franck et al., 2017), a great share of which arise from construction and civil engineering contracts (Drahozal and Ware, 2010).

The ICC, the leading arbitration institution in the world, was the main theatre of the gigantic construction arbitrations arising from the construction boom in the Arab countries in the 1970s and 1980s. In the 1970s, international construction arbitration represented 30% of the commercial disputes referred to the ICC Court of Arbitration (Thompson, 1977). In the 1980s, construction disputes represented more than 20% of the commercial cases submitted to ICC arbitration each year (Seppala, 1998). Recent records show that construction arbitration has maintained its position at the top. In 2012, construction and engineering cases comprised 17% of all cases submitted to the ICC (Webster and Buhler, 2014). Since 2017, the ICC has made its annual statistical reports available to the public free of charge (ICC, 2018). In 2017, 2018, 2019, and 2020, construction and engineering cases accounted for almost 23% (ICC, 2018), 27% (ICC, 2019), 20% (ICC, 2020), and 24% (ICC, 2021) of the cases, respectively.

The caseload statistics of the London Court of International Arbitration (LCIA) show that around 16% of the arbitrations that proceeded under the LCIA Rules in 2016 were related to construction and infrastructure projects (LCIA, 2017). However, in the most recent years, the construction and infrastructure cases dropped to 10% or less of the total cases (LCIA, 2018; LCIA, 2019; LCIA, 2020; LCIA, 2021).

The caseload statistics of the Hong Kong International Arbitration Centre (HKIAC) indicate a high representation of construction cases. In the period between its inauguration in 1985 and 2002, HKIAC received 2,764 cases, of which 1,144 were construction cases (i.e., more than 40% of the cases) (Moser and Cheng, 2004). However, this declined in the most recent years to almost 19% of the cases in 2016 and 2017, 14% of the cases in 2018, 15% of the cases in 2019, 11% of the cases in 2020, and 9% of the cases in 2021 (HKIAC, 2022).

According to the Cairo Regional Centre for International Commercial Arbitration (CRCICA), construction disputes represented the highest proportion of commercial disputes referred to the centre: 25% of the cases in 2015 and 2016, 32% of the cases in 2017, 25% of the cases in 2018, 32% of the cases in 2020, and 17% of the cases in 2021 (CRCICA, 2022). Construction disputes also tend to have the greatest sums. The largest dispute referred to the centre in 2015 (~ $1 billion) arose from a construction contract (CRCICA, 2016). Earlier statistics, reported by El-adaway, Ezeldin, and Yates (2009), show that more than 30% of the disputes referred to arbitration under the auspices of CRCICA between 2000 and 2006 were construction disputes.

Although the percentage of construction cases fluctuates over time, overall, it seems that construction arbitrations have the highest representation. In addition to its highest representation in terms of the number of cases submitted to institutional arbitration, it is notable that international construction arbitration involves the largest amounts of claims, which can run into billions of dollars or pounds (Flood and Caiger, 1993).

1.3 The need for this book

As international construction arbitration expands and has become, indeed, the default and fundamental dispute resolution method (Friedland and Mistelis, 2015), contracting parties and their counsel have become more concerned about the substantive norms arbitrators apply to decide their disputes (Schneider, 2012; Turner, 2005; Brekoulakis, 2013).

Understanding how arbitrators decide and the substantive norms they rely on to reach their decisions helps in the realisation of a justice system that produces predictable outcomes. The predictability of arbitration outcomes is fundamental to the performance of international construction as a significant cross-border economic activity and to the survival of international arbitration itself. Interestingly, when international arbitration was still in its infancy, Domke (1965) (cited in Karton, 2012a) pronounced the 'predictability of the result' as the main challenge facing international arbitration. This challenge is also evident in some scholars' belief that international arbitrators are less predictable in their decisions than national judges (Gaillard and Savage, 1999).

A better understanding of arbitral decision-making also assists the parties in contract negotiation and drafting, enables advocates to provide credible legal advice to make the arbitrate/no arbitrate decision, and helps the parties to settle their disputes to the predictable outcome and maintain their business relationship (Karton, 2012a; Ossman, 2003; Karton, 2013; Park, 2015). The predictability of arbitration outcomes is expected to minimise the transaction cost, which is beneficial to all parties involved in international construction contracting.

A British solicitor based in Dubai, who was interviewed by the author, described the problem regarding the unpredictability of arbitration outcomes as follows:

> In international arbitration, decisions are typically confidential. So it is difficult to work out how a particular arbitrator may decide a case, and this adds an element of uncertainty.

A theory of arbitral decision-making can also assist parties to make more informed decisions regarding what arbitration rules to select and what arbitrators to appoint (Karton, 2013). This book illustrates how international arbitrators interpret certain arbitration rules in a way that affects their substantive decisions (e.g., rules regarding trade usages) (see Chapter 4). It also discusses in an entire chapter how arbitration outcomes may depend on the characteristics of the arbitrator making the decision (see Chapter 8).

A further reason for the parties' need to understand how arbitrators decide is that, in the vast majority of jurisdictions, arbitration awards are final and binding and the parties have no opportunity to appeal based on the decision on the merits (Andrews, 2016; Blackaby et al., 2015; Natanson, 2013; Park, 2010).

International arbitrators themselves would also benefit from a greater understanding of their fellow arbitrators' approach to substantive decision-making (Schneider, 2012; Drahozal, 2003). Many international arbitrators told the author that they could articulate how they make their decisions, but they have little knowledge of how other arbitrators decide. This understanding would promote consistency in arbitral decision-making, which underpins the legitimacy of arbitration.

Given all these reasons, and the central role arbitrators play in international trade and commerce, including in international construction, it is necessary to understand how arbitrators decide. This is vital to maintain the legitimacy of arbitration (Franck et al., 2017) and to ensure the sustainability and growth of international construction projects and international construction arbitration.

However, the author's review of relevant literature finds that arbitral decision-making has received scant attention from scholars, with most attention being given to procedural and conceptual matters. This finding has support from leading arbitration scholars and practitioners, as the remaining part of this section will show.

In addition, most literature related to arbitral decision-making is theoretical (i.e., non-empirical), which involves debates on how arbitrators should decide rather than how arbitrators do, in fact, decide. The ongoing debate reflects a lack of consensus within the arbitration community on the 'appropriate' substantive norms that should underpin the reasoning of arbitrators and guide them to the 'right' solution. Accordingly, the extant literature reveals that arbitral decision-making lacks a solid theoretical foundation (see Section 2.8).

Further, the author's review of relevant literature finds that empirical literature is lacking. There are two reasons for the lack of empirical knowledge concerning arbitral decision-making.

The first reason for the lack of empirical knowledge seems to be the inherent privacy and confidentiality of arbitration proceedings and awards. Unlike court judgements, the resolution of construction disputes via arbitration means that there is a shortage of reported opinions in the form of published or accessible reasoned awards. It is impossible to tell, without publications of awards, whether international arbitrators apply the substantive law in a similar manner to national judges (Karton, 2012a). The publication of arbitral awards would permit insight into the secretive and mysterious process of arbitral decision-making. However, unfortunately, the arbitration system fails to bring to light arbitrators' decisions, which could provide access to how these private judges – the arbitrators – make their decisions (Weidemaier, 2009; Karton, 2012a).

The proportion of published international commercial arbitral awards remains tremendously small but even those awards that manage to 'see the light' are only available in extract or sanitised form most of the time (Schneider, 2012; Karton, 2013; Moloo and King, 2014; Drahozal, 2005). Even if arbitral awards are not in a summarised or redacted form, there are two limitations to relying on them as a source of data.

First, arbitral awards are usually insufficiently detailed. As such, it becomes difficult to tell how arbitrators decide cases (Drahozal, 2000; Turner, 2005). In this regard, Turner (2005, p. 110) noted:

> Too many award-drafters ... write the foregoing background, and what follows, at excessive length, ... but all too little as to how and why the arbitrator has reached a conclusion ... if a reasoned award is required... a separate 'reasons' section must clearly demonstrate those reasons. It is inappropriate to set out all the reasoning.

Second, the reasons provided in the award may not reflect the reasoning underpinning the decision arrived (Turner, 2005). In other words, the stated reasons may not be the actual reasons that led to the decision (Drahozal, 2000). Lord Mansfield is believed to have made such a distinction between the decision and the justification of that decision around 200 years ago (Bishop, 2012).

These difficulties restrict doctrinal research that is characterised by the study of legal texts or, in this context, arbitration awards, in order to reveal the rules and principles that govern the decision-making on the merits of the case (Karton, 2013), or at least used to justify the awards.

The second reason for the lack of empirical knowledge on how arbitrators make their decisions is the scarcity of empirical research. This has allowed anecdotes to constitute the main part of knowledge in this area with little structured empirical evidence to justify it.

Some scholars (Schultz, 2015; Stipanowich and Ulrich, 2014; Karton, 2013) documented the challenge of the scarcity of primary data to undertake empirical research on arbitral decision-making. Then, they followed different methodologies to address the knowledge gap.

At the beginning of his article, Schultz (2015) said:

> We often lack the empirical data to conduct such empirical investigations. Yet, we should not hold back our understanding of arbitral decision-making while we wait for such data to become available. It clearly is more helpful for the advancement of knowledge to engage in satisficing, rather than pursuing optimality. In this context, this means accepting validation by rational assent ... instead of being content with nothing short of empirical verification.

Then, he followed a non-empirical legal-realist approach to shed some light on what the case might be, as opposed to what the case actually is.

The author's review of extant literature found no empirical study that specifically investigates arbitral decision-making on international construction disputes. However, there is one study that embraced empiricist methodologies of the social sciences to offer insight into how international commercial arbitrators make their decisions on the merits of disputants' claims. This study was undertaken by Karton (2010, 2012b, 2013, 2015) and examined international commercial arbitrators' approaches to contractual interpretation. At the outset of his work, Karton (2012b) documented his observation regarding the neglect of arbitral decision-making in most writings on international commercial arbitration:

> The last several years have produced an explosion of academic treatments of international commercial arbitration. However, the overwhelming majority of this literature considers jurisdictional and procedural matters… little is known about the decisions of international arbitrators on the merits of international commercial disputes.

One of the earliest calls in the literature to steer away from the dominant procedural writings to try to explore arbitral decision-making was made by the former president of the American Arbitration Association, Robert Coulson:

> In view of the increasing importance of arbitration, it is surprising how little attention has been focused upon exactly how arbitrators make decisions.
>
> *(Coulson, 1989, p. 1)*

> Most studies of arbitration are devoted to discussions about the applicable law or the various procedural rules. It seems far more important to try to analyse how and why arbitrators make up their minds.
>
> *(Coulson, 1990, p. 1)*

Two decades later, Blackaby et al. (2009) noted that the abundant writings in the field did not pay attention to arbitral decision-making:

> In all that is written and said about arbitration–and nowadays a great deal is written and said–there is very little about how a tribunal of arbitrators goes about reaching its decision.

The critique of the little attention paid to arbitral decision-making still holds true. Schneider (2012, p.1), the former president of the Swiss Arbitration Association, acknowledges that the question of how arbitrators reach their decisions still persists and endures:

> The question of how arbitral tribunals' decisions are reached – the process itself – is shrouded in darkness. The little that is known about arbitral decision-making remains anecdotal.

In recognition of the importance of the topic and the necessity to fill this gap in knowledge, the Swiss Arbitration Association made arbitral decision-making the subject of its annual conference in 2013 in order to gather and share some of the experiences of a number of arbitration practitioners (Schneider, 2012).

The author's research finds that the foregoing statements still hold true. The successive calls to shift focus to the substantive aspects of arbitral decision-making have not been responded to and the questions remain substantially unanswered. The findings of the literature search (see Section 2.8), show that arbitral decision-making lacks solid theoretical as well as empirical foundations. The lack of a solid theoretical foundation is a result of the lack of consensus on the underlying normative standards that should guide arbitral decision-making. The lack of a solid empirical foundation results from the inherent privacy and confidentiality of arbitration proceedings and awards as well as the shortage of empirical research. The sparse quantitative and doctrinal studies that are related to international construction arbitration decision-making have methodological drawbacks and give inconclusive answers (see Section 2.8).

Therefore, based on all the reasons set out earlier, this book follows an empirical approach that draws on interpretivism, as the underlying epistemology, and interviews, as the primary data collection method, in order to empirically contribute towards a theory of decision-making in international construction arbitration.

1.4 The book's focus

This book responds to successive calls by the arbitration community for more empirical research that offers evidence-based insight into arbitral decision-making. It proposes an arbitral decision-making conceptual framework that identifies the substantive norms international arbitrators apply, assesses the weight or effect arbitrators give to these norms, and explains the reasons for their decision-making approaches and preferences. The conceptual framework is intended to constitute a significant contribution towards developing a theory of international construction arbitration decision-making.

This book is concerned with the following general question: 'how do international construction arbitrators make their decisions on the substance of construction disputes?'

To be more specific, this book seeks to answer the following question: 'What are the substantive norms that influence arbitrators' decisions on the substance of international construction disputes, and why do arbitrators follow these norms?'. It is descriptive and explanatory in nature.

The main question unfolds to the following subquestions:

1. To what extent do substantive law norms influence arbitral decision-making, and what is the rationale for this?
2. To what extent do commercial norms influence arbitral decision-making, and what is the rationale for this?
3. To what extent do 'international construction law' norms influence arbitral decision-making, and what is the rationale for this?
4. To what extent do international arbitrators follow their own sense of fairness to arrive at their decisions, and what is the rationale for this?
5. To what extent do foreign mandatory rules of law influence arbitral decision-making, and what is the rationale for this?
6. To what extent do the background characteristics of international arbitrators influence their substantive decision-making?

Those sub-questions shape the structure of this book. While Chapter 2 provides the reader with a brief introduction to the field of international construction arbitration and the debate and lack of certainty regarding arbitral decision-making, the remaining chapters address the above sub-questions in turn.

1.5 The book's scope

As the topic concerning arbitral decision-making is vast, it is important to delineate the boundaries of this book. This section clarifies what this book is not about, which is a lot, and, hence, what it does not attempt to address.

First, arbitral decisions can be examined from four viewpoints: (1) normative (asking how decisions ought to be made according to a value position), (2) prescriptive (asking how better decisions might be made), (3) descriptive (asking how decisions are made) (Ossman, 2003), and (4) explanatory (asking why decisions are made in a particular way). This book does not intend to engage with the debate concerning how arbitrators should decide, which is a question of philosophy rather than epistemology. This book provides descriptive and explanatory accounts of substantive decision-making in international construction arbitration.

Second, as a further confinement, this book does not inquire into the effect of the tripartite dynamic on decision-making. The use of three-member tribunals, which is common in international arbitration, adds an extra layer of complexity to arbitral decision-making. This additional dimension involves deliberation and dynamic interaction between the tribunal members to agree on the outcome of a dispute (Berger and Schneider, 2014; Blackaby et al., 2009). This book is concerned with how arbitrators make their decisions individually as sole arbitrators or panel members.

Third, this book does not attempt to venture into the domain of psychology and cognitive science to inquire about certain aspects of arbitral decision-making. Few studies have attempted to do so in international arbitration (e.g. Diamond, 2003; Drahozal, 2004) in parallel to similar research on judicial decision-making (e.g. Guthrie, Rachlinski, and Wistrich, 2007; Klein and Mitchell, 2010; Tumonis, Šavelskis, and Žalytė, 2013). The empirical work underpinning this book is positioned in the field of social science and, hence, aims to understand how arbitrators, as social actors functioning in a social system, make their decisions.

Fourth, except for a small number of references to domestic construction arbitration, this book is specifically concerned with international construction arbitration. The two environments are largely different, and, hence, the key arguments of this book neither draw upon evidence from domestic construction arbitration nor intend to be applicable and transferable to domestic contexts.

Fifth, although construction contracts could qualify as investment agreements (Uff, 2014; Uff and Uff, 2010; Nazzini, 2018), or administrative contracts (Ismail, 2016; Atallah, 2005), they are essentially commercial contracts. As such, this book deals with arbitrations of disputes arising from commercial contracts concluded between commercial entities or between commercial and non-commercial (e.g., government) entities. Commercial contracts and disputes are subject to general rules of contract law. Administrative contracts and investment arbitrations involve states that are bound to take care of the public interest and therefore distinct rules of law could apply (Ismail, 2016; Karton, 2013). The origin of commercial arbitration is often traced back to the resolution of commercial disputes between merchants in the Middle Ages. Investment arbitration is viewed as markedly different from commercial arbitration (Kläger, 2011). Accordingly, this book treats international construction arbitration as a subset of international commercial arbitration and excludes from consideration investment arbitrations.

Sixth, notwithstanding falling into the category of commercial arbitration, construction arbitration is distinct and could have different characteristics from other commercial sectors' arbitrations, as discussed in Section 2.3. As such, discussions of certain classes of international commercial arbitration that have their own specialty norms, such as commodities arbitration (Karton, 2013), are beyond the scope of this book.

To state what could be obvious, this book excludes literature on decision-making in non-commercial arbitration, such as labour arbitration, employment arbitration, and sports arbitration (Levin, 1997).

1.6 Terminological choices

Mustill (2014) notes that the use of the word 'arbitration' in a single form is a misnomer because this field is vast, and arbitration, as a dispute resolution method, is used in a wide spectrum of diverse fields.

Therefore, to avoid confusion, a reference in this book to arbitration or arbitrator denotes a reference to international construction arbitration or international commercial arbitration as understood from the context and unless explicitly provided otherwise (e.g., the text expressly refers to domestic commercial or construction arbitration).

Accordingly, the terms 'arbitration' or 'arbitrator', unless accompanied with specific adjectives, should be construed narrowly to exclude all different types of arbitration, such as investment arbitration or labour arbitration.

1.7 Methodology

1.7.1 Research approach

The purpose of this section is to present the methodological aspects of the empirical work underlying this book. As this book is aimed primarily at professionals, it does not discuss the philosophical aspects of the research methodology that underpins this work, such as the nature of knowledge (i.e., ontology) and the manner of its production (i.e., epistemology). This section briefly explains the research strategy, the research approach, the data collection methods, and the sources of data that were used in this work.

This book aims to develop a deeper understanding of 'how' arbitrators make their substantive decisions and 'why' they decide in a particular manner. To be able to achieve the aim of providing a description and an explanation of arbitral decision-making, the research underlying this book uses the qualitative approach. The qualitative approach has allowed the author to gain access to arbitrators' perspectives and perceptions as to how they give meaning to their experiences in arbitrating disputes (i.e., how they think they make decisions). It has also enabled him to acquire insight into the reasons (in the form of motivations, intentions, role perception, or external institutional factors) that make arbitrators decide in the manner they do. This understanding makes it possible to conceptualise arbitrators' approaches to deciding disputes.

A quantitative approach lacks the descriptive and explanatory power to study human constructs relating to a social process such as arbitral decision-making. It fails to represent the human experience by reducing it to a numerical form. Likert-type or Yes/No questionnaires would not be appropriate as this would require the development of hypotheses prior to data gathering. As there are few preexisting studies relevant to substantive decision-making in international construction arbitration, induction and theorem development rather than testing is required.

Theory development requires inductivism and an exploratory approach. Inductive reasoning (also called inductive logic or inductive inference) moves from the more specific to the more general. As such, it begins with specific observations and moves towards developing broad generalisations (Naoum, 2007; Saunders, Lewis, and Thornhill, 2012). The conclusions reached by inductive reasoning may turn out to be false even if all of the premises or observations are true because the conclusions are built on a limited number of cases. This kind of reasoning is fallible and does not guarantee the truth of the conclusion (Sinnott-Armstrong, 2017). Despite its flaw, the inductive approach is rational in its reasoning, and it is still an effective way of making inferences and likely conclusions, particularly in the interpretive paradigm that seeks meanings and understandings of reality as opposed to generalisation to the entire population.

1.7.2 Research strategy

The research underpinning this book used 'grounded theory' as the research strategy. Grounded theory is beneficial when there is not much information about the social phenomenon under investigation (Auerbach and Silverstein, 2003). The review of the literature demonstrates that there is little understanding of how international construction arbitrators make their decisions. Therefore, due to the exploratory nature of this research, the grounded theory strategy was selected. This strategy enables building a theory that is grounded in qualitative data (arbitrators' statements and perceptions on how they make their decisions) (Glaser and Strauss, 1967).

The grounded theory approach requires the research to start with no preconceived ideas or hypotheses (Glaser and Strauss, 1967). The research underpinning this book started with a general question, which was 'how do international construction arbitrators make their decisions on the substance of construction disputes?'. As long as the researcher does not start the investigation with a preconceived hypothesis, but with a generic question, then the research conforms to grounded theory methodological requirements (Corbin and Strauss, 2015; Strauss and Corbin, 1998).

1.7.3 Sources of data

This book relies on data gathered from three sources, which are explained in the following subsections.

1.7.3.1 Semi-structured interviews

The author undertook 28 semi-structured interviews to gather rich primary data on arbitrators' perceptions of their decision-making approach. The interview method was the main data collection method. The semi-structured nature of interviews allows the interviewer to change the wording of questions, alter the order of questions, skip questions, or add questions depending on what happens in the interview (Saunders, Lewis, and Thornhill, 2009). As such, the interviews included both a list of pre-defined open-ended questions (see Appendix A) in addition to new questions the interviewer raised in response to emerging themes. These characteristics of semi-structured open-question interviews fit grounded theory's goals of discovery.

The sampling method that has been used to select participants in the research underpinning this book is theoretical sampling. Theoretical sampling is associated with the grounded theory approach. It involves the purposeful selection of a sample (participants with specific characteristics) in the initial stages (Goulding, 2002). Like purposive sampling, it involves selecting people who have specific knowledge and expertise relevant to the research question (Naoum, 2012). As this book intends to provide insight into how arbitrators make their decisions, the participants must have the experience relevant to the research question to be able to give worthy information. Hence, the main inclusion criterion for recruiting participants was 'arbitrators who have an experience in international construction arbitration'.

The qualified arbitrators, who satisfy the selection requirements, were identified and their contact information was obtained from lists of leading arbitration practitioners published by 'Who's Who Legal' (www.whoswholegal.com) as well as 'Chambers and Partners' (www.chambersandpartners.com). The author also searched the websites of various chambers and law firms as well as arbitration institutions and forums that make arbitrators' profiles available. These include the websites of the International Arbitration Institute (www.iaiparis.com), the Swiss Arbitration Association (https://profiles.arbitration-ch.org), the German Arbitration Institute (DIS) (http://www.dis-arb.de), and the Canadian-based arbitration place (www.arbitrationplace.com). Some interviewees were identified via personal contact, LinkedIn, or from their publications. There are other sources to identify international arbitrators, such as 'The Roster of International Arbitrators', updated in 2017 and that contains information about more than 1,200 international arbitrators (Smit and Mistelis, 2017).

In fact, finding international construction arbitrators, specifically the big names, was an unexpectedly easy task. International arbitrators are keen to maintain a strong online presence and visibility on different platforms, which is important to be approached and recruited by parties in dispute. Many arbitrators have personal web pages, LinkedIn profiles, and detailed resumes available at their chambers or law firms' websites or arbitration institutions' lists. Many of them also write significantly in academic journals, conferences, professional outlets, and blogs.

The author interviewed 28 international construction arbitrators. They are nationals of the following countries (Canada, United States, United Kingdom, Ireland, Australia, Denmark, Germany, Switzerland, Egypt, Lebanon, and Palestine). Table 1.1 shows the interviewees' countries of nationality:

Although the international arbitrators the author interviewed come from a small number of countries, they practice in a wide range of jurisdictions, and they were trained in various legal systems. They sit in major international or regional arbitration institutions, such as ICC, LCIA, SIAC, HIAC, AAA/ ICDR, DIAC, and CRCICA. As such, most major trading regions and, in particular, major hubs for international construction are represented.

Few interviewees work as full-time arbitrators. Most of the interviewees work as counsel and/or academics and receive arbitration appointments. Some of them also act as adjudicators, expert witnesses, or mediators in domestic or international disputes. Two interviewees are national court judges at the commercial court division in their respective countries and a third was a judge at the Technology and Construction Court in England.

Table 1.1 The nationalities of international arbitrators interviewed by the author

Country of nationality	No. of interviewees
United Kingdom	6
Canada	5
United States	3
Ireland	1
Australia	2
Switzerland	4
Germany	1
Denmark	1
Egypt	3
Lebanon	1
Palestine	1

Most interviewees are chartered arbitrators. The rest are fellows or members of the Charted Institute of Arbitrators. Some of them are presidents or former presidents of various arbitration institutions. A number of interviewees are listed as 'most in-demand arbitrators' and/or appear on 'Who's Who in Arbitration' and 'Who's Who in Construction' and/or are recognised by 'Legal 500' and 'Chambers & Partners' as leaders in the field of international construction arbitration. Also, some interviewees have been named among the best international construction lawyers, American construction lawyers, or Canadian construction lawyers by various arbitration and professional bodies.

The interviewees range in age from their late thirties to their early eighties. As such, some of them have extensive arbitration experience while others began to receive appointments as international arbitrators only in recent years. Finding an appropriate measure of experience is problematic. There are two choices to express an individual's experience in arbitration: the number of years of practice as an arbitrator or the number of arbitration cases the arbitrator was actually involved in. The former measure fails to account for the arbitrator's workload, while the latter fails to account for the size, complexity, and nature of the disputes (e.g., subject matter of disputes, legal frameworks, and applicable laws). In Appendix B, the interviewees' set of experiences in arbitration is described in accordance with the number of arbitrations they participated in and the arbitration rules they operated under. The combined experience of those who participated in the interviews amounted to hundreds of international construction arbitrations (~ 300 cases) in addition to several hundreds of international commercial arbitrations. While some are generalist international arbitrators (i.e., arbitrate international commercial disputes and even investment disputes), most of them work largely or exclusively in international construction arbitration.

Only two interviewees were women. The author tried to secure more participation from women arbitrators, but they are still a minority in the international arbitration field.

A table providing more anonymous information about the background of the international arbitrators interviewed by the author is included in Appendix B.

Besides national, professional, and legal backgrounds, experience in international arbitration was an important parameter for selection. The principal aim was to recruit arbitrators with extensive experience in international arbitration. As most of the international arbitrators interviewed by the author have such a rich experience, the author has obtained access to a vast range of accumulated experiences, extending over a multitude of jurisdictions and covering a multiplicity of construction disputes, substantive laws, and so on. Accordingly, the data obtained are rich, thick, and more reliable. The data also have a representational sense as some of those experienced arbitrators are amongst the main and repetitive players, and, hence, their points of view are more important and more representative of what is going on than those who are less experienced. However, as the spirit of grounded theory is to search for negative instances and variations, it is important to be keen to have a diverse sample. Hence, the author has included a few arbitrators with relatively little experience in international arbitration to examine how the experience might shape arbitral decision-making.

As such, and despite the limitations in the research sample, the participants were selected to represent a diverse range of backgrounds (nationality, professional background, legal background, and experience) as much as possible. The main aim behind recruiting a diverse sample is to reveal similarities and differences in their arbitral decision-making and to search for potential patterns of decision-making approach vis-à-vis an arbitrator's background that might show a correlation between the arbitral decision-making approach and the background of the arbitrator.

1.7.3.2 Published awards as data

A number of published international construction arbitration awards were used to supplement data gathered by interviews. The study of these arbitration awards aimed at finding evidence related to arbitrators' decision-making on the substance of disputes. This evidence can be found in the 'reasons' part of the award, even though it may be necessary to examine the entire case to have a greater understanding.

The selection of the arbitration awards for the purpose of data analysis was based on classifying them as 'international construction arbitration awards' (i.e., the construction project itself involved more than one legal system or the parties to a construction contract came from different jurisdictions) (Nazzini, 2018). It follows that domestic construction arbitration awards and international commercial arbitration awards were excluded.

There are three sources (listed in Table 1.2) for the arbitral awards that were collected and reviewed for relevance. These awards range in their level of detail from brief extracts to full arbitral awards, as is the case in Alam Eldin (2010) and Alam Eldin (2014). It is important to mention that not all of these awards ended up being used. For more detailed information on the awards that were cited in this book, please see Appendix C.

Despite the value of the evidence obtained from the arbitration awards analysed in this book, the analysis of the awards does not enable us to make generalisable conclusions about arbitral decision-making for three reasons.

First, the percentage of arbitration awards that are published remains minute. For instance, by the end of 2004, the ICC, which publishes more arbitral awards than any other institution, had published only 3% of its international commercial arbitration cases in the five-volume Collection of ICC Arbitral Awards (Karton, 2013).

Second, it is next to impossible to determine whether the sample of published awards is representative of the entire population of arbitral awards. The total number of arbitration awards rendered remains a mystery because there is no way to know the number of ad hoc arbitrations and not all arbitral institutions report their caseload statistics (Karton, 2013). Moreover, it is highly likely that the sample of published awards is biased because arbitral institutions do not publish a random sample. Rather, they publish awards, after receiving the parties' consent, that appear to be interesting to the arbitration community. For instance, there is a greater tendency to publish awards involving the jurisdiction of arbitral tribunals than awards addressing general principles of law or *amiable composition*. A former secretary-general of the ICC Court of International Arbitration commented on this selective publication policy in saying: 'Only those awards in which arbitrators have felt least constrained to apply national law have been published' (Karton, 2013). These factors altogether make it difficult to know whether certain awards are representative of the mainstream prevailing practice.

Third, epistemologically, deriving knowledge about arbitral decision-making from arbitral awards (i.e., the end product of the decision-making process) is not as simple as it may appear. It is possible for arbitrators to reach their decisions based on certain considerations, but to justify their decisions using completely different reasons (see Section 1.3). In this case, the arbitrator reaches a conclusion and then searches for supporting evidence.

Table 1.2 References for international construction arbitration awards

Author/ Editor	Reference
Christopher Seppälä	International Construction Contract Disputes: Commentary on ICC Awards Dealing with the FIDIC International Conditions of Contract – *ICC International Court of Arbitration Bulletin*, Vol 9/No 2 (1998). International Construction Contract Disputes: Second Commentary on ICC Awards Dealing Primarily with FIDIC Contracts – *ICC International Court of Arbitration Bulletin*, Vol 19/No 2 (2008). International Construction Contract Disputes: Third Commentary on ICC Awards Dealing Primarily with FIDIC Contracts – *ICC International Court of Arbitration Bulletin*, Vol 23/No 2 (2012). International Construction Contract Disputes: Fourth Commentary on ICC Awards Dealing Primarily with FIDIC Contracts – *ICC International Court of Arbitration Bulletin*, Vol 24/No 2 (2013).
Mohi-Eldin Alam-Eldin	Alam Eldin, M.E. (2000). *Arbitral Awards of the Cairo Regional Centre for International Commercial Arbitration I*, Kluwer Law International. Alam Eldin, M.E. (2003). *Arbitral Awards of the Cairo Regional Centre for International Commercial Arbitration II*, Kluwer Law International. Alam Eldin, M.E. (2010). *Construction Arbitral Awards Rendered Under the Auspices of CRCICA*, Lambert Academic Publishing. Alam Eldin, M.E. (2014). *Arbitral Awards of the Cairo Regional Centre for International Commercial Arbitration IV*, Kluwer Law International.
Albert Jan van den Berg (1986 – present) Sanders (1977–1985)	The International Council for Commercial Arbitration (ICCA) Yearbook Commercial Arbitration (1976–to date) published by Kluwer Law International.

This type of reasoning can be genuine, but it can also be a result of the arbitrator's predisposition to one party or to the subject matter in dispute.

1.7.3.3 Scholarly commentaries and academic writings

Secondary data were obtained from scholarly commentaries and academic writings, such as journal papers and conference presentations. It is noteworthy that, unlike traditional legal research in which secondary sources of data (e.g., scholarly commentaries) are considered inferior to the primary sources of data (e.g., treaty, statute, and case law), both sources of data are equally helpful for the study of arbitral decision-making. The reasons are that in arbitration, probably more than any other field, the division between a scholar and a practitioner is blurred as many arbitrators give conference presentations and write academic papers and books and many scholars act as arbitrators or are practitioners of arbitration (Karton, 2013). The practitioners of arbitration normally play different roles; they can act as arbitrators, counsel, or experts. This combination of the practice of and the writing about arbitration is part of the symbolic capital that arbitrators are keen to develop (Dezalay and Garth, 1998).

1.8 Structure of the book

The book is comprised of nine chapters. Each chapter starts with a section titled 'Introduction,' which outlines the objectives of the chapter and introduces its structure. Each chapter ends with a conclusion section that summarises the main findings and puts forward the chapter's arguments.

1.8.1 Chapter 1: Introduction

This chapter sets the scene and explains the importance of the book. It argues for the need to explore arbitral decision-making in the context of international construction arbitration. Then, it presents the aim and objectives of the book and demarcates its scope. Thereafter, it explains the key methodological aspects of the research underpinning the book. The coverage of the methodology is brief as it is not intended for an academic audience. Finally, it provides a preview of the remaining chapters.

1.8.2 Chapter 2: Background

This chapter offers a definition of international construction arbitration and explains why it is a unique category within international commercial arbitration. Then, it presents a historical outline of the evolution of international construction arbitration and outlines the main advantages that underpin its prevalence and dominance. The rest of the chapter is dedicated to problematising the current knowledge on arbitral decision-making in international construction disputes and thereby demonstrating the knowledge gap in the existing studies. This justifies the need for the book.

1.8.3 Chapter 3: Law as a substantive norm

This chapter discusses to what extent international arbitrators adhere to substantive law when deciding the parties' disputes. It examines how arbitrators view their duty to apply substantive law, including ascertainment of its content. It discusses the effect of the substantive law on arbitrators' decisions on the substance of international construction disputes. It sheds light on the tension between party autonomy and competing considerations to properly apply substantive law, including its mandatory provisions. Thereafter, this chapter explores how arbitrators decide when substantive law is incomplete or indeterminate. Then, it provides an explanatory framework for arbitrators' decision-making behaviour.

1.8.4 Chapter 4: Commercial norms

This chapter critically reviews the debate surrounding the best approach to contract interpretation in an arbitration setting. The scholarly discussion in the arbitration literature suggests that there are two schools of thought; one that supports a legal approach to contract interpretation and another that defends a commercial approach to contract interpretation. At the heart of this debate is the role and status of commercial norms such as custom and trade usages in arbitral decision-making. Hence, this chapter discusses the application of custom and trade usages in international commercial arbitration and the meaning and effect of the arbitration rules in international arbitration instruments (e.g., national arbitration laws, institutional arbitration rules) requiring arbitrators to consider custom and trade usages when they determine the parties' dispute. It provides empirical insight into whether arbitrators depart from substantive law and apply commercial norms in order to achieve a commercially sensible outcome that is consistent with construction business common sense.

1.8.5 Chapter 5: International construction law

Given the long academic and professional debate surrounding *lex mercatoria* (or international commercial law), this chapter explores this notion in the context of international construction arbitration. It examines how legal norms that do not belong to the governing law (i.e., transnational legal norms) might have an impact on arbitral decision-making. It empirically constructs the concept of 'international construction law' and discusses its sources, authority, and application in international construction arbitration.

1.8.6 Chapter 6: Fairness

Justice and fairness are surely prime considerations for parties involved in a dispute. Scholarly writings on arbitration sometimes suggest a close relationship between arbitration and equity-based decisions, especially in certain contexts. This chapter examines the extent to which notions of fairness have an impact on arbitrators' decisions. Parties can empower the tribunal to decide in accordance with notions of fairness. Fairness or equity-based decisions are normally understood to be related to two approaches to decision-making that are historically associated with arbitration: *amiable composition* and *ex aequo et bono.* This chapter reviews the theoretical and practical aspects of these approaches and how they shape arbitral decision-making.

1.8.7 Chapter 7: Mandatory rules of foreign law

International construction contracts usually involve multiple legal systems that have a connection to the construction project or the resolution of a dispute arising from it. They include the law of the place of performance (i.e., construction), the law of the seat of arbitration, the laws of the places of domicile of the parties to the construction contract, and the law of the place of enforcement. The laws of these jurisdictions are considered 'foreign' when they are different from substantive law. The effect of the mandatory rules of foreign law on arbitral decision-making is one of the most controversial aspects of arbitration theory and practice. This chapter offers empirical insight into this issue.

1.8.8 Chapter 8: The arbitrator's background

There is a general acceptance in the arbitration community that 'arbitration is as good as the arbitrator'. This well-known saying is applicable not only to the quality of the arbitration procedure but also to the quality of the arbitration outcome. In other words, the arbitrator's decision might be influenced by the arbitrator's background characteristics. This chapter explores the relationship between the arbitration outcome and the arbitrator's background. It examines the factors, other than the merits of the case as presented by the parties, that may influence arbitrators' decisions and the outcome of the dispute.

1.8.9 Chapter 9: Conclusion

This chapter summarises how arbitrators make their decisions on the substance of international construction disputes. It presents answers to the questions raised in Chapter 1 and throughout the book. It argues that international construction arbitrators tend to follow a 'transnational legal model' when deciding disputes arising from international construction contracts. Then it highlights the book's contributions to knowledge, implications for practice, and limitations.

References

Alam Eldin, M. E. (2000). *Arbitral Awards of the Cairo Regional Centre for International Commercial Arbitration I*. The Hague: Kluwer Law International.

Alam Eldin, M. E. (2003). *Arbitral Awards of the Cairo Regional Centre for International Commercial Arbitration II*. The Hague: Kluwer Law International.

Alam Eldin, M. E. (2010). *Construction Arbitral Awards Rendered Under the Auspices of CRCICA*. Saarbrücken: Lambert Academic Publishing.

Alam Eldin, M. E. (2014). *Arbitral Awards of the Cairo Regional Centre for International Commercial Arbitration IV*. The Hague: Kluwer Law International.

Andrews, N. (2016). *Arbitration and Contract Law*. Cham: Springer.

Atallah, B. (2005). Egypt. *In:* Knutson, R. (ed.) *FIDIC: An Analysis of International Construction Contracts*. The Hague: Kluwer Law International.

Auerbach, C. & Silverstein, L. B. (2003). *Qualitative Data: An Introduction to Coding and Analysis*. New York: New York University Press.

Berger, B. & Schneider, M. E. (2014). *Inside the Black Box: How Arbitral Tribunals Operate and Reach Their Decisions*. New York: JurisNet, LLC.

Bishop, R. D. (2012). Luncheon presentation: The quality of arbitral decision-making and justification. *World Arbitration & Mediation Review*, 6(4), 801–812.

Blackaby, N., Partasides, C., Redfern, A. & Hunter, M. (2009). *Redfern and Hunter on International Arbitration*. 5th ed. Oxford: Oxford University Press.

Blackaby, N., Partasides, C., Redfern, A. & Hunter, M. (2015). *Redfern and Hunter on International Arbitration*. 6th ed. Oxford: Oxford University Press.

Brekoulakis, S. (2013). Systemic bias and the institution of international arbitration: A new approach to arbitral decision-making. *Journal of International Dispute Settlement*, 4(3), 553–585.

Cairo Regional Centre for International Commercial Arbitration (CRCICA) (2016). *CRCICA Annual Reports*. Available: https://crcica.org/annual-reports/ [Accessed 12 December 2022].

Cairo Regional Centre for International Commercial Arbitration (CRCICA) (2022). *CRCICA Annual Reports*. Available: https://crcica.org/annual-reports/ [Accessed 12 December 2022].

Charrett, D. (2012). A common law of construction contracts: Or vive la différence? *International Construction Law Review*, 29(1), 347–356.

Corbin, J. & Strauss, A. (2015). *Basics of Qualitative Research*. Thousand Oaks, CA: SAGE.

Coulson, R. (1989). Do we know how arbitration panels decide? *Journal of International Arbitration*, 6, 7.

Coulson, R. (1990). The decision making process in arbitration. *Arbitration Journal*, 45(3).

Dezalay, Y. & Garth, B. G. (1998). *Dealing in Virtue: International Commercial Arbitration and the Construction of a Transnational Legal Order*. Chicago: University of Chicago Press.

Diamond, S. S. (2003). Psychological aspects of dispute resolution: Issues for international arbitration. *In*: Berg, A. J. V. D. (ed.) *International Commercial Arbitration: Important Contemporary Questions*. The Hague: Kluwer Law International.

Domke, M. (1965). *Commercial Arbitration*. New Jersey: Prentice-Hall.

Drahozal, C. R. (2000). Commercial norms, commercial codes, and international commercial arbitration. *Vanderbilt Journal of Transnational Law*, 33, 79.

Drahozal, C. R. (2003). Of rabbits and rhinoceri: A survey of empirical research on international commercial arbitration. *Journal of International Arbitration*, 20(1), 23–34.

Drahozal, C. R. (2004). A behavioral analysis of private judging. *Law and Contemporary Problems*, 67(1), 105–132.

Drahozal, C. R. (2005). Contracting out of National Law: An Empirical Look at the New Law Merchant. *Notre Dame Law Review*, 80(2), 523.

Drahozal, C. R. & Naimark, R. W. (2005). *Towards a Science of International Arbitration: Collected Empirical Research*. The Hague: Kluwer law international.

Drahozal, C. R. & Ware, S. J. (2010). Why do businesses use (or not use) arbitration clauses. *Ohio State Journal on Dispute Resolution*, 25, 433.

El-adaway, I. H., Ezeldin, A. S. & Yates, J. (2009). Arbitral tribunal proceedings case study: Egyptian large-scale construction project. *Journal of Legal Affairs and Dispute Resolution in Engineering and Construction*, 1(3), 147–153.

Flood, J. & Caiger, A. (1993). Lawyers and arbitration: The juridification of construction disputes. *The Modern Law Review*, 56(3), 412–440.

Franck, S. D., van Aaken, A., Freda, J., Guthrie, C. & Rachlinski, J. J. (2017). Inside the arbitrator's mind. *Emory Law Journal*, 66, 1115.

Friedland, P. & Mistelis, L. (2015). *2015 International Arbitration Survey: Improvements and Innovations in International Arbitration*. Queen Mary University of London and School of International Arbitration. https://arbitration.qmul.ac.uk/media/arbitration/docs/2015_International_Arbitration_Survey.pdf. [Accessed 10 October 2022].

Gaillard, E. & Savage, J. (1999). *Fouchard, Gaillard, Goldman on International Commercial Arbitration*. The Hague: Kluwer law international.

Glaser, B. & Strauss, A. (1967). *The Discovery of Grounded Theory*. New Brunswick: Transaction Publishers.

Goulding, C. (2002). *Grounded Theory: A Practical Guide for Management, Business and Market Researchers*. Thousand Oaks, CA: SAGE.

Guthrie, C., Rachlinski, J. J. & Wistrich, A. J. (2007). Blinking on the bench: How judges decide cases. *Cornell Law Review*, 93(1), 1.

Hernandez-Garcia, R. (2009). Globalization of construction. *In*: Venoit, W. K. (ed.) *International Construction Law: A Guide for Cross-border Transactions and Legal Disputes*. Chicago: American Bar Association Publishing.

Hoffmann, B. (1989). International construction arbitration. *In*: Sarcevic, P. (ed.) *Essays on International Commercial Arbitration*. London: Graham & Trotman.

Hong Kong International Arbitration Centre (HKIAC) (2022). *Statistics*. Available: https://www.hkiac.org/about-us/statistics [Accessed 12 December 2022].

International Chamber of Commerce (ICC) (2018). *2017 Dispute Resolution Statistics* [Online]. Available: https://iccwbo.org/publication/2017-icc-dispute-resolution-statistics/ [Accessed 12 December 2022].

International Chamber of Commerce (ICC) (2019). *2018 Dispute Resolution Statistics* [Online]. Available: www.iccwbo.org/dr-stat2018 [Accessed 12 December 2022].

International Chamber of Commerce (ICC) (2020). *2019 Dispute Resolution Statistics* [Online]. Available: https://iccwbo.org/media-wall/news-speeches/icc-releases-2019-dispute-resolution-statistics/

International Chamber of Commerce (ICC) (2021). *2020 Dispute Resolution Statistics* [Online]. Available: https://iccwbo.org/publication/icc-dispute-resolution-statistics-2020/

Ismail, M. A. (2016). *Globalization and New International Public Works Agreements in Developing Countries: An Analytical Perspective*. Abingdon: Routledge.

Karton, J. (2010). *The Culture of International Arbitration and the Evolution of Contract Law*. Doctor of Philosophy, University of Cambridge.

Karton, J. (2012a). A conflict of interests: Seeking a way forward on publication of international arbitral awards. *Arbitration International*, 28(3), 447–486.

Karton, J. (2012b). International commercial arbitrators' approaches to contractual interpretation. *International Business Law Journal*, 383.

Karton, J. (2013). *The Culture of International Arbitration and the Evolution of Contract Law*. Oxford: Oxford University Press.

Karton, J. (2015). The arbitral role in contractual interpretation. *Journal of International Dispute Settlement*, 6(1), 4–41.

Kläger, R. (2011). *'Fair and Equitable Treatment' in International Investment Law*. Cambridge: Cambridge University Press.

Klein, D. E. & Mitchell, G. (2010). *The Psychology of Judicial Decision Making*. New York: Oxford University Press.

Lagerberg, G. & Mistelis, L. (2013). *Corporate Choices in International Arbitration: Industry Perspectives*. Queen Mary University of London and School of International Arbitration. https://www.pwc.com/gx/en/arbitration-dispute-resolution/assets/pwc-international-arbitration-study.pdf. [Accessed 12 December 2022].

Levin, M. S. (1997). The role of substantive law in business arbitration and the importance of volition. *American Business Law Journal*, 35(1), 105–180.

London Court of International Arbitration (LCIA) (2017). *Facts and Figures - 2016: A Robust Caseload* [Online]. Available: https://www.lcia.org/lcia/reports.aspx [Accessed 12 December 2022].

London Court of International Arbitration (LCIA) (2018). *2017 Casework Report* [Online]. Available: https://www.lcia.org/lcia/reports.aspx [Accessed 12 December 2022].

London Court of International Arbitration (LCIA) (2019). *2018 Annual Casework Report* [Online]. Available: https://www.lcia.org/lcia/reports.aspx [Accessed 12 December 2022].

London Court of International Arbitration (LCIA) (2020). *2019 Annual Casework Report* [Online]. Available: https://www.lcia.org/lcia/reports.aspx [Accessed 12 December 2022].

London Court of International Arbitration (LCIA) (2021). *2020 Annual Casework Report* [Online]. Available: https://www.lcia.org/lcia/reports.aspx [Accessed 12 December 2022].

Molineaux, C. (1997). Moving toward a construction lex mecatoria. *Journal of International Arbitration*, 14(1), 55–66.

Moloo, R. & King, B. (2014). International arbitrators as lawmakers. *New York University Journal of International Law and Politics*, 46(3).

Moser, M. J. & Cheng, T. Y. (2004). *Hong Kong Arbitration: A User's Guide*. The Hague: Kluwer Law International.

Mustill, M. J. (2014). The history of international commercial arbitration: A sketch. *In*: Newman, L. W. & Hill, R. D. (eds.) *The Leading Arbitrators' Guide to International Arbitration*. 3rd ed. New York: Juris Publishing.

Naoum, S. G. (2007). *Dissertation Research and Writing for Construction Students*. Abingdon: Routledge.

Naoum, S. G. (2012). *Dissertation Research and Writing for Construction Students*. Abingdon: Routledge.

Natanson, R. (2013). *The Choice of the Applicable Law as a Strategy in International Commercial Arbitration*. M.Sc., Toulouse Capitole University.

Nazzini, R. (2018). *Transnational Construction Arbitration: Key Themes in the Resolution of Construction Disputes*. New York: Informa Law from Routledge.

Ossman, G. (2003). *Construction Arbitration Consistency and Reliability: An Empirical Study*. M.Sc., Pepperdine University School of Law.

Park, W. W. (2009). Arbitrator integrity: The transient and the permanent. *San Diego Law Review*, 46, 629.

Park, W. W. (2010). Arbitrators and accuracy. *Journal of International Dispute Settlement*, 1(1), 25–53.

Park, W. W. (2015). The predictability paradox: Arbitrators and applicable law. *Transnational Dispute Management*, 12(6).

Saunders, M., Lewis, P. & Thornhill, A. (2009). *Research Methods for Business Students*. Harlow: Pearson Education Ltd.

Saunders, M., Lewis, P. & Thornhill, A. (2012). *Research Methods for Business Students*. Harlow: Pearson Education Ltd.

Schneider, M. (2012). President's message: Arbitral decision making: A look into the black box. *ASA Bulletin*, 30(3), 509.

Schultz, T. (2015). Arbitral decision-making: Legal realism and law & economics. *Journal of International Dispute Settlement*, 6(2), 231–251.

Seppala, C. R. (1998). International construction contract disputes: Commentary on ICC awards dealing with the FIDIC international conditions of contract. *ICC International Court of Arbitration Bulletin*, 9(2).

Sinnott-Armstrong, W. & Neta, R. (2017). *Think Again I: How to Understand Arguments* [Online]. Available: https://www.coursera.org/learn/understanding-arguments [Accessed 15/01/2017].

Smit, H. & Mistelis, L. (2017). *Roster of International Arbitrators*. 2nd ed. New York: Juris Publishing.

Stipanowich, T. & Ulrich, Z. (2014). Arbitration in evolution: Current practices and perspectives of experienced commercial arbitrators. *The American Review of International Arbitration*, 25, 395–480.

Strauss, A. & Corbin, J. (1998). *Basics of Qualitative Research: Procedures and Techniques for Developing Grounded Theory*. Thousand Oaks, CA: SAGE.

Thompson, R. (1977). International chamber of commerce-arbitration of disputes arising under international construction contracts. *International Business Lawyer*, 5(2), 225.

Tumonis, V., Šavelskis, M. & Žalytė, I. (2013). Judicial decision-making from an empirical perspective. *Baltic Journal of Law & Politics*, 6(1), 140–162.

Turner, R. (2005). *Arbitration Awards: A Practical Approach*. Oxford: Blackwell Publishing Ltd.

Uff, J. (2014). Arbitrating International Construction Disputes. *In*: Newman, L. W. & Hill, R. D. (eds.) *The Leading Arbitrators' Guide to International Arbitration*. 3rd ed. New York: Juris Publishing, Inc.

Uff, J. & Uff, A. (2010). The availability of treaty arbitration in construction. *International Construction Law Review*, 27(4).

Webster, T. H. & Buhler, M. (2014). *Handbook of ICC Arbitration: Commentary, Precedents, Materials*. London: Sweet & Maxwell.

Weidemaier, W. M. C. (2009). Toward a theory of precedent in arbitration. *William and Mary Law Review*, 51, 1895.

CHAPTER 2

Background

2.1 Introduction

This chapter has two main objectives.

First, this chapter introduces the reader to international construction arbitration. To do so, it proposes a working definition of international construction arbitration (Section 2.2) and explains how arbitration in construction disputes is distinct from arbitration in commercial disputes (Section 2.3). Subsequently, it outlines the main advantages of arbitration that have made it the fundamental dispute resolution method in international construction disputes (Section 2.4). Then, it presents a brief history of international construction arbitration (Section 2.5).

Second, this chapter problematises the extant knowledge concerning how international construction arbitrators make their substantive decisions. To do so, it synthesises the scarce publications that are relevant to arbitral decision-making in international construction disputes (Section 2.8).

2.2 Definition of international construction arbitration

Originally, the word 'arbitrator' comes from the Latin *arbitratus* (to be a hearer) (Wright, 1913). However, some authors state that arbitrators are so called because they have an arbitrary power and authority derived from the parties' arbitration agreement (Ossman, 2003).

In his paper titled 'British Experience with Arbitration', Nordon (1935) cited the first definition he found for arbitrator in Giles Jacob's law dictionary published in 1729 and attributed to Robert Raymond (Lord Chief Justice of England):

> An arbitrator is a private extraordinary judge between party and party, chosen by their mutual consents, to determine controversies between them. And arbitrators are so called because they have an arbitrary power; for if they observe the submission and keep within due bounds their sentences are definite, from which there lies no appeal.

Stephenson (2001) states that this definition is still valid particularly if the phrase 'due bounds' is considered to mean 'the law'.

The Chartered Institute of Arbitrators defines arbitration as (CIArb, 2018b):

> A non-judicial process for the settlement of disputes where an independent third party – an arbitrator – makes a decision that is binding.

Arbitration is a very wide field dealing with disputes of different natures, such as business, commerce, intellectual property, and basically all arbitrable matters in civil and administrative law, including even disputes on non-monetary matters but excluding criminal matters (Gaillard and Savage, 1999).

DOI: 10.4324/b22975-2

Commercial arbitration covers many disputes in business and commerce. The drafters of the UNCITRAL Model Law (2006) considered putting forward a definition of the term 'commercial' but then they abandoned the attempt (Blackaby et al., 2015). They noted the difficulty of devising a clear-cut definition of the word 'commercial', but they agreed that the term should be broadly interpreted (UNCITRAL Working Group on International Contract Practices, 1982). Instead of defining the term 'commercial', the Model Law describes it in a footnote to Article 1 as follows:

> Matters arising from all relationships of a commercial nature, whether contractual or not. Relationships of a commercial nature include, but are not limited to, the following transactions: any trade transactions for the supply or exchange of goods or services; distribution agreements; commercial representation or agency; factoring; leasing; construction of works; consulting; engineering; licensing; investment; financing; banking; insurance; exploitation agreements or concessions; joint ventures, and other forms of industrial or business cooperation; carriage of goods or passengers by air, sea, rail, or road.

This book will focus on the arbitration of disputes arising from construction and engineering contracts. There is no authoritative definition of the term 'construction arbitration'. Even textbooks dedicated to the topic, such as Nazzini (2018) and Hinchey and Harris (2008), and professional institutions, such as the Society of Construction Arbitrators, have not provided such a definition.

H.H. Judge Humphrey Lloyd QC noted that (Lloyd, 2001):

> We understood the term 'construction arbitrations' to mean arbitrations that concern all kinds of disputes arising out of projects for construction work, but mainly those relating to the execution of the services (e.g., engineering services) and work necessary for the implementation of the project.

After all, as construction arbitration concerns arbitrations of disputes arising from construction contracts, it is inevitable to define the latter. Again, this book finds no generally accepted definition of what constitutes a construction contract. However, a useful resource to look at for guidance is the broad definition provided in the UK Housing Grants, Construction and Regeneration Act 1996 ('the Construction Act'). The Construction Act defines the term 'construction contract' to include contracts for carrying out construction operations as well as services (e.g., surveying, architecture, consultancy, construction management, project management) (Jenkins and Stebbings, 2006).

The term 'international' is the last term that needs to be defined in order to have a working definition of international construction arbitration. The term 'international' denotes the difference between arbitrations that are 'national' or 'domestic' and those that are 'international'. However, there is no one definition of what constitutes international arbitrations. Each jurisdiction has its own test to determine if an arbitral award is domestic or international (Blackaby et al., 2015).

The Model Law (2006), in Article 1(3), defines international arbitration expansively to cover four situations as follows:

> An arbitration is international if:
>
> (a) the parties to an arbitration agreement have, at the time of the conclusion of that agreement, their places of business in different States; or
> (b) one of the following places is situated outside the State in which the parties have their places of business:

   (i) the place of arbitration if determined in, or pursuant to, the arbitration agreement;
   (ii) any place where a substantial part of the obligations of the commercial relationship is to be performed or the place with which the subject-matter of the dispute is most closely connected; or

(c) the parties have expressly agreed that the subject matter of the arbitration agreement relates to more than one country.

Most national arbitration laws adopt similar definitions (Born, 2015). This book adopts a broad definition of international arbitration similar to that of the Model Law.

According to the foregoing, international construction arbitration can be defined as arbitrations of disputes arising out of or in connection with construction works and engineering services in which:

- the parties have different nationalities or places of domicile; or
- the place of performance of the construction contract is different from the place of domicile of at least one of the parties; or
- the seat of arbitration is a jurisdiction that is different from at least one of the parties' places of domicile.

2.3 International construction arbitration vis-à-vis international commercial arbitration

As international commercial arbitration expands and becomes more diverse, it becomes necessary to differentiate between certain commercial activities in which their disputes are normally referred to arbitration (Kaufmann-Kohler, 2007; Uff, 2014). Each area of commerce tends to have its own peculiarities (Turner, 2005) and set of norms against which the disputants' conduct is to be measured (Mentschikoff, 1961). These commercial norms might ultimately have an impact on how arbitrators make their decisions on the substance of disputes (Landolt, 2012). In this context, Flood and Caiger (1993) succinctly say:

> The world of arbitration varies according to the context in which it takes place. The main dichotomies are between subject fields, i.e., whether the dispute is in shipping or construction, and between domestic and international arbitration. To make sense of these issues the topic must be studied within a particular context.

Likewise, some scholars assert that the wide range of arbitration contexts that are available today complicates any meaningful evaluation of the role of substantive norms, including the substantive law, in arbitration (Levin, 1997). Landolt (2012) suggests that the evolution in the field of international commercial arbitration leads to 'differentiation' between different species of arbitrations. This differentiation is important because, in some divisions, such as trade association arbitrations or commodities arbitrations, commercial parties still contract out national laws and often select commercial people (as opposed to legal people) who are more concerned about the commercial practice and trade usages to arbitrate their disputes (Landolt, 2012; Karton, 2013). Yet, according to Landolt's (2012) proposition, in most other divisions, substantive decision-making in international commercial arbitration has evolved towards a position more favourable to the application of the law within the limits of the role of arbitrators.

This book takes the view that engineering and construction arbitration has several salient features that make it distinct from the rest of commercial arbitrations. These features are discussed in the following paragraphs.

First, a typical construction project involves many entities, such as the government, the financers, the employer, the designer, the engineer, the contractor, the subcontractors, the material suppliers, the manufacturers, etc. As such, construction contracts are connected with several contracts throughout the supply chain (Uff, 2014; Winter, 2016).

Second, the contractual relationship between parties to a construction contract is dependent upon the procurement route and the payment method (Uff, 2014; Jenkins and Rosenberg, 2013). The procurement route refers to the high-level approach of structuring contractual arrangements and risk allocation from the perspectives of financing, design, construction, operation, and maintenance of the completed works (Jenkins and Rosenberg, 2013). The payment method could be either price-based (lump-sum or re-measurement) or cost-based (cost-reimbursable or target-cost) (Potts and Ankrah, 2008).

Third, many construction contracts run over much longer periods than most other forms of commercial contracts. This brings significant risks and uncertainties to the contracting parties at the time of contract formation and generates extensive facts extending over a number of years. Also, construction works take place in an open environment (the construction site) that is difficult to control (Gregory and Berg, 2013). This brings whole new types of risks and, hence, disputes over unforeseen ground conditions, weather conditions, work disruption, interferences, and so on.

Fourth, construction contracts are usually comprised of extensive documents, including bills of quantities, drawings, specifications, conditions of contracts, etc. (Dunham, 2010; Harmon, 2003). Further, considerable documents are typically produced during the design and construction implementation phase of the project, such as shop drawings, correspondence, and reports (Harmon, 2003). In addition, piles of documents are produced during arbitration proceedings, such as technical reports prepared by experts. Given the huge volume of documents produced during the pre-contract phase, implementation phase, and post-implementation dispute-resolution phase, construction arbitrations are document intensive and characterised by voluminous pleadings, factual records, and witness statements (Lane, 2012).

One English arbitrator interviewed for this book stated that in an arbitration case he was involved in and related to the construction of an oil refinery, the documents filled an entire room! He added that in arbitrations of this size and scale, arbitrators may have to read thousands of pages to understand what happened, and what are the claims and counterclaims. As an international arbitrator with a wealth of experience spanning more than three decades, he underscored the importance of finding the facts in construction arbitrations as follows:

> Well, 90% of cases in my view are decided based on facts … once you sort out the facts the answer is relatively obvious … I think many arbitrators, particularly the less experienced ones, do not realise how important facts are … it is often more difficult to decide the facts of the case than the law and it is certainly more time-consuming, painstaking, and laborious.

There is a consensus among arbitrators that construction arbitrations have ‘a lot more paper’ than arbitrations related to other commercial activities. It follows that arbitration awards themselves will be lengthy. According to an Egyptian arbitrator interviewed by the author, the large size of construction arbitration awards makes construction arbitration distinct from generic commercial arbitration. Referring to an arbitration case concerning the construction of an airport in the Middle East, he stated:

> Sometimes, you are confronted with hundreds of claims in one arbitration. This is a source of bread and butter for lawyers because they are complicated and time-consuming. I remember in one case, there were over 300 different claims. Believe me if I tell you that some awards were over 500 pages. When you devote 4 pages for each claim, believe me it will be even more than that.

Many interviewees said that the large size of bidding and contract documents often leads to contradictions or discrepancies between contract documents or within contract documents. Although it may sound counterintuitive, an English arbitrator observed that this is a typical situation in large-scale construction projects that suffer from this problem the most. Large-scale projects usually involve many people working in different teams, at different places, and perhaps in different time zones. The tender documents constantly evolve and change, and the inconsistent incorporation of various versions leads to contradictory or inconsistent documents.

Almost all arbitrators interviewed by the author concur that finding the facts is probably the most important part of deciding construction disputes. Most construction disputes that reach international arbitration require finding the facts and an interpretation of the contract. At the beginning of arbitration proceedings, the facts are often not clear. The arbitral tribunal asks the claimant to submit their claims in detail with all supporting evidence and then asks the respondent to respond and counterclaim. The whole point here is to get to the facts because quite often the reason why the parties have entered into a dispute is that each side has its own version of what it believes the facts to be.

Fifth, construction disputes over quality, time, and quantum involve complex questions of factual causation and legal causation (Baatz, 2016). The proof of a cause–effect relationship between an event and an outcome (defects, delay, additional costs/expenses) is daunting because there are usually multiple events that potentially contribute to the outcome. It may be impossible or impractical to break down a complex factual network to isolate a chain of causation for each individual claim (Jenkins and Rosenberg, 2013; Gregory and Berg, 2013). According to an English arbitrator interviewed by the author, causation is probably the most difficult question that an arbitrator has to deal with in a construction case as it presents all sorts of intellectual problems. The complex causation problems coupled with the intensive facts surrounding construction disputes have resulted in a prevalence of programming evidence in construction arbitration. Delay analysis experts get on board to identify the cause and quantify the duration of a delay event to the project completion date using a multiplicity of delay analysis techniques. Concurrent delay is a classic area where there are concurrent causes of delay and different legal systems take different views of how to approach concurrency. In conjunction, as construction projects are technologically complex and involve a wide variety of applied sciences (geotechnical, structural, electrical, mechanical, etc.), expert evidence is at the heart of fact-finding in construction arbitration (Lane, 2012).

Sixth, it is common for construction contracts to be based upon standard forms of contract published by professional organisations such as FIDIC (Uff, 2014). These standard forms produce a second layer of legal principles that are superimposed on the governing law of the contract (Bunni, 2000). In addition, standard forms bring more challenges to disputes related to or arising out of contract interpretation (O'Reilly, 1999).

Seventh, international construction contracts normally have a tiered dispute resolution clause that provides for a multi-stage dispute resolution process. This includes an engineer determination and an adjudicator (or dispute adjudication board) decision (Uff, 2014).

The foregoing points demonstrate that construction contracts differ in important respects from other commercial contracts. Thus, there might be differences between construction disputes and other commercial disputes in arbitral decision-making concerning the application of the law, customs and usages, and other substantive norms. The internal variations within the international commercial arbitration field (Flood and Caiger, 1993; Landolt, 2012) make it a worthwhile exercise to examine the particularities of decision-making in particular industries, especially the construction industry, which, as Blankenship (2010) asserts, has the largest representation and the longest experience in commercial arbitration.

2.4 Advantages of international construction arbitration

The success story of arbitration as outlined in the previous section has left a significant legacy. Today, arbitration has become the norm in the resolution of international construction disputes. Anecdotal evidence suggests that almost all international construction contracts have an arbitration clause (Uff, 2014). Similarly, Rechsteiner (2001), cited in Nunes et al. (2005), states:

> In international contracts that refer to the construction of an industrial complex or similar project the number of these contracts where arbitration clauses are inserted reaches 100%. In this area, we can say that, basically, the decisions are made by the Arbitration Courts and not the State courts.

Empirical evidence suggests that arbitration is the fundamental and preferred dispute resolution method in international construction projects (Friedland and Mistelis, 2015; Lagerberg and Mistelis, 2013).

The wide acceptance and the steady increase in the use of international construction arbitration are due to certain advantages, of which the two chief are neutrality and enforceability (Friedland and Mistelis, 2015). The advantages of arbitration that have led to the dominance of arbitration in the resolution of cross-border construction disputes are outlined in the following subsections.

2.4.1 Neutrality

Neutrality is a paramount consideration in dispute resolution, including international arbitration (Nazzini, 2018). A party to an international construction contract will normally refuse to resolve a dispute in the other party's national courts, particularly when the other party is a government, because of fear of bias (Nazzini, 2018). If the other party is a government, there is another obstacle to sovereignty. A government would not submit its dispute to the court of another state (Thompson, 1977). Arbitration is a neutral dispute resolution mechanism that provides a neutral forum for dispute resolution. The seat of arbitration is often selected to be a neutral country and the chair of the arbitration tribunal is usually from neither party's nationality (Andrews, 2016; Moses, 2008).

2.4.2 Enforcement

The widespread and relatively easy enforceability of arbitration awards is one of the most attractive benefits of international arbitration (Andrews, 2016; Lagerberg and Mistelis, 2006). The enforcement of a foreign arbitral award is much easier than a foreign court judgement (Andrews, 2016) primarily as a result of the New York Convention acceded to by 169 countries (Biresaw, 2022). Further, the binding decisions of decision-makers under other alternative dispute resolution methods, such as adjudication or expert determinations, cannot be enforced like arbitral awards because of the absence of an automatic enforcement regime. They may require the winning party to initiate arbitration or court proceedings to obtain an arbitration award or a court judgement (Hobeck, Mahnken, and Koebke, 2008).

2.4.3 Finality

In almost all jurisdictions, there is no right of appeal for the parties against international arbitration awards (Andrews, 2016). Also, arbitration awards cannot be challenged, set aside, or non-enforced on the basis that arbitrators erred either as to the law or as to the facts (Blackaby et al., 2015; Natanson, 2013; Park, 2010). The finality of arbitration awards is a controversial feature of international arbitration (Andrews, 2016). It could be viewed as an advantage or a disadvantage depending on the viewpoints of the winner and the loser.

The idea that the parties are left at the mercy of an arbitrator, who could be biased or incompetent, would be frustrating to the losing party if the arbitrator erred in their findings of facts or conclusions of law (Moss, 2004; Moses, 2008). This is understood given that someone's final victory is someone else's irreversible defeat (Andrews, 2016). Almost 175 years ago, a Scottish judge warned about this feature of arbitration in his judgement in the case of *Mitchell v. Cable [1848]* (Born, 2001):

> An arbitrator may believe what nobody else believes, and he may disbelieve what all the world believes. He may overlook or flagrantly misapply the most ordinary principles of law, and there is no appeal for those who have chosen to submit themselves to his despotic power.

However, although the finality of arbitration awards remains a highly contested advantage in theory (Andrews, 2016), it appears to have decisive support in practice. Recent empirical evidence, based on questionnaire surveys, suggests that parties to international arbitration are overwhelmingly supportive of its finality and against an appeal mechanism (Lagerberg and Mistelis, 2006).

2.4.4 Confidentiality

The confidentiality of arbitration proceedings and awards is viewed as one of the advantages of arbitration (Andrews, 2016). Contracting parties prefer to not disclose to the public information related to their commercial activities and disputes. If the arbitration law and rules are silent on confidentiality, the parties can still agree on it and its scope (Moses, 2008).

2.4.5 Arbitrator's expertise

The parties' selection of their arbitrators is probably the most important decision they make which has a significant impact on the decision-making process (substantive and fact-finding norms) and thereby the outcome of a dispute (Dezalay and Garth, 1998; Mentschikoff and Haggard, 1977).

Arbitrators are normally selected based on their knowledge of the governing law of the contract and their commercial awareness of the sector (Friedland and Mistelis, 2015). The disputants' ability to select their private judge who has relevant knowledge and experience is one of the original premises of construction arbitration (Wright, 1913), which may still hold true (Nazzini, 2018). Lloyd (2001) points out that, in the international construction sector, it is still possible to remain faithful to one of the fundamental rationales of arbitration as it is highly desirable that an arbitral tribunal be comprised of construction practitioners who are familiar with construction contracts and disputes. Nevertheless, there is no empirical or statistical evidence to substantiate this assertion. In fact, the opposite seems to be true.

2.4.6 Party autonomy and arbitration flexibility

Arbitration is an informal and flexible dispute resolution method that highly respects the parties' autonomy. Arbitrators have wide discretion to tailor the procedure to a particular dispute (nature, size) and to accommodate the parties' requirements regarding the timeline, hearing venue, language, and so on. Arbitrators are not bound by strict rules of civil procedure or rules of evidence (Stephenson, 2001; Nazzini, 2018). In addition to this procedural flexibility, the parties have the liberty to choose the substantive norms to be applied to their dispute (Stephenson, 2001).

2.5 History of international construction arbitration

A comprehensive account of the history of international construction arbitration entails a review of the history of 'arbitration', 'construction', and then the internationalisation of both. A detailed examination of them falls outside the scope of this book. This section presents only a brief historical outline of them.

Lord Mustill (1989) and Mentschikoff and Haggard (1977) opine that commercial arbitration must have existed since the dawn of commerce. The concept and the procedure from the start (arbitration agreement) to the end (enforcement or arbitral award) might have been different from arbitration as it is known today (Mustill, 1989). However, Mustill (1989) concedes that the story of arbitration is lost forever. It is impossible to piece together the reality not only because of the temporal remoteness but also because arbitration has always been a private dispute resolution. Mustill (2014) also notes that arbitration has been radically transformed since the 1950s and that transformation is more significant than all the changes that took place in its entire recorded history. For these reasons, in following the outline of what is believed to be the story of arbitration, more emphasis will be put on the modern era and, specifically, the post–World War II period.

The literature on the history of arbitration suggests that this dispute resolution technique is not a modern invention. The earliest origins of commercial arbitration are claimed to go back as far as ancient Babylon (now Iraq) dating to 2800 BCE, ancient Egypt dating to 2500 BCE, and ancient Greece dating to 500 BCE (Blankenship, 2010; Natanson, 2013; Roebuck, 2001). Further, scholars believe that arbitration was practised in the Roman Empire (Böckstiegel, 2009; Roebuck and de Fumichon, 2004), the Byzantine Empire

(Wright, 1913), Arabia, and the Islamic Caliphate (Ahdab and Ahdab, 1998). At that time, it was not uncommon for arbitrators to rely on scripture to decide disputes.

Centuries after the collapse of the Roman Empire, the kingdoms of medieval Europe revived Roman arbitration (Böckstiegel, 2009). The Middle Ages witnessed the growth of arbitration between merchants trading between the East and the West and passing from a trade fair to a trade fair and from market to market (Noussia, 2010). It is viewed as the first time that arbitration became international (Natanson, 2013), following political and economic changes in Europe that made markets more accessible (Gucer, 2009). At that time, arbitration provided a level playing field – a neutral dispute resolution method – whereby an arbitrator was selected from the ranks of the merchant class according to their commercial expertise and sound judgement. The arbitrator's decision was not based on national law as such a thing did not exist at the time (Gucer, 2009; Horwitz, 1974; Glennm, 2016). Rather, the arbitrator's decision was in accord with the Law Merchant, or merchant law (Trakman, 1983, cited in [Ossman, 2003]). The Law Merchant was comprised of a set of commercial rules and principles that were distinct from the law of the land. This extra-national mercantile law represented an autonomous system of rules that were developed by merchants and applied by arbitrators, who were fellow merchants, throughout Europe (Serbest, 2013; DiMatteo, 2013; Mustill, 1989; Berman and Kaufman, 1978).

Centuries later, during the Renaissance, European nations passed laws to regulate and govern arbitration. For instance, England adopted the Arbitration Act of 1697 and France put in place a compulsory system of commercial arbitration in 1560, which was revamped during the French Revolution. During the French Revolution the resort to arbitration was declared to be a natural right for all citizens protected by the 1791 constitution (Noussia, 2010; Blackaby et al., 2015; Böckstiegel, 2009).

Parallel to this legislative recognition and regulation of arbitration, the industrial revolution was taking place. The industrial revolution brought with it sweeping changes to the construction field. The new technology of the industrial age made it possible to construct large-scale canals in England in the 18th century (Derrington, 1987).

The design and construction of canals gave rise to a new important discipline called civil engineering. The Society for Civil Engineers was founded in 1771 and, decades later, the Institution of Civil Engineers, the first engineering institution in the world, was founded in 1818 (Derrington, 1987). At the same time, the railway era came into existence. The first public railway in the world, connecting Liverpool and Manchester, was opened in 1830 (Derrington, 1987).

Parallel to these developments at the national level, construction began to enter the international stage. Since the industrial age, the mechanisation of construction has led to the construction of large civil engineering projects, such as canals and railways and artificial harbours (Linder, 1994). These vital infrastructure assets made construction, for probably the first time, a cross-border commercial activity. Britain, France, and other European nations began to export construction know-how and technology to build other countries' railways and canals. One of the largest international construction projects in this era was the Suez Canal in Egypt, a geographic crossroad from Europe to India that was designed and financed by Britain and France and opened in 1869 (Milner, 2011).

The end of the 19th century and most of the 20th century witnessed winds of significant changes concerning both the construction sector and arbitration.

On the construction level, for the first time an interest in construction contracts, construction law, and construction arbitration in the industrialised nations increased (Thomas and Wright, 2016).

In the 19th century, civil engineering and building projects significantly grew. To serve the needs of industrialisation, large civil engineering projects to build canals and railways were on the rise. Parallel thereto, there was an increasing level of construction activities to deliver mills, factories, and houses for the growing working population in the industrial towns and cities. Civil engineering and building works were governed by contracts regulating various matters, such as price, time for completion, and specifications of the works to be done (Thomas and Wright, 2016).

The increased complexity and pressure for timely completion, among other things, revealed a need for the standardisation of building and civil engineering contracts. The first standard contract was published by the Royal Institution of British Architects (RIBA) in 1870 (Broome and Hayes, 1997). Thereafter, several standard forms of construction contracts were published in England and elsewhere. RIBA was the forerunner of the Joint Contracts Tribunal (JCT) forms of contract, which were originally published in 1963. The Institution of Civil Engineers (ICE) conditions of contract were in print in 1945 (Bunni, 2005). The ICE standard form provided the basis for the first standard form of international construction contract known as the Conditions of Contract (International) for Works of Civil Engineering Construction, which was published in 1957 by FIDIC (Bunni, 2005). These standard forms have gone through several revisions and updates over the last decades. The standard forms of construction contracts in use today can be traced back to the conditions of contracts that were drafted in the 19th century.

In addition to the growing interest in standard forms of construction contracts, a large body of construction case law was developed during the industrial revolution (Thomas and Wright, 2016). This led to the publication of textbooks aiming to explain the contractual and legal aspects of construction. The first textbook to be dedicated to construction contracts as distinct from commercial contracts was *Hudson Building and Engineering Contracts*, which was first published in 1891 (Dyson, 2018). Hudson's book remains one of the leading authorities in the field. Its 13th edition was published in 2017 (Clay and Dennys, 2017). In the late 19th century, textbooks dedicated to construction arbitration started to appear in print. The first textbook devoted to construction arbitration appears to be *Wright on Building Arbitrations*, which was published in 1894 (Wright, 1913).

On the international arbitration level, an unprecedented reform movement was taking place. England led the nations in the modernisation of arbitration legislation and passed a new Arbitration Act in 1889. The City of London Chamber of Arbitration (later, the London Court of International Arbitration) was formed in 1891 (LCIA, 2018). The Chartered Institute of Arbitrators was founded in 1915 (CIArb, 2018a). Following the aftermath of World War I, the International Chamber of Commerce (ICC) International Court of Arbitration was established in 1923 (ICC, 2018). In the same year, in contemplation of resolving the problem concerning the lack of enforceability of arbitration agreements, the Geneva Protocol on Arbitration Clauses of 1923 was adopted by the League of Nations. This was shortly followed by the Geneva Convention on the Execution of Foreign Awards of 1927 in order to tackle the challenge of enforcement of foreign arbitration awards (Moses, 2008; Serbest, 2013; Mustill, 1989).

Following World War II, and in light of the subsequent expansion of international trade, the limitations of the Geneva Convention became evident. The enforcement of awards was a cumbersome and time-consuming process (Serbest, 2013). Further, the convention was not ratified by several large trading nations, such as the United States (Gaillard and Savage, 1999). Accordingly, the newly born United Nations drafted a new instrument intended to address these problems related to the enforcement of foreign arbitral awards. The UN hosted an international conference in New York. As a result, the New York Convention on the Recognition and Enforcement of Foreign Arbitral Awards ('New York Convention') came into being in 1958 (Gaillard and Savage, 1999; Serbest, 2013; Nazzini, 2018).

Today, the New York Convention is considered the most successful and fundamental international instrument in the entire history of international commercial arbitration (Moses, 2008; Serbest, 2013; Mustill, 1989). By 2021, it had been ratified by 169 nations, including all important trading nations (Biresaw, 2022).

According to some scholars (Dezalay and Garth, 1998; Nazzini, 2018), the modern era of international arbitration started after World War II. Dezalay and Garth (1998), in their famous sociological work concerning the emergence of international commercial arbitration, assert that the success of international commercial arbitration as it is known today is attributed to the major arbitrations that happened between the Euro-American conglomerates and the Arab states in the mid-20th century that took place in a rapidly changing political, economic, and legal world order.

The fallout from World War II led to the end of colonialism, the rise of nation-states, and the creation of a new world order respecting the sovereignty of nation-states. These independent countries lacked vital infrastructure. At the same time, enormous amounts of oil were discovered in the Arab Gulf states. The governments of the newly born nations lacked the technology and the know-how to make use of the discovered oil or to build their infrastructure. As such, to harness the oil wealth, they had to enter into concession agreements with multinational oil companies. The enormous oil revenues, which skyrocketed after the oil crisis in 1973, made it possible for the Arab states to enter into contracts with multinational engineering and construction companies to build their infrastructure (Dezalay and Garth, 1998). Statistical evidence from that period shows that international construction projects greatly increased in the 1970s and afterwards (Hoffmann, 1989). The vast majority of these projects took place in the Arab states (Hoffmann, 1989). According to Linder (1994), the massive construction programmes initiated by the oil-producing Arab states played a key role in the internationalisation of the construction industry.

The discovery of oil and the subsequent change in the economic landscape of the region (Hoffmann, 1989) have also led to gigantic international commercial and investment disputes related to commercial contracts and concession agreements. These disputes were referred to international arbitration.

In the 1950s and 1960s, a series of high-profile arbitration cases arising out of the nationalisation of oil concessions were lost by the Arab states in favour of the seven sisters (Dezalay and Garth, 1998). One noteworthy case is *Sheikh of Abu Dhabi v. Petroleum Development Ltd [1952]*. In this case, the Emirate was the losing party. This was shocking for the Emirate and others on many levels. Most importantly, the decision of the English arbitrator, Lord Asquith, to disregard the applicable law of the Emirate and apply English law instead was inflammatory and derogatory. It appeared as a form of neo-colonialism (Bishop et al., 2005; Gaillard and Savage, 1999). The arbitrators of other high-profile disputes regarding oil concessions in the Gulf region (*Ruler of Qatar v. International Marine Oil Co. Ltd. [1953]*, and *Saudi Arabia v. Arab American Oil Co. (ARAMCO) [1963]*) also disregarded the national laws of these countries that governed the oil concession agreements (see Section 5.5.3). Therefore, the Arab states viewed arbitration as biased towards the former colonial powers and their large oil companies (Dezalay and Garth, 1998).

As in the case of the petroleum disputes, arbitration was used to resolve the mega-construction disputes that followed the huge petrodollar international construction projects of the 1970s and 1980s (Dezalay and Garth, 1998; Hoffmann, 1989). Similar to oil arbitrations, the Arab states suffered from a string of losses in ICC arbitration cases arising from large construction contracts in the 1970s. This reinforced the perception that international arbitration was unfair and existed solely to maintain the interest of the old colonial powers (Dezalay and Garth, 1998).

The period between the 1950s and 1970s represented a tremendous challenge to this new world order (i.e., international arbitration as a post-colonial international private justice system). The series of unpleasant outcomes of the huge oil and construction arbitrations made the Arab states sceptical about international arbitration. They viewed it as an alternative tool to colonialism and Western domination. Some Arab states retaliated by resisting agreement on arbitration clauses in their contracts with multinational petroleum companies and construction companies. This attitude was, of course, subject to the relative bargaining power between multinationals and host governments (Dezalay and Garth, 1998).

Nevertheless, several favourable arbitration awards in the 1970s and 1980s gradually restored the confidence of the Arab states that arbitration is perhaps the most appropriate dispute resolution technique for cross-border disputes. Beginning in the 1970s and accelerating in the 1980s, the ICC became the focal point for major arbitrations, with gigantic sums in controversy, which were tied to the large-scale construction projects that were mostly located in the Arab states. In that period, the Western-Arab arbitrations represented a significant part of international commercial arbitration cases, which were dominated by construction arbitration cases. Following the acceptance of arbitration as an adequate technique for the resolution of international disputes, the ICC international arbitration cases of the 1970s and 1980s – mostly related to the mega construction projects in the Arab states – fuelled the growth of the entire field of international commercial arbitration (Dezalay and Garth, 1998; Hoffmann, 1989).

Overall, it is fair to conclude that these gigantic petroleum and construction arbitrations paved the way for a worldwide acceptance of arbitration as the legitimate way to resolve transnational business disputes. Events in the political, economic, and legal fields, especially decolonisation, the oil crisis, the petrodollar mega-construction projects, the growth of international trade, the power of Anglo-American law firms, and the transnational legal development have all combined to produce the new legal order (Dezalay and Garth, 1998).

In 1985, following a worldwide acceptance of international arbitration, a further landmark advancement in international arbitration, and perhaps the final breakthrough up to now, was the United Nations Commission on International Trade Law (UNCITRAL) Model Law on International Commercial Arbitration ('the UNCITRAL Model Law') which many countries have adopted, sometimes with some modifications, as their national arbitration acts. This has brought considerable harmonisation in arbitration practice throughout the world (Moses, 2008; Serbest, 2013).

Overall, this brief overview of the history of international construction arbitration shows that arbitration has always been at the heart of the growth of international trade and commerce, including international construction. Today, arbitration is as essential to international construction as international construction was vital for the success of arbitration in being accepted as an international private justice system.

2.6 Arbitral decision-making on the substance of disputes

Arbitrators make substantive and procedural decisions. The scope of research on substantive arbitral decision-making is broad indeed. It includes questions on how arbitrators find facts (Landolt, 2012), the difference between individual decision-making and group decision-making and the influence of a tribunal deliberation on the dispute outcome (Berger and Schneider, 2014), the influence of appointment method (party-appointed vs. institutional) (Bishop and Reed, 1998; Diamond, 2003; Karton, 2013), the influence of arbitration type (ad hoc vs. institutional), the role of precedent (Kaufmann-Kohler, 2007; Moloo and King, 2014; Guillaume, 2011; Weidemaier, 2009), the influence of an arbitrator's background or unconscious bias (Ossman, 2003; Berger and Schneider, 2014; Flood and Caiger, 1993; Callahan, 1982; Brekoulakis, 2013; Coulson, 1990), or other extra-legal factors (Schultz, 2015) on the arbitration outcome.

It is obviously not possible to cover at one time all aspects of arbitral decision-making on the merits. Therefore, the emphasis of this book is on the substantive norms that arbitrators rely on to reach or justify their decisions.

2.7 The substantive norms international arbitrators apply to resolve construction disputes

To determine a dispute, an arbitrator needs to form a reasonably clear picture of the 'is' and the 'ought'. In other words, an arbitrator needs to determine what the parties 'did' and what they 'should have done'. The first part (i.e., is/did) concerns determining the facts of the dispute i.e., what probably (not necessarily certainly) happened. The second part (i.e., ought/should have done) concerns determining what should, or should not, occur in particular circumstances and, hence, it guides an arbitrator's decision on how a particular behaviour is to be judged (Haggard and Mentschikoff, 1977). When an arbitrator determines the extent to which each party is in the right or the wrong, based on the extent to which the conduct of each party coincides with or is discrepant with what the arbitrator believes each should have done, then the decision has been reached even though it may not have been articulated (Haggard and Mentschikoff, 1977).

Any decision on the question of 'who is right' in a dispute situation, however, requires the use of a set of norms or standards against which the conduct involved in the dispute is to be measured by the decision-makers because wrongness or rightness can never be a question of fact but it is always a matter of judgement as to values (Mentschikoff and Haggard, 1977). Substantive norms are those used to make a normative judgement as to the wrongness or rightness of the parties' behaviour at the time the dispute arose

(Mentschikoff and Haggard, 1977). Arbitrators need to apply substantive norms to the facts in order to make their judgement on how meritorious the parties' claims are.

If a dispute reaches a court, the normative standard a judge applies is prescribed by the law (Levin, 1997). However, if a construction dispute is referred to international arbitration, the normative standard that will be applied by a tribunal is seemingly less certain. Do arbitrators base their decisions on a toss of a coin, personal wisdom and a sense of fairness, commercial norms, or legal norms? This is the question that this book sets out to answer.

The uncertainty surrounding how international construction arbitrators make their substantive decisions is discussed in the next section.

2.8 Arbitral decision-making: The theoretical and empirical accounts[1]

This section provides a glimpse into the extant knowledge relevant to international construction arbitration decision-making. For a better understanding, it is important to make a distinction between the available knowledge in accordance with epistemological foundations. The author proposes a taxonomy of arbitration decision-making scholarship that divides the literature into theoretical and empirical research. The theoretical literature examines arbitral decisions from normative (i.e., discussing how decisions ought to be made according to a value position) and prescriptive (i.e., discussing how decisions are required to be made) accounts. While normative accounts are philosophical in nature, prescriptive accounts are pragmatic. The empirical research seeks to provide informative, descriptive (asking how decisions are made), and explanatory (asking why decisions are made in a particular way) accounts.

2.8.1 How should arbitrators decide on construction disputes?

The extant literature offers theoretical prescriptive and normative accounts of 'how' arbitrators 'ought to' decide commercial or construction disputes. These arguments are conflicting because the values that are proposed to guide decision-making can be inconsistent. The absence of a common normative ground is problematic for the construction parties and their legal advisors as it paves the way for inconsistency in and unpredictability of arbitral decision-making. In particular, it appears that there is no full consensus in the arbitration scholarship on whether arbitrators should follow the law while deciding on the substance of disputes. The debate on the legal vis-à-vis commercial standards to govern arbitral reasoning and judgement has been ongoing for centuries.

Evidence of the traditional perspective of arbitral decision-making in US construction arbitration can be found in the textbook *Wright on Building Arbitrations*, which was first published in 1894 and then in a second edition in 1913. Wright (1913) asserted that technical arbitrators, not obstructed by law, are to render awards based on the evidence and using their own common-sense technical knowledge and commercial practice. He rejected early arguments to legalise arbitration by appointing attorneys as arbitrators and

1 Note: Section 2.8 is based on Besaiso, H., Fenn, P. and Emsley, M. (2017). International construction arbitration: A need for decoding the black box of decision making. *International Construction Law Review*, *34*(3), pp. 288–308.

putting emphasis on legal procedure. He fiercely argued that 'no class of men, probably, are more competent on the whole and technically to act as an arbitrator in the building and engineering disputes than the experienced architect, contractor or engineer'. His arguments regarding the desirable background of an arbitrator and the normative standards that should underpin arbitral decision-making in construction disputes rested on the grounds that most questions that frequently came up before arbitration tribunals were not questions of law but questions of fact. These factual controversies involved matters related to construction techniques, drawings, trade customs, the value of works, etc., which the technical arbitrator usually has at his fingertips. Hence, the construction professional, as an arbitrator, can decide the normative question 'What is right and proper to be done under certain conditions and circumstances?' (Wright, 1913). A century after Wright's book, the same debate remains ongoing. Chapter 4 provides a more detailed insight into this debate.

2.8.2 How are arbitrators 'required' to decide construction disputes?

Mitchell (2012) reexamined the old-age question of whether arbitrators are 'required' to follow the law in the context of international arbitration. He started his article by stating:

> A shocking string of emails circulated within a very credible Listserv disclosed that a number of full-time arbitrators took the position that arbitrators need not follow the law in drafting awards. The author strongly disagrees.

Mitchell (2012) examined international institutional arbitration rules (e.g., AAA, ICC, LCIA), the UNCITRAL Model Law, and the New York Convention and concluded that arbitrators are required to follow the law and the terms of the parties' contract. He argued that arbitrators should meet the parties' expectations of proper adherence to the law that the parties bargained for when they negotiated and entered into their contract (Mitchell, 2012). Likewise, Webster and Buhler (2014) assert that arbitrators are expected and required to apply the law because, even though courts will probably not review arbitrators' interpretation of the law, a failure to apply the law can result in an annulment of the award.

However, the reality is much more complex, and it is not in perfect alignment with these conclusions and assertions. In fact, and unlike court litigation, there is little opportunity to appeal or challenge an arbitral award on substantive grounds (i.e., on the basis that an arbitral tribunal made a mistake of law). The arbitration statutes of many countries and most institutional arbitration rules, reflecting the policy of the New York Convention and the Model Law, do not provide for appeal based on erroneous legal conclusions or factual findings. The available grounds for challenge, nullification, or setting aside of awards at the place of arbitration or for non-enforcement of awards at the place of enforcement (the state in which enforcement is sought, which will be a state where the losing party has recoverable assets) are limited and narrow and almost entirely procedural or jurisdictional (Blackaby et al., 2015; Kaufmann-Kohler, 2005). In annulment or recognition and enforcement proceedings, the court's focus is on procedural matters, and, hence, judges will probably not set aside an award or refuse enforcement on meritorious grounds that the arbitrators made a wrong decision based on an error of law or contract interpretation or fact (Karton, 2013).

As a case in point, in 2013, the High Court of Australia refused to overturn an arbitration award 'due to an error of law on the face of the award' (DiMatteo, 2013). The court noted that Article 28 of the UNCITRAL Model Law does not require an arbitral award to be correct in law. The court also stated that the instructions of both the UNCITRAL Model Law and the New York Convention are to enforce foreign arbitral awards and not to review such awards for errors in the application of the law (DiMatteo, 2013).

In addition, the Guide to the UNCITRAL Model Law on International Commercial Arbitration notes that, under Article 28 of the UNCITRAL Model Law, 'an arbitral tribunal is not required to apply the law chosen by the parties in a manner that a competent court would have applied it' (Holtzmann and Neuhaus, 1989 cited in DiMatteo, 2013). This probably implies a more relaxed approach to applying the law, which permits a deviation from legal principles or accommodation of commercial considerations.

The exclusion of substantive grounds as legitimate grounds to challenge arbitral awards by national arbitration laws and institutional arbitration rules tends to vest arbitrators with a broad and virtually unreviewable decision-making power (Jenkins and Stebbings, 2006; McConnaughay, 1999). Even obvious legal mistakes in arbitration awards are virtually immune from appellate review (Rogers, 2001). The absence of formal constraints on the arbitrators' ability to err in finding the facts, determining the content of the law, or applying the law to the fact may pave the way for inconsistent and unpredictable arbitration awards. DiMatteo (2013) similarly suggests that the flexibility of arbitral reasoning based on both hard law and soft law (i.e., legal arguments and commercial arguments) flows naturally from the protection and immunity granted by the narrow grounds for appealing an arbitration award.

The foregoing discussion shows that there is a disconnection between the arbitration rules requiring arbitrators to follow the law in rendering arbitral awards and the national arbitration laws, the UNCITRAL Model Law, and the New York Convention providing no grounds for setting aside or for non-enforcement of arbitral awards in case arbitrators do not follow the law. This disconnection reveals a gap in the arbitral decision-making system. The vacuum left by the absence of a mechanism to ensure compliance with the requirement to apply the law in making decisions casts some doubt on the seriousness of this requirement or at least indicates a defect in the international arbitration system. This defect is probably a natural outcome of trying to reconcile genuinely irreconcilable goals: getting it right (correctness) and getting it done (finality).

2.8.3 How do arbitrators decide construction disputes? Empirical evidence from socio-legal empirical research

> Much of our understanding of what happens in arbitration proceedings is based on anecdotal sources of information such as reported court cases, published arbitral awards, and attorney 'war stories'. The problem with anecdotes, of course, is that it is difficult to evaluate whether the event described is typical or atypical, frequent or infrequent, ordinary or extreme.
>
> *(Drahozal, 2003, p. 1)*

In an epistemological revolution against the longstanding paradigm in our knowledge of the arbitral decision-making process, few empiricists went beyond the theoretical debate or anecdotal evidence. Empirical research seeks empirical evidence (i.e., seeks an answer based on what arbitrators actually do or what arbitrators think they do). The author's review of relevant literature finds four empirical attempts to challenge the frontier of existing knowledge in the domain of domestic construction arbitration (Stipanowich and Ulrich, 2014; Ossman, Bayraktar, and Cui, 2009; Bartlett, 2000; Thomson, 1994). It is worth mentioning that Stipanowich and Ulrich's (2014) study was limited neither to 'construction' arbitration nor to 'domestic' arbitration in the United States as almost half of the commercial arbitrators who participated in the study were involved in domestic and international construction arbitrations. These four studies are supplemented by what appears to be the only relevant empirical study that examined contract interpretation in the context of international commercial arbitration: Karton (2013).

Empiricists have sought to answer whether arbitrators follow the law (Karton, 2013; Thomson, 1994; Stipanowich and Ulrich, 2014) and whether arbitrators render consistent and predictable awards (Bartlett, 2000; Ossman, Bayraktar, and Cui, 2009). These studies contribute to a better empirical understanding, and they are summarised in the following paragraphs.

The earliest study was undertaken by the American Arbitration Association (AAA) in 1994. It relied on a large-scale quantitative survey to obtain empirical evidence as to how construction arbitrators think they decide (Thomson, 1994). The study was prompted by a prevailing concern amongst many users of US construction arbitration regarding the arbitrators' non-adherence to legal standards and their tendency to engage in unjustifiable compromise decisions (Stipanowich, 1987). So, the study asked an empirical question to construction arbitrators: 'Do you always follow the law in formulating your awards?'. This question is different from the theoretical questions debated earlier: 'Should arbitrators follow the law?' (Section 2.8.1) and 'Are arbitrators required to follow the law?' (Section 2.8.2). The survey found that 20% of construction arbitrators did not always follow the law in formulating arbitral awards while 72% of construction arbitrators did. If arbitrators have no obligation to follow the substantive law when rendering an award, then they may not necessarily be bound to follow the terms of the parties' contract as the law normally requires. In this regard, the survey asked the following question to the construction arbitrators: 'Do you always enforce the parties' contract according to its terms in formulating your awards?'. The survey found that 25% of construction arbitrators did not always enforce the parties' contract according to its terms while 67% of construction arbitrators applied it. In this case, it is legitimate to question the point of having a contract in the first place given that some arbitrators may not enforce it. The arbitrators who responded that they enforced the parties' contracts in all disputes they arbitrated considered this as part of their obligation. The arbitrators who responded otherwise noted that contracts were often incomplete (i.e., ambiguous or silent on the matters in dispute) or unfair and, hence, would lead to inequitable outcomes (Thomson, 1994).

Although arbitration was one of the most preferred dispute resolution techniques in the US construction industry, the AAA's study concluded that arbitration users were discontented with arbitration that was not only expensive and lengthy but also produced awards that were not based on facts, contract, and law. In a situation like this, what good is it to opt for arbitration when it is not only more expensive and time-consuming but also more uncertain and unpredictable than litigation? The finding that some arbitrators did not always follow the law or the parties' contract in rendering their awards is alarming. When a contract or an arbitration agreement specifies the substantive law applicable to the dispute, arbitrators would be exceeding their authority if they render an award to the contrary of what the law requires. The paradox here is that appeal, whether in domestic or in international settings, is generally possible on the ground of arbitrators' excess of their authority (*ultra petita*) but not on the ground of a substantive error as a result of ignoring the contract or law (da Silveira and Levy, 2008).

Although the AAA survey marked a commendable start in giving a glimpse into construction arbitration decision-making, it had some methodological drawbacks. Drahozal (2006) points out that the survey results provide little or no evidence of how often arbitrators deviate from the provisions of the parties' contract and its governing law. The survey questions did not attempt to solicit such information either in quantitative or in qualitative terms. The wording of the two questions, starting with 'Do you always...', generated answers that did not distinguish between an arbitrator who deviated once and an arbitrator who deviated all the time from the parties' contract and the law. Accordingly, the results of the survey were inconclusive (Drahozal, 2006). In addition, it is important to be mindful that the context of the AAA study was limited to US domestic construction arbitration.

In addition to this study, recent empirical studies on US commercial arbitration indicate that the same users' concerns, which may reduce demand for arbitration services, still linger (Stipanowich and Lamare, 2014). The main concerns still revolve around the possibility that arbitrators will not follow the applicable legal standards in rendering awards, the perceived tendency of arbitrators to indulge in inappropriate compromises in award-making, and the difficulty of successfully appealing arbitration awards based on those two concerns (Stipanowich and Lamare, 2014).

However, it is unclear to what extent these concerns are relics of past decades when the environment of construction arbitration was different. In the present day, the environment of construction arbitration has changed since the AAA's 1994 survey and has much changed since Wright's books of 1891 and 1913. One key change relates to the configuration of construction arbitration tribunals. Construction professionals or multidisciplinary panels have long been used in the arbitration of construction disputes in the United States. Recent evidence (Stipanowich, 2014; Stipanowich and Ulrich, 2014) suggests that these panels are diminishing as there is an increasing emphasis on appointing arbitrators with legal backgrounds instead of construction professional arbitrators. The construction arbitration 'drift' towards a legal model that flows from the increasing intrusion by legal professionals sitting as arbitrators or representing the parties. This change will probably transform the landscape of construction arbitral decision-making because the background of arbitrators may affect their application of the contract and the law and the weight they give to commercial practice.

To assess the extent to which these concerns were still justified, Pepperdine's Straus Institute for Dispute Resolution in cooperation with the College of Commercial Arbitrators undertook a study on commercial arbitration practice in 2013 (Stipanowich and Ulrich, 2014). The researchers, Stipanowich and Ulrich, 2014, criticised the emphasis in the arbitration literature on the 'process' rather than the 'outcome'. They used a survey to examine several aspects of arbitral decision-making, including the application of substantive law. The survey targeted the most experienced arbitrators in the United States who have arbitrated domestic and international disputes. However, the survey questions made no distinction between domestic and international arbitration. Almost half of the respondents arbitrated construction cases.

The survey responses indicate, contrary to the users' perceptions and concerns, that nearly all of the experienced arbitrators tend to be meticulous in paying heed to legal arguments and that they do whatever they can to ascertain and follow the law in rendering an award. The greater consideration given to legal authority in arbitral decision-making could be explained by the legal background and orientation of the arbitrators who responded to the survey as all of them claimed a legal or judicial background (Stipanowich and Ulrich, 2014). The same observation or hypothesis can be extrapolated to real-life settings. The increased emphasis on appointing arbitrators with legal backgrounds and the commensurate de-emphasis on appointing arbitrators with construction backgrounds, in practice, will probably elevate the status of legal standards in construction arbitral decision-making.

However, the responses to the survey add a puzzling caveat that leaves the question of whether arbitrators apply the law with no definitive answer. A quarter of the respondents said that at least 'sometimes' they feel 'free to follow their own sense of equity and fairness in rendering an award even if the result would be contrary to applicable law' (Stipanowich, 2014). This statement blurs our understanding for two reasons. First, the semantic ambiguity inherent in the word 'sometimes' makes it uncertain in meaning. It has different meanings to different individuals. People have different interpretations of the same numeric frequency depending on the context and the general expectation connected with the phenomenon (Bühring-Uhle, 2005). Second, it remains unclear how those arbitrators interpret their mandate or conceptualise their role. In some situations, they may believe that to achieve fairness they are left with no choice but to refuse to apply the law. This is problematic because the arbitrators' choice to ignore the law in favour of their own sense of fairness may be contrary to the parties' expectations. The fact that arbitral awards are almost entirely immune to an annulment on substantive grounds should not be exploited by arbitrators to impose their own sense of fairness. Stipanowich (2014) argues that arbitrators should be mindful of their 'ethical obligation' to ensure that they are acting in accordance with the parties' expectations. This argument proposes that the benchmark for measuring the effectiveness of arbitral awards should be the parties' expectations, whether grounded in the legal model, the commercial model, or something else. In other words, there is no universal 'right' approach to render arbitral awards. It depends on the parties' choices, thus reflecting the principle of 'party autonomy'.

Despite the empirical insight the study of Stipanowich and Ulrich (2014) provides, it has some methodological limitations. First, the survey questions made no distinction between domestic and international arbitration: making it difficult to ascertain the transferability of the findings to the specific context of international commercial and construction arbitration as opposed to the domestic context of US arbitration. Second, this quantitative study offers little understanding of how arbitrators make their decisions. This is because the quantitative methodology restricts our ability to explore in depth the complex and multifaceted reality of certain aspects of arbitral decision-making.

The two empirical studies discussed in the previous paragraphs (Thomson, 1994; Stipanowich and Ulrich, 2014), which focus on the extent to which US construction arbitrators adhere to the parties' contract and the governing law, suggest that some arbitrators, at least sometimes, may not apply the substantive law. Nevertheless, the results are far from conclusive due to methodological and epistemological limitations.

In addition to these two survey-based studies, two studies examined whether construction arbitrators render consistent and predictable awards (Bartlett, 2000; Ossman, Bayraktar, and Cui, 2009).

The first study, known as *Meadowsweet v. Bindweed* case and published in the journal of the Chartered Institute of Arbitrators, involved a hypothetical multi-claim construction dispute scenario distributed to five distinguished arbitrators in England (Bartlett, 2000). The five arbitrators reached different findings of facts and conclusions of law, including variant determinations of liability and quantification of damages.

The second study (Ossman, Bayraktar, and Cui, 2009) involved a hypothetical construction-delay dispute scenario summarised in two pages and distributed to a pool of construction professionals in the United States, amongst which 429 responded. The dispute included uncontested facts, but it was not an either-or dichotomous situation with short and simple facts. The respondents were asked to decide on liability and damages. Although facts were uncontested, the arbitrators rendered inconsistent awards, including different apportionments of liability and quantifications of damages.

The previous four studies examine construction and commercial arbitral decision-making in the domestic contexts of the United Kingdom and the United States. A literature search found no empirical study attempting to explore decision-making in international construction arbitration.

Therefore, readers who want to assess the transferability of the findings of these empirical studies need to be mindful of the possible contextual variations. For instance, the environment of international construction or commercial arbitration seems to be dominated by the legal profession. The arbitrators tend to be law professors, senior barristers, senior partners in law firms, or retired judges. Second, the available evidence suggests that the construction parties do not enter into international arbitration to avoid legal determinations for their disputes. Rather, they are keen to get their disputes decided on legal grounds. The main reason for choosing international arbitration is because parties from different nationalities do not wish their rights and obligations to be determined by the courts of the other party's state of nationality (Dezalay and Garth, 1998). Hence, the application of the law and other standards in decision-making could have a more serious treatment in international arbitration than in domestic arbitration.

The author found only one empirical study that examines substantive decision-making in the context of international commercial arbitration. Karton's empirical work, which was introduced in his PhD thesis (Karton, 2010), updated in a book (Karton, 2013), published in two journal papers (Karton, 2012; Karton, 2015) and a book chapter (Karton, 2014), examines how international commercial arbitrators decide and whether they follow the law in the interpretation of contracts. Karton analysed a number of international commercial arbitration awards (43 in Karton (2010); 53 in Karton (2012); 73 in Karton (2015)) to examine whether international arbitrators follow the interpretive methods dictated by the governing law or follow the interpretive methods they prefer. He finds that international arbitrators are geared towards subjective interpretation (also referred to as contextual interpretation). As a result of this phenomenon, some arbitrators would admit or accept evidence of the parties' subjective intent even if the rules of contract interpretation laid down in the governing law provide otherwise. This is clearly different from the way national court judges apply the law. Although Karton's work offers useful insight, it has some methodological limitations. First, the sample of arbitration awards he analysed was small, and, hence, it makes his conclusions tentative. Second, even if there are an adequate number of arbitral awards to permit doctrinal works on arbitration, this on its own is not sufficient to provide a full understanding of how arbitrators make their decisions and normative choices (Schultz, 2015). Third, his study provides a description but little explanation of why international arbitrators decide in a particular way.

Overall, the theoretical and empirical evidence provided in Section 2.8 illustrates that the application of substantive law should not be treated as taken for granted in arbitration settings. Arbitrators have different reasons or incentives to depart from the applicable legal rules. Gaillard and Savage (1999) point out that there are three theories that are used to justify, in certain circumstances, arbitrators' deviation from the stipulations of the substantive law. These are (1) incompleteness of the chosen law, (2) expansive application of international trade usages, and (3) international mandatory rules or international public policy. These theoretical propositions are critically discussed in Chapters 3, 4, and 7, respectively.

2.9 Conclusion

This chapter provides a working definition of international construction arbitration and argues that it is a distinct subset of international commercial arbitration. It outlines the main drivers for its popularity and recognition as the most fundamental dispute resolution technique in international construction contracts.

This is followed by a brief overview of the history of international construction arbitration. Embedded in this historical narrative are evolving views on the standards applicable to arbitral decision-making. The historical overview puts more emphasis on modern times, especially the era following World War II. One of the key challenges that faced international arbitration at that time was the developing world's distrust of the international arbitration process and its outcomes. In particular, the new nation-states were concerned about international arbitrators' bias and attitudes towards the application of substantive law to the parties' disputes.

Then, this chapter focuses on the core concern of this book (i.e., arbitral decision-making in international construction disputes). It discusses the different views on how arbitrators should decide, how they are required to decide by arbitration laws and rules, and how they actually decide based on the limited available empirical evidence. The lack of theoretical consensus and empirical understanding of arbitral decision-making in international construction disputes constitutes the knowledge gap that this book intends to fill.

The next chapter discusses in more detail the question of whether international arbitrators apply the substantive law the parties agreed to in the contract to resolve their disputes.

2.10 References

Ahdab, E., Hamid, A. & El Ahdab, J. (1998). *Arbitration with the Arab Countries*. The Hague: Kluwer Law International.

Andrews, N. (2016). *Arbitration and Contract Law*. Cham: Springer.

Baatz, N. (2016). 'Factual' and 'legal' causation in construction and infrastructure law: A thorny subject. *A Paper Based on Talks Given in Manchester on 22nd February 2016*. The Society of Construction Law.

Bartlett, A. (2000). A complete and unabridged facsimile of papers as seen by the honourable and illustrious arbitrator in the frequently perplexing and oft-times diverting case of Meadowsweet v Bindweed. *Arbitration*, 66(2), 83–163.

Berger, B. & Schneider, M. E. (2014). *Inside the Black Box: How Arbitral Tribunals Operate and Reach Their Decisions*. New York: JurisNet, LLC.

Berman, H. J. & Kaufman, C. (1978). The law of international commercial transactions (Lex Mercatoria). *Harvard International Law Journal*, 19(1), 221.

Besaiso, H., Fenn, P. and Emsley, M. (2017). International construction arbitration: A need for decoding the black box of decision making. *International Construction Law Review*, 34(3), 288–308.

Biresaw, S. M. (2022). Appraisal of the success of the instruments of international commercial arbitration vis-a-vis international commercial litigation and mediation in the harmonization of the rules of transnational commercial dispute resolution. *Journal of Dispute Resolution*, 2022(2), 1.

Bishop, D. & Reed, L. (1998). Practical guidelines for interviewing, selecting and challenging party-appointed arbitrators in international commercial arbitration. *Arbitration International*, 14(4), 395–430.

Bishop, R. D., Crawford, J. & Reisman, W. M. (2005). *Foreign Investment Disputes: Cases, Materials, and Commentary*. The Hague: Kluwer Law International.

Blackaby, N., Partasides, C., Redfern, A. & Hunter, M. (2015). *Redfern and Hunter on International Arbitration*. 6th ed. Oxford: Oxford University Press.

Blankenship, J. T. (2010). Isomorphism of construction arbitration: The key to its prevention and reversal. *Dispute Resolution Journal*, 65(2), 114.

Böckstiegel, K.-H. (2009). Past, present, and future perspectives of arbitration. *Arbitration International*, 25(3), 293–302.

Born, G. (2001). *International Commercial Arbitration: International and USA Spectscommentary and Materials*. The Hague: Kluwer Law International.

Born, G. (2015). *International Arbitration: Law and Practice*. 2nd ed. Alphen aan den Rijn: Kluwer Law International

Brekoulakis, S. (2013). Systemic bias and the institution of international arbitration: A new approach to arbitral decision-making. *Journal of International Dispute Settlement*, 4(3), 553–585.

Broome, J. & Hayes, R. (1997). A comparison of the clarity of traditional construction contracts and of the New Engineering Contract. *International Journal of Project Management*, 15(4), 255–261.

Bühring-Uhle, C. (2005). A survey on arbitration and settlement in international business disputes: Advantages of arbitration. *In*: Drahozal, C. & Naimark, R. (eds.) *Towards a Science of International Arbitration: Collected Empirical Research*. The Hague: Kluwer Law International.

Bunni, N. G. (2000). Recent developments in construction disputology. *Journal of International Arbitration*, 17(4), 105.

Bunni, N. G. (2005). *The FIDIC Forms of Contract*. 3rd ed. New Jersey: Blackwell Publishing.

Callahan, M. T. (1982). Procedures in construction arbitration: From an arbitrator's view. *Construction Lawyer*, 3(2), 3.

CIArb. (2018a). *The History of the Chartered Institute of Arbitrators* [Online]. Available: http://www.ciarb.org/about/history [Accessed 12 March 2018].

CIArb. (2018b). *What is Arbitration?* [Online]. Available: http://www.ciarb.org/dispute-appointment-service/arbitration/what-is-arbitration [Accessed 08 May 2018].

Clay, R. & Dennys, N. (2017). *Hudson's Building and Engineering Contracts*. 13th ed. London: Sweet & Maxwell.

Coulson, R. (1990). The decisionmaking process in arbitration. *Arbitration Journal*, 45(3), 37–41.

da Silveira, M. & Levy, L. (2008). Transgression of the arbitrators' authority: Article V (1)(c) of the New York convention. *In*: Gaillard, E. & Pietro, D. (eds.) *Enforcement of Arbitration*

Agreements and International Arbitral Awards: The New York Convention in Practice. London: Cameron May.

Derrington, J. (1987). Arbitration and the civil engineer. *Arbitration*, 53(2), 77–84.

Dezalay, Y. & Garth, B. G. (1998). *Dealing in Virtue: International Commercial Arbitration and the Construction of a Transnational Legal Order*. Chicago: University of Chicago Press.

Diamond, S. S. (2003). Psychological aspects of dispute resolution: Issues for international arbitration. *In*: Berg, A. J. V. D. (ed.) *International Commercial Arbitration: Important Contemporary Questions*. The Hague: Kluwer Law International.

DiMatteo, L. A. (2013). Soft law and the principle of fair and equitable decision making in international contract arbitration. *The Chinese Journal of Comparative Law*, 1(2), 221–255.

Drahozal, C. R. (2006). Is arbitration lawless. *Loyola of Los Angeles Law Review*, 40(1), 187.

Drahozal, C. R. (2003). Of rabbits and Rhinoceri: A survey of empirical research on international commercial arbitration. *Journal of International Arbitration*, 20(1), 23–34.

Dunham, K. F. (2010). Construction arbitration: Collected works. *Faulkner Law Review*, 2(2), 311.

Dyson, L. (2018). The contribution of construction cases to the development of the common law. *In*: Dyson, L. (ed.) *Justice: Continuity and Change*. 1st ed. Oxford: Hart Publishing.

Flood, J. & Caiger, A. (1993). Lawyers and Arbitration: The Juridification of Construction Disputes. *The Modern Law Review*, 56(3), 412–440.

Friedland, P. & Mistelis, L. (2015). *2015 International Arbitration Survey: Improvements and Innovations in International Arbitration*. Queen Mary University of London and School of International Arbitration. https://arbitration.qmul.ac.uk/media/arbitration/docs/2015_International_Arbitration_Survey.pdf. [Accessed 10 October 2022].

Gaillard, E. & Savage, J. (1999). *Fouchard, Gaillard, Goldman on International Commercial Arbitration*. The Hague: Kluwer law international.

Glennm, H. P. (2016). The law merchant and choice of law. *In*: Gélinas, F. (ed.) *Trade Usages and Implied Terms in the Age of Arbitration*. Oxford: Oxford University Press.

Gregory, D. W. & Berg, P. A. (2013). Construction lawyer: Problem or problem solver? The need for cost-effective dispute resolution in the construction industry. *Construction Lawyer*, 33(4), 16.

Gucer, S. (2009). Lex Mercatoria in international arbitration. *Ankara Bar Review*, 1(1), 30.

Guillaume, G. (2011). The use of precedent by international judges and arbitrators. *Journal of International Dispute Settlement*, 2(1), 5–23.

Haggard, H. & Mentschikoff, S. (1977). Responsible decision making in dispute settlement. *In*: Tapp, J. L. & Levine, F. J. (eds.) *Law, Justice, and the Individual in Society: Psychological and legal issues*. New York: Holt, Rinehart and Winston

Harmon, K. M. (2003). Resolution of construction disputes: A review of current methodologies. *Leadership and Management in Engineering*, 3(4), 187–201.

Hinchey, J. W. & Harris, T. L. (2008). *International Construction Arbitration Handbook*. Minnesota: Thomson West.

Hobeck, P., Mahnken, V. & Koebke, M. (2008). Time for Woolf reforms in international construction arbitration. *International Arbitration Law Review*, 11(2), 84.

Hoffmann, B. (1989). International construction arbitration. *In*: Sarcevic, P. (ed.) *Essays on International Commercial Arbitration*. London: Graham & Trotman.

Holtzmann, H. M. & Neuhaus, J. E. (1989). *A Guide to the UNCITRAL Model Law on International Commercial Arbitration: Legislative History and Commentary*. Alphen aan den Rijn: Kluwer Law International.

Horwitz, M. J. (1974). The historical foundations of modern contract law. *Harvard Law Review*, 87(5), 917–956.

ICC. (2018). *History* [Online]. Available: https://iccwbo.org/about-us/who-we-are/history/ [Accessed 12 March 2018].

Jenkins, J. & Rosenberg, K. (2013). Engineering and construction arbitration. *In*: Lew, J. D. M., Bor, H., Fullelove, G. & Greenaway, J. (eds.) *Arbitration in England: with Chapters on Scotland and Ireland*. The Hague: Kluwer Law International.

Jenkins, J. & Stebbings, S. (2006). *International Construction Arbitration Law*. 2nd ed. Alphen aan den Rijn: Kluwer Law International.

Karton, J. (2010). *The Culture of International Arbitration and the Evolution of Contract Law*. Doctor of Philosophy, University of Cambridge.

Karton, J. (2012). International commercial arbitrators' approaches to contractual interpretation. *International Business Law Journal*, 383.

Karton, J. (2013). *The Culture of International Arbitration and the Evolution of Contract Law*. Oxford: Oxford University Press.

Karton, J. (2014). International arbitration culture and global governance. *In*: Mattli, W. & Dietz, T. (eds.) *International Arbitration and Global Governance: Contending Theories and Evidence*. Oxford: Oxford University Press.

Karton, J. (2015). The arbitral role in contractual interpretation. *Journal of International Dispute Settlement*, 6(1), 4–41.

Kaufmann-Kohler, G. (2005). The arbitrator and the law: Does he/she know it? Apply it? How? And a few more questions. *Arbitration International*, 21(4), 631–638.

Kaufmann-Kohler, G. (2007). Arbitral precedent: Dream, necessity or excuse?: The 2006 freshfields lecture. *Arbitration International*, 23(3), 357–378.

Lagerberg, G. & Mistelis, L. (2006). International Arbitration: Corporate Attitudes and Practices. Queen Mary University of London and School of International Arbitration. Available at https://arbitration.qmul.ac.uk/media/arbitration/docs/IAstudy_2006.pdf [Accessed 12 December 2022].

Lagerberg, G. & Mistelis, L. (2013). *Corporate Choices in International Arbitration: Industry Perspectives*. Queen Mary University of London and School of International Arbitration. Available at https://www.pwc.com/gx/en/arbitration-dispute-resolution/assets/pwc-international-arbitration-study.pdf. [Accessed 12 December 2022].

Landolt, P. (2012). Arbitrators' Initiatives to Obtain Factual and Legal Evidence. *Arbitration International*, 28(2), 173–224.

Lane, P. M. (2012). Can construction arbitration learn from adjudication? *Proceedings of the Institution of Civil Engineers: Management, Procurement and Law*, 165(1), 35–39.

LCIA. (2018). *History* [Online]. Available: http://www.lcia.org/LCIA/history.aspx [Accessed 30 March 2018].

Levin, M. S. (1997). The role of substantive law in business arbitration and the importance of volition. *American Business Law Journal*, 35(1), 105–180.

Linder, M. (1994). *Projecting Capitalism: A History of the Internationalization of the Construction Industry*. Westport, CT: Greenwood Press.

Lloyd, H. (2001). Final report on construction industry arbitrations. *ICC International Court of Arbitration Bulletin*, 12(2).

McConnaughay, P. J. (1999). The risks and virtues of lawlessness: A second look at international commercial arbitration. *Northwestern University Law Review*, 93(2), 453.

Mentschikoff, S. & Haggard, E. (1977). Decision making and decision consensus in commercial arbitration. *In*: Tapp, J. L. & Levine, F. J. (eds.) *Law, Justice, and the Individual in Society: Psychological and Legal Issues*. New York: Holt, Rinehart and Winston.

Mentschikoff, S. (1961). Commercial arbitration. *Columbia Law Review*, 61(5), 846–869.

Milner, L. (2011). *The Suez Crisis* [Online]. Available: http://www.bbc.co.uk/history/british/modern/suez_01.shtml [Accessed 30 May 2018].

Mitchell, R. (2012). Must Arbitrators Follow the Law? *JAMS Global Construction Solutions Newsletter*. 1–2. Available at https://www.jamsadr.com/files/uploads/documents/gec-newsletter/jams-gec-news-2012-spring.pdf [Accessed 12 December 2016].

Moloo, R. & King, B. (2014). International arbitrators as lawmakers. *New York University Journal of International Law and Politics*, 46(3), 875–909.

Moses, M. L. (2008). *The Principles and Practice of International Commercial Arbitration*. Cambridge: Cambridge University Press.

Moss, G. (2004). Introductory materials on international commercial law. *Transnational Dispute Management*, 1(3), 1–161.

Mustill, M. J. (1989). Arbitration: History and background. *Journal of International Arbitration*, 6(2), 43–56.

Mustill, M. J. (2014). The history of international commercial arbitration: A sketch. *In*: Newman, L. W. & Hill, R. D. (eds.) *The Leading Arbitrators' Guide to International Arbitration*. 3rd ed. New York: Juris Publishing

Natanson, R. (2013). *The Choice of the Applicable Law as a Strategy in International Commercial Arbitration*. M.Sc., Toulouse Capitole University.

Nazzini, R. (2018). *Transnational Construction Arbitration: Key Themes in the Resolution of Construction Disputes*. New York: Informa Law from Routledge.

Nordon, C. L. (1935). British experience with arbitration. *University of Pennsylvania Law Review*, 83(3), 314–325.

Noussia, K. (2010). The history, importance and modern use of arbitration. *In*: Noussia, K. (ed.) *Confidentiality in International Commercial Arbitration: A Comparative Analysis of the Position Under English, US, German and French Law*. Cham: Springer

Nunes, F., Alvarenga, M., Rea, A. & Castejon, F. (2005). Brazil. *In*: Knutson, R. (ed.) *FIDIC: An Analysis of International Construction Contracts*. The Hague: Kluwer Law International.

O'Reilly, M. (1999). *Civil Engineering Construction Contracts*. London: Thomas Telford.

Ossman, G., Bayraktar, M. E. & Cui, Q. (2009). Consistency and reliability of construction arbitration decisions: Empirical study. *Journal of Management in Engineering*, 26(2), 56–64.

Ossman, G. (2003). *Construction Arbitration Consistency and Reliability: An Empirical Study*. M.Sc., Pepperdine University School of Law.

Park, W. W. (2010). Arbitrators and accuracy. *Journal of International Dispute Settlement*, 1(1), 25–53.

Potts, K. & Ankrah, N. (2008). *Construction Cost Management: Learning from Case Studies*. Abingdon: Taylor & Francis.

Rechsteiner, B. W. (2001). *Arbitragem Privada Internacional no Brasil*. São Paulo: Editora Revista dos Tribunais.

Roebuck, D. & de Fumichon, B. D. L. (2004). *Roman Arbitration*. Oxford: Holo Books.

Roebuck, D. (2001). *Ancient Greek Arbitration*. Oxford: Holo Books.

Rogers, C. A. (2001). Fit and Function in Legal Ethics: Developing a Code of Conduct for International Arbitration. *Michigan Journal of International Law*, 23(2), 341–423.

Schultz, T. (2015). Arbitral decision-making: Legal realism and law & economics. *Journal of International Dispute Settlement*, 6(2), 231–251.

Serbest, F. (2013). *Is There Scope for the Wider Application of Fast-track Arbitrations in the Resolution of International Commercial Disputes?* Doctor of Philosophy, King's College London.

Stephenson, D. A. (2001). *Arbitration Practice in Construction Contracts*. 5th ed. Oxford: Blackwell Science Ltd.

Stipanowich, T. J. (1987). A Preliminary Analysis of Responses to the Questionnaire on Construction Industry Arbitration. *The Construction Lawyer*, 7, 17.

Stipanowich, T. J. & Lamare, J. R. (2014). Living with ADR: Evolving perceptions and use of mediation, arbitration, and conflict management in fortune 1000 corporations. *Harvard Negotiation Law Review*, 19(1), 1.

Stipanowich, T. & Ulrich, Z. (2014). Arbitration in evolution: Current practices and perspectives of experienced commercial arbitrators. *The American Review of International Arbitration*, 25, 395–480.

Stipanowich, T. J. (2014). Managing construction conflict: Unfinished revolution, continuing evolution. *The Construction Lawyer*, 34(4), 13.

Thomas, R. & Wright, M. (2016). *Construction Contract Claims*. 4th ed. London: Palgrave Macmillan.

Thompson, R. (1977). International chamber of commerce-arbitration of disputes arising under international construction contracts. *International Business Lawyer*, 5(2), 225.

Thomson, D. B. (1994). Arbitration theory and practice: A survey of AAA construction arbitrators. *Hofstra Law Review*, 23, 137.

Trakman, L. E. (1983). *The Law Merchant: The Evolution of Commercial Law*. Littleton: Fred B. Rothman & Co.

Turner, R. (2005). *Arbitration Awards: A Practical Approach*. Oxford: Blackwell Publishing Ltd.

Uff, J. (2014). Arbitrating international construction disputes. *In*: Newman, L. W. & Hill, R. D. (eds.) *The Leading Arbitrators' Guide to International Arbitration*. 3rd ed. New York: Juris Publishing, Inc.

UNCITRAL Working Group on International Contract Practices (1982). *Report of the Working Group on International Contract Practices on the Work of its Third Session*. New York. Available at https://digitallibrary.un.org/record/30077?ln=en. [Accessed 25 December 2022].

UNCITRAL (2006). *UNCITRAL Model Law on International Commercial Arbitration 1985 With amendments as adopted in 2006*. Available at https://uncitral.un.org/sites/uncitral.un.org/files/media-documents/uncitral/en/19-09955_e_ebook.pdf [Accessed 25 December 2022].

Webster, T. H. & Buhler, M. (2014). *Handbook of ICC Arbitration: Commentary, Precedents, Materials*. London: Sweet & Maxwell.

Weidemaier, W. M. C. (2009). Toward a theory of precedent in arbitration. *William and Mary Law Review*, 51, 1895.

Winter, J. (2016). Resolving time sensitive construction disputes: Are attorneys just getting in the way? *Pepperdine Dispute Resolution Law Journal*, 16(3), 463.

Wright, G. A. (1913). *Wright on Building Arbitrations: A Manual for Architects, Students, Contractors and Construction Engineers*. San Francisco: Wale Printing Co.

CHAPTER 3

Law as a substantive norm[1]

3.1 Introduction

Some scholars concede that a persisting question within the increasingly important topic of arbitral decision-making concerns whether arbitrators apply the law or make their decisions based on different standards and norms (Schultz, 2015). This uncertainty concerning whether arbitrators apply the rules of the governing law or extra substantive norms is problematic to the parties at the time of both contract negotiation and dispute resolution (Moss, 2004).

This chapter examines to what extent international arbitrators apply the law as the substantive norm and provides an explanation for that.

To do so, this chapter has the following objectives:

1. to examine how arbitrators view their duty to apply the law (Section 3.3);
2. to discuss how arbitrators ascertain the content of the law (Section 3.4);
3. to find how the law affects arbitral decision-making on the merits of claims (Section 3.5);
4. to discuss arbitral decision-making when the law is indeterminate (Section 3.6);
5. to explain the reasons for arbitral decision-making behaviour (Section 3.7).

3.2 Choice of law

Unlike litigation in national courts, by virtue of the principle of party autonomy, disputants in international arbitration are free to choose the substantive norms to be applied to their dispute (Gaillard and Savage, 1999).

Usually, parties to an international construction contract select a national law to govern their contract. This law is referred to as substantive law, governing law, proper law, applicable law, or *lex causae* (Nazzini, 2018). It creates, defines, and regulates the substantive rights of the parties (Levin, 1997). It governs the examination of the contract's validity, the construction of its clauses, and the determination of remedies for breach (Nazzini, 2018; Gaillard and Savage, 1999). It represents an important contractual decision because the outcome of a dispute may depend on the governing law (Jaffe and McHugh, 2009).

The national law the parties may choose to govern the construction and interpretation of their contract and any dispute arising out of or in connection with the contract could be a 'neutral law' with no connection to the parties or their dispute (Gaillard and Savage, 1999; Moses, 2008). The choice of the national law of a third country could be

1 Some parts of this chapter draw on material from Besaiso, H. and Fenn, P. (2020). How do international construction arbitrators make their decisions? The status of substantive law. *International Construction Law Review*, 37(3), 199.

DOI: 10.4324/b22975-3

because of its neutrality or because it is well developed and suitable to govern an international construction contract (UNCITRAL, 1988; Moses, 2008). This was noted by the arbitral tribunal in ICC Case No. 4629/1989, which was reported in the ICCA Yearbook Commercial Arbitration in 1993. This arbitration case concerned a construction contract to finish and furnish a hotel in a Middle Eastern country. The owner was a Middle Eastern party and the contractor was a European company. The parties entered into a work contract in 1981 and agreed on submitting their contractual disputes to the Swiss Code of Obligations in any case for which the contract did not provide a specific solution. In the arbitration award, the tribunal stated that 'in an international contract like the present one, involving parties of different nationalities, the choice of law is entirely free, and the parties could freely decide that their relations were to be governed by Swiss law, even though the case has no connection whatsoever with Switzerland'.

Although the parties may agree on a neutral law to govern their contractual relationship, it is normally the case that the governing law is the national law of one of the parties (Moses, 2008). In construction contracts, it is usually the case that the parties agree to apply the law of the country where the works are to be constructed (i.e., place of performance). This is normally the law of the purchaser's country (UNCITRAL, 1988). This is especially true for the main construction contract between a main contractor and a government. However, different laws may govern subcontracts. The choice of a law to govern a subcontract which is different from the law governing the main contract can be problematic. The different laws applicable to different tiers in the supply chain may disrupt back-to-back contractual arrangements to pass liability down the supply chain and therefore lead to divergent or discontinued liability and remedy chains (Jaffe and McHugh, 2009).

Under several arbitration laws and arbitration rules, parties have the choice to select not only a national law to govern the substance of their dispute but also non-national 'rules of law'. The notion of 'rules of law' has been interpreted to refer to transnational rules, general principles of law, or *lex mercatoria* (Gaillard and Savage, 1999). The parties can also authorise arbitrators to decide a dispute as *amiable compositeur* or *ex aequo et bono*. There is no consensus on what acting as *amiable compositeur* or *ex aequo et bono* entails. However, it is generally understood that it grants arbitrators the power to temper a strict application of the parties' contract or its governing law for the sake of fairness and equity (Ayoğlu, 2012; Park, 2009; Park, 2010; Gaillard and Savage, 1999; Błaszczak and Kolber, 2013; Waincymer, 2011; Park, 2015; Moses, 2008).

Empirical evidence indicates that contracting parties rarely opt for non-national rules of law to govern the resolution of their disputes. According to data published by the ICC, parties agreed on the application of non-national rules of law or *lex mercatoria* in about 2% of its arbitrations. In the majority of ICC arbitrations, the parties selected a national law to govern their contracts (Drahozal, 2005).

To sum up, parties to international arbitration have the freedom to choose the substantive norms that arbitrators need to apply to determine their dispute. These substantive norms fall into three categories: national law, transnational rules of law, and non-legal rules.

3.3 Arbitrators' duty to apply the law

The duty of international arbitrators to apply the law (Mitchell, 2012; Kirsh, 2012; Rau, 2007), the extent to which they should adhere to the law (Levin, 1997), the exact scope of such a duty (Moses, 2008; Karton, 2013) and whether arbitrators do actually apply the law (Thomson, 1994; Stipanowich and Ulrich, 2014; Karton, 2013; Mentschikoff, 1961) are the subjects of an ongoing debate. The literature is not short of arguments that arbitrators do not have to follow the law in determining the parties' dispute (Weidemaier, 2009; Brunet, 1992). Rather, they may decide according to what they deem is just and fair in the circumstances (Weidemaier, 2009; Brunet, 1992). On the contrary, some scholars (e.g., Kurkela and Turunen, 2010; Landolt, 2012; Mitchell, 2012; Caron, 2015) argue that it is the arbitrators' duty to apply the governing law of the contract to decide the parties' disputes. Kaufmann-Kohler (2005) notes that the status of the substantive law (i.e., how arbitrators apply it) is one of the few areas that are still unresolved and lack consensus in international arbitration practice. Similarly, Sakr (2009) states that what is missing in arbitration scholarship is a glimpse of light into the way arbitrators apply national laws.

Given this uncertainty regarding the status of the substantive law in international arbitration, the author interviewed 28 international arbitrators and asked them whether they apply substantive law strictly. All arbitrators affirmed they do so unless the parties have agreed otherwise (i.e., to apply non-legal criteria). This is the case despite reservations expressed by some of them that the law is rarely black or white. In other words, legal questions rarely have an objectively correct solution that is incontestable. This idea finds support in the legal realism school of thought, which views the law as rarely providing determinate answers to legal questions (Schultz, 2015). Hence, the notion of a 'strict application' could be inaccurate.

This viewpoint, that the law is sometimes a grey area, is by no means limited to arbitrators. In commercial disputes, judges often deal with incomplete contracts that require interpretation. The interpretation may not be a straightforward exercise and judges can be and, indeed, should be creative when searching for an answer to the contractual dispute. This is especially the case in complex cases that involve legal problems that do not have direct answers within existing law. However, creativity must be constrained by the boundaries of the existing legal principles. Judges cannot distort legal principles to achieve a result that they think is commercially reasonable. Legal reasoning is an intellectual exercise that aims to find a legal answer to resolve a legal problem within a specific framework of rules (Mitchell, 2013).

A Canadian arbitrator, who was interviewed by the author, expressed a similar view and rejected the notion of a 'strict application of the law'. In his view, this notion is misleading and indicates a misunderstanding of how the common law method works. Unlike civil law, common law is not a codification of the law. The common law method provides the dispute resolver, whether a judge or an arbitrator, with a conceptual framework to understand and resolve problems without being strict to a black letter code. The notion of an objective legal truth and a single correct legal answer hardly sits well with the common law method. The large number of legal precedents and the judges' ability to distinguish between them allow some leeway in judgements (Mitchell, 2013)

Notwithstanding the limitation with the phrase 'strict application of the law', all interviewed arbitrators confirmed that they apply the law to construe the parties' contract. This concurs with anecdotal evidence provided by leading authorities in international arbitration that arbitrators apply substantive law in the vast majority of cases (Gaillard and Savage, 1999).

However, the finding that arbitrators follow the law in their decisions must be further analysed since 'how arbitrators apply the law' comprises a key part of the inquiry. As such, after establishing, as a point of departure, that arbitrators do follow the law in their decision-making, it is important to understand how they ascertain the content of the law. The answer to this question provides insight into the arbitrators' conceptualisation of what their duty to apply the law entails.

3.4 Substantive law: Ascertainment of content

To apply a law, an arbitrator needs to ascertain its relevant content first (Karton, 2013). This topic has attracted little attention in the literature. The thin literature on the topic provides no specific guidance to arbitral tribunals on how to determine the content of the law (Landolt, 2012; Kaufmann-Kohler, 2005; De Ly, di Brozolo, and Friedman, 2008). Although this is an important aspect that affects the substantive decision on the matters in dispute, it falls under the procedural domain (Landolt, 2012). Accordingly, this section will neither venture into this area in detail nor make comparisons with courts' procedures in common law and civil law. Rather, this section briefly discusses the arbitral practice in the ascertainment of the content of the governing law, which sheds more light on arbitral decision-making and more specifically on arbitrators' understanding of the scope of their duty to apply the law.

A tribunal may neither be familiar with nor have sufficient knowledge of the law governing the contract because its members are lawyers trained in another jurisdiction or are engineers with no legal training. In this case, the parties may appoint their own legal experts or the tribunal may appoint its own legal expert, who is normally a practising lawyer or a law professor, to give a legal opinion on the legal point in dispute (Park, 2010; Kurkela and Turunen, 2010; Park, 2015). This could be in the form of a written opinion (a practice preferred by civil law) or in the form of testimony before the tribunal (a practice preferred by common law). Both forms are used in international arbitration. The advantage of the latter is that it gives the parties an opportunity to test and cross-examine the strength of each other's legal arguments (Park, 2015; Gaillard and Savage, 1999).

However, it is normally the case that arbitrators are selected based on their knowledge and familiarity with the applicable law (Lagerberg and Mistelis, 2006). As such, they are able to make their conclusions of law based on the applicable legal authorities. The identification of applicable legal authorities is the concern of this section.

Arbitrators have wide discretion on a number of procedural matters, including the initiatives they may take to determine the content of the law, for three reasons. First, international arbitrators do not follow strict rules of civil procedure and evidence as a court of law (Landolt, 2012). Second, most arbitration laws and rules of procedure do not provide guidance on how arbitrators should determine the content of the substantive law. Those that provide some guidance, however, do so in ill-defined ways that leave arbitrators with broad discretion (Karton, 2013). Third, parties rarely agree on the procedural basis upon which the tribunal should proceed in obtaining evidence of law and evidence of fact (Landolt, 2012; De Ly, di Brozolo, and Friedman, 2008).

Despite this wide authority, the arbitrators interviewed in the study underpinning this book appear to have a largely uniform approach with respect to their interaction with the parties to locate legal authorities that are relevant to the dispute. Their approach is generally consistent with the best practice recommendations of the International Law Association Report (the 'ILA Report') published in 2008 (De Ly, di Brozolo, and Friedman, 2008). The ILA Report recognises the scarcity of commentaries on the topic. Hence, it attempts to fill this gap and provides guidelines to international arbitrators on how to ascertain the content of the substantive law (De Ly, di Brozolo, and Friedman, 2008).

In international arbitration, the interaction between arbitrators and the parties is closer to the adversarial model of litigation that originated in the common law world. It means that the parties have the primary responsibility to submit legal arguments that support their cases. In the civil law world, an opposite model of litigation referred to as inquisitorial is used whereby the judge is assumed to know the law. It follows that the parties are primarily responsible to plead the facts and then the judge will ascertain and apply the law in the 'correct' manner (De Ly, di Brozolo, and Friedman, 2008; Landolt, 2012). The judge has the obligation to find the right legal rule applicable to the facts and to apply it to these facts regardless of the legal arguments put forward by the parties in support of their claims, counterclaims, or defences.

The arbitral closeness to the adversarial model was apparent throughout the interviews the author undertook with arbitrators. The arbitrators made it clear that it is up to the parties to raise and plead with the legal authorities (whether a legal provision, an implied term, a precedent, a customary practice, etc.) they believe to be relevant and to prove their content and applicability. Then, they will decide in accordance with the pleadings of the parties. Below are two quotes from two arbitrators interviewed by the author which demonstrate the inclination towards the adversarial model.

The following quote is from an interview with an English arbitrator. It is extracted from his response on how he ascertains the content of the substantive law, particularly if it is a law he is less familiar with:

> It is up to the parties to tell me how they want me to deal with the legal question in dispute ... it is up to the parties to plead it and raise it ... but if it was not raised for me to determine ... I would not open that inquiry by myself ... on my own, I am not going to do that.

The following quote is from an interview with a Canadian arbitrator. It is extracted from his response on how he deals with customs and trade usages in international arbitration:

> I would expect somebody to come forward and prove these customs... on my own, I will not say whether this or that is a customary practice ... I will never do that ... I would expect the parties to provide me with an expert ... I would hear such evidence but I would not imply it into a contract on my own.

This approach is in accordance with the ILA Report recommendation that places the primary responsibility on the parties to identify the legal authorities that are relevant to the dispute.

The arbitral preference for the adversarial model appears to be due to a number of factors. First and foremost, it respects the core principle of international arbitration: party autonomy. Party autonomy refers to the parties' wish to keep their control of the process and to some extent the outcome to avoid a legal solution they may not have envisaged and which perhaps contravenes their commercial expectations. Second, the adversarial model satisfies procedural considerations to control time and cost and substantive considerations to maintain the predictability of the dispute outcome (Landolt, 2012). Third, commercial parties involved in international commerce are better able to defend their interests.

The finding that arbitrators appear to be closer to the adversarial model is the starting point but not the end of the inquiry. There are a number of thorny intellectual and practical questions that need answers. For instance, what would arbitrators do when the submitted legal material is not sufficient to reach a decision? Also, what would arbitrators do if they know that relevant legal authorities are missing, whether deliberately or not, from the parties' submissions? Lastly, would arbitrators make their own legal research about the content of the law to make sure that their award is legally correct?

In international arbitration, parties have the incentive to provide as many legal authorities supporting their cases as they can. It follows that it is rarely the case that arbitrators are left with a normative void to make a decision (Landolt, 2012). In this rare case, arbitrators may take the initiative to determine what the law is. In so doing, arbitrators may ask the parties to submit additional legal arguments, seek a legal opinion to be submitted by tribunal-appointed or parties-appointed legal experts, or search the law by themselves (Landolt, 2012). If the normative void is due to a lack of guidance in the governing law, then there are a number of techniques to find a legal solution (see Section 4.6). In light of the tribunal's large flexibility and the outcome's high uncertainty in this event, arbitrators are clear that they have to give the parties a reasonable opportunity to comment on how their dispute should be resolved.

In the event that the parties' submissions are missing relevant legal authorities, then there are two possibilities. It is either that arbitrators do know or that they do not know about the missing legal authorities that could be relevant.

If arbitrators know of missing legal authorities that are relevant to the determination of the parties' dispute, they may raise legal points by their own initiatives. It is notable that some arbitrators consider that it is their 'duty' to do so while others are of the opinion that it is something they can do but not something they must do. It follows that some arbitrators tend to be more interventionist than others. Below are two exemplary quotes from two arbitrators interviewed by the author.

In response to the author's question on how he deals with situations when relevant legal authorities are missing, an English arbitrator stated:

> If I do know that the parties missed a relevant part of the law, then it is my duty to raise the matter ... so if I find that a party has missed something, I would normally invite submissions by both parties ... I have to give the parties the opportunity to make submissions on the point.

In response to the same question, a Scottish arbitrator suggested a softer duty as follows:

> In court, judges are responsible for the law of the land and so they will bring a relevant case that has not been advanced by the parties to the parties' attention...arbitrators ought to do so but they do not have the same duty as that of a judge... so, if arbitrators knew of a case that was applicable, and not argued by the parties, they ought to bring that case to the parties' attention.

In either case, arbitrators are mindful that they have to invite the parties to make submissions on any point of law they raise. In so doing, they are keen to give the parties a reasonable opportunity to discuss and address these legal points. They are certainly cautious not to 'take the parties by surprise' by applying legal principles that have not been invoked by the parties. They do so to protect the award from the risk of an annulment or non-enforcement on the grounds of a curtailment of the parties' rights to be heard.

Arbitrators are also attentive to not deciding on legal grounds different from those raised by the parties even if they think that these legal grounds provide for the right legal solution. They do so to protect the award from the risk of an annulment or non-enforcement on the grounds of an excess of mandate (or the doctrine of *extra petita* and *ultra petita*) or unequal treatment of the parties (or undue process or even bias).

In this respect, an English arbitrator stated:

> In a recent arbitration case, I said to the chairman: you know the best way to look at this issue is this way … he said yes, I agree with you entirely but they did not argue in this way, so we had to find a way to decide the case in accordance to their arguments.

Likewise, another English arbitrator said that tribunals are attentive to deciding within the boundaries of parties' submissions even if they feel for some reason or another that the parties' arguments do not reflect 'the legal reality':

> I was one of the counsel in an international arbitration … arbitrators raised whether or not Vienna convention on the sales of goods apply and neither party had submitted that it did and therefore the arbitrators did not proceed on the basis that it did apply. So, although they might have felt that it did apply, and this is why they raised it with the parties … when both parties showed no enthusiasm for it applying, they appeared to have dropped it.

In the same vein, an arbitrator who was interviewed by the author stated that, while acting in the capacity of a counsel in a case, he obtained an annulment on the ground of the tribunal's excess of its mandate. In that case, the parties were arguing that the contract was terminated because of a breach of contract and blamed each other for the breach. The tribunal, however, raised legal arguments on its own and concluded that there was no breach of contract by any of the parties. Rather, the tribunal found that the contract was terminated according to the civil law concept of 'disappearance of the basis/cause of the contract' during contract performance. In other words, the tribunal decided based on legal grounds that were not submitted by the parties.

This summarises the state of affairs with respect to the arbitrators' initiatives when they are aware that there are applicable legal authorities that are missing. It seems that they will not do more than that if they do not know that the parties have failed to include certain legal principles or cases that are relevant to the dispute. They might carry out legal research to be sure about the inclusion of relevant legal materials but most likely they will not. In either case, they have to bring the result of their legal research to the parties' attention and ultimately decide in accordance with the parties' legal arguments and not in accordance with what they believe is the correct legal solution. After all, an objective measure of legal correctness is lacking. The criteria for a 'correct decision' and what counts as a 'legal error' depend on the legal reasoning approach that is being followed to resolve the dispute. The criterion for correctness could be finding 'the single right legal answer' that can be derived from the applicable legal rules and principles, or an answer that accords with the common intentions of the parties, or something else (Mitchell, 2013).

Accordingly, there is a general understanding that an arbitral duty to apply the law does not entail a duty to apply it correctly in the sense of an objective legal truth, but to apply it properly according to a subjective legal truth based on the parties' submissions. Arbitrators conceptualise their duty to apply the law to require them to apply the law but within the submissions of the parties. This approach is an adequate application of the law in their opinion. Moreover, they seem to be reluctant to search the content of the law by themselves to satisfy themselves that the award is legally correct mainly because of cost, time, and due process considerations. It is the parties' private dispute, they should have control over the time and cost involved in its resolution, and they are best able to defend their interests by arguing how their dispute should be resolved. Furthermore, arbitrators appear to be more eager to render an enforceable award than a 'legally correct' one. The following quote is an excerpt from an interview with an English arbitrator which illustrates this position:

> Civil law courts raise points by their own initiatives on issues of law that the parties have never raised and never addressed … for me, this is completely wrong in principle but certainly wrong in the context of international arbitration … because this can be challenged on the grounds of the tribunal deciding a case based on a legal basis that has not been raised by the parties … and my mission is not to give an award that is legally correct because any arbitrator can make a mistake … my mission is to give an award that is enforceable … so there is a margin of appreciation for legal error in the New York convention.

The international arbitration regime provides no assurance measures to make sure the arbitral award is 'legally correct'. There is no guarantee that a tribunal will reach the correct decision. A relevant legal rule may be misinterpreted, misapplied, or not considered at all. Of course, the risk is higher if an arbitrator is not familiar with the applicable law, which is not unheard of in international arbitration. This leads to the argument that perhaps what is required from international arbitrators is not perfection in the application of the law but a better understanding of business and commercial practice.

For the aforementioned reasons, it seems that arbitrators rarely take the initiative to search the law by themselves or invoke their own legal solutions. They conceptualise their job to apply the law to be limited to deciding within the parties' submissions on the law. In other words, their duty is discharged by applying the more convincing view of the law within the parties' submissions. This agrees with some scholarly writings on international arbitration that doing so is an adequate application of the law and there is no professional embarrassment for arbitrators who do so (Landolt, 2012). Landolt (2012) also argues that there is no empirical evidence or a convincing non-empirical argument in favour of the view that disputants seek an award that is 'legally correct' beyond what they themselves submit. This also concurs with arguments in the literature that arbitrators have the power but not an obligation to take the initiative to bring legal authorities to the table (Landolt, 2012; Kaufmann-Kohler, 2005). Arbitrators have little incentive in having a proactive approach because, as far as arbitration is concerned, the only interests that matter are those of the parties to control the procedure and the outcome of their dispute resolution. A state's interest in the right application of its law is less relevant (Landolt, 2012). Further, arbitrators' awards rendered based on the parties' submissions on contractual and legal provisions have virtually no danger of annulment or non-enforcement. There are less compelling reasons for arbitrators to go beyond these submissions because they may risk being viewed as exceeding their mandate, violating the parties' right to be heard and biased (Landolt, 2012).

The arbitrators' preference to stay within the parties' legal arguments is understandable as long as there are reasonable views of what the law is. However, if a dispute involves a mandatory rule of law or a matter of public policy, then the issue becomes more controversial. The controversy surrounding the nature of the arbitral role is rooted in the tension between two competing theories: the contractualist and jurisdictionalist theories of international arbitration. Are arbitrators accountable to the parties or the state the law of which is at stake?

Overall, the ILA Report admits that there is no single correct approach to address the ascertainment of law questions and that the lack of consensus stems from a deeper division on the very concept of the arbitrator's role (De Ly, di Brozolo, and Friedman, 2008):

> The way in which arbitrators approach the applicable law and its contents is thus a vital issue for international commercial arbitration. It is also, in some sense, a fundamental one. It alludes to the question of the very role of the arbitrator. If an arbitrator's sole function is to resolve the dispute presented by the parties, then the arbitrator presumably may – perhaps must – determine the law based solely on what the parties tell him it is. If, however, the arbitrator has supplementary obligations – derived from professionalism, a pledge to the parties or an institution to decide a dispute according to law, or public policy considerations – then the arbitrator may have to retain the ability to probe beyond what the parties say about the applicable laws and rules.

3.5 The impact of the governing law on contract interpretation

3.5.1 Strict vis-à-vis non-strict application of the parties' contract

When a construction dispute is referred to an arbitral tribunal, the first source of substantive norms or rules to look at are those provided in the contract. In international construction projects, the contracting parties normally enter into a comprehensive contract that provides a detailed regulation of their obligations and allocation of risks that may materialise (Moss, 2004). They price their contracts based on their set of defined obligations and assumed risks. As such, it is vital that the contracting parties be confident that their agreement will be honoured and enforced (Charrett, 2012). Accordingly, the author started the inquiry concerning arbitral decision-making by asking the arbitrators he interviewed whether they strictly apply the parties' contract in international construction arbitration.

The answers received from some arbitrators reveal a methodological impasse. Acquiring knowledge on whether arbitrators apply contracts strictly or not is epistemologically challenging, certainly in positivist quantitative research, but also in interpretive qualitative research. This is because the distinction between a strict and a non-strict application of contracts is problematic and seems rather artificial for three reasons.

First, arbitrators have different notions of what strict is and different perceptions of what a strict application of a contract entails. It seems that some arbitrators associate a 'strict application' with a 'literal interpretation' while others associate it with a 'correct construction of contract'. For the latter group, an interpretation that looks at extrinsic evidence of the parties' intent outside the four corners of the contract, or construction that renders a clause in the parties' contract ineffective is still a strict application because this is the right way to interpret or construct a contract.

For example, a Scandinavian arbitrator interviewed by the author stated that the parties' contract is an important document, but it does not always lead to a strict application of its terms and conditions. This is because contracts are inherently incomplete (and need to be understood in light of the parties' correspondence, conduct, etc.), or they may have unfair and unreasonable clauses that are hard to apply. The arbitrator gave an example of a typical situation where he does not tend to apply the contract strictly or may deviate from its literal wording. Sometimes construction contracts state that variations must be ordered in writing from the employer to the contractor, for the contractor to be entitled to payment for variations. He observed that this provision is not usually strictly applied by arbitrators in Scandinavian countries because the contractor is often entitled to additional payment even if the variation is not given to the contractor in writing. As long as the contractor can substantiate or prove that they have actually performed additional works and that this has been done as instructed or as agreed by the employer then the contractor is entitled to payment. It is worth mentioning that this is a typical situation that several arbitrators interviewed in this work referred to when explaining situations involving deviation from the literal wording of the contract.

For some commentators, this may still be understood as a 'strict interpretation' of the contract even though it may not be expressed as a 'strict application' in the sense of a direct and literal adherence to the words of the contract in detachment of what the governing law requires. Accordingly, it is highly likely for two arbitrators to have the same approach in applying the parties' contract even though they think they are at polar ends in terms of the extent to which they follow the parties' contract. These divergent conceptualisations render the question, as to whether arbitrators strictly apply the parties' contract, methodologically invalid as it does not answer what it intends to answer.

Second, the application of implied terms can be viewed differently. Some arbitrators view implied terms as external norms while others view them as falling within the boundaries of the contract. As an American arbitrator interviewed by the author said, there are express terms that the parties have agreed upon in their agreement, but there are implied terms such as the duty of good faith and fair dealings in civil law countries and the US federal contracts. In his opinion, the implication of terms is part and parcel of a strict application of the contract even though the parties may end up obliged by something that is not expressly included in their contract. Below is an excerpt from his interview that shows how arguments on the strict application of a contract can easily drift towards a redefinition of the borders of a contract:

> Generally speaking, I apply the contract strictly … everybody wants the contract enforced. That is why they entered into it to begin with ... but the question you are really asking is; what is in the contract? Is it limited to the four corners of the printed words or is it obligations above and beyond, and the answer is both.

This view should not be surprising as some academics make a distinction between an 'agreement' and a 'contract'. In this distinction, the agreement means what the parties agreed on while the contract is broader in scope and it includes obligations implied in the contract from the law (Charrett, 2012).

Third, some arbitrators refused to answer the question in the abstract because the binary classification of contract application to either strict or non-strict appears to be, at best, simplistic and, at least, a false dichotomy. In this regard, an English arbitrator noted:

> But you cannot say as a matter of principle either you would always comply literally with the wording of the contract, or you would never reject a particular clause… you cannot say that as a matter of English law which is probably the most literal in the world … because there is a doctrine under English law that if something is repugnant to the commercial purpose, then it is possible to disregard it in strict circumstances.

Therefore, it is a more valuable exercise to try to understand how arbitrators interpret contracts instead of pointless inquiries in a 'check the box' format about whether arbitrators apply contracts in a strict way. In the end, it has become crystal clear that any inquiry about how arbitrators apply the contract will swiftly travel to the territories of contractual interpretation. A British arbitrator described this state of affairs in response to the author's question on whether he strictly enforces the parties' contract as follows:

> I strictly apply the contract. The difficulty, of course, is that the parties often have different interpretations of the contract, so you get different arguments on how the contract should be interpreted and hence applied.

Further, some arbitrators added another variable by connecting the concepts of 'strict application of a contract', 'contract interpretation', and 'substantive law' together. As such, any inquiry into how strict arbitrators are in their adherence to the terms of the parties' contract will be necessarily paraphrased to reflect how arbitrators interpret the parties' contract and will potentially end up investigating the effect of the substantive law on contract interpretation (which is the purpose of the next section). A Lebanese arbitrator succinctly answered the author's question as to whether he strictly applies the terms of the parties' contract as follows:

> I am not sure there is a yes/no answer … it depends on the governing law of the contract …. there are two situations where you have to go to sort of interpretation and depart from the strict text of the contract. First, if you have a contractual provision that clearly contradicts a mandatory provision of the substantive law, you cannot apply it. Second, when the contract provision is not very clear, then it requires interpretation and the substantive law itself gives directions to arbitrators on how to interpret the contract. So, those are two situations where an arbitrator cannot say well I have the text of the contract saying this and I cannot depart from it … and it will depend on the contract provision itself because it might be unreasonable.

In response to the same question (i.e., whether he strictly applies the parties' contract), a Swiss arbitrator stated:

> The general answer is yes because the parties have a bargain: the contract allocates risks, and this results in a price … but the qualified answer would be that there might be issues where the contract is not clear and needs interpretation, and there may be issues where the party insisting on strict adherence to the contract is in a situation whereby its behaviour contradicts its previous behaviour, so it is clear to me that they waived certain contractual requirements, and it does not make sense for me to apply the contract absolutely strictly … this conclusion is a legal conclusion and needs to be supported by law.

In light of the aforementioned discussion, this book escapes the ontological and epistemological dilemmas of arbitral strictness in applying the contract and the law. It rather explores how arbitrators interpret the contract and how arbitrators ascertain and apply the law. The next section discusses how arbitrators interpret international construction contracts.

3.5.2 Contract interpretation and construction

Some legal theorists make a distinction between an 'interpretation' and a 'construction' whereby the first is more concerned with the meaning while the latter is more concerned with the legal effect to be given to the meaning (Lawrence, 2010). On the other hand, other scholars tend to use the term 'interpretation' to refer to both tasks (Mulcahy, 2015). This book uses the two terms interchangeably to refer to both tasks of determining the meaning and the legal effect of contract terms.

Also, legal systems have different views on the exact boundaries of contractual interpretation. Generally speaking, contractual interpretation has a narrower scope in common law countries than in civil law countries. For instance, the rules relating to implied terms are considered to be part of the contract interpretation process in civil law countries but they are deemed to belong to a distinct set of doctrines in common law countries (Vogenauer, 2007). This book uses the term 'interpretation' in a narrow sense. As such, it uses the terms 'supplementation' or 'gap-filling' to designate the arbitrator's task of incorporation or implication of legal rules or implied terms into the parties' contract.

When a construction dispute is referred to an arbitral tribunal, the first source of substantive norms or rules to look at are those provided in the contract. If the provisions of the contract provide the solution to the dispute, then arbitrators do not need to go any further than that to ascertain the law (Moss, 2004). However, as discussed earlier, what happens most of the time is that the parties during the performance of the contract do not agree on how contract provisions should be interpreted. In this instance, arbitrators may need to rely on rules of substantive law to guide the interpretation of the meaning of contract provisions (see Section 3.5.3) (Moss, 2004; Gaillard and Savage, 1999). Further, during the negotiation of the contract, the parties may not regulate certain matters through contract provisions. Then, if a dispute arises on a matter the contract is silent on, arbitrators may rely on the regulation provided by the governing law to fill the gaps in the parties' contract (see Section 3.5.4) (Moss, 2004; Gaillard and Savage, 1999). Furthermore, arbitrators may refuse to give effect to contract terms that are considered invalid or unenforceable according to the mandatory provisions of the governing law (see Section 3.5.5) (Moss, 2004; Gaillard and Savage, 1999).

So far, this chapter demonstrates that international arbitrators hold the opinion that they have a duty to apply substantive law even though the boundaries of this duty are by no means uncontroversial. The three subsequent sections in this chapter discuss how the substantive law affects the parties' obligations and hence the arbitrators' decisions on the substance of disputes concerning contract interpretation.

3.5.3 Rules of interpretation in the governing law

The interpretation of contracts is probably the most significant topic in commercial contract law (Andrews, 2016) and it is believed to be the most common issue in international commercial arbitrations (Karton, 2015; Mulcahy, 2015). Nevertheless, it is largely neglected in the literature (Rosengren, 2013). Typically, contract interpretation is a matter of law and, hence, follows the governing law of the parties' contract (Rosengren, 2013). The research underpinning this book finds that international arbitrators tend to adhere to rules of interpretation laid out in the substantive law. This finding concurs with Karton's (2012b) conclusion on international arbitrators' approaches to contract interpretation.

The assertion that contractual interpretation depends on the substantive law was a theme running throughout the interviews the author undertook with international arbitrators. Below are some excerpts from the interviews showing that arbitrators rely on substantive law to obtain guidance on 'how' to construe or interpret international construction contracts.

An English arbitrator clarified how the contractual interpretation exercise differs according to the law the contract is subject to:

> When you are interpreting the contract ... it depends on the legal system under which you are functioning...you use different tools depending on the toolbox the parties have given

> you ... it can be an English toolbox or an Egyptian toolbox, but you use the tools in each case to interpret the contract ... each legal system has its own rules as to the way you can interpret the contract ... so the common law system is more geared towards the literal words of the contract ... whereas the civil law system looks for the spirit of the contract and the subjective intention of the parties ... the exercise under any system is to interpret what the contract means, but each legal system approaches the questions of contract interpretations in a different way.

Likewise, a Canadian arbitrator asserted that the contract interpretation exercise differs according to the substantive law. It follows that he adjusts his approach to contract interpretation according to the substantive law. According to him, this is a part of the job and he has no difficulty in changing lenses to interpret contracts governed by different substantive laws. Some lenses focus more on contextual analysis while other lenses focus more on textual analysis. For instance, he stated that whereas contract interpretation under Canadian law requires arbitrators to look at the whole context of the provision they are interpreting, English law does not allow extrinsic evidence to be brought in.

The differences between national laws in contract interpretation methodologies arise from two sources. The first source concerns the interpretive approach (objective vs. subjective) for ascertaining the parties' intention and the type of evidence that is admissible in this process. The second source concerns the effect of legal doctrines or principles that are applicable under each system of law (Rosengren, 2013).

The following quote from an interview the author undertook with an Australian arbitrator provides a brief explanation of contract interpretation and how it differs across civil law and common law jurisdictions:

> Now, the process of thinking about what a clause says must start with the words, the natural and ordinary meaning of the words. What do the words together mean? ... then, there are different rules that apply to the interpretation of contracts to help you work out what a clause means ... you probably get more assistance in contract interpretation in common law countries than you do in civil law countries ... in the common law world, there are a handful of rules of contract interpretation... such as Parol rule that excludes evidence outside the contract (e.g., prior communications and negotiations on a particular clause) ... and the exclusion of the subjective view of the parties on what they think the contract means ... then, of course, the overlay ... in contract interpretation you may have other notions that may or may not apply depending on which tradition you come from ... in civil law countries there is a big emphasis on what is called an implied duty of good faith and fair dealing. In the common law countries, courts have read into construction contracts many implied duties.

The arbitrator clarified that the essence of contract interpretation is a search for the common intention of the parties, but it excludes evidence of what each party understood the contract to mean. Interpretation theories recognise that 'there is no window into a person's mind to discover what they actually intended'. As this information is not accessible to a judge or an arbitrator, they can only rely on external manifestations of intentions (Mitchell, 2013).

This sample of arbitral accounts provided in the preceding paragraphs shows that contract interpretation depends on the legal rules set out in the governing law. The arbitrators' narratives as well as extant literature tend to generalise that the common law system has an objective approach (that emphasises a textual or literal interpretation), while the civil law system has a subjective approach (that emphasises a contextual interpretation that looks beyond the wording of the contract) (Rosengren, 2013).

According to this perceived difference in the contract interpretation approach between civil law and common law, some commentators contend that the outcomes of contract interpretation may be widely different depending on the governing law (Borris, 1994 cited in Rosengren, 2013). Similarly, some participants asserted that different national laws have different emphases on the parties' objective vis-à-vis subjective intentions and therefore have different interpretive rules and guidelines on whether certain categories of extrinsic evidence (e.g., a party's opinion as to what it thinks the contract means, prior negotiation and communication to entering into a contract, a party's subsequent conduct, etc.) can be considered to assist an arbitrator in interpreting what a contract means. They opine that this difference in the method and its accompanying rules on evidence can lead to different outcomes.

Moreover, some participants maintain that the 'outcome' of interpretation can be different depending on the governing law because national laws sometimes have legal principles that affect the interpretation or have interpretive rules that are genuinely different. A prime example of a legal principle that heavily influences contract interpretation is good faith in contract performance, which exists in many but not all jurisdictions. The application of this principle could allow an arbitrator to reach a construction that would not have been possible without it (Rosengren, 2013). Contrary constructions could also result from the application of interpretive rules concerning ambiguous clauses. According to a Lebanese arbitrator interviewed by the author, most civil law codes have an interpretive rule that directs a judge or an arbitrator to construe the contract in favour of the debtor in case of doubt. Common law jurisdictions, on the other hand, have a *contra proferentem* rule that provides that an ambiguous term shall be construed against the party that drafted the contract.

On the other hand, there are contrary views expressed by the interviewed arbitrators and in scholarly writings that the practical effect of the differences between common law and civil law is overstated (Vogenauer, 2007; Rosengren, 2013). It is true that common law and civil law have conceptual differences as to the purpose of interpretation (attain certainty and predictability vs. reveal the true intent of the parties) and therefore methodological differences in the approach to contract interpretation (objective vs. subjective) (Karton, 2015). However, the outcomes of the interpretation appear to be substantially similar in practice (Vogenauer, 2007; Valcke, 2009; Knutson, 2004). Also, although some scholars (e.g., Karton, 2015) do not rule out the possibility that the substantive law can be decisive to the interpretation result, they concede that the significance of the substantive law is not noticeable with respect to matters of contract interpretation as it is the case in the impact of mandatory rules on the validity of certain contract provisions. The scepticism about the actual difference in the outcomes of contractual interpretation in practice due to the methodological difference between legal systems was also raised by a number of interviewed arbitrators from the common law world.

For example, an English arbitrator asserted that the common law system 'claims' that it reaches an objective view while at the same time it looks at the intention of the parties but in the form of the 'intention of a reasonable person in the position of the contracting parties'.

Likewise, an Australian arbitrator suggested that the common law system appears at first glance to achieve an objective view of what a contract means. However, she emphasised some aspects of the common law's approach to contract interpretation that might temper the perceived objectivity. For instance, interpreting the contract based on the objective test of 'what a reasonable person having all the background knowledge which would have been available to the parties would have understood' allows and, in fact, requires a better understanding of the context surrounding the dispute. It leads towards an interpretation that makes sense to commercial people as opposed to ordinary people. Moreover, the common law system requires the judge to look at the matrix of facts surrounding the entry into a contract. The facts may include the events leading up to entering into that contract, such as the tendering stage (including parties' communications and tender clarification meetings and correspondence). As a result, a judge or arbitrator thinking about the meaning of a clause may be influenced by these contextual facts whether consciously or not.

Although the common law rules of interpretation intend to limit subjectivity in contract interpretation, it can be argued in light of the previous arbitrators' accounts that the common law does not lead to as literal and objective interpretation as it might appear to be as a first impression.

Bridging the gap from the other end, an American arbitrator downplayed the practical difference between common law and civil law approaches to contract interpretation as the latter still endeavours to reach an objective interpretation that is somehow based on a reasonable person's view. As the parties' subjective intentions do not meet, and this is the reason they have a dispute in the first place, there is a need to look at what the contract means from the point of view of a reasonable third party. Parties in a dispute typically assert they have different understandings – whether honest or not – as to the meaning of the contract. Then, the arbitrator needs to ascertain the parties' presumed intention depending on contextual evidence as understood by himself or herself as a reasonable person. Below is an excerpt from the American arbitrator's interview:

> Coming from a common law jurisdiction, I have to look at it from an objective perspective of what any reasonable person would have understood the contract to mean ... You cannot allow one party to say here is what I really intended, and hence the other party is bound by it. The parties are bound only to the extent that some reasonable third party is going to agree on what their obligations are... now, in civil law jurisdictions they talk about the subjective intent, i.e., what the parties themselves agreed. But in interpreting a contract, in looking at what the parties agreed, you tend to have to look objectively at what the intent was ... therefore, I think it [the objective/subjective divide] is more of a cosmetic distinction ... It could be that arbitrators will arrive at the same result but simply express different paths to reach the same result.

Likewise, Mitchell (2013) concurs that drawing a line between objective and subjective approaches in legal reasoning is difficult. This is because these two approaches are not binary. They lie across a continuum, overlap, and shade into each other. The objectivity or subjectivity required by any system of law is a matter of degree (Mitchell, 2013).

In the same vein, a Canadian arbitrator interviewed by the author minimised the effect of the substantive law on contract interpretation results. In response to the author's question about whether he might make two different decisions on the same dispute if it was governed by two different substantive laws, he stated:

> I have never seen that happening and I have trouble even in envisioning a case in which that would happen but it is theoretically possible.

In short, although different systems of law may follow different approaches and apply different rules, maxims, or canons of construction, it is neither easy to say in the abstract nor to empirically verify the extent to which the practical effect differs (Rosengren, 2013).

In addition to the scepticism shown in the aforementioned accounts of some arbitrators towards the practical effect that is sometimes claimed to result from the difference between the legal approaches to contract interpretation (objective vs. subjective), the relaxed rules of evidence in international arbitration bring the two legal systems even closer to each other (Karton, 2012b). Relaxing the rules of evidence, especially those related to admissibility, may have the effect of moving the common law closer to civil law. International arbitrators tend to be liberal in letting a wide range of evidence in, including evidence that could be inadmissible under the governing law, because they are concerned about procedural challenges in case of dismissing evidence (Drahozal, 2004; Karton, 2015; Moses, 2008; Sussman, 2014).

Further, Karton (2015) presents evidence from arbitral awards and interviews that suggests that international arbitrators play down the role of substantive law in contract interpretation. He quoted a French scholar and practitioner asserting that rules of interpretation are not really rules of law, but they are guidelines for a sound and reasonable interpretation. Likewise, in ICC Case No. 12745/2010, the arbitral tribunal noted that rules for the construction of contracts set out in the French Civil Code are not mandatory, but they are sensible guidelines to ascertain the intent of the parties (Karton, 2015). Besides, some scholars consider that rules of contract interpretation are malleable and flexible enough to enable arbitrators to reach, more or less, similar reasonable interpretations (Rosengren, 2013).

Furthermore, assertions on the extent to which substantive laws guide or control the interpretation exercise give the impression that interpretation is a mechanistic process. This neglects the significant influence of an arbitrator's background (legal, commercial, and cultural) on both the process and the outcome of contract interpretation (Rosengren, 2013). From this perspective, Rosengren (2013) suggests that an arbitrator's own view of common sense may have a greater impact than the rules or principles of interpretation set out in the substantive law.

In fact, there is evidence from arbitral practice that many international arbitrators do not rely on substantive law to interpret contracts. Karton (2015) examined 73 international commercial arbitration awards and found that in 40% of the awards arbitrators interpreted the contracts without citing any interpretive rule or legal principle of contract interpretation or relevant legal authority (precedent or code provision).

These findings are compatible with the note to ICC Case No. 2291/1975 (Karton, 2013) of Yves Derains, the then secretary general of the ICC Court of Arbitration:

> The interpretation of contracts is one of the areas in which international commercial arbitrators are most inclined to disengage from national laws in order to resort to general principles of law.

In the same vein, Webster and Buhler (2014) state that arbitrators, in some awards, appear to avoid relying on the principles of interpretation set out in the substantive law. They criticise this approach in the interpretation of contract provisions as contract terms cannot be interpreted in a legal vacuum; they may have special meanings according to the applicable law.

The research underpinning this book finds that the majority of arbitrators follow the rules of interpretation laid down in the substantive law. However, there are a few exceptions. Some arbitrators seem to be less attached to the substantive law in questions of contract interpretation and more attentive to commercial practice (see Chapter 4) or transnational interpretation (see Chapter 5) in an attempt to achieve a commercially sensible result.

3.5.4 Contract supplementation: Non-mandatory law

In addition to its interpretation rules, the governing law of the contract matters because the set of obligations of the parties and the remedies the parties are entitled to claim are not limited to those available under the contract. In addition to the 'contractual' claims, a party may assert 'legal claims' under the law governing the contract. The most important type of legal claims are claims related to a breach of contract (Seppala, 2005). The outcome of these legal claims can be different depending on the substantive law. The substantive law the parties choose to govern their obligations provides a default allocation of risks in the form of legal rules (Knutson, 2005). This risk allocation varies depending on the substantive law. For example, different national laws have distinct legal theories for the wrongful termination of a contract (Knutson, 2005). Also, some civil law jurisdictions have hardship, *force majeure*, and *imprévision* doctrines, while common law jurisdictions embrace stricter concepts that have a narrower scope of application, such as frustration, impossibility, and impracticability. The specific regulation of these legal rules may vary from country to country and, thus, provide for different legal solutions including a modification of the contract, an excuse of performance, or ultimately a termination of contract (Knutson, 2005; Park, 2015; Seppala, 2005; Moss, 2004).

The body of legal rules under any system of law is classified into two types. These legal provisions can be non-mandatory (i.e., regulatory) or mandatory. Different legal systems may regulate the same matter in different ways. This shows the importance of the choice of law decision and that a contract should be drafted having in mind the law that will govern it (Moss, 2004).

The non-mandatory law is used only to fill gaps in the parties' contract when the contract is incomplete (i.e., silent on the issue in dispute) (Moss, 2004; Charrett, 2012). There is a whole body of scholarship on incomplete contracts theory that is dedicated to unpacking the reasons for and the implications of the incompleteness of contracts (e.g., Scott and Triantis, 2005; Williamson, 1979; Hart and Moore, 1988; Spier, 1992). The governing law of the contract provides default rules to plug the gap left by incomplete contracts. Rules on contract interpretation, implied terms in the common law, or non-mandatory rules in civil codes provide solutions to the inevitable problem of incomplete contracts (Mitchell, 2013).

Unless the parties include an express term to the contrary, non-mandatory legal provisions in civil law countries or implied terms in common law jurisdictions may end up being part of the parties' set of obligations even though the parties may not be aware of their existence (Moss, 2004; Charrett, 2012). This is particularly relevant to civil law jurisdictions that intend to provide a comprehensive codification of the law on certain matters. Civil law codes provide a default set of rules should the parties fail to include express terms (Charrett, 2012).

A number of non-mandatory rules are of particular relevance and importance to international construction contracts (Brunner, 2009). For instance, the parties may agree on a contractual regulation or risk allocation of *force majeure* events that is different from what the governing law stipulates. This contractual regulation will prevail over the regulation provided in the law (Moss, 2004). Concurrency is another legal concept that is often applied to the resolution of construction disputes. A typical example of concurrent causes in construction disputes is a concurrent delay. A concurrent delay is a delay that has concurrent causes (Burr, 2016). Different legal systems take different views on how concurrency problems should be decided. There is also a wide range of non-mandatory construction law rules providing a default allocation of risks that can be altered by the parties. These can be related to unforeseen ground conditions, weather conditions, currency exchange and devaluation, termination, and so on.

3.5.5 Mandatory rules of substantive law

3.5.5.1 The dilemma of mandatory law's application in international arbitration

One key aspect of the substantive law that may affect the construction of contracts involves mandatory provisions of the substantive law. According to the arbitrators interviewed by the author and some commentators (e.g., Charrett, 2012), most construction law rules are non-mandatory. They maintain that mandatory rules in private law relations such as contract law are rare and have narrow applications in practice, whether in civil law or in common law jurisdictions, because the legislator respects the autonomy of contracting parties to agree on the rules, they wish to govern their commercial relationship. However, there are some mandatory rules the parties cannot derogate from, and a judge has to apply them regardless of the wishes of the parties (Charrett, 2012; Moss, 2004). National laws may have mandatory provisions that have different effects on the parties' set of obligations and on the validity and enforceability of their contractual terms (Moss, 2004). A contractual clause might be binding or not depending on what the governing law is (Moss, 2004). The following paragraphs briefly showcase a sample of construction law mandatory rules.

In some jurisdictions, time-bar clauses tend to be strictly construed in accordance with *pacta sunt servanda* (agreements must be kept). Under other jurisdictions, these clauses can be interpreted in a more relaxed way or even ruled out as contrary to the mandatory law. In the latter case, time-bar clauses can be construed as an attempt to prevent a party from claiming its right because of the elapse of time or can be construed as an indirect decrease of the prescription period provided for in the law itself. Either construction can be against public policy (Burr, 2016; Sakr, 2009).

Liquidated damages (LAD) is another legal concept that different legal systems approach in different ways. For instance, the English approach to liquidated damages is binary. They are either on or off. They are off if they offend the law against penalty. In other legal systems, including both civil law and common law, liquidated damages can be increased or decreased by an arbitrator depending on the circumstances of the case (Burr, 2016).

In addition to time-bar and LAD clauses, a governing law typically comes into play when it prohibits the enforcement of particular types of clauses such as a pay-when-paid clause (e.g., UK Construction Act 1996) (Burr, 2016), a no-damage-for-delay clause (Thomas and Messner, 2003), or an allocation of risk intended to limit or exclude liability (Charrett, 2012). For instance, a clause intending to shift the risk of ground conditions or errors in site information delivered by an employer to a contractor, as is the case under subclause 4.10 of FIDIC conditions of contract for EPC/Turnkey Projects 1999, may be null and void according to certain national laws, such as the German law (Charrett, 2012; Knutson, 2005).

Knutson (2005) points out that there are some inconsistencies or contradictions between some clauses in FIDIC contracts and the substantive law in some jurisdictions. These include rules regarding the allocation of ground risk, payments of penalties, exclusions, and limitations of liability clauses that will not be enforced in jurisdictions that do not, for instance, accept the concept of penalties or permit contractual waiver of liability in certain matters.

There are other mandatory provisions the parties cannot exclude concerning direct payment to subcontractors by the principal (e.g., in Victoria, Australia) (Charrett, 2012), the obligation to act in good faith (Charrett, 2012), the duty of mitigation of damages (UNCITRAL, 1988), or the modification of a contract when a major change in economic conditions occurs that destroys the contractual equilibrium (*imprévision* or unforeseen circumstances) (e.g., in France and Arab countries) (Charrett, 2012; Sakr, 2009).

Given that, there could be a situation in which a contract term is in conflict with a mandatory provision of the governing law. In this case, the parties' intention could arguably be best reflected in the express terms of their contract. However, at the same time, they agreed on a law to govern the interpretation and construction of their contract which invalidates one of their contract terms (Park, 2015; Moss, 2004; Gélinas, 2016). In this instance, a national judge would normally interpret such a term under the governing law that renders it ineffective (i.e., the mandatory law supersedes contrary contractual provisions). An international arbitrator, on the other hand, is not a national judge. There are institutional differences between them. After all, arbitrators derive their power from the parties, they are often selected and get paid by the parties, and, hence, they should presumably give more consideration to their 'private law' that is their contract (Park, 2010). Consequently, arbitrators may depart from the mandatory provisions of the governing law in favour of the parties' *ex-ante* expectation that their contract terms will be enforced.

In light of this, the author discussed with the arbitrators interviewed in this work how they would approach this dilemma, and whether in this situation they would be concerned about applying the law in a manner that resembles a national judge's approach. The following subsections discuss the arbitrators' responses and show that different approaches to this problem are possible.

3.5.5.2 The prevailing view: Apply the mandatory law

Almost all interviewed arbitrators stated they would generally apply the law in the correct way (i.e., the mandatory law supersedes contrary contractual provisions). They affirmed that they would not attempt to ascertain the parties' expectations and apply them in disregard of the law.

For example, an Egyptian arbitrator stated that the choice of law is one of the most important clauses in the contract which has a direct impact on the parties' obligations and risks allocation:

> If there is a fair provision of the contract that is contrary to a mandatory provision of the substantive law, I have to apply the law and strike down the contractual provision ... It is not our job to change the law. It is not our function to undermine the law … my view is to uphold the substantive law agreed by the parties, regardless of what is written in the contract because the choice of law is one of the most important things on which the parties agreed. Unfortunately, there are arbitrators who consider the rules of arbitration as the key thing, the seat of arbitration as an important thing, and the substantive law as something of minimal concern, and I think that is ridiculous.

The following three international construction arbitration awards demonstrate the arbitral practice of applying mandatory rules of the governing law of the contract.

AD HOC ARBITRATION CASE: PIPELINE CONTRACTOR VERSUS OIL COMPANY

The contradiction between the parties' contract and the governing law's position on interest was one of the issues that were decided in an ad hoc arbitration case reported in the *Yearbook Commercial Arbitration* in 1989. In 1983, the claimant and the respondent entered into a contract for the construction of a pipeline in Saudi Arabia. The parties agreed on the law of Saudi Arabia to govern their agreement and to have the seat of arbitration in Dammam, Saudi Arabia. One of the claims in this arbitration concerned the cost of non-payment of the amounts claimed when they were due. The claimed cost and expenses were related to bank charges and interest which the claimant alleged it had paid due to the respondent's failure to pay the claimant's entitlements in full. On the other hand, the respondent asserted that the basis of this claim was illegal as it contradicted the Shari'a/Islamic law that was applicable to the contract. The respondent argued that the Shari'a/Islamic law expressly forbids any charging of interest because it involves usury. The arbitral tribunal found that interest is a matter of public policy, and, for this reason, it rejected the claim.

CRCICA CASE NO. 43/1995

The Cairo Regional Centre for International Commercial Arbitration (CRCICA) Case No. 43/1995 also concerns, amongst other things, a dispute concerning the applicable interest rate. The dispute arose from a contract between a European Company (claimant) and an African Tourism Company (respondent). The governing law of the contract was Egyptian law. The arbitral tribunal was composed of three arbitrators; a Swiss Chairman and two members from Egypt.

The tribunal concluded that interest rate is governed by mandatory provisions of the law. It referred to Article 266 of the Egyptian Civil Code, which provides that interests are due at the rate of 4% in civil matters and 5% in commercial matters. The tribunal also noted that, according to Article 227 of the Egyptian Civil Code, the parties can agree on another rate of interest provided that it does not exceed 7%. Also, as a matter of public policy, Article 232 of the Egyptian Civil Code does not allow interest to run on outstanding interest.

ICC CASE NO. 6230/1990

ICC Case No. 6230/1990, which is reported in the *Yearbook Commercial Arbitration* in 1990 (also available at ICC Digital Library) is another case that involves a mandatory provision in the governing law and a contradictory clause in the parties' contract.

The claimant (subcontractor) entered into a civil works subcontract with the respondent (main contractor) which incorporated FIDIC Conditions of Contract (International) for Works of Civil Engineering Constructions (2nd edition 1969). The main contract concerning the construction of a power plant was signed between the respondent (main contractor) and a government entity.

The subcontract included a pay-when-paid (PWP) clause (that is, a clause providing that the subcontractor would be paid only when the contractor had been paid by the employer). The respondent (main contractor) received an advance payment of 15% of the main contract price from the owner and, consequently, transferred to the claimant (subcontractor) 15% of the subcontract value. No further payments were made by the respondent to the claimant. The owner run into financial difficulties in the early stages of the project. Nevertheless, both the respondent (main contractor) and the claimant (subcontractor) continued to work for several months despite not getting paid for the work done. After 14 months of unpaid work, the claimant (subcontractor) stopped the works under the subcontract and in the same period respondent (main contractor) ceased work under the main contract.

A dispute arose between the parties regarding the unpaid work on the project. The claimant initiated ICC arbitration in 1988. Both the main contract and the subcontract provided that Swiss law was the substantive law and Zurich was the seat of arbitration. The claimant demanded payment of all due amounts plus interest. The respondent relied on the PWP clause to not pay. The tribunal considered that this clause requires interpretation. The question was whether the PWP clause is to be interpreted strictly in accordance with its wording or instead by considering the atypical allocation of the risk between the contractor and the subcontractor. The tribunal found that, under Swiss construction law, the risk of outstanding payments by the owner normally lies with the contractor and that the contractual assignment of the risk of non-payment by the owner using PWP clauses has the character of an exception. They commented on the validity of PWP clauses under the governing law as follows:

> The exceptional character of PWP clauses under Swiss subcontractor law does not, however, mean that such clauses are generally void (as is the case under German or French subcontractor law). Nevertheless, one finds narrow boundaries on their interpretation, although the Arbitral Tribunal is not aware of any Swiss case law on the subject.

The preceding evidence from arbitrators' accounts and arbitration awards suggests that arbitral tribunals apply mandatory provisions of the substantive law to determine the validity and effect of the terms the parties agreed on in their contract.

On the other hand, some arbitration commentators and scholars argue that international arbitrators should be more concerned about the parties' expectations than upholding a national law that governs their contract. Sometimes, the parties may choose a neutral law to govern their contract, which they are not aware of or familiar with its content. In this sense, it is difficult to imagine that they deliberately choose a governing law that makes their contract or part of it null and void. This outcome will probably be contrary to the parties' intentions, and, hence, the tribunal should live up to the parties' expectations (Moss, 2004; Cuniberti, 2014; Gaillard and Savage, 1999; Gélinas, 2016). This reasoning seems to have more merit and to be more convincing in international arbitration as opposed to national litigation because arbitrators derive their power from the parties (Gaillard and Savage, 1999). After all, arbitrators make their awards for the parties and not for society at large. They are 'problem solvers' and not 'policy makers' (Karton, 2013). In the context of international arbitration, promissory theories of contract support the argument that arbitrators should give more weight to the parties' contract than contrary stipulations by the substantive law. Promissory theories of contract consider the contract as the 'creature of the parties', and the court's function is to uphold and enforce what the parties agreed on rather than factoring in the wider implications of their judgements on the commercial community as a whole (Mitchell, 2013).

Nevertheless, the research underpinning this book finds that this argument has not been widely accepted in arbitration practice. The counterargument as expressed by many arbitrators interviewed by the author is that the choice of law also reflects the parties' expectations and it is an objective indication of their expectations. For instance, an English arbitrator emphasised that the choice of law clause is to be treated no less than any other clause in the contract. He argues that the choice of law clause is an objective expression of the parties' intentions and, hence, has a greater weight than contrary subjective intentions claimed ex-post:

> The parties might not know what the implications of their choice of law are but as I understand it they said that the proper law is X and we want our agreement to be construed as if it was made in country X by reference to law X … so you know it is their choice … I do not see there is a conflict between the parties' expectation and the right application of mandatory law ... and if there is a choice of law clause, then the parties have chosen that proper law as much they have chosen any other term in the contract.

Similarly, a Canadian arbitrator commented on a situation that involved a contradiction between a term in the parties' contract and a mandatory rule in the governing law of the contract as follows:

> If the parties are from different parts of the world, and for whatever reason, they made the decision to choose a neutral third law and did not appreciate that its mandatory law has a particular consequence, then that is not a sufficient reason to not apply the mandatory provision.

Other arbitrators from common law tradition expressed similar views and rejected arguments to give preference to the parties' contract. According to them, the parties must satisfy themselves that the contract they sign including the choice of law clause represents their intentions. It follows that applying the law would not be contrary to the parties' expectations. Further, parties to international arbitration are sophisticated commercial parties (this is different from a consumer-type setting), legally advised and should understand whether the clauses in their contract are enforceable under the governing law. At the end of the day, arbitrators need to be comfortable that there is a legal basis to not strike down a contractual clause that is seemingly contrary to a mandatory provision.

One Canadian arbitrator maintained that:

> understanding the contract clauses and the law you agree on is as important as understanding the project you agree to build or the price you agree to pay for it.

Emphasising that it is up to the parties to understand what their legal rights are, an Australian arbitrator stated that the governing law is the most important source for determining the parties' obligations. The parties must understand the limitations of the governing law they choose and the consequences of their choice on their set of obligations. The following is an excerpt from her interview:

> The governing law is at the highest level in terms of the parties' obligations. Have they chosen the law of another country, then their expectations might have been fulfilled.

The preceding discussion shows that the arbitrators interviewed by the author appear to concur that mandatory provisions of the substantive law should be upheld. This arbitral approach accords with the judicial approach. Judges will give effect to mandatory provisions of the law over the contract terms (Moss, 2004). The rationale for this stance is twofold. First, arbitrators appear to hold the opinion that an arbitrator's duty resembles a judge's duty to apply the law properly and consistently. Second, despite several arguments in international arbitration scholarship that a non-application of mandatory provisions of the governing law will rarely expose the award for judicial intervention (Landolt, 2012), arbitrators remain concerned that such awards will be vulnerable to challenge.

This arbitral approach also accords to arbitration jurisprudence that is reflected in arbitration awards and arbitrators' writings. The current arbitration jurisprudence largely considers that mandatory provisions of the substantive law chosen by the parties shall prevail over the terms of the parties' contract and shall be applied even if the parties may not be aware of the legal effect or even their very existence (Gaillard and Savage, 1999; Charrett, 2012; Barraclough and Waincymer, 2005; Mayer, 1986; Derains, 1987). Likewise, Born (2014) proposes that the arbitral duty to apply the law includes a duty to apply its mandatory provisions.

Gaillard and Savage (1999) reject certain views expressed in the literature providing that arbitrators may depart from the mandatory provisions of the governing law in favour of the parties' expectations. The reason is that such views are based on mistaken premises of the parties' intention when they choose the law to govern their contract. The parties' intention, when they agree on a choice of law clause, even if they are unfamiliar with its content, should be rightly construed to mean their acceptance of the legal solutions achieved by applying this law even if the solutions declare a term of their contract void (Gaillard and Savage, 1999).

However, it is less certain whether arbitrators would apply mandatory provisions of the governing law in all circumstances. The next two subsections show that arbitrators might not always apply mandatory provisions of the substantive law. The rationale for this 'dissenting opinion' is also presented.

Before examining the rationale for not applying mandatory rules, it is necessary to distinguish between a number of scenarios. The tribunal approach to dealing with a conflict between a clause in the contract and a mandatory rule of the substantive law is less controversial if the issue is raised by the parties. In this case, the tribunal needs to decide it as any other legal question (Waincymer, 2011). The following quote is from an interview with an American arbitrator that clarifies arbitrators' preference to apply the mandatory substantive law when at least one party argues for its application:

> If the law of the jurisdiction says X, and it gives no discretion, but the parties had said anti-X, … it seems to me that the parties had put the arbitrator in a difficult situation… It seems to me that an arbitrator in that case, no matter what he or she does, is gonna make one of the parties furious … the arbitrator will either enforce the law or ignore the law in lieu of one of the parties' expectation. Either way, the arbitrator is going to be criticised. I think it is more accurate for the arbitrator to comply with the mandatory law and strike down the contrary contract provision.

On the other hand, it is more problematic if the parties do not raise the issue of the conflict between a contract term and a mandatory rule of the governing law. There is a view that arbitrators must refrain from raising issues related to mandatory rules of the substantive law as the tribunal mandate is limited to the issues the parties raise (Mayer, 1986). However, the mainstream view seems to be that the tribunal may decide to raise the issue keeping in mind several considerations before doing so as discussed earlier in Section 3.4. The discussion in Section 3.4 gives the impression that the parties' consent may be determinative. Some scholars (e.g., Barraclough and Waincymer, 2005; Derains, 1987) also contend that if an arbitrator thinks a mandatory rule must be applied but the parties submit otherwise, then the arbitrator should not interfere with the parties' autonomy. Even if an arbitrator believes a mandatory rule must be applied based on implied consent *ex-ante* but the parties expressly revoke that consent *ex-post*, then an arbitrator should not disregard the parties' directions. After all, the parties are fully aware of their rights and interests and the non-application of these mandatory rules will have no effect on third parties (Barraclough and Waincymer, 2005; Derains, 1987). Further, even if the parties intended *ex-ante* to subject themselves to a specific national law in its entirety, but then changed their minds *ex-post*, there is nothing wrong in permitting them to modify the arbitration agreement and the arbitrator's mandate (Barraclough and Waincymer, 2005). However, this view to prioritise the parties' *ex-post* expectations over mandatory provisions of the governing law remains a controversial area in international arbitration (Waincymer, 2011). The parties may decide *ex-ante* to exclude mandatory provisions of the governing law. In this case, Barraclough and Waincymer (2005) opine that it is easier for arbitrators to apply the parties' *ex-ante* expectations as expressed in their contract to exclude mandatory provisions of the governing law than to apply the parties' *ex-post* expectations to disregard the law.

3.5.5.3 The qualifying view: The contract might prevail over the mandatory law

The mainstream arbitral opinion, as found in the study underpinning this book, is to apply the mandatory provision as it takes precedence over the parties' contract. However, some arbitrators maintained that they would approach this issue with an open mind. Although their starting point would be to give effect to the mandatory provision, they might shift their position and enforce the contract term in certain circumstances.

A few Swiss arbitrators interviewed by the author rationalised this flexible approach by reference to the fact that contracting parties sometimes choose a national law on the basis of its neutrality. Sometimes, in an international context, one party may come from country A, the other party may come from country B and then they choose the law of country C as a compromise. The law may contain a mandatory rule that the parties did not consider and is in contradiction to what the parties had expressly agreed. The question an arbitral tribunal must answer in this situation is whether to apply this mandatory rule in spite of the fact that the parties clearly wanted something else. In this case, the application of the mandatory provision of the law chosen by the parties might lead to a result that was not intended by the parties. If both parties were not aware of the mandatory legal provision that contradicts a term in their contract, the Swiss arbitrators stated that they do not find it compelling to strictly apply a mandatory legal provision that was clearly not intended by the parties and belongs to a country that neither party has a particular connection to.

This is especially the case in international arbitration where parties come from different backgrounds. In this specific circumstance, the arbitrators might give more weight to the contractual term than the mandatory provision of the substantive law. They find it more convincing to enforce the term the parties negotiated and agreed on as it better represents their common intention. The emphasis here is on the mutual intention, because if it is not a mutual intention then it is simply irrelevant. To these arbitrators, the parties' contract is a better indication of their intent and, hence, may take precedence over the substantive law. For this reason, the arbitrators stated that they do not apply the substantive law as strictly as the contract. The arbitrators' attitude towards the substantive law would be different in domestic arbitration. In domestic arbitration, as both parties operate in the same jurisdiction, they are expected to be aware of the requirements of the law of the land.

The following text is an excerpt from the author's interview with a Swiss arbitrator that illustrates the inclination of some arbitrators to give more weight to the parties' contract. In his search for the parties' common intention, the arbitrator said that he would determine as a preliminary matter whether the parties really intended to have all mandatory rules of the substantive law applicable to their contract, with the possible consequence that some express terms of their contract become ineffective:

> If the parties selected a substantive law that considers a clause in their contract void ... that is their problem ... this is my first reaction, but I will try to solve it somehow ... you have to look at how the law was chosen, and whether it was negotiated because sometimes people choose a law, like Swiss law, for considerations that have nothing to do with the substantive concept of the legislation ... they choose it because it is neutral and they do not realise that they are agreeing to do something that does not work under the substantive law ... so I take the position that when the parties enter into a contract, they try to enter into a valid contract ... I try to salvage it... I will find a way to uphold the common intent if it relates to a private law issue and not public policy...if there is a way for me to interpret the contract in a way that does not contravene the mandatory provision, then I will do that.

The arbitrator noted that he may find that a mandatory rule of the substantive law overrides an express term in the parties' contract rendering it invalid only as a solution of last resort. In his experience, parties focus on the terms of the contract during the negotiation process and spend much less time researching the substantive law and its effect on the contract. He concluded the explanation of his approach to solving the problem of contradiction between the parties' contract and mandatory provisions of the substantive law as follows:

> In summary ... I am open to the idea that I may depart from a strict application of the law if it makes sense, and both parties agreed on carefully negotiated terms, and I have evidence on that, and evidence that there was not much concentration on the law.

Another Swiss arbitrator interviewed by the author elaborated on what may affect his decision on whether to apply a mandatory rule of the substantive law. One factor that affects his decision is whether the mandatory rule is usual or not. If the substantive law has an unusual rule that is not found in other legal systems, particularly the legal systems of the parties' home jurisdictions, then he will be less likely to enforce the mandatory rule. This line of reasoning is related to the argument of the parties' intention and whether the rule was within the expectations of the parties. Another factor that affects his decision is the relatedness of the substantive law to the parties and their dispute. The more connection the substantive law has to the parties and their contract, the more likely that he would apply the mandatory rules of the substantive law. The following is an excerpt from his interview that illustrates, by a hypothetical example, that the extent to which he would strictly apply the mandatory rules of the substantive law depends on how close the law is to the facts of the dispute:

> If, for example, an English company and a French company contracted to deliver a construction project in Germany and they chose German law, I would probably be more likely to strictly apply German law including its mandatory rules. If the construction project was in Turkey and the English and the French companies simply chose German law because it was a neutral law and otherwise there was absolutely no relationship with that law, I would probably be less likely to strictly apply German law. The closer the law to the facts of the dispute, the more likely I would enforce it.

The Swiss arbitrator acknowledged that different arbitrators have different viewpoints on this particular issue, and it is not black or white, but he was critical of those arbitrators, especially those who come from common law tradition, who pronounce that their mission is just to apply the law as follows:

> In general, English arbitrators would say: 'I would just apply the law. I'm not there to try to arrive at any different answer. It's not my job to be more creative or to try to figure out a better outcome'.

A further argument to support applying the parties' contract despite contrary stipulations by the governing law relies on the good faith principle. According to the Swiss arbitrators, if a party contends it was aware, during contract negotiation, of a mandatory provision that contradicts a contractual clause, but demands its application during or after contract performance, then they might construe this as 'negotiating in bad faith' and, hence, would be reluctant to support the application of this mandatory provision.

In addition to the preceding arbitral interview accounts, there is support for the viewpoint of enforcing a contractual clause that is contrary to a mandatory rule of the governing law in the literature.

This viewpoint derives its merits from the distinction between two classes of mandatory provisions of law: those that govern the obligations of private parties and those that also relate to the state's public policy (Rau, 2007; De Ly, di Brozolo, and Friedman, 2008). Although the parties cannot derogate from the application of mandatory provisions of private law (e.g., contract law, tort law, etc.) in domestic court litigation (Moss, 2004; McConnaughay, 1999), these provisions may not be mandatory, in the traditional sense, in international arbitration. This is because the parties may opt out of them by subjecting themselves to any other law. As such, it is not radical to argue that these provisions become elective in international arbitration and, hence, could be treated as akin to non-mandatory provisions, the non-application of which has almost no risk for challenge (McConnaughay, 1999; De Ly, di Brozolo, and Friedman, 2008; Derains, 1987; Voser, 1996).

Derains (1987) maintains that if it was the parties' intention to exclude a mandatory rule of the substantive law, then the arbitral tribunal ought to respect their will. This is because they could have chosen a law that did not contain a mandatory rule with the same undesired effect on the terms of their agreement. Barraclough and Waincymer (2005) commented that arbitrators who believe that the only limit to the autonomy of the parties is transnational public policy are likely to agree with Derains's view. On the other hand, if arbitrators believe that party autonomy does not go that far, then the intent of the parties would be a relevant but not decisive factor in the tribunal's decision.

This viewpoint also derives its merits from a need to meet the parties' expectations. Given the contract interpretation rule providing that a specific stipulation trumps general ones, and as the parties' clause in the contract is more specific than a general reference to a governing law, an arbitrator may decide to give more weight to the parties' intention as specifically written down in their contract. The argument based on the parties' intent is particularly relevant to international contracts where two foreign parties may agree on a third law merely because of its neutrality (Park, 2015).

There is also evidence from arbitration awards that arbitral tribunals may enforce a contractual clause that is contrary to a mandatory rule of the governing law in specific circumstances. The following text summarises ICC Case No. 7528/1993. This arbitration case illustrates a situation where international arbitrators may give effect to the parties' expectations even if their contract seems to contradict mandatory provisions of the substantive law.

ICC CASE NO. 7528/1993

This arbitration case concerns a dispute that arose between two French companies regarding a construction project in Pakistan. The dispute concerns the subcontractor's alleged poor performance, which led the main contractor to terminate the subcontract. The special conditions of the subcontract provided for ICC arbitration in Paris and French law as the governing law of the subcontract. The subcontractor (claimant) initiated arbitration proceedings seeking to secure payments for the work it has carried out. However, at the same time, and in an attempt to escape counterclaims regarding the poor performance of the subcontract, the subcontractor (claimant) argued that the subcontract was void because it did not comply with a mandatory provision of the governing law of the subcontract (Law no. 75-1334 of 31 December 1975). The main contractor (defendant) asserted that the subcontract was valid as the mandatory law under consideration did not apply to the subcontract. In order to determine the parties' dispute, the arbitral tribunal first had to determine the applicability of the mandatory provisions of French law.

The arbitral tribunal noted that under French case law the subcontractor cannot simultaneously rely on the subcontract to obtain payments for the work it has performed and assert that the subcontract is void to escape its contractual obligations.

The arbitral tribunal stated that parties to an international contract are allowed to avoid the application of a mandatory provision of the substantive law they select to govern their contract. It stated that under French private international law, the principle of party autonomy is not limited to allowing the parties to choose a law to govern their contract, but it also allows them to depart from the governing law. They cited a French seminal case on party autonomy in which the court upheld the validity of a limitation of liability clause despite its invalidity under the substantive law the parties chose to govern their contract (American law) on the ground that when the claimant agreed to the clause, 'it was not unaware that this clause would be enforced on a French territory where it is considered as valid'.

The tribunal reached a similar conclusion in this arbitration case. It found that the spirit of the parties' agreement indicated that it was their common intention that the mandatory provision did not apply. It found that the parties intended to apply French contract law other than this particular mandatory rule. The tribunal stated, 'It is difficult to accept that the parties meant to refer to French law while concluding a contract which would be void under that same law'. It follows that the parties have consciously deselected the mandatory provision of the governing law that contradicts their agreement.

The tribunal confirmed that international arbitration, as a private system for the resolution of international commercial disputes, should not allow the parties' agreement to prevail over all mandatory rules of national laws and in all circumstances. The tribunal excluded certain overriding mandatory rules (i.e., rules that relate to the public policy of a state) from the scope of party autonomy and noted that international arbitrators must be prepared to enforce them irrespective of the contrary intention of contracting parties.

Regarding the mandatory rule under consideration in this arbitration case, the tribunal found that the mandatory rule had a mandatory character in domestic transactions, but it was not the legislature's intent to extend its application to international contracts. Although the subcontract was concluded between two French companies, the tribunal found that the subcontract was more closely connected to Pakistan than to France and had an international character because the employer was a government entity in Pakistan and the works were to be performed in Pakistan.

In summary, the tribunal concluded that the parties' agreement was valid, and it superseded the contrary mandatory provision of the governing law on the ground that (1) the agreement reflected the parties' true intention, (2) the international character of their subcontract and its place of performance and (3) the mandatory provision was not intended to apply to international contracts. The tribunal stated that the parties clearly intended to avoid the mandatory provision relating to the formation of the subcontract, and, given the international character of the subcontract, the parties' true intention must be upheld. Hence, the tribunal decided to enforce the parties' agreement.

3.5.5.4 The lack of consensus over the effectiveness of a contractual clause excluding any contradictory rules in the substantive law

Imagine a case where the parties' contractually exclude mandatory provisions of the governing law from arbitrable issues and explicitly direct the tribunal to not apply them (Waincymer, 2011). Due to the considerable freedom the parties enjoy in international arbitration by virtue of the principle of party autonomy, a question arises as to whether the parties are free to go as far as to exclude mandatory provisions of the governing law. To be more specific, what if the parties agree that in case of contradiction between a contractual clause and a mandatory provision of the substantive law, then the contract clause shall prevail? This question is not academic as similar clauses with similar wordings are sometimes inserted in international contracts (e.g., the unpublished ICC Case No. 6257 and ICC Case No. 6136) (Gaillard and Savage, 1999).

Based on that, the author asked the arbitrators interviewed in the study underpinning this book the following question: 'If the parties agree that in the event of a contradiction between a contractual clause and a mandatory provision of the substantive law, then the contract provision takes precedence … how will you decide?'. This question, or other questions of a similar effect, raised a thorny debate about the very concept of arbitration and the exact role of an arbitrator. As far as arbitration is concerned, is it an alternative dispute resolution method or supplementary to court proceedings? As far as arbitrators are concerned, is their allegiance to the parties or to the proper application of the law under consideration? The arbitrators interviewed by the author have put forward two views to address the validity of such clauses: one against and one in favour.

For many arbitrators, this anomaly clause alters the classical hierarchy between a contract and its governing law and changes upside down how the law works. They asserted that mandatory provisions of the law, by definition, cannot be derogated by the parties' consent. The very idea of a mandatory provision of law is that the parties cannot contract it out. For them, this clause would not be enforced by a court of law and arbitrators should decide in accordance with the law as judges do. Further, they questioned the enforceability of the award in this case. The following quote from an interview with an Australian arbitrator reflects this opinion:

> It is a general principle of law that … if there are mandatory provisions of the substantive law, then the parties are not allowed to derogate from them ... as an international arbitrator, I would make a decision on the same basis as a judge would, applying the governing law of the contract … you cannot apply this clause based on an assumption that there is no risk of a challenge, annulment or non-enforcement ... so, why would I hand down an award that has a basic legal flaw?

Likewise, an English arbitrator indicated that arbitrators should not be viewed as instruments of the parties because there are other considerations that matter alongside the parties' will:

> It is my role to apply the law like a judge. I am not there to give someone what he or she wants regardless of the law so, to enter into a contract in which we agree to ignore the law, especially mandatory law, would be to enforce an unenforceable contract ... the award would be in danger of non-enforcement.

Similarly, an American arbitrator expressed his concerns regarding the risk of non-enforcement if arbitrators follow the parties' agreement that contradicts mandatory law:

> The parties cannot simply by agreement disregard mandatory provisions of the substantive law … The reason for that is, if an award is issued, it could be that a reviewing court would find that the arbitrators exceeded their powers in a manifest disregard of the law. So that goes really to the enforcement of the award itself.

Gaillard and Savage (1999) agree with the view that contractual clauses aiming to evade the application of mandatory provisions of the substantive law will not necessarily be effective. The reason is that to give effect to such a clause that is in conflict with the governing law means that this particular clause will no longer be governed by any law. Despite the parties' broad freedom to select the law or the rules of law to govern their contract, this does not extend to choosing no law at all. The option of a self-sufficient contract that is governed by no law at all is not available to the parties. This is because contracts cannot exist in a legal vacuum and international arbitration cannot be fully detached from all legal jurisdictions. They asserted that even arbitrators, who support the theory of floating contracts or contracts with no governing law, do, in fact, resort to general principles of law in their awards. Accordingly, based on these premises, Gaillard and Savage (1999) argue that a clause the parties insert to exclude contrary mandatory provisions of the governing law will break down and have no effect.

The preceding arbitral accounts suggest that some arbitrators endorse the position that arbitration is to supplement but not supplant court litigation. It follows that arbitrators should decide like judges in giving effect to the mandatory provisions' higher precedence over contract terms. However, the research underpinning this book reveals an exception to what appears to be the mainstream view. Some arbitrators interviewed by the author stated that they may enforce a contractual clause that requires altering the classical hierarchy between the law and contracts by making the parties' contract supersedes mandatory provisions in the law. In so doing, they pronounce that they are not gatekeepers of any state's mandatory provisions as states' judges are. As such, their respect for the principle of party autonomy, their concern for not exceeding their mandate and their dedication to meeting the parties' expectations may trump arguments that it is their duty to apply the law in a manner consistent with that of a national judge. The following interview excerpts illustrate the opinions of arbitrators who hold this view.

An Irish arbitrator, who has a long experience in the UK construction industry, emphasised his respect for the parties' autonomy to make such a choice:

> I would say the contract is dominant … I would be open-minded to the autonomy of the parties to make such a decision, but my experience is that most lawyers would not be open-minded to that. I met many lawyers who would say hang on this is not the way the law works and that is an unreasonable clause because it turns upside down the way the law works.

Likewise, an American arbitrator stated:

> If the parties in their arbitration agreement say in the event of a conflict between the mandatory law and the contract, the contract will prevail, then that is fine. They laid down the ground rules under which the arbitration panel is empowered. Then obviously the contract would prevail … in this instance, I would not be concerned that this is an incorrect application of the law … because remember the arbitrator's jurisdiction is really governed by a contract as opposed to a judge.

Similarly, a Canadian arbitrator maintained that he would be primarily concerned to reach a conclusion that meets the parties' expectations:

> In that case, it is arguable that the parties have not chosen the law of country X, but they have chosen the law of country X except to the extent that it is contrary to a contractual provision that is void under the law of X.… As an arbitrator, I will come back to my principle that you are trying to get a fair result … I will try to enforce what appears to be their current intention … if the parties had to choose the law but they did not intend themselves to be caught up in traps such as legal provisions that consider their clauses unenforceable … then it seems to me that they have demonstrated a clear intention that they directed their minds to the outcome they both wanted.

It is noteworthy that some of these arbitrators linked the possibility to enforce a clause pertaining to excluding a contrary mandatory provision in the governing law to award enforcement. They stated that if there was no threat for annulment at the seat or non-enforcement at the place where parties intend to enforce, then they would probably apply this clause. For instance, a Lebanese arbitrator pointed out:

> If it is not something that may threaten the award and there is a clear agreement by the parties on that, I would apply the parties' agreement. The main condition is that there is no threat of annulment or non-enforcement of the award … in such a case, I would not be acting as a court judge … because I should not forget that the arbitration process is consensual by nature ... but the parties' autonomy is not without limits.

Some arbitration commentators agree with the view that arbitrators should enforce the parties' agreement to exclude the application of a mandatory rule of law that contradicts a term in their contract or renders it void.

Departing from the principle of party autonomy that imposes limits on arbitrators' authority, Park (2015) argues that a contractual provision directing the tribunal to not apply mandatory provisions of the governing law that are contrary to the contract imposes a limit on the tribunal's jurisdiction and mandate, the disregard of which may put the award in danger of challenge.

Rau (2007) warns that arbitrators who ignore a contractual provision excluding a statutory cause of action from the scope of arbitrable issues, and proceed to decide on the issue in dispute would see their awards refused enforcement on the grounds of 'excess of power'. This is because the parties have withheld from them the jurisdiction to decide on the issue in dispute (that involves the applicability of mandatory law). He added that rules of law may be mandatory but arbitration is not, and contracting parties have the power to agree on which mandatory rules are included or excluded from the submission to arbitration. It follows that the parties' agreement to exclude specific mandatory rules from the tribunal's mandate can be understood as an agreement to reserve their right to submit a dispute concerning that rule to a national court that might apply it. The exclusion of certain mandatory rules from the arbitrators' jurisdiction does not exclude them from national courts' jurisdictions (Rau, 2007).

3.5.5.5 The essence of the debate

Overall, the debate on the best course of action, in this case, boils down to two matters.

First, what is the conception of arbitration itself? Is it an alternative system to courts that underpins the autonomy of the parties or is it supplementary to litigation in applying the law (Barraclough and Waincymer, 2005)? To put it differently, is arbitrators' allegiance to the parties who give them their decision-making power or to their own dedication or duty to apply the law (Gaillard and Savage, 1999; Landolt, 2012)? If it is the latter, then to whom exactly do arbitrators owe this duty and what is the source of this duty? In this regard, Rau (2007) referred to the tension between the contractual and jurisdictional concepts of arbitration as the classic 'arbitrator's dilemma' that lies at the heart of each interesting question in arbitration (see Section 3.7.4).

Second, what is the danger of non-enforceability of the award? If the award is going to be detached from states' jurisdictions by virtue of the losing party's voluntary compliance (Moss, 2004), then some arbitrators appear to be more attentive to the parties' expectations. If, on the other hand, the winning party needs to seek a court intervention to enforce an award, then some arbitrators appear to be less enthusiastic to meet the parties' expectations and more concerned about the enforceability of the award as their primary duty. In practice, it is difficult to tell if parties will voluntarily comply with the award. It follows that in practice arbitrators' interest in rendering an enforceable award generally has more weight than a competing goal to satisfy the parties' expectations.

Therefore, the question of whether arbitrators will give greater weight to the parties' contract over contrary mandatory law needs to be answered in light of these two main considerations.

3.6 Substantive law is silent

Some scholars argue that one of the cases whereby an arbitrator may deviate from the governing law is when the governing law itself has no guidance or regulation on the matter in dispute (Gaillard and Savage, 1999). If the governing law does not provide the arbitrator with a clear rule, according to which criteria should the arbitrator then decide? This section concerns a situation when both the contract and the law are silent on the issue in dispute. The author asked the arbitrators interviewed in this work how they would decide in this situation.

Some arbitrators asserted that the law can never be silent and there has to be an answer somewhere. The reason is that even if the legislator has not thought about a specific legal problem and its solution (i.e., there is no specific rule), there has still to be a legal theory to derive an answer from. For instance, an Egyptian arbitrator stated that in case there are no contractual or statutory provisions regulating the matter in dispute, guidance can be sought from the general rules of contract in the general theory of obligations in the Egyptian civil and commercial codes. This exercise involves deductive and analogical legal reasoning to derive an unstated legal rule.

A Canadian arbitrator made a similar point, maintaining that an answer must exist in the law:

> If there is no legal case on the point, you have to extrapolate from the existing law to determine what the law should be on this point or what the law is although not yet stated. I mean you have got to resolve the dispute … there has got to be a law in one way or another.

Along the same line, an English arbitrator noted that in a situation where the applicable law provides no explicit answer, arbitrators can still work out what the implicit answer is by analogy (which is a common technique in English law, i.e., working by analogy on established case law to answer the legal question and resolve the dispute):

> I was once acting in a case for a foreign country and its law was very rudimentary. The choice of law was a religious law … the dispute was about delays to the construction of a major infrastructure project, and the contract was based on FIDIC … so, there was no obvious answer in the chosen law but with the help of a legally qualified person from that jurisdiction, it was possible to work out by analogy what the answer would have been, what the implicit answer was, not the express answer because there was not one … It is very rare that you come to a conclusion that there is no answer … I cannot think of a case in which the tribunal would simply say we ran out of laws so we might decide it as we feel.

In case both the contract and its governing law are silent, which is very rare, the outcome tends to be highly uncertain. Arbitrators will be inclined to find a solution that is fair and meets the parties' expectations. In so doing, they would expect the parties, their counsel and law-expert witnesses to argue by 'analogy' and analogy can take four forms as follows.

First, the parties can argue based on the contractual risk allocation (i.e., the spirit of the contract). A Canadian arbitrator noted that in a situation where the parties' contract and its governing law provide no clear answer to the dispute, arbitrators would have great leeway in deciding the dispute and one party may argue based on the dominant pattern of risk allocation in the parties' contract:

> In this case, as neither party has thought about it ... I think you are more into taking a fair approach by asking, how would the parties have dealt with this based on how they have dealt with everything else. If the contract clearly shifts a lot of the risks of unforeseen events to one party, you might be inclined to say: have they directed their minds to this, they would have done the same with this risk.

Second, the parties can argue by analogy not based on the governing law but based on foreign jurisprudence. The participants stated that this is acceptable in both arbitral as well as juridical practice. They gave several examples of how they do so in international arbitration. For instance, if the parties chose the law of a common law country to govern their contract, parties would make submissions based on a number of national laws, such as English law, Canadian law, Australian law, etc. An English arbitrator interviewed by the author confirmed that this practice happens in England whereby the English courts look at jurisprudence from all over the world as foreign law has a persuasive authority in English law. The same thing applies to civil law jurisdictions. For instance, in the Arab world, it is common in disputes arising from construction contracts governed by an Arab law (e.g., UAE, Qatar, Kuwait, etc.) to have submissions from the parties based on the Egyptian jurisprudence. This is because Egyptian law is quite sophisticated, more developed, and more supported by commentary and courts' decisions than the laws of some other Arab states.

By the same token, a Canadian arbitrator mentioned that there are two approaches the parties may follow to attempt to convince the tribunal of a reasonable solution to their dispute in case both the contract and the governing law contain no explicit solution. One approach is to argue by analogy based on the applicable law and the other approach is to argue by analogy based on foreign law. The following interview excerpt illustrates this point:

> If the applicable law the parties have chosen does not deal with the issue in dispute … I think two things may happen. Either they are going to argue by analogy within that same law, and say apply the law which we have chosen, even if the law does not exactly talk about the matter in dispute, it talks about that thing which is similar, so extrapolate from what exists already and determine what the law might be on the matter in dispute … .or the parties may say apply another law which we have not chosen but which we think it provides some guidance here, and that is what it says. One may suggest one thing, and the other might suggest another thing. There will be some flexibility in deciding … I have a choice to make, and I am going to make a choice which I think comes down to what is fair under the circumstances. ... I need to decide which one makes more sense.

In so doing (i.e., relying on foreign legal authorities), arbitrators are mindful that they need to demonstrate in their award that such foreign authorities fit into the governing law. In ICC arbitrations, the ICC will scrutinise its awards and ask arbitrators for clarification on their reliance on a law different from the governing law. In their response, arbitrators normally explain the historical ties between the two national laws and cite legal authorities from the governing law that express that another law has a persuasive authority and so on. Therefore, even though arbitrators could partially or fully rely on foreign authorities to determine a dispute, they tend to strive to embed them in the governing law. Otherwise, it could be a breach of duty to determine a dispute according to rules of law that do not belong to the governing law (Karton, 2015). Nevertheless, Gaillard and Savage (1999) opine that arbitrators are entirely entitled to refer to national laws that were the source of inspiration for the governing law under consideration.

Third, some arbitrators suggested that transnational rules can be used to supplement the parties' contract and its governing law. This book uses the term 'transnational rules' as exclusive of customs and trade usages because these can be interpreted as part of the law or the parties' arbitration agreement or contract. The terms 'transnational rules' or 'international construction law' are used in this book to refer to a wide range of legal norms that could be applied to international construction contracts (see Section 5.2). Anyhow, the arbitrators interviewed by the author confirmed that they might rely on either trade usages and customs or transnational rules in the event the parties' contract and its governing law have no express regulation.

Fourth, a Canadian arbitrator did not rule out the possibility to look at the laws of the countries where the parties come from because they might provide an indication of the intent of the parties and their normal expectations:

> If the national laws of the parties have a way of dealing with the matter in dispute but it is not the law of the contract, you might say that they came from jurisdictions where this matter is handled this way, so their mutual expectations might have been to do something both of them are familiar with. I mean we do that in procedural issues, where both parties are from jurisdictions where production/disclosure of documents is very limited, then your starting proposition tends to be that those are their expectations. So, it seems to me that you can do the same with respect to the substance as well.

Overall, almost all arbitrators interviewed by the author confirmed that it is rare to deal with a dispute where both contract and law are silent. On this rare occasion, as shown above, there is a number of gap-filling tools the parties can use to convince a tribunal that they have a right and therefore to decide in their favour. However, according to some participants, it is also possible that a tribunal will find that there is no basis in law or contract for a claim and thereby dismiss the claim. From this perspective, it is inconceivable to impose a risk allocation that was not contemplated by the parties at all.

This stance has been followed by the arbitral tribunal in an arbitration case that was reported in the *Yearbook Commercial Arbitration* in 1979 (Volume 4, page 202). The tribunal decided that there is no guidance or basis from the substantive law that gives a source of right to the claimant. The tribunal stated:

> The question whether currency loss can be qualified from a legal point of view as damages resulting from delay ... To the knowledge of the arbitral tribunal, there is no leading decision concerning the latter question. The arbitral tribunal is of the opinion that this question must be answered in the negative.

At the end of the day, arbitrators do not make law, but they must make a decision based on existing law.

3.7 Explanatory framework for the legal model of arbitral decision-making

Up until now, this book demonstrates that arbitrators apply the parties' contract and the governing law when deciding the parties' dispute. In so doing, they do not attempt to rewrite the parties' contract or ignore the governing law in favour of their own notions of fairness or reasonableness. Rather, they are keen to apply the law properly taking into consideration procedural limitations and party-autonomy constraints.

This section provides an answer to the 'why' question. In other words, it unpacks arbitrators' motivation and incentive to adhere to the law in their decisions on the merits.

The research underpinning this book finds nine reasons that explain the dominant legal model of arbitral decision-making.

3.7.1 Arbitral duty to apply the law

The arbitrators interviewed by the author asserted that it is their mission to apply the law unless the parties have authorised them not to. There is no shortage of scholarly opinion that arbitrators have a duty to apply the law unless the parties have agreed otherwise (e.g., Natanson, 2013; Mayer, 2001; Buys, 2005).

The problem here concerns the source of this obligation. In national litigation, judges have a duty towards the state to apply its law to its citizens. In international arbitration, it is highly unlikely that arbitrators have the same duty (Mayer, 2001; Park, 2010). This duty stems from the international arbitration's social institution as explained in the next sections.

3.7.2 Arbitration's institutional framework

Arbitration, as a private dispute resolution method, is not governed by an institution. However, it operates within a framework of institutional rules, national laws, and international conventions. These altogether set out the rules of the game (i.e., arbitration decision-making).

In this regard, the arbitrators interviewed by the author and arbitration scholars (e.g., Buys, 2005; Mitchell, 2012) noted that their duty to apply the law is expressed in various institutional rules (e.g., ICC, LCIA) and national arbitration acts.

For instance, the ICC 2012 arbitration rules provide in Article 21.1:

> The parties shall be free to agree upon the rules of law to be applied by the arbitral tribunal to the merits of the dispute. In the absence of any such agreement, the arbitral tribunal shall apply the rules of law which it determines to be appropriate.

Also, the UNCITRAL Model Law provides in Article 28.1:

> The arbitral tribunal shall decide the dispute in accordance with such rules of law as are chosen by the parties as applicable to the substance of the dispute.

Similarly, the English arbitration Act 1996 provides in Article 46.1(a):

> The arbitral tribunal shall decide the dispute in accordance with the law chosen by the parties as applicable to the substance of the dispute.

Nevertheless, the absence of a mechanism to ensure arbitrators' compliance with their duty to apply the law is problematic. The New York Convention, the UNCITRAL Model Law and most national arbitration acts do not provide a supervisory mechanism to sanction arbitrators' disregard or misapplication of the law. This gap or defect in the international arbitration regime is problematic. It is rather hard to see the point of laying down obligations that cannot be enforced.

Nonetheless, it is challenging to 'get it right' and 'get it done' at the same time. The correctness of the arbitral award and its finality seem to be irreconcilable aims that made the architects of international arbitration content with a compromise that favours finality. Further, opening the door for courts' review on the merits will bring back national courts to the resolution of the parties' dispute which the parties wanted to avoid in the first place because of neutrality concerns (Cuniberti, 2008).

3.7.3 Valid and enforceable award

Arbitrators' duty to provide an enforceable award is widely recognised in arbitration scholarship and institutional rules as the value of an unenforceable award is negligible (Natanson, 2013; Karton, 2013; Moses, 2008; Platte, 2003). For many arbitrators, the duty to apply the law is independent of the duty to render a valid and enforceable award. However, the majority of arbitrators interviewed by the author implied a subtle connection between the two duties in the sense that not complying with the former could lead to a breach of the latter. In other words, they are concerned that making a decision that deviates from or contravenes the stipulations of the governing law might put their award in danger of annulment or non-enforcement.

This contrasts with the overwhelming opinion in arbitration scholarship that concurs that arbitral awards are virtually immune from a challenge based on erroneous legal conclusions or mistakes of law (Natanson, 2013; Park, 2010; Rubino-Sammartano, 2008; McConnaughay, 1999; Moses, 2008; Weidemaier, 2009; Blackaby et al., 2015; De Ly, di Brozolo, and Friedman, 2008). Although they vary from one jurisdiction to another, there are limited grounds for the challenge of arbitral awards in the seat of arbitration or in the jurisdiction where enforcement is sought. According to the UNCITRAL Model Law and the arbitration laws of most countries, courts have no power to review awards on the merits (i.e., arbitrators' conclusions of law and findings of facts) (Cuniberti, 2008; Gaillard and Savage, 1999; Andrews, 2016; Moloo and King, 2014). Similarly, the New York Convention and, hence, courts of acceding countries have no grounds for non-recognition or non-enforcement based on a mistake of law, however serious or blatant (Park, 2010; Gaillard and Savage, 1999; McConnaughay, 1999; da Silveira and Levy, 2008). The premise behind this limited judicial review is to maintain an essential feature of arbitration that is the finality of the award (McConnaughay, 1999).

Nonetheless, there are three areas of concern relating to the risk of award non-enforcement that make arbitrators thoughtful of their substantive decisions. These concerns are primarily directed towards courts of enforcement jurisdictions because they normally have a significant connection with the losing party. Courts of the seat are of less concern in this respect because the seat is normally chosen due to its neutrality (McConnaughay, 1999).

The first concern arbitrators and arbitration scholars (e.g., Moses, 2008; Van den Berg, 2005) have is that a disregard of the governing law provisions might be construed as an excess of authority by the tribunal that entitles a reviewing court to set aside or refuse to enforce the award. In this sense, an English arbitrator interviewed by the author noted:

> If an arbitrator does not decide in accordance with the law, then there is a significant risk that he has not in fact complied with the jurisdiction he has been given, and the award could be set aside.

However, this argument has been criticised as it would defeat the purpose of arbitration in providing a final and enforceable award (da Silveira and Levy, 2008). da Silveira and Levy (2008) argue, based on a series of courts' decisions in various jurisdictions, that arbitrators' misapplication of the law cannot be broadly construed as an excess of the limits of their mandate or the scope of their jurisdiction and, hence, is not reviewable by courts at jurisdictions where enforcement is sought. Likewise, Moss (2004) finds that, based on an analysis of arbitral awards concerning the application of the UNCITRAL Model Law and the New York Convention, an excess of power has rarely been successful to challenge arbitrators' determinations of law.

The second concern arbitrators have is that despite all protection afforded to arbitrators' decisions on the substance, they are alert that courts can invoke public policy to challenge arbitral awards. The right of states to do so is recognised by the New York Convention and the UNCITRAL Model Law (Karton, 2013). In the opinion of some arbitrators, it is against public order not to enforce the law, especially in civil law countries.

In this regard, an English arbitrator stated:

> I do not accept the premise that an award cannot be challenged based on the tribunal's deviation from the law. I believe there are many jurisdictions that do not permit this … so under English law, you have a right of appeal, subject to the admission of the court, to expressly challenge the findings of law of the arbitral tribunal … but even under jurisdictions where there are no express rights in the arbitration law, the question of public order and public policy comes into play ... in many civil law countries, it is against public order not to enforce the law.

However, there is a general agreement in arbitration scholarship that public policy should be applied restrictively and construed narrowly to refer to procedural or substantive defects that contradict the fundamental principles of society and natural justice (Cuniberti, 2008; McConnaughay, 1999; Moss, 2004). There is also evidence from practice that courts' decisions setting aside or refusing to enforce arbitral awards on the ground of public policy are not many. In these limited cases, courts have, generally speaking, consistently interpreted public policy to refer to matters violating states' rules on bribery, corruption and the like (Moss, 2004). It follows that public policy would not be used to scrutinise the soundness of an arbitrator's conclusions of law (Gaillard and Savage, 1999; McConnaughay, 1999; Moss, 2004). Nevertheless, the concept of public policy remains elastic and indeterminate in many jurisdictions (Moss, 2004; Kurkela and Turunen, 2010). As such, in practice, it seems some arbitrators feel more comfortable not taking the risk, even if it has a small chance of occurring, of departing from the law.

The third area of concern is that a few jurisdictions, England and the United States in particular, might review an arbitrator's application of the law. However, arbitration scholarship and courts' practice suggest that courts will review the merits of awards under both jurisdictions in exceptional circumstances. In England, a court may review the merits of the tribunal's decision according to the English Arbitration Act 1996. However, to do so, the court needs to find that (1) the parties have agreed to keep their right to appeal; (2) the tribunal's decision is patently wrong on a point of law; (3) the point of law is limited to English law; and (4) the matters at stake are of general public importance (Moses, 2008; Andrews, 2016). Evidence from practice suggests that English courts do not grant an appeal in the majority of cases (Andrews, 2016). In the United States, some courts devised a non-statutory ground to vacate or set aside an arbitral award based on 'manifest disregard of the law'. However, this doctrine has been rarely applied (Kaufmann-Kohler, 2005) because of the high threshold of the proof required (a party needs to demonstrate that an arbitrator deliberately disregarded the law). Also, it has been rejected and disapplied in some states (Moses, 2008).

Based on the aforementioned reasons, arbitrators tend to be mindful of the importance of properly applying the law to protect their awards from the risk of challenge based on a number of grounds. Arbitrators apply the law not only to fulfil their duty to render an enforceable award but also to avoid the embarrassment of failing to see their awards enforced. For arbitrators, having their awards annulled or refused enforcement may harm their reputation and could be detrimental to their career (Schultz, 2015; Basaran, 2014; Natanson, 2013; Karton, 2013; Moses, 2008). In this regard, an Irish arbitrator commented:

> The most humiliating thing in your arbitration career is that your decision is challenged and not upheld in court which means there is something wrong.

3.7.4 Arbitration is supplementary, not alternative, to courts

The classic arbitrator's dilemma concerns the longstanding debate on the arbitrator's role and the arbitration's nature (Rau, 2007; Barraclough and Waincymer, 2005). There are two distinct formulations for this conceptual problem. Is arbitration an alternative/substitute or a supplement to courts' justice (Kirgis, 2006)? To put it differently, is arbitration contractual or jurisdictional (Barraclough and Waincymer, 2005)? Consequently, is an arbitrator a service provider (i.e., an agent who is hired by the parties to resolve their dispute based on their rules), or is an arbitrator a quasi-judge who is responsible for the right application of the law regardless of the wishes of the parties (Kirgis, 2006)?

This is the most fundamental problem in arbitration theory and practice that has not been resolved in theory and not settled in practice. It is problematic in practice because it leads to different views on the parties' rights and obligations and the extent of arbitrators' power and authority (Barraclough and Waincymer, 2005).

There is a wide range of opinions that support either model (e.g., Kirgis, 2006; Rau, 2007), but the main view seems to support a hybrid model that includes elements of both models: contractual and jurisdictional (Barraclough and Waincymer, 2005). The dilemma, however, remains as to where to draw the dividing line. So, if the nature of arbitration is represented by a continuum, with the contractual view and the jurisdictional view at the two ends of the spectrum, then there is a wide margin for individual choice of where to draw the line that represents the hybrid model (Barraclough and Waincymer, 2005).

This theoretical division or conceptual tension underpinning arbitration explains most of the controversial views that arbitrators hold in relation to their decision-making approach, as this book finds.

It follows that the closer an arbitrator is to the contractual view, the more he or she is respectful of party autonomy. In turn, the arbitrator would have a greater tendency to apply the law as the parties see it and plead it, and vice versa is true.

Arbitrators who are closer to the other end of the spectrum maintain that the arbitral mission entails a duty to apply the law in the same manner as that of a national judge. This duty, they believe, is derived from the very concept of arbitration as supplementary to court justice and not a substitution or a replacement to substantive justice as administered by courts. As such, by selecting arbitration, there is a basic assumption that the parties have not given up their legal rights. Rather, they wish their legal rights to be determined but in a neutral setting. If the parties do not wish their dispute to be resolved according to the law and their contract, then they should seek mediation or other forms of alternative dispute resolution (ADR) techniques whereby a dispute resolver is not bound by the law. Likewise, there is a considerable scholarly opinion that arbitration is a procedural but not substantive alternative to court litigation (Karton, 2013; Ridgway, 1999). The parties opt for arbitration for procedural reasons (e.g., enforceability of arbitral awards, the neutrality of the forum, the flexibility of procedure, etc.) and not for substantive reasons (Drahozal and Ware, 2010; Naimark and Keer, 2002; Bühring-Uhle, 1996).

3.7.5 Parties expectations

It is often said that arbitration should sever commerce. It should enable businesspeople to make sensible commercial arrangements and thereby further international trade.

Commercial people must be given the utmost liberty of contracting. They shall be left free to decide on the allocation of commercial risks in their contracts. When disputes arise, arbitrators should be sensitive to the commercial purpose of the deal and decide in accordance with the parties' expectations. But what are the parties' expectations? What does a solution according to the parties' expectations require? This is a matter of empirical verification but so far there is no empirical study, to the best of the author's knowledge, that solicits the parties' expectations as to how they think their disputes should be resolved in international arbitration. This is a normative inquiry. Normative claims tell us or affirm what ought to be the case under a specific circumstance. There is also little attempt to provide a theoretical explanation as to what parties' expectations might be in the context of international arbitration. The literature contains several assertions concerning parties' expectations that have been allowed to pass with no empirical evidence.

For instance, some authors opine that commercial parties expect a commercial decision and that is the reason for choosing arbitration in lieu of court litigation. In this sense, a decision based on a black-letter analysis of the law would be contrary to their commercial expectations (Vogenauer, 2006; Hermann, 1983; Ossman, 2003; Ridgway, 1999; McConnaughay, 1999).

There is another assertion that parties in international commerce pay little attention to the law while closing the deal. They negotiate the terms of the contract and leave the choice of law to the end. Sometimes, they insert a choice of law clause without a careful analysis of its impact on their contractual allocation of risks or agree on a third law when they are not familiar with its content simply because of its neutrality. Sometimes, they even do not agree on the law to govern their contract or forget it and end up with no choice of law. This indicates that the parties expect their contract terms to be enforced no matter what legal rules may be applied by arbitrators (Moss, 2004; Cuniberti, 2014). This viewpoint finds support from the promissory theory of contract law. The promissory theory underscores the importance of party autonomy and supports the idea that the agreement as understood by the parties should be upheld (Mitchell, 2013).

However, the available evidence discredits this claim and suggests otherwise. Parties prefer arbitration to national litigation because of the advantages of neutrality and enforceability (Lagerberg and Mistelis, 2006; Nazzini, 2018; Friedland and Mistelis, 2015; Bühring-Uhle, 2005), and the parties' expectations are seemingly to have their disputes determined according to the law. The parties' expectations, as inferred from the law they choose in their arbitration clauses (Drahozal, 2005; Bond, 2005), is that they wish for a decision based on a specific and predictable national law. They do not desire an 'extra-legal' resolution to their disputes (Bond, 2005). Neither do they want their legal rights and obligations to be decided by the courts of the other party's state of nationality (Dezalay and Garth, 1998; Bond, 2005).

Arbitrators interviewed by the author as well as arbitration scholars (Mayer, 2001; Karton, 2015; Karton, 2012a; Kaufmann-Kohler, 2007) opine that arbitrators' duty to apply the law also draws from commercial parties' appreciation of the certainty of their rights and obligations, predictability of the outcome of their dispute and the stability in commercial dealings in the long run. Predictability and stability go hand in hand with the finality of arbitration, which is one of the most attractive aspects of international arbitration. Otherwise, if arbitrators entertain wide discretion to decide as they prefer, people will lose confidence in the arbitration process. Therefore, to protect arbitration as an international private justice system that provides disputants with decisions that are final and binding with limited grounds for appeal, arbitrators need to assure predictability, and this can be achieved only by applying the law.

Further, if the parties truly expected a commercial decision, then they would be expected to structure their dispute resolution process to produce such an outcome. For instance, they could appoint commercial people as arbitrators. Although, in principle, all arbitrators have the same duty to apply the law, some participants noted that, as a practical matter, arbitrators' different backgrounds may lead to somewhat different results. This is because industry people will generally have more difficulty applying the law and more tendency to consider the commercial merits of the parties' claims. Some arbitrators interviewed by the author noted that there is an implicit understanding between the disputants and the arbitrators they select with respect to the nature of the decision they expect. If the parties choose arbitrators with legal backgrounds, then this indicates that they expect a legal decision. If, on the other hand, the parties choose arbitrators from the construction industry, then this implies that they expect a decision that is more attentive to commercial practice. It is true that national arbitration acts and institutional arbitration rules do not require arbitrators to have legal training, but. in practice, most international arbitrators are distinguished lawyers or law professors (Cuniberti, 2008).

In addition to appointing commercial people as arbitrators, the parties could direct the tribunal to decide based on non-legal criteria (e.g., trade usage, *lex mercatoria, ex aequo et bono*, etc.). However, this cannot be further from the truth. Often, the parties appoint legal professionals (lawyers, barristers, law professors, judges, etc.) to arbitrate their disputes (Cuniberti, 2008; Karton, 2015; Franck, 2005) and select a national law to govern their disputes (Karton, 2015; Drahozal, 2005; Berger et al., 2005; Bond, 2005). The arbitrators interviewed in the study underpinning this book asserted that the choice of law clause is one of the most important contractual decisions. The parties are presumed to be knowledgeable and aware of the implications of their choices, and they should draft their contract in a way that is consistent with its governing law in order to avoid undesirable results. Moreover, the available empirical evidence suggests that the parties make their decision to initiate arbitration based on their assessment of the strength of their legal position (Lagerberg and Mistelis, 2013).

Therefore, the way the parties structure their arbitration decision-making process indicates that it is their intention and expectation to receive a decision according to the law (Park, 2011). As such, the argument that the parties' expectations are not to have their dispute determined according to the law fails to be convincing.

3.7.6 Informal control: ICC and scholarly scrutiny

One thing that makes ICC arbitration different from other institutional arbitrations is that the ICC Court of Arbitration scrutinises arbitral awards rendered under its auspices.

In ICC arbitration, an arbitral tribunal submits its draft award to the secretary. Then, the court, through one of its weekly subcommittees or monthly plenary sessions, reviews it and either approves it or asks the tribunal to revise its award. In the latter case, the court might recommend or require a change. Although the court's feedback mainly concerns the form of the award, it also touches upon matters of substance. Article 33 (Scrutiny of the Award by the Court) of the ICC 2012 Rules of Arbitration provides that:

> before signing any award, the arbitral tribunal shall submit it in draft form to the Court. The Court may lay down modifications as to the form of the award and, without affecting the arbitral tribunal's liberty of decision, may also draw its attention to points of substance. No award shall be rendered by the arbitral tribunal until it has been approved by the Court as to its form.

It follows that a court may recommend the tribunal revise certain findings or conclusions that are seemingly flawed or inconsistent. Although the court will normally not require tribunals to change their decisions on the substance, it remains a professional embarrassment for some arbitrators to receive such remarks. It is even more embarrassing if their arbitral awards get publicised and receive scholarly criticism. In this regard, a Lebanese arbitrator said:

> Even if the court has no power to oblige arbitrators to change their decisions, there is another informal control that constraints international arbitrators. Arbitration awards may be published in redacted form or even complete. For instance, the ICC publishes its awards in the ICC bulletin. You do not want a scholar or an arbitrator to write a case note criticising the way you applied the law. So, it would not look good for me as an arbitrator. I am talking about the particular context of institutional arbitration where arbitrators are appointed by arbitration institutions. So, if these things get repeated very often, I think an arbitrator may worry about not getting more appointments. You see, it is a market control which is exercised by the market itself. International arbitration is becoming a market actually.

This statement regarding the court's scrutiny of essentially the form but also the substance of arbitral awards concurs with many scholarly writings (e.g. Nazzini, 2018; Verbist et al., 2015). Zlatanska (2015) asserts that the publication of awards will provide a sort of external scrutiny and soft control over arbitral decision-making. This form of social control and social sanction of arbitrators' misapplication of the law is paramount in international arbitration as a justice system lacking formal control of its substantive outcomes (Zlatanska, 2015). Overall, the court and scholarly scrutiny form a soft power incentivising arbitrators to properly apply the law.

3.7.7 Not my job! It is the parties' choice

In the interaction between law and parties' expectations, some arbitration scholars (Mandziuk, 2014) believe that, in many cases, there is a misalignment between the stipulations of the governing law of the contract and the expectations of the parties. Nonetheless, most arbitrators interviewed by the author maintain that they would apply the law even if it turns out to be contrary to the parties' expectations. Throughout the interviews, the arbitrators maintain that it is not their job to rewrite the parties' contract or ignore the stipulations of the law they chose to govern their contract. Their arbitral mission does not give them the jurisdiction to decide on a basis different from that which the parties agreed to. Rather, they have to respect the parties' agreement and enforce their contract, including the choice of law clause as an objective statement of their intent.

In addition, according to the interviewed arbitrators, construction parties are usually not small players and are assumed to have had legal advice before entering into a contract. As such, the parties should be able to look after themselves and perhaps undergo an internal review to find who was accountable for agreeing on certain terms during contract negotiation or for failing to administer and manage the contract during contract performance.

3.7.8 Concern for reputation and appointments

Some interviewed arbitrators stated that they are keen to apply the law and adhere to the parties' contract for the sake of their own reputation. This indicates the arbitrators' perception that it is the parties' expectation to have their contract terms enforced according to the governing law. As such, they believe a fulfilment of the parties' expectations in addition to their compliance with their duty to apply the law enhances their reputation. Further, they believe that this decision-making approach safeguards their awards from the risk of challenge, which could otherwise cause them reputational damage and negatively affect the demand for their services.

The rationale arbitrators provided for applying the law demonstrates that arbitration services are governed by market forces and arbitrators, as service providers are subject to market rules of competition. It follows that the arbitral decision-making behaviour is shaped by the arbitrators' incentive to receive appointments. What arbitrators do to attract business and increase their market value is to win the parties' confidence that, if appointed, they will apply the terms of the parties' contract and comply with the stipulations of the law they chose to govern their contract (Karton, 2013; Drahozal, 2005; Weidemaier, 2009). Even though arbitral awards are rarely published, arbitrators believe that their decision-making approach has an effect on their market value and, thus, their income.

Schultz (2015) analysed arbitral decision-making behaviour from a law and economics perspective. According to this theoretical framework, decision-making behaviour is a function of incentives and constraints. The main incentive arbitrators have is to maximise their own utility. As such, their decision-making behaviour will conform to what they envisage to be in their self-interest. He argues that the arbitration field is regulated by market forces, and arbitrators respond to these market forces. To attract more business (i.e., arbitral appointments) and increase their market value, arbitrators need to make decisions that are sound, reasonable, and legally accurate (Schultz, 2015).

However, there is a paradox in that the parties sometimes prefer an arbitrator who does not have legal acumen and integrity, is disposed to their arguments, and will help them to win the case (Schultz, 2015; Park, 2014).

The following quote from an interview with an Irish arbitrator illustrates the market forces paradox in international arbitration:

> I think most arbitrators will make decisions based on their own 'self-preservation' and this comes from deciding on what the parties agreed on in their contract because this is an objective criterion and easy to reach a consensus on whereas what is fair or unfair is very subjective … as an arbitrator you seek to be seen as someone who writes sensible and reasonable decisions … it is all about reputation … about being seen doing the job properly and thoroughly, and giving a decision in a professional way that explains to the parties the reason for your decisions … that's it frankly … no arbitrator wants to be seen doing a bad job, you want people to ask you to arbitrate another dispute … but again, having said that, I imagine there are parties in international arbitration who will choose a party-appointed arbitrator simply because they know this arbitrator is going to be biased towards their position … in arbitration, like anywhere else, there are corrupt people.

However, the available evidence on the extent to which legally correct decisions on the substance assist arbitrators to attract more business is inconclusive. There is empirical evidence that suggests when parties are on the lookout for arbitrators, they are primarily concerned about an arbitrator's competence in procedural matters, with little concern for the quality of the decision on the substance (Schultz and Kovacs, 2012). Yet, contrary empirical evidence suggests that the two most important factors in the selection of international arbitrators are their understanding of the relevant industry and knowledge of the governing law; both of which concern the substantive outcome (Lagerberg and Mistelis, 2013). Overall, it appears that the real effect of arbitrators' substantive decisions on the demand for their services is uncertain (Schultz, 2015).

3.7.9 A pledge to professionalism and reputation protectionism

Some arbitrators interviewed by the author suggested that a duty to apply the law comes from a pledge to professionalism in the conduct of arbitration services.

Even if the arbitration award does not get publicised or commented on, some arbitrators still believe that they have a professional duty to apply the law. Otherwise, they would be viewed as negligent (i.e., in breach of their professional duty). However, this should not be construed narrowly as a breach of legal duty because arbitrators are immune from liability and claims based on professional negligence (Salahuddin, 2017).

By the same token, some scholars argue that the arbitrator's contract obliges him or her to comply with the parties' arbitration agreement, including the substantive norms the parties agreed to apply to their dispute (Onyema, 2010). Again, this should not be construed in a strict sense because arbitrators are immune from legal action. Therefore, even if arbitrators do not adhere to the criteria the parties elect to govern their dispute, they will not be in a breach of contract that gives rise to legal recourse (Salahuddin, 2017).

As such, the arbitrators' duty to apply the law should be construed broadly to mean a moral duty and a commitment to the professionalism of arbitration. In this sense, an arbitrator interviewed by the author said that, in some cases, he was applying a national law that was different from the law of the seat and the laws of the potential enforcement jurisdictions. Despite the lack of supervisory power on his decision, he remained keen to properly apply the law due to his commitment to what he called 'intellectual honesty' and 'professionalism' in the performance of his job.

3.8 Arbitrators' perception of the practical impact of the governing law on the dispute outcome

How important is substantive law in international construction arbitration? The answer is always going to be 'it depends' on the circumstances of the case. Sometimes, the dispute largely concerns contested facts or different interpretations of the contract. Hence, the arbitrator's job would be to find the facts and interpret the contract. In other cases, a dispute could involve a complex legal controversy (Moses, 2008).

Nonetheless, to generalise, some arbitrators interviewed by the author opine that the substantive law will not normally have a significant impact on the outcome of a construction dispute despite the differences between national laws on interpretation rules, regulatory rules, and mandatory rules. There are four reasons for this.

First, most construction disputes can be resolved based on the facts and terms of the contract. According to one English arbitrator, 90% of construction disputes are decided based on facts (i.e., if the facts are determined then the answer is straightforward). Second, normally, international construction contracts are comprehensive, and, hence, there is little need for supplementation or implication from the substantive law. Third, mandatory rules of law applicable to construction contracts are not many. Fourth, the ultimate goal of all legal systems is to guide the decision-maker to arrive at a fair and just solution. They do so using different means. For instance, an eminent Egyptian arbitrator with international arbitration experience spanning five decades stated:

> I can confidently tell you that certainly legal systems have differences, but they more or less would lead to the same result by different techniques. The techniques used in common law would be alien to someone from a civil law country ... but if you apply them and go to the end, in my humble opinion, I think in 95% of the cases you will arrive at the same result by a different type of reasoning...this is because the law of contracts is based on very simple legal premises, the respect of pacta sunt servanda and good faith ... you are bound to follow those guidelines in dealing with interpretation ... under English law, I was involved in cases where we [the tribunal] were discussing Hoffmann's canon of contract interpretation and I found them more or less arriving at the same result through vocabulary that was not the same as that which the French court of cassation or the Egyptian court of cassation would use.

This opinion has much support in the literature. In many cases, arbitrators proclaim in their awards that the outcome of the dispute would not have been different if other national laws or general principles of law had been applied (Karton, 2013). Some legal systems provide for a general duty of good faith to attain a particular result while other legal systems make available a set of implied terms or extensive rules of contract interpretation to arrive at substantially the same fair and reasonable result. They principally differ in the approach to the reasoning process (Rosengren, 2013). At the end of the day, the contract will determine the liabilities and entitlements of the parties in the majority of international construction arbitrations (Knutson, 2004; Dunham, 2010).

3.9 Conclusion

This chapter finds that international construction arbitrators concur that they have a duty to apply the law, and they tend to properly apply the law unless the parties have agreed otherwise. The application of the law involves applying the rules in the governing law that govern the interpretation of the meaning of a contract, filling the gaps in a contract and constructing the legal effect and the validity of a contract.

This chapter finds that the majority of arbitrators follow the rules of interpretation laid down in the substantive law. Nonetheless, there are dissenting opinions on the extent to which contract interpretation should be governed by the governing law. This is to be further explored in the next chapters.

Also, this chapter finds that matters involving mandatory rules of the governing law seem to be highly controversial. This is especially the case when the parties resist their application *ex-post* during arbitration proceedings or try to exclude their applicability *ex-ante* through an exclusion clause in their contract. The core of the controversy boils down to the very concept of arbitration and accordingly the role an arbitrator is presumed to fulfil. The tension is between party autonomy and competing principles concerning the arbitrators' duty to apply the law, the arbitrators' duty to render an enforceable award and the arbitrators' own conceptualisation of their role as substantially similar to a judicial role in, among other things, the right application of the law. This chapter demonstrates that arbitrators strike the balance between these competing concepts differently.

The finding that arbitrators follow and apply the governing law does not necessarily mean they apply it in a manner that is identical to national judges. This is attributed to procedural as well as conceptual differences. Nonetheless, the prevailing arbitral opinion supports the orthodox approach in giving higher precedence to mandatory legal provisions over contractual provisions.

Then, as some scholars cite the incompleteness of national laws as a ground that entitles arbitrators to deviate from the governing law, this chapter examines how arbitrators decide in this situation. Some arbitrators assert that the law is never silent as a matter of legal theory. However, as a practical matter, if the law is unclear or indeterminate, arbitrators have a number of options to devise a legal solution. The sources of inspiration or supplementation include foreign law, transnational rules of law and customary practices.

Finally, this chapter unpacks the reasons behind the dominance of the legal model in international construction arbitration decision-making. The legal model fulfils the parties' aspirations for predictability of the outcomes of their disputes and, hence, stability in commercial and business dealings. It respects the parties' choice of law, which is an outcome of their negotiations and part of their risk allocation. Also, the legal model meets the arbitrators' desire to discharge their duties to apply the law and to render enforceable awards, which, in the arbitrators' opinion, has a positive impact on their career in arbitration. The legal model also complies with most arbitration rules and arbitration laws requiring arbitrators to apply the law or the rules of law chosen by the parties.

On a more abstract level, the evolution of this legal model appears to be the result of the interaction between a number of forces in the field: (1) the disputants, (2) the arbitrators, (3) arbitration institutions and national legislators setting out rules to guide arbitrators on how to decide, and (4) national courts setting and/or implementing rules relating to the level of scrutiny and control over arbitrators' decisions.

3.10 References

Andrews, N. (2016). *Arbitration and Contract Law*. Cham: Springer.

Ayoğlu, T. (2012). Application of trade usages in international institutional arbitration–some reflections. *ASA Bulletin*, 30(3), 539–547.

Barraclough, A. & Waincymer, J. (2005). Mandatory rules of law in international commercial arbitration. *Melbourne Journal of International Law*, 6, 205.

Basaran, H. R. (2014). Is international arbitration universal. *ILSA Journal of International & Comparative Law*, 21, 497.

Berger, K., Dubberstein, H., Lehmann, S. & Petzold, V. (2005). The CENTRAL enquiry on the use of transnational law in international contract law and arbitration: Background, procedure and selected results. *In*: Drahozal, C. R. & Naimark, R. W. (eds.) *Towards a Science of International Arbitration: Collected Empirical Research*. The Hague Kluwer law international.

Blackaby, N., Partasides, C., Redfern, A. & Hunter, M. (2015). *Redfern and Hunter on International Arbitration*. 6th ed. Oxford: Oxford University Press.

Błaszczak, Ł. & Kolber, J. (2013). General principles of law and equity as a basis for decision-making in arbitration. *Comparative Law Review*, 15, 189–208.

Bond, S. R. (2005). How to draft an arbitration clause. *In*: Drahozal, C. R. & Naimark, R. W. (eds.) *Towards a Science of International Arbitration: Collected Empirical Research*. The Hague: Kluwer law international.

Born, G. (2014). *International Commercial Arbitration.* 2nd ed. The Hague: Kluwer Law International.

Borris, C. (1994). Common law and civil law: Fundamental differences and their impaction arbitration. *Arbitration*, 60, 78–78.

Brunet, E. (1992). Arbitration and constitutional rights. *North Carolina Law Review*, 71, 81.

Brunner, C. (2009). *Force Majeure and Hardship Under General Contract Principles: Exemption for Non-performance in International Arbitration.* The Hague: Kluwer Law International.

Bühring-Uhle, C. (1996). *Arbitration and Mediation in International Business.* The Hague: Kluwer Law International.

Bühring-Uhle, C. (2005). A Survey on Arbitration and Settlement in International Business Disputes - Advantages of Arbitration. *In:* Drahozal, C. & Naimark, R. (eds.) *Towards a Science of International Arbitration: Collected Empirical Research.* The Hague: Kluwer Law International.

Burr, A. (2016). *Delay and Disruption in Construction Contracts.* Oxford: Informa Law from Routledge.

Buys, C. G. (2005). The arbitrators' duty to respect the parties' choice of law in commercial arbitration. *St. John's Law Review*, 79(1), 59.

Caron, D. (2015). Regulating opacity: Shaping how tribunals think. *King's College London Dickson Poon School of Law Legal Studies Research Paper Series*, Paper No. 2015-07.

Charrett, D. (2012). A common law of construction contracts: Or vive la différence? *International Construction Law Review*, 29(1).

Cuniberti, G. (2008). Beyond contract: The case for default arbitration in international commercial disputes. *Fordham International Law Journal*, 32, 417.

Cuniberti, G. (2014). The international market for contracts: The most attractive contract laws. *Northwestern Journal of International Law & Business*, 34(3), 455.

da Silveira, M. & Levy, L. (2008). Transgression of the arbitrators' authority: Article V (1)(c) of the New York convention. *In*: Gaillard, E. & Pietro, D. (eds.) *Enforcement of Arbitration Agreements and International Arbitral Awards: The New York Convention in Practice*. London: Cameron May.

De Ly, F., di Brozolo, L. & Friedman, M. (2008). Ascertaining the Contents of the Applicable Law in International Commercial Arbitration. International Commercial Arbitration Committee of the International Law Association. Available at https://www.ila-hq.org/en_GB/committees/international-commercial-arbitration-1989 [Accessed 12 December 2016].

Derains, Y. (1987). Public policy and the law applicable to the dispute in international arbitration. *In*: Sanders, P. (ed.) *Comparative Arbitration Practice and Public Policy in Arbitration.* Alphen aan den Rijn: Kluwer Law International.

Dezalay, Y. & Garth, B. G. (1998). *Dealing in virtue: International commercial arbitration and the construction of a transnational legal order.* Chicago: University of Chicago Press.

Drahozal, C. R. (2004). A behavioral analysis of private judging. *Law and contemporary problems*, 67(1), 105–132.

Drahozal, C. R. (2005). Contracting out of national law: An empirical look at the new law merchant. *Notre Dame Law Review*, 80(2), 523.

Drahozal, C. R. & Ware, S. J. (2010). Why do businesses use (or not use) arbitration clauses. *Ohio State Journal on Dispute Resolution*, 25, 433.

Dunham, K. F. (2010). Construction arbitration: Collected works. *Faulkner Law Review*, 2(2), 311.

Franck, S. (2005). The role of international arbitrators. *ILSA Journal of International & Comparative Law*, 12, 499.

Friedland, P. & Mistelis, L. (2015). 2015 International Arbitration Survey: Improvements and Innovations in International Arbitration. Queen Mary University of London and School of International Arbitration. Available at https://arbitration.qmul.ac.uk/media/arbitration/docs/2015_International_Arbitration_Survey.pdf. [Accessed 10 October 2022].

Gaillard, E. & Savage, J. (1999). *Fouchard, Gaillard, Goldman on International Commercial Arbitration*. The Hague: Kluwer law international.

Gélinas, F. (2016). Trade usages as transnational law. *In*: Gélinas, F. (ed.) *Trade Usages and Implied Terms in the Age of Arbitration*. Oxford: Oxford University Press.

Hart, O. & Moore, J. (1988). Incomplete contracts and renegotiation. *Econometrica: Journal of the Econometric Society*, 56(4), 755–785.

Hermann, A. H. (1983). *Judges, Law and Businessmen*. Deventer: Kluwer

Jaffe, M. & McHugh, R. (2009). International construction disputes in today's economy. Available at http://fidic.org/sites/default/files/2%20jaffe09.pdf [Accessed 22 October 2017].

Karton, J. (2012a). A conflict of interests: Seeking a way forward on publication of international arbitral awards. *Arbitration International*, 28(3), 447–486.

Karton, J. (2012b). International commercial arbitrators' approaches to contractual interpretation. *International Business Law Journal*, 383.

Karton, J. (2013). *The Culture of International Arbitration and the Evolution of Contract Law*. Oxford: Oxford University Press.

Karton, J. (2015). The arbitral role in contractual interpretation. *Journal of International Dispute Settlement*, 6(1), 4–41.

Kaufmann-Kohler, G. (2005). The arbitrator and the law: Does he/she know it? Apply it? How? And a few more questions. *Arbitration International*, 21(4), 631–638.

Kaufmann-Kohler, G. (2007). Arbitral Precedent: Dream, Necessity or Excuse?: The 2006 Freshfields Lecture. *Arbitration International*, 23(3), 357–378.

Kirgis, P. F. (2006). Contractarian model of arbitration and its implications for judicial review of arbitral awards. *Oregon Law Review*, 85(1), 1.

Kirsh, H. J. (2012). Pitfalls, perceptions and processes in construction arbitration. *The Advocates' Quarterly*, 40(3).

Knutson, R. (2004). Recent treatment of construction awards by the ICC international court of arbitration. A paper given to a meeting of the Society of Construction Law. London.

Knutson, R. (2005). *FIDIC: An Analysis of International Construction Contracts* (2nd ed.). The Hague: Kluwer Law International.

Kurkela, M. & Turunen, S. (2010). *Due process in international commercial arbitration* (2nd ed.). New York: Oxford University Press.

Lagerberg, G. & Mistelis, L. (2006). International Arbitration: Corporate Attitudes and Practices. Queen Mary University of London and School of International Arbitration.

Lagerberg, G. & Mistelis, L. (2013). Corporate choices in International Arbitration: Industry perspectives. Queen Mary University of London and School of International Arbitration. Available at https://www.pwc.com/gx/en/arbitration-dispute-resolution/assets/pwc-international-arbitration-study.pdf. [Accessed 12 December 2022].

Landolt, P. (2012). Arbitrators' initiatives to obtain factual and legal evidence. *Arbitration International*, 28(2), 173–224.

Lawrence, B. S. (2010). The interpretation: Construction distinction. *Georgetown Public Law Research Paper No. 11-95*, 27, 95–118.

Levin, M. S. (1997). The role of substantive law in business arbitration and the importance of volition. *American Business Law Journal*, 35(1), 105–180.

Mandziuk, S. N. (2014). Book review: Contract law and contract practice: Bridging the gap between legal reasoning and commercial expectation, by Catherine Mitchell. *Osgoode Hall Law Journal*, 52(2), 660–669.

Mayer, P. (1986). Mandatory rules of law in international arbitration. *Arbitration International*, 2(4), 274–293.

Mayer, P. (2001). Reflections on the international arbitrator's duty to apply the law: The 2000 Freshfields lecture. *Arbitration International*, 17(3), 235–248.

McConnaughay, P. J. (1999). The risks and virtues of lawlessness: A second look at international commercial arbitration. *Northwestern University Law Review*, 93(2), 453.

Mentschikoff, S. (1961). Commercial arbitration. *Columbia Law Review*, 61(5), 846–869.

Mitchell, R. (2012). Must arbitrators follow the law? *JAMS Global Construction Solutions Newsletter.*

Mitchell, C. E. (2013). *Contract Law and Contract Practice: Bridging the Gap Between Legal Reasoning and Commercial Expectation.* Oxford: Bloomsbury Publishing.

Moloo, R. & King, B. (2014). International Arbitrators as Lawmakers. *New York University Journal of International Law and Politics,* 46(3), 875–909.

Moses, M. L. (2008). *The Principles and Practice of International Commercial Arbitration.* Cambridge: Cambridge University Press.

Moss, G. (2004). Introductory materials on international commercial law. *Transnational Dispute Management*, 1(3), 1–161.

Mulcahy, C. (2015). What does it mean-contractual interpretation in international commercial arbitration. *Dispute Resolution International*, 9, 15.

Naimark, R. W. & Keer, S. E. (2002). What do parties really want from international commercial arbitration? *Dispute Resolution Journal*, 57(4), 78.

Natanson, R. (2013). *The Choice of the Applicable Law as a Strategy in International Commercial Arbitration.* M.Sc., Toulouse Capitole University.

Nazzini, R. (2018). *Transnational Construction Arbitration: Key Themes in the Resolution of Construction Disputes.* New York: Informa Law from Routledge.

Onyema, E. (2010). *International Commercial Arbitration and the Arbitrator's Contract.* Abingdon: Routledge.

Ossman, G. (2003). *Construction Arbitration Consistency and Reliability: An Empirical Study.* M. Sc., Pepperdine University School of Law.

Park, W. W. (2009). Arbitrator integrity: The transient and the permanent. *San Diego Law Review*, 46, 629.

Park, W. W. (2010). Arbitrators and accuracy. *Journal of International Dispute Settlement*, 1(1), 25–53.

Park, W. W. (2011). Arbitration in autumn. *Journal of International Dispute Settlement,* 2(2), 287–315.

Park, W. W. (2014). A fair fight: Professional guidelines in international arbitration. *Arbitration International*, 30(3), 409–428.

Park, W. W. (2015). The predictability paradox: Arbitrators and applicable law. *Transnational Dispute Management*, 12(6).

Platte, M. (2003). An arbitrator's duty to render enforceable awards. *Journal of International Arbitration*, 20(3), 307–313.

Rau, A. (2007). The arbitrator and mandatory rules of law. *The American Review of International Arbitration*, 18, 51–88.

Ridgway, D. A. (1999). International arbitration: The next growth industry. *Dispute Resolution Journal*, 54(1), 50.

Rosengren, J. (2013). Contract interpretation in international arbitration. *Journal of International Arbitration*, 30(1), 1–16.

Rubino-Sammartano, M. (2008). Decision-making mechanism of the arbitrator vis-a-vis the judge. *Journal of International Arbitration*, 25(1), 167.

Sakr, M. (2009). Turnkey contracting under the ICC model contract for major projects: A middle eastern law perspective. *International Construction Law Review*, 26(2), 146.

Salahuddin, A. (2017). Should arbitrators be immune from liability? *Arbitration International*, 33(4), 571–581.

Schultz, T. (2015). Arbitral decision-making: Legal realism and law & economics. *Journal of International Dispute Settlement*, 6(2), 231–251.

Schultz, T. & Kovacs, R. (2012). The rise of a third generation of arbitrators? Fifteen years after Dezalay and Garth. *Arbitration International*, 28(2), 161–172.

Scott, R. & Triantis, G. (2005). Incomplete contracts and the theory of contract design. *Case Western Reserve Law Review*, 56(1), 187–201.

Seppala, C. (2005). Contractor's claims under the FIDIC contracts for major works. *Construction Law Journal*, 21(4), 278.

Spier, K. E. (1992). Incomplete contracts and signalling. *The RAND Journal of Economics*, 23(3), 432–443.

Stipanowich, T. & Ulrich, Z. (2014). Arbitration in evolution: Current practices and perspectives of experienced commercial arbitrators. *The American Review of International Arbitration*, 25, 395–480.

Sussman, E. (2014). What lurks in the unconscious: Influences on arbitrator decision making. *Alternatives to the High Cost of Litigation*, 32(10), 149–155.

Thomas, H. R. & Messner, J. I. (2003). No-damages-for-delay clause: Evaluating contract delay risk. *Journal of Professional Issues in Engineering Education and Practice*, 129(4), 257–262.

Thomson, D. B. (1994). Arbitration theory and practice: A survey of AAA construction arbitrators. *Hofstra Law Review*, 23, 137.

UNCITRAL. (1988). *UNCITRAL Legal Guide on Drawing Up International Contracts for the Construction of Industrial Works*. New York: United Nations Publication.

Valcke, C. (2009). Contractual interpretation at common law and civil law: An exercise in comparative legal rhetoric. *In*: Neyers, J. W., Bronaugh, R. & Pitel, S. (eds.) *Exploring Contract Law*. Oxford: Hart Publishing.

Van den Berg, A. J. (2005). Failure by arbitrators to apply contract terms from the perspective of the New York convention. *In*: Aksen, G., Böckstiegel, K. H., Mustill, M. J., Whitesell, A. M. & Patocchi, P. M. (eds.) *Global Reflections on International Law, Commerce and Dispute Resolution: Liber amicorum in honour of Robert Briner*. Paris: ICC Publishing.

Verbist, H., Schäfer, E. & Imhoos, C. (2015). *ICC Arbitration in Practice*. 2nd ed. The Hague: Kluwer Law International.

Vogenauer, S. (2006). Sources of law and legal method in comparative law. *In*: Reimann, M. & Zimmerman, R. (eds.) *The Oxford Handbook of Comparative Law*. Oxford: Oxford University Press.

Vogenauer, S. (2007). Interpretation of contracts: Concluding comparative observations. *In*: Burrows, A. & Peel, E. (eds.) *Contract Terms*. Oxford: Oxford University Press.

Voser, N. (1996). Mandatory rules of law as a limitation on the law applicable in international commercial arbitration. *The American Review of International Arbitration*, 7, 319.

Waincymer, J. (2011). International arbitration and the duty to know the law. *Journal of International Arbitration*, 28(3), 201–242.

Webster, T. H. & Buhler, M. (2014). *Handbook of ICC Arbitration: Commentary, Precedents, Materials*. London: Sweet & Maxwell.

Weidemaier, W. M. C. (2009). Toward a theory of precedent in arbitration. *William and Mary Law Review*, 51, 1895.

Williamson, O. E. (1979). Transaction-cost economics: The governance of contractual relations. *The Journal of Law and Economics*, 22(2), 233–261.

Zlatanska, E. (2015). To publish, or not to publish arbitral awards: That is the question. *Arbitration: The International Journal of Arbitration, Mediation and Dispute Management*, 81(1), 25–37.

CHAPTER 4

Commercial norms[1]

4.1 Introduction

So far, this book finds that international construction arbitrators construe international construction contracts in accordance with the governing law of the contract. Nonetheless, as discussed in Chapter 2, there is a thorny debate in the literature on whether arbitrators should depart from the law in favour of notions of commercial reasonableness and business common sense. This chapter briefly reviews this debate in Section 4.2. There is also thin empirical evidence, discussed in Chapter 2, proposing that international arbitrators do not always apply the law or may deviate from the law on matters of contract interpretation.

In light of this theoretical debate and empirical uncertainty, this chapter provides insight into whether arbitrators in fact lean towards commercial norms to construe the parties' contract. To do so, this chapter meets the following objectives:

1. to discuss the extent to which arbitrators apply the notion of commercial reasonableness as distinct from applicable legal norms (Section 4.3);
2. to determine the extent to which arbitrators apply the notion of commercial reasonableness as a manifestation of the supremacy of customs and trade usages (Section 4.4).

Of course, the start of the inquiry on the extent to which arbitrators draw upon notions of commercial reasonableness should ideally begin with defining what it is all about. However, this book finds that a precise definition of 'commercially reasonable' or 'commercially sensible' interpretation is lacking. As such, this chapter also constructs the concept of commercial reasonableness alongside discussing its effect on arbitral decision-making.

4.2 Debate on commercial vs. legal interpretation

There is a long-standing debate in arbitration scholarship and practice over the preferred approach to contract interpretation.

One school of thought views arbitration as a supplement, not a substitute to court litigation. They view it as procedurally different but not substantively different. Accordingly, arbitrators must apply the law as judges do to resolve the parties' dispute.

The other school of thought draws on the history of arbitration as a method of resolving commercial disputes between commercial people. The proponents of the 'commercial model' in arbitral decision-making argue that the ultimate purpose of arbitration should

1 Some parts of this chapter draw on material from Besaiso, H. and Fenn, P., (2022). How international construction arbitrators make their decisions: Status of commercial norms and international construction law. *Journal of Construction Engineering and Management*, *148*(9). Used with permission from ASCE.

 DOI: 10.4324/b22975-4

be serving the commercial world. They suggest, more or less candidly, that arbitral justice as a private justice system is different from court justice as a national justice system. As arbitration is rooted in commerce, they suggest that arbitral justice 'is' closer to commerce (Landolt, 2012). As such, they assert that commercial parties prefer the 'commercial reasoning' followed by arbitrators to the 'private law reasoning' followed by courts. The rationale is that the former is concerned with the parties' expectations that are grounded in their business relationships, while the latter is concerned with the letter of the law that is entrenched in a parochial legal analysis (Collins, 1999 cited in Karton (2013)). The proponents of the commercial model still view arbitration as it originally was during the Middle Ages. At that time, the merchants preferred a decision that would be inspired by a personal knowledge of the trade and therefore would be fair and sensible in commercial terms (Mustill, 1989).

The argument that the law and legal reasoning do not match the commercial expectations of the parties has empirical support. Empirical studies of contracting behaviour suggest that contracting parties give little attention to contracts and their formal legal enforcement regime. They rely on trust, implicit understanding, and informal sanctioning. This misalignment between the law and the practice of commercial parties has led to critiques of the law as largely irrelevant to commercial practice (Mitchell, 2013). However, these studies were not undertaken in the context of international contracting where the parties' contracting behaviour may be different and more legally sophisticated.

The contract-law reasoning has been critiqued by some scholars (Campbell and Collins, 2003) because it fails to support the new and innovative models of commercial contracting of project delivery, such as partnering and alliancing. These contracting models require the parties to work in the spirit of trust and cooperation. The law, on the other hand, assumes contracting parties work to satisfy their own individual interest. However, the critics of the classical law foundation of self-interest do not provide a clear and complete proposal on the required changes to allow the law and legal reasoning to reflect different realities of commercial contracting.

Several arbitration scholars and commentators suggested, with little or no empirical evidence, that there is an arbitral preference for commercial reasoning. Some arbitration commentators consider that it is the arbitrator's mission to provide 'commercial justice' for commercial parties (Karton, 2015). Typically, the rationale for this argument is phrased in terms of the parties' commercial expectations from choosing arbitration. Otherwise, if the parties desired a legal solution, they would go to court. Karton (2013) noted that the goal some arbitrators aim to achieve is to meet the parties' legitimate commercial expectations and make their awards acceptable to the parties. This leads them to put less emphasis on legal formalism and more emphasis on commercial reasonableness. The absence of courts' scrutiny over their substantive decisions in international arbitration facilitates the achievement of this goal. It is not a secret that many arbitrators seek to reach a fair and just result, but they may disagree on how this can be achieved. Vogenauer (2006) asserts that the concern some arbitrators have to deliver an award that will be considered fair and just in a particular business community makes them seek a 'business interpretation' that considers commercial practice as a legitimate source for substantive norms. Similarly, Hermann (1983) considers arbitration to be a common-sense method of resolving business disputes according to commercial practice. He argues that parties choose arbitration because they seek an arbitrator who is knowledgeable about their business and capable of resolving disputes according to sound business sense rather than a literal legal analysis of the text. Alike, Levin (1997) notes that commercial parties choose arbitration because they are more trusting of commercial experts to make a decision that is sympathetic to commercial merits than judges, who are more concerned about legal rules for contract interpretation.

Karton (2015) asserts that 'many' international arbitrators consider the greater attention given to commercial practices over legal rules to be an important comparative advantage for arbitration over litigation. They consider that businesspeople prefer judgements in accordance with the standards of their industries and not according to a set of rigid rules of contract law imposed upon them by a legal system. In what seems to be an attempt to meet the parties' expectations, arbitrators tend to open the door for contextual evidence (including evidence on prevailing customs and usages) and follow a subjective interpretation of the contract regardless of its express terms.

Similarly, Ossman (2003) argues, based on personal experience in US construction arbitration, that businesspeople tend to prefer resolutions based on commercial norms rather than legal norms. Notwithstanding their preference, he states that construction parties are frequently disappointed by the actual process that is contrary to their expectations.

Karton (2012b; 2014) analysed 53 international commercial arbitration awards to examine international arbitrators' approaches to contract interpretation and whether they follow the interpretive methods dictated by the governing law or follow the interpretive methods they prefer. Karton finds that there is a civil law bias in contract interpretation. In other words, international arbitrators tend to interpret the contract in a subjective way to determine the subjective intention of the parties by admitting extrinsic evidence. In some cases, where the law governing the contract interpretation and performance is that of a common law jurisdiction that seeks objective interpretation, the tribunal admitted some extrinsic evidence of the parties' subjective intent. Hence, in general, international arbitrators are likely to consider all materials that may help to reveal the subjective understandings of the parties, even if the substantive law is that of a common law jurisdiction (Karton, 2012b; 2014). This is different from the way judges would act and is probably a failure to apply the law in the correct manner, i.e., similar to the national courts.

To supplement and corroborate his findings from these cases, Karton interviewed 20 international commercial arbitrators to understand their approaches to contract interpretation. He finds that a 'commercial mentality exists alongside a legal mentality in the minds of arbitrators' and that they would try, if at all possible, to bring commercial reasoning to the decision-making toolbox. One international arbitrator reflected this mindset by affirming that contractual interpretation has only two rules: common sense and commercial sense.

Along the same lines, DiMatteo (2013) argues that the optimal approach in contract interpretation in international commercial arbitration is 'contextualism' because contextual evidence (on customs, trade usage, commercial practice, prior dealings, etc.) helps arbitrators to understand the nature of the transaction, ascertain the parties' intent, and examine whether a party acted in good faith. Contextualism is a legal reasoning method that reflects the pragmatic realities of contracting practices. It acknowledges the importance of context in legal reasoning. The text representing the parties' agreement is not the starting point and end point of legal reasoning, but a factor. Despite the importance of the parties' written agreement, there are other aspects of the parties' relationship that are important to understand what they intended (Mitchell, 2013).

The economics of dispute resolution are also relevant to understanding the differences between the two approaches of contract interpretation. An efficiency-based argument favours a contextual approach to contract interpretation because it has the potential to reduce transaction costs. The parties do not have to produce lengthy and detailed contract documents. They can draft simpler and shorter contracts leaving it to the courts to fill gaps through the process of contextual interpretation or incorporation of applicable legal or commercial norms. Indeed, the contracting practice in civil law countries (that follow a subjective approach to contract interpretation) is to produce shorter contracts in comparison to the contracting practice in common law countries (that follow an objective approach to contract interpretation). However, the caveat is that relying on the court's gap-filling function may reduce the *ex-post* cost of contract drafting but increase the *ex-ante* cost of contract interpretation and enforcement when disputes arise. An inquiry that goes beyond the four corners of the contract to ascertain the parties' subjective intent is more time-consuming and, hence, costly. This is because there are more things to argue about and more evidence to examine (e.g., the parties' prior communication and negotiation and their prior business dealings).

Although a contextual approach to contract interpretation is more costly, parties in international arbitration fund their dispute resolution process. Thus, they may demand and pay for an interpretive regime that is more sensitive to their own commercial circumstances. Further, the parties may prefer the contextual approach because it allows them to certainly spend less today and probabilistically spend more tomorrow (i.e., they pay to resolve disputes that actually happened rather than disputes that may happen). However, the counterargument is that detailed contracts assist the parties to avoid or minimise disputes so they might be money worth spending.

Whereas the foregoing discussion illustrates that some arbitration scholars and practitioners support a flexible approach to contract interpretation, which allows them to depart from the applicable legal rules to achieve a commercially sensible outcome, other commentators (e.g., DiMatteo, 2013; Thomson, 1994; McConnaughay, 1999) are less subtle in asserting that a substantive law does not matter much in arbitration. McConnaughay (1999) described international arbitration as being 'lawless' because arbitrators may determine a dispute based on their view of what constitutes a commercially reasonable solution rather than a strict legal solution, and for such a decision to escape courts' review on the merits. Thomson (1994), referring to the US domestic context, and DiMatteo (2013), referring to the international context, contend that one of the unique hallmarks of arbitration is that arbitrators do not have to follow the law. They opine that arbitrators have the discretion to make their decisions upon legal, commercial, or extra-legal grounds because the object of arbitration is to determine the facts and render a fair settlement.

On the other hand, not everyone in the arbitration community considers the failure to follow the established law as a benefit of arbitration. Several commentators on international commercial arbitration (e.g., Webster and Buhler, 2014; Mitchell, 2012) and US commercial arbitration (Stipanowich and Lamare, 2014; Stipanowich and Ulrich, 2014; Thomson, 1994) consider that the arbitrators' failure to follow the law or the terms of the parties' contract to be frustrating to the parties' expectations. This is because the parties seem to prefer the application of known legal principles, ensuring, to a certain extent, certainty and predictability of the outcome of a dispute that is submitted to arbitration. Certainty and predictability of the dispute outcome make it easier for the parties to quantify risks and price their contracts *ex-ante* and assist them to negotiate a compromise once a dispute arises *ex-post* (Karton, 2012a). The main reason for choosing arbitration is because parties from different nationalities do not wish their rights and obligations to be determined by the courts of the other party's state of nationality (Drahozal and Naimark, 2005; Dezalay and Garth, 1998).

While the aforementioned scholars speak on behalf of the users of arbitration, the author of this book found no study that directly solicits the actual preferences and expectations of the parties themselves. This vacuum has allowed random theorising to pass unchallenged and to become received wisdom. There is little structured empirical evidence available to justify the assertions concerning the parties' expectations. It is desirable to undertake a study to better understand the standards the parties expect tribunals to apply while making their decisions.

Overall, the available evidence suggests that at least some arbitrators tend to prefer a commercial interpretation of a contract. This requires contextual evidence of the parties' intent, which can be drawn from trade usages and customs. Why do arbitrators do so? To understand how arbitrators decide, it is necessary to understand the ultimate goal that guides them.

DiMatteo (2013) argues that the primary goal of most commercial arbitrators is to render fair and just decisions. To achieve this, it is imperative to achieve a commercially reasonable interpretation of a contract. To do so, arbitrators need to ascertain the 'hypothetical intent' of a 'hypothetical entity', called a 'reasonable commercial person'. As a benchmark guiding the arbitrators, this commercial person has the background commercial knowledge (informed by customs and usages, etc.) that would reasonably have been available to the parties at the time of the contract. The understanding of this person should be the same as the understanding of the parties, and, hence, they should have formed the same intent. This is the intent that should govern contractual interpretation as it is likely to give effect to the true intention of the parties who act in good faith (DiMatteo, 2013).

4.3 Commercial reasonableness as a legal concept

Arbitrators who defend the occasional need to depart from the substantive law justify this on the necessity to avoid commercially absurd results (Karton, 2015). However, a common theme that emerged from the narrative of the arbitrators interviewed by the author regarding their conception of commercial reasonableness shows that, contrary to the widely held opinion in the literature (Hermann, 1983; Vogenauer, 2006; Landolt, 2012), commercial judgement is not the antithesis of the law.

One notion of commercial reasonableness seems to associate it with the civil law legal tradition and distance it from the common law legal system. For example, a Danish arbitrator stated that he follows a commercially sensible interpretation as opposed to a rigid legal interpretation. According to him, commercial interpretation means the pragmatism that is permitted under the civil law system to take into account commercial parties' intentions and expectations and leads to a commercially sensible result. The arbitrator emphasised that commercial interpretation does not mean ignoring the law or contract.

He believes that his duty as an arbitrator is to find a commercially sensible result within the borders of the contract and the applicable legal framework. Below is an excerpt from his interview:

> I follow a commercially sensible interpretation … that does not mean I don't have a legal approach … but I think one of the fundamental differences between the common law approach and the civil law approach in reaching a legal conclusion is that common law judges and arbitrators are formalist in their strict application of the contract, and anything in advance of the contract or beyond the contract or after the contract has no relevance at all … we have a somewhat different approach which is: ok this is a contract, but the parties have a life besides the contract, they had negotiations before the contract, they had correspondence, meetings and certain conduct beside the contract…all of that might have an impact and must be included in reaching a legal conclusion.

An Australian arbitrator also suggested a linkage between the commercial common-sense approach to contract interpretation and the civil law legal philosophy. The key connection point, as he proposed, is the civil law's good faith obligation. The following is an excerpt from his interview:

> I suspect the debate on the proper approach of contract interpretation (commercial vis-à-vis legal) might be a civil law/common law divide because one of the big differences between the civil law and the common law is that the civil law has an overarching principle of good faith, which is definitely not the case in English law, Australian law, and most of the common law countries. In certain cases, the good faith obligation can be applied in the construction of the terms of the contract to alleviate what might otherwise be very unfair provisions.

Arbitrators with a common law background maintained that commercial common sense is not necessarily the antithesis of legal interpretation. Rather, it is embedded in the law itself whether it belongs to the civil law system or the common law system. For example, an English arbitrator stated that contract interpretation starts with examining the meaning of the words and whether they make sense in light of the overarching commercial purpose of the contract. Based on his extensive multi-jurisdiction experience covering many national laws (including European, Arab, and Central and Far East Asian laws), he noted that each national law approaches the questions of contract interpretations in different ways, but, if a particular analysis goes contrary to the commercial purpose of the contract, then national laws normally provide different tools to challenge that. The following is a quote from what he said:

> Contract interpretation depends on the law the contract is subject to … the exercise under any system of law is to interpret what a contract means… but what I think is in common between all legal systems I have come across is that if something has gone wrong with the words … I am not aware of any legal system that would enforce a commercially absurd result … even under English law which is probably the most literal in the world'… because there is a doctrine under English law that if something is repugnant to the commercial purpose, then it is possible to disregard it… in strict circumstances.

Although the English law of contracts is often described as literal by legal commentators, English judges have long regarded it as a facilitator of commerce. Such a claim gives the impression that English law allows and even requires judges to consider the effect of their decisions on commercial contractors and how they can achieve commercially sensible results through legal means (Mitchell, 2013).

In the same vein, a Canadian arbitrator asserts that legal interpretation does not result in unreasonable outcomes that are contrary to commercial common sense. He said:

> I think that almost all common law systems have some version of the principle that if you are presented with two possible interpretations of an ambiguous provision, a judge and hence an arbitrator is entitled to prefer the interpretation which is consistent with business common sense … so, hopefully, the law is reflecting common sense in interpreting the contract.

The arbitrator rejected the idea that the law requires a strict and literal interpretation regardless of the commercial reasonableness of the outcome. He stated that the law in Canada requires reading the contract purposefully to try to understand the purpose of the contract and to uphold the reasonable expectations of the parties. However, the flexibility permitted under the law does not extend to bending the contract to another shape.

Similarly, an Egyptian arbitrator who stated that he leans towards a commercial approach in contract interpretation explained that this approach does not mean ignoring the mandatory provisions of the governing law. Instead, commercial interpretation means when an arbitrator is interpreting the words of the contract, and there are alternative interpretations, the arbitrator should always go with the interpretation that makes more sense from a commercial point of view.

The arbitral approach in contract interpretation as exemplified in the aforementioned accounts concurs with the scholarly opinion that arbitrators' duty to scrupulously follow the governing law in matters of contract interpretation does not rule out business common sense. This is because, as a matter of principle, the application of the law should never produce commercially absurd results. A layer of protection is provided by legal rules that require contracts to be interpreted according to the reasonableness test or good faith lens (Karton, 2015). To determine whether the parties acted in good faith or in a reasonable way, the law directs judges or arbitrators to look at commercial norms as a baseline. This brings law and business closer to each other (Drahozal, 2000).

Overall, the majority of arbitrators interviewed by the author said they will try to achieve commercial justice but within the confines of the applicable law. An English arbitrator summed up his approach that was representative of the interviewed arbitrators as follows:

> As long as the law of the contract allows me, and to the extent it allows me, I will apply commercial reasoning … but I am bound by the law that governs the contract.

While the arbitrators quoted above are confident that legal interpretation does not compromise the commercial reasonableness of the outcome, other arbitrators have different views. Some arbitrators appear less attached to the substantive law in questions of contract interpretation and more attentive to commercial practice (see Section 4.4) or transnational norms (see Chapter 5) in an attempt to achieve a commercially sensible interpretation.

4.4 Commercial reasonableness as a product of commercial norms

4.4.1 Introduction

Although customs, usages, and practices may have different connotations (Kadens, 2012) and different effects under different legal systems (Gélinas, 2016a), this book uses them interchangeably.

As this book demonstrates (see Section 2.8 and Section 4.2), consensus is lacking on the fundamental basis of arbitral decision-making. The division is between two schools of thought: the commercial school and the legal school. Both sides assert that they meet the parties' expectations; an assertion that this book finds no empirical evidence to support.

The proponents of the legal model assert that the parties expect arbitrators to adhere to the law because this is an assurance of the predictability of dispute resolution outcomes, which is necessary for stability in commercial and business dealings (Karton, 2012a). They argue that this is what arbitrators are instructed to do in arbitration rules and statutes (Mitchell, 2012). In their view, legal solutions do not deviate from reasonable commercial expectations because the fundamental purpose of commercial contract law is to facilitate commerce. These or similar assertions can be found in contract law scholarship and judicial decisions. There are many court judgements that state that the function of commercial contract law is to uphold the commercial purpose of the contract and to give effect to commercial practice. However, these assertions made by contract law scholars and judges lack empirical support (Mitchell, 2013). For a full discussion of the rationale underpinning arbitrators' preference to follow the legal model, please see Section 3.7. The empirical research underpinning this book finds nine reasons underpinning arbitrators' preference to adhere to the applicable legal rules.

On the other hand, the proponents of the commercial model assert that parties expect arbitrators to be more attentive to commercial practice and to follow business common sense (e.g., Hermann, 1983; Landolt, 2012; Vogenauer, 2006). Mitchell (2013) asserts that there are 'two mutually exclusive worlds regulating the process of economic exchange'. The first is a world that is socially constructed by the parties based on their commercial expectations. The second is an artificial world that is created by lawyers. In other words, there is a significant gap between the 'real deal' and the 'paper deal'. The gap between the commercial expectations of the parties and the law is problematic, and not everyone agrees that it is the law that should follow the commercial practice to close the gap. This is because the law is not solely concerned with commercial practice. The law is also rooted in morality and moral philosophy. What contracting parties actually do is not necessarily a reflection of what they ought to do. That is why empirical studies of what contracting parties do have limited value as to what the law should be. For example, an empirical observation that commercial parties in a specific industry do not generally keep their promises and breach their contracts may not change our view on the morality of promise-keeping (Mitchell, 2013).

It is surprising that almost all scholars arguing for or against the commercial model, which supposedly meets the parties' commercial expectations, do so without trying to define it first. However, the literature provides an implicit but imprecise notion of what this concept entails. Mitchell (2013) suggests that the parties' commercial expectations could be derived from commercial practice. Commercial practice refers to a recurring pattern of contracting behaviour either between two contracting parties or within an industry. Over time, repeated practices may become norms that represent how things should be done in a specific context and are implicitly agreed on by the parties. Similarly, Karton (2015) seems to associate the commercial model of decision-making with commercial practice, trade usage, business customs, and industry norms. The exact meaning and effect of this association are, nevertheless, not clear (see Section 4.4.3).

4.4.2 Role of customs

As a starting point, the custom theory is an important part of the law (Ayoğlu, 2012). In this sense, the term 'law', under any legal system, comprises all sources of rules, including statute, case law, and custom as well as the authority attributed to each source (Gaillard and Savage, 1999). It follows that a strict legal interpretation of a construction contract may apply customs.

The law's attitude towards customs and trade usages arises from the widely accepted assumption that commercial law should support and facilitate commerce and not impede it. The law should provide an efficient and effective governance framework for commercial exchange. It should provide legal solutions to commercial problems that meet the legitimate needs of the market. The incorporation of commercial norms into legal reasoning allows 'decentralised lawmaking' in the commercial community. These norms assist judges and arbitrators to determine what is sensible from a commercial point of view (Mitchell, 2013).

The law's relationship with customs and trade usages can also be understood in light of their common history. The origins of commercial law can be traced to longstanding and widely accepted practices by the commercial community. These commercial practices or norms, referred to as the law merchant (*lex mercatoria*), were eventually recognised and absorbed by the common law in England or codified into civil law in Europe (Mitchell, 2013).

Although the incorporation of custom and trade usage into the law provides an assurance that the law stays in touch with commercial practice and expectation, the problem with relying on these commercial norms is that they are difficult to prove (Mitchell, 2013). The question of whether trade usages are known to commercial people is a question of fact (Teramura, 2020). To successfully argue that a commercial practice is elevated to the status of a custom or usage, and, hence, the parties intended to imply them into their contract, the claimant should provide sufficient evidence that the practice has been widely used for a long period of time. This difficulty in discharging the burden of proof limits their application in practice (Mitchell, 2013), but it begs the question as to what may be used as evidence of applicable trade usages in international commercial arbitration.

Teramura (2020) argues that there are different sources that could be used to prove the existence of international trade usages. In addition to expert evidence and the arbitral tribunal's own knowledge of the trade, international conventions (such as CISG) and soft law instruments (such as the UNIDROIT Principles) could be relied on by arbitral tribunals as evidence of applicable international trade usages (Teramura, 2020).

The United Nations Convention on Contracts for the International Sale of Goods (CISG), sometimes known as the Vienna Convention, governs contracts for the international sale of goods, and it has been accepted by most of the leading trading nations. Teramura (2020) cited several ICC arbitration awards (ICC Case No. 5713/1989, ICC Case No. 7710/1995, ICC Case No. 8502/1996, ICC Case No. 11320/2001) to support his argument that CISG can be relied on as evidence of applicable trade usages. In these arbitration cases, the arbitral tribunals noted that the CISG reflects the generally recognised or widely accepted international trade usages.

Further, Teramura (2020) cited several ICC arbitration awards (ICC Case No. 10022/2001, ICC Case No. 12226/2004, ICC Case No. 13919/2007) to demonstrate that the UNIDROIT Principles were considered authoritative sources of international trade usage by arbitral tribunals. However, there is no consensus on treating the UNIDROIT Principles as a codification of international trade usage. Some arbitration awards (e.g., ICC Case No. 9029/1999, ICC Case No. 11256/2003) reflect this reality. This book, as we will see in Chapter 5, treats the UNIDROIT Principles as a potential source for international principles of commercial contract law rather than as a source of international trade usage.

The arbitrators interviewed by the author hold the opinion that the parties' arguments based on customs are not uncommon in construction arbitrations. However, they noted that customs and trade usages do not usually have a significant effect on the arbitration outcome because international construction contracts tend to be comprehensive. Generally speaking, customs can be used as an aid for interpretation or supplementation (gap-filling) (Karton, 2015; Gélinas, 2016a; Drahozal, 2000). The following three interview excerpts illustrate this point.

An American arbitrator summarised the two possible roles of customs as an aid for interpretation or supplementation in solving the incomplete contract problem as follows:

> Sometimes, you are looking at a contract that does not include clauses that might normally be included. Now if the parties simply forgot to include something, every arbitrator I know will look at the situation and say ok what is the custom in that industry and they will impose that … but if there is evidence that the parties intentionally excluded something, then that is a different story … also, sometimes, it could be that the terms of the contract can only make sense if you interpret them in accordance with trade usages.

An English arbitrator explained the rationale behind using commercial practice as evidence of the parties' intention and their reasonable expectations as follows:

> If I am interpreting a contractor's obligations, the customary practice would have an effect for two reasons … first, if there is a normal way of doing things, then an employer would reasonably expect the contractor to follow the norm … second, the reason why this is the way it is usually done is because it is the good practice … so the normal ways of doing things and the good practice tend to coincide very often.

An Egyptian arbitrator gave an example of how customs might be used in contract interpretation as it adds a further context to what the parties reasonably, and originally, have intended:

> After the final completion of the project, the employer shall promptly take over the site and issue a taking-over certificate to the contractor. If this is delayed … and the contract does not stipulate the timing … what can I do? There are usages of the trade … it is widely understood in the practice of construction contracts, whether domestic or international, that an employer must promptly do so.

This possible role of trade usages and customs in contract interpretation and contract supplementation is unanimously accepted by the arbitrators interviewed by the author. Almost all national laws acknowledge the role of customs, in contractual interpretation or gap-filling, but they confer them with different scope and authority (Ayoğlu, 2012). The civil law school deems trade usages to be a 'secondary source of law' that may be taken into consideration in the determination of the rights and obligations of the parties. The common law school does not treat trade usages as an independent source of obligation

(Mitchell, 2013). It deems trade usages that are known or ought to be known by the parties to be a 'part of the contract', i.e., incorporated into the contract under the 'implied terms' doctrine (Ayoğlu, 2012).

In this regard, an English arbitrator interviewed by the author, who arbitrated disputes in several jurisdictions, maintains that customs constitute a helpful source for contract interpretation under civil law legal systems, whereas they are hardly admissible as an aid in contract interpretation in the common law world. Under English law, a term will be implied into the parties' contract on the basis of custom and trade usage if the usage is 'invariable, certain, and general' or 'notorious, certain, and reasonable' and not contradicted by express terms. Custom and trade usage can be used under English law to understand the factual matrix or background context according to which a contract could be interpreted, or to judge the reasonableness or onerousness of specific terms (Mitchell, 2013).

The perceived superior status customs have under the civil law system compared to the common law system is in line with the perception some arbitrators expressed in Section 4.3 that the civil law is closer to commerce and commercial practice than the common law and hence is more capable to produce a commercially sound judgement.

The aforementioned differences between national legal systems regarding the effect of custom and trade usages are probably not directly transferable to international arbitration. In international arbitration, the exact status and hierarchy of trade usages and customs with respect to the parties' contract and the governing law is a matter of controversy. This is discussed in the next section.

4.4.3 The arbitral authority of customs vs. the legal authority of custom

Scholars as well as the arbitrators interviewed by the author have reached no consensus on the authority customs and trade usages have in international arbitration.

The lack of consensus appears to stem from the core debate on the very concept of arbitration; is it supplementary or alternative to court justice? The latter view is deeply rooted in the legacy of arbitration as a dispute resolution method that is intended to serve merchants, values commercial expertise, and aspires to commercial justice (Ayoğlu, 2012). The very existence of the notion of *lex mercatoria*, the new law merchant, might indicate a long-lasting consensus between arbitrators and merchants or businesspeople on the primacy of usages and customs in the arbitration of disputes arising from international commerce (Karton, 2014). According to an English arbitrator interviewed by the author, the question of whether an arbitrator should follow legal norms or commercial norms is still unresolved. He said:

> I think there is an unresolved question about what the principal purpose of commercial arbitration is, keeping in mind its historical background that it is in some way a commercial process … I mean it is certainly resolved in the context of English arbitration because the obligation is clearly imposed by the law to apply the law … but I am not sure if it is as clear as that in international arbitration.

In addition to this unresolved question, the stance adopted by international institutional arbitration rules and national arbitration laws appears to be fuelling this debate. Most international arbitration rules (e.g., ICC, DIAC, HKIAC, UNCITRAL arbitration rules) and national arbitration laws (the UNCITRAL Model Law and many national statutes that adopt it or are modelled on it) consider customs and trade usages as a source of obligations. They require that arbitrators shall take into account the relevant trade usages, along with the substantive rules applicable to the substance of the dispute (Ayoğlu, 2012; Drahozal, 2000; Gama, 2016).

For instance, Article 21.2 of the ICC 2012 Arbitration Rules provides that:

> the arbitral tribunal shall take account of the provisions of the contract, if any, between the parties and of any relevant trade usages.

Alike, Article 28.4 of the UNCITRAL Model Law provides that:

> in all cases, the arbitral tribunal shall decide in accordance with the terms of the contract and shall take into account the usages of the trade applicable to the transaction.

On the face of it, the requirement to take customs and trade usages into account suggests that regardless of whatever legal rules may apply to the dispute, arbitrators will draw on commercial practice to determine the parties' dispute (de Boisséson, 2015). An alternative way to look at the requirement of international arbitration rules and national arbitration laws to consider customs and trade usages is that they are a reflection of a longstanding preference by arbitrators to apply relevant commercial norms (Karton, 2014).

The 'institutional requirement' to take trade usages into account or the perceived 'arbitral preference' to apply trade usages brings into question the actual meaning and implications of such a requirement or preference on arbitral decision-making. Does that imply that arbitrators may reshuffle the hierarchy of norms under a governing law by placing customary rules above legal rules? In other words, may arbitrators give greater weight to commercial arguments than legal arguments? If so, would this be a result of construction that deems the parties' agreement on such arbitration rules and arbitration laws to have the effect of incorporating trade usages into their contract, notwithstanding the effect conferred to them by the applicable law? The author's research into this finds that there are three arbitral opinions on the status of customs and usages in international arbitration.

At one end of the spectrum, there is an opinion that the express requirement by arbitration laws and arbitration rules to consider trade usages probably confers on them a more significant role compared to that available under national legal systems (Ayoğlu, 2012). According to this opinion, customs and usages of a particular trade or industry should be given more weight than and be applied in preference to the rules of national law (DiMatteo, 2013). Webster and Buhler (2014) state that Article 21(2) of the 2012 ICC Rules appears to place 'trade usages' on the same level as the contract terms. They opine that the parties' agreement on this article means that relevant trade usages have become a part of their contract by incorporation of the rules. Nevertheless, they maintain that the available evidence, obtained from parties' pleadings and tribunals' reasons in arbitral awards, indicates that arbitrators tend to rely on the terms of the contract rather than trade usages to determine disputes arising from international commerce. According to Gélinas (2016b), it is not convincing to follow a narrow interpretation of the requirement to take trade usages into account, which accords them the same authority they already entertain under the governing law. Such an interpretation would be redundant. Instead, Gélinas (2016b) argues for a broad conception of trade usages that might disrupt normative hierarchies.

He maintains that there is a 'common understanding' that trade usages should be viewed as implied terms in the parties' contract and thereby displace contrary supplementary provisions in the governing law. In other words, trade usages would have a higher normative authority than non-mandatory legal rules. In fact, there is tentative evidence, based on a few non-construction arbitral awards, that shows that arbitrators used trade usages to override seemingly clear express terms in the parties' contract or to overrule legal provisions in the governing law (Drahozal, 2000; Karton, 2013).

Drawing on evidence from ICC arbitration cases, Karton (2012b; 2014) finds that arbitrators may unilaterally invoke general principles of international commercial practice and business norms to govern the parties' rights and obligations even if the parties have neither raised them nor are actually aware of them. For instance, they may use these customs and usages to interpret the terms of the contract and to examine their 'commercial reasonableness'. In other words, they examine whether the terms are consistent with the prevailing commercial practice and, hence, can survive (e.g., ICC Case No. 9443/1998, where the tribunal disregarded the literal plain meaning of the term the parties agreed to and applied the customary practice). Further, what sounds to be unthinkable for commercial parties is that arbitrators may also use trade usages to override an express term in the contract, a legal provision in the code or a judicial precedent (e.g., ICC Case No. 7063/1993, ICC Case No. 3820/1981).

There is a second opinion whereby some authors (e.g., DiMatteo, 2013; Drahozal, 2000) suggest that arbitrators 'may' or even 'should' view sources of law in a less hierarchical way. This means arbitrators should not be constrained by the approach of most legal systems that recognise a strict hierarchy of sources of law, in which higher sources take precedence over lower sources. They argue that the interpretation of the phrase 'to take into account' is consistent with this stance. This phrase does not mean an obligation to apply usages but merely requires taking them into consideration. In other words, it grants arbitrators discretion and flexibility in the interplay between rules of law and usages to provide a commercially just outcome in case a black-letter law analysis would lead to unjust and unintended results considering the circumstances of each case (DiMatteo, 2013; Drahozal, 2000). By the same token, Jean Robert, a former vice president of the International Court of Arbitration, described the ICC rule on trade usages as 'a door for freeing arbitrators from legalistic constraints' (Craig, Park and Paulsson, 2000 cited in Jolivet, Marchisio, and Gélinas, 2016). Commenting on the ICC rules, Yves Derains, the then secretary general of the ICC Court of Arbitration, asserted that arbitration can fulfill the aspirations of commercial people only if it allowed 'the broadest possible scope for the application of usages' (Gélinas, 2016b).

Amongst the 28 international arbitrators interviewed by the author, only a few construed this phrase as empowerment for them to be more flexible and less constrained by the contract and the law. They did not firmly reject the proposition that a trade usage may have greater weight than a contract clause. Accordingly, their stance appears to be consistent with the second opinion outlined in the previous paragraph.

For instance, a Dubai-based Palestinian arbitrator, whose background is in the construction business, indicated that a customary practice may trump an express term of the parties' contract. The Palestinian arbitrator noted that a commercially reasonable interpretation must draw on a good understanding of the commercial practice. Customs and trade usages, in his words, can be used to test the reasonableness of contract terms. He observed that the reality of construction contracting is that contracts are never executed to the letter. Some technical or contractual requirements always appear in construction contracts, but they are rarely if ever complied with. This repeated contracting behaviour can be used as evidence of the parties' implicit understanding and intention at the time they entered into the contract. The arbitrator maintained that what matters the most when interpreting contracts is revealing the real intention of the parties and this requires a broader understanding of contracting behaviour and commercial practice in the construction industry. He said:

> You have to look at contracts, not as words and phrases that are as rigid as rocks ... you need to understand how things are done in real life.

Similarly, a Canadian arbitrator with a dual formation in common law and civil law said that a trade usage may trump an express term of the parties' contract provided that the usage is very prevalent, and the contract allows the arbitrator to apply trade usages:

> If the contract says X, but the usage in that particular industry is actually Y and everyone knows it all the time ... and no one ever paid attention to that X in the contract ... and the parties have been working on the basis of Y ... , then there is a reason to discard X in favour of Y ... and you MIGHT be able to persuade me that in fact the trade usage is strong enough to trump the contract provision that was contrary to that ... I think it is possible because a trade usage can be very strong ... if you do not want it you can somehow exclude it, but if you put into your contract that you want to apply trade usages then you need to be prepared that they will be applied ... then a trade usage is in direct competition with a contractual provision. Then it will be a question of how strong is this in a particular industry ... but normally, the contract itself will trump trade usages. It comes first in most cases.

Despite keeping an open mind regarding the relative status and effect trade usages have on her interpretation of the parties' obligations, the Canadian arbitrator emphasised that the normal hierarchy would be the general law, the parties' contract, trade usages, and fairness as the underlying principle. It is only when the parties authorise her to apply trade usages that the latter becomes in direct competition with the contractual provisions and might be more convincing as to how the contract should be interpreted.

One of the conditions the Canadian arbitrator referred to above in order to apply trade usages is an authorisation from the parties to do so. In her opinion, it is hard to imagine how a trade usage would trump an actual contract provision unless the contract itself allows her to consider trade usages in construing it. It seems this is a situation where some arbitrators would interpret the arbitration rules that require arbitrators to consider customs as an authorisation to make a custom overrule a term in the parties' contract in certain situations.

In this regard, another Canadian arbitrator concurred with this proposition and said that the parties' can make his job to apply trade usages easier if they choose arbitration rules that give the arbitrator the authority to do so. The following quote is from his interview:

> In the construction of a contract, I would start with the governing law. Certainly, a number of laws would say that you look at the industry's practice ... but even if it is not possible under the governing law, the arbitration rules the parties have chosen often become part of the contract. If the ICC rules or whatever rules the parties adopted call for a certain way for interpreting the contract, then in fact the parties have agreed to it ... that would make it easier because

> then you have an agreement between the parties directing the tribunal that they should be considering the industry's practice.

Nevertheless, there is a dilemma here. The parties agree on both the governing law of the contract and the arbitration rules. The former provides that legal provisions take precedence over customs, while the latter is interpreted by some arbitrators to give them the power to let customs take precedence over legal rules. How this contradiction can be resolved remains to be seen.

On the other end of the spectrum lies the third arbitral opinion. Some scholars assert that the choice of institutional rules shall neither be construed to give trade usages a privileged status (Ayoğlu, 2012; Lew, Mistelis and Kröll, 2003) nor considered as an invitation to disregard the law (Karton, 2015) in arbitration settings. They disagree with the argument mentioned earlier that suggests that the parties' intention in referring to institutional rules is to incorporate trade usages into their contract. Their counterargument is that such a reference is a procedural choice and certainly not a choice to imply or supplement additional substantive terms into their contract.

Ayoğlu (2012) noted that the arbitral tribunal's obligation is merely "to take into account" the relevant trade usages. In other words, the tribunal does not have to apply them. All it needs to do is to deliberate on the applicability and effect of the trade usages in question. This view finds support in the documented deliberations of the drafters of the UNCITRAL Model Law as shown in the following paragraphs.

The report of the UNCITRAL Working Group on International Contract Practices published in 1982 documents the group's deliberations and decisions regarding a draft model law on international commercial arbitration (UNCITRAL Working Group on International Contract Practices, 1982). One of the issues the drafting group had to discuss and agree on was whether to include an article requiring the arbitral tribunal to 'decide in accordance with the contract and to take into account the usages of the relevant trade'. There were divergent views as to whether such a requirement should be included in the Model Law.

Regarding the phrase concerning contract terms, the prevailing view was that there was no need to include an article in the Model Law because (1) the requirement to decide according to the parties' contract was self-evident, and (2) such an article can be misleading or flawed since a term in the parties' contract could be invalid under the substantive law. However, it seems that another view in favour of including an express requirement to decide in accordance with the parties' contract was accepted and used in the published version of the Model Law.

Regarding the phrase concerning trade usages, one view opposed the inclusion of an article in the Model Law because the status and effect of trade usages was a matter of substantive law and including such an article could create conflict with the substantive law. The prevailing view, however, was to include an article in the Model Law that keeps the legacy of the 1961 Geneva Convention that required the arbitral tribunal in Article VII, paragraph 1 to ('take account of the … trade usages'). It was suggested that such an article in the Model Law could be modelled on Article VII, paragraph 1 of the Geneva Convention or Article 33, paragraph 3 of the UNCITRAL Arbitration Rules, which requires the arbitral tribunal to ('take into account the usages of the trade applicable to the transaction'). An express requirement to take trade usages into account was accepted and used in the published version of the Model Law.

It is notable that the phrase 'in accordance with' was used for contractual terms, while the phrase 'take into account' was used for the trade usages under Article 28.4 of the Model Law. The drafters' discussion that is summarised in paragraph 9 of the report reflects their understanding that the phrase 'in accordance with' has a stronger effect than the phrase 'take into account'. In this respect, Teramura (2020) opines that the text in this report indicates the drafters' view that contract terms take precedence over trade usages in the event that they conflict with each other. He asserts that trade usages are inferior not only to the terms of the parties' contract but also to mandatory provisions of the governing law. This is because customs and trade usages could be used as an indication of the implied intention of the parties only while the contract terms and its governing law express the parties' objective intention.

Overall, the scholars supporting the third arbitral opinion assert that trade usages shall be applied in accordance with the status conferred to them by the substantive law chosen by the parties to govern their contract – no more or less. This means that arbitrators shall determine the legal effect of trade usages pursuant to the hierarchy of sources as valid in the substantive law.

The interviews the author conducted with international arbitrators reveal that the majority opinion of the interviewed arbitrators rejects the idea that customary practice should have greater consideration than legal provisions.

For instance, an Egyptian arbitrator clarified that the Egyptian Civil Code makes a distinction between mandatory rules and supplementary rules. He explained how these legal rules work in both litigation and arbitration settings. The mandatory rules prevail over the contract provisions by default. The supplementary or regularity rules apply if the parties have not agreed otherwise in the contract (i.e., when there is a gap in the contract). These legal rules have more weight than customs and usages. It is only when the law is not clear or does not regulate a particular matter that the parties then try to convince the tribunal to fill in the gaps using customs.

Another Egyptian arbitrator noted that custom theory is an important part of the law that assists in interpreting the contract because sometimes the subjective intentions of the parties can be revealed from the customs and usages of the trade. However, he emphasised that he has to apply them 'within the contract provisions'.

An American arbitrator suggested that if the parties are not happy with an interpretation approach that gives higher priority to legal rules and contract provisions, then they can change that. He suggested that the parties can provide clear instructions to the tribunal to give more weight to customs and trade usages in case they are in conflict with legal rules.

All in all, it appears safe to conclude that, for most arbitrators, a customary rule would not take precedence over a legal rule or contractual term. They might consider it to interpret or supplement the parties' contract as long as it does not contradict a legal or contractual provision. In so doing, arbitrators will most likely give weight to customs and trade usages according to what the governing law confers to them.

The real intent and actual effect of arbitration rules' requirement to take trade usage into account remains largely unknown (Błaszczak and Kolber, 2013). However, it could be plausible to argue that it intends to moderate the strictness of some systems of law that attempt to exclude or minimise the role of customs, but not to give them greater weight than legal provisions or contractual terms. In other words, its object could be to elevate the status of customs under common law to match their status under civil law and use it as a source of obligation not only as a tool for interpretation. This permits the admissibility of evidence on customs and trade usages in international arbitration without constraints imposed by a particular legal system.

4.5 Conclusion

This chapter examines how trade usages and customs might have an impact on arbitral decision-making. As the application of these norms is often justified on the ground of achieving commercially reasonable results, this chapter seeks to uncover international arbitrators' views of commercial reasonableness in contract interpretation.

The extant literature generally makes a simplistic either-or representation of international arbitrators' approaches to contract interpretation. According to this dichotomous conceptualisation, commercial interpretation and legal interpretation are mutually exclusive. This chapter challenges this dichotomy and puts forward an alternative view that does not necessarily consider commercial reasonableness as the antithesis of the law. The prevailing arbitral opinion seems to consider that commercial reasoning does not displace legal reasoning because commercial common sense is built into the law. In this context, some arbitrators follow the view that commercial common sense, as a legal construct, has a broader application under the civil law legal system than the common law legal system. They opined that civil law is closer to commercial practice and customs.

This chapter contributes to the long theoretical debate on the nature of arbitration and, hence, the substantive norms that should govern arbitrators' decisions. It contributes to the discussion concerning the role and authority of customs and trade usages in arbitral decision-making. While the discussion in the extant literature is largely theoretical, this chapter provides empirical insight into how international arbitrators construe the requirement expressed in various arbitration rules and laws to take trade usages into consideration, and how they apply customs and usages in international construction arbitration practice.

The real intent of the architects of the articles requiring arbitrators to take into account trade usages remains unknown. However, what is known is that this requirement obscures the classification of custom and trade usages in international arbitration (i.e., is it part of the law or an external norm?) and intensifies the tension between the legal and commercial models. These commercial norms may be used to interpret or supplement construction contracts. However, their authority as substantive norms in international construction arbitration is not resolved. Arguments exist that customs and usages should have a privileged status to achieve outcomes that are reasonable according to commercial standards. Although international arbitrators tend to be meticulous in applying the law the parties agree to govern their contract, it is possible that some arbitrators can be persuaded to disregard an express term in the parties' contract or a provision in the governing law in favour of a dominant customary practice. However, the prevailing opinion appears to accord customs and usages the authority they entertain under the governing law.

4.6 References

Ayoğlu, T. (2012). Application of trade usages in international institutional arbitration–some reflections. *ASA Bulletin*, 30(3), 539–547.

Błaszczak, Ł. & Kolber, J. (2013). General principles of law and equity as a basis for decision-making in arbitration. *Comparative Law Review*, 15, 189–208.

Campbell, D. & Collins, H. (2003). Discovering the Implicit Dimensions of Contracts. In: Campbell, D., Collins, H. and Wightman, J. (eds.) *Implicit Dimensions of Contract: Discrete, Relational, and Network Contracts. International studies in the theory of private law*. Oxford: Hart Publishing Ltd., pp. 25–50.

Collins, H. (1999). *Regulating Contracts*. Oxford: Oxford University Press.

Craig, W. L., Park, W. W. & Paulsson, J. (2000). *International Chamber of Commerce Arbitration*. 3rd ed. New York: Oceana Publications.

de Boisséson, M. (2015). Chapter 8: Substantive applicable law in international arbitration: An arbitrator's perspective. In: Bortolotti, F. & Maye, P. (eds.) *The Application of Substantive Law by International Arbitrators*. Paris: ICC Publication.

Dezalay, Y. & Garth, B. G. (1998). *Dealing in Virtue: International Commercial Arbitration and the Construction of a Transnational Legal Order*. Chicago: University of Chicago Press.

DiMatteo, L. A. (2013). Soft law and the principle of fair and equitable decision making in international contract arbitration. *The Chinese Journal of Comparative Law*, 1(2), 221–255.

Drahozal, C. R. (2000). Commercial norms, commercial codes, and international commercial arbitration. *Vanderbilt Journal of Transnational Law*, 33, 79.

Drahozal, C. R. & Naimark, R. W. (2005). *Towards a Science of International Arbitration: Collected Empirical Research*. The Hague: Kluwer law international.

Gaillard, E. & Savage, J. (1999). *Fouchard, Gaillard, Goldman on International Commercial Arbitration*. The Hague: Kluwer law international.

Gama, L. (2016). Usages and implied obligations under the UNIDROIT principles of international commercial contracts. *In*: Gélinas, F. (ed.) *Trade Usages and Implied Terms in the Age of Arbitration*. Oxford: Oxford University Press.

Gélinas, F. (2016a). *Trade Usages and Implied Terms in the Age of Arbitration*. Oxford: Oxford University Press.

Gélinas, F. (2016b). Trade usages as transnational law. *In*: Gélinas, F. (ed.) *Trade Usages and Implied Terms in the Age of Arbitration*. Oxford: Oxford University Press.

Hermann, A. H. (1983). *Judges, Law and Businessmen*. Deventer: Kluwer

Jolivet, E., Marchisio, G. & Gélinas, F. (2016). Trade usages in ICC arbitration. *In*: Gélinas, F. (ed.) *Trade Usages and Implied Terms in the Age of Arbitration*. Oxford: Oxford University Press.

Kadens, E. (2012). The myth of the customary law merchant. *Texas Law Review*, 90(5), 1153.

Karton, J. (2012a). A conflict of interests: Seeking a way forward on publication of international arbitral awards. *Arbitration International*, 28(3), 447–486.

Karton, J. (2012b). International commercial arbitrators' approaches to contractual interpretation. *International Business Law Journal*, 383.

Karton, J. (2013). *The Culture of International Arbitration and the Evolution of Contract Law*. Oxford: Oxford University Press.

Karton, J. (2014). International arbitration culture and global governance. *In*: Mattli, W. & Dietz, T. (eds.) *International Arbitration and Global Governance: Contending Theories and Evidence*. Oxford: Oxford University Press.

Karton, J. (2015). The arbitral role in contractual interpretation. *Journal of International Dispute Settlement*, 6(1), 4–41.

Landolt, P. (2012). Arbitrators' initiatives to obtain factual and legal evidence. *Arbitration International*, 28(2), 173–224.

Levin, M. S. (1997). The role of substantive law in business arbitration and the importance of volition. *American Business Law Journal*, 35(1), 105–180.

Lew, J. D., Mistelis, L. A. & Kröll, S. (2003). *Comparative International Commercial Arbitration*. The Hague: Kluwer Law International.

McConnaughay, P. J. (1999). The risks and virtues of lawlessness: A second look at international commercial arbitration. *Northwestern University Law Review*, 93(2), 453.

Mitchell, R. (2012). Must Arbitrators Follow the Law? *JAMS Global Construction Solutions Newsletter*, pp. 1–2. Available at https://www.jamsadr.com/files/uploads/documents/gec-newsletter/jams-gec-news-2012-spring.pdf [Accessed 12 December 2016].

Mitchell, C.E. (2013). *Contract Law and Contract Practice: Bridging the Gap Between Legal Reasoning and Commercial Expectation*. Oxford: Bloomsbury Publishing.

Mustill, M. J. (1989). Arbitration: History and background. *Journal of International Arbitration*, 6(2), 43–56.

Ossman, G. (2003). *Construction Arbitration Consistency and Reliability: An Empirical Study*. M.Sc., Pepperdine University School of Law.

Stipanowich, T. J. & Lamare, J. R. (2014). Living with ADR: Evolving perceptions and use of mediation, arbitration, and conflict management in fortune 1000 corporations. *Harvard Negotiation Law Review*, 19(1), 1.

Stipanowich, T. & Ulrich, Z. (2014). Arbitration in evolution: Current practices and perspectives of experienced commercial arbitrators. *The American Review of International Arbitration*, 25, 395–480.

Teramura, N. (2020). *Ex Aequo et Bono as a Response to the 'Over-Judicialisation' of International Commercial Arbitration*. Kluwer Law International BV.

Thomson, D. B. (1994). Arbitration theory and practice: A survey of AAA construction arbitrators. *Hofstra Law Review*, 23, 137.

UNCITRAL Working Group on International Contract Practices (1982). Report of the Working Group on International Contract Practices on the work of its third session, New York. Available at https://digitallibrary.un.org/record/30077?ln=en. [Accessed 25 December 2022].

Vogenauer, S. (2006). Sources of law and legal method in comparative law. *In*: Reimann, M. & Zimmerman, R. (eds.) *The Oxford Handbook of Comparative Law*. Oxford: Oxford University Press.

Webster, T. H. & Buhler, M. (2014). *Handbook of ICC Arbitration: Commentary, Precedents, Materials*. London: Sweet & Maxwell.

CHAPTER 5

International construction law[1]

5.1 Introduction

The literature suggests that transnational law is closely associated with international arbitration. Some authors suggest that transnational law constitutes a transnational legal order or governance framework for transnational transactions and that international arbitrators prefer to rely on transnational law to make their decisions. The sheer volume of publications on transnational law in the international arbitration environment makes it necessary to investigate the relevance and application of transnational law in arbitral decision-making. This chapter begins with a brief discussion of the transnational law concept (Section 5.2) and the role it plays in international arbitration (Section 5.3). Then, it takes a closer look into the segment of transnational law that is relevant to international construction contracts (referred to in this book as international construction law). This chapter presents the attitudes and opinions of international arbitrators about the concept of international construction law (Section 5.4). The majority of this chapter focuses on the nature and sources of international construction law (Section 5.5). A tentative list of international construction law principles is suggested (Section 5.6). Finally, this chapter discusses how international arbitrators apply this concept in practice (Section 5.7).

5.2 Transnational law: The concept

There is a plethora of terms that are used in the literature to refer to transnational law, such as *lex mercatoria* (also known as the new law merchant or mercantile law), transnational commercial law, transnational commercial contract law, rules of transnational law, general principles of international commercial/trade law, general principles of contract law, etc. (Karton, 2013; Drahozal, 2005b; Gaillard and Savage, 1999; DiMatteo, 2013).

Some authors use the term *lex mercatoria* or one of its similar expressions as inclusive of transnational legal rules as well as international trade usages (Drahozal, 2007; Moses, 2008; Drahozal, 2000; Gélinas, 2016b). In this context, some scholars (de Boisséson, 2015; Derains and Schwartz, 2005; Gaillard and Savage, 1999) noted that there is terminological confusion in the area and spoke of the need to make a clear distinction between transnational legal rules and international trade usages. This terminological distinction is important to ease the discussion on how certain concepts related to substantive norms fit together (Gaillard and Savage, 1999). Transnational legal rules refer to legal norms that are common to many nations, while international trade usages refer to commercial norms generally accepted and observed in a specific industry (Gaillard and Savage, 1999).

1 Some parts of this chapter draw on material from Besaiso, H. and Fenn, P., (2022). How international construction arbitrators make their decisions: Status of commercial norms and international construction law. *Journal of Construction Engineering and Management, 148*(9). Used with permission from ASCE.

DOI: 10.4324/b22975-5

This book uses the term 'general principles of international commercial law' or 'transnational law' to refer to legal rules that are widely accepted between nations and, hence, could be applicable in international commerce. This terminological choice is consistent with the choice made by some scholars (e.g., Gaillard, 2001; Derains and Schwartz, 2005). Trade usages are not part of these transnational legal rules. As a distinct concept, they are discussed in Chapter 4.

Further, the terminological choice adopted in this book is deliberately made between numerous interchangeable terms to attract the least possible criticism. Some scholars (e.g., Gaillard, 2001; Karton, 2013) declare their preference to use the term 'transnational', as it indicates that the legal rules have their roots in national laws. The term 'international commercial law' has been described as misleading on the ground that it conveys an impression that there is, in fact, a unified body of legal rules created by an international institution with an appropriate authority to supervise and maintain its application to international commercial contracts (Moss, 2004). To a greater extent, the term *lex mercatoria* has generated much controversy, as shown hereunder.

The very existence of *lex mercatoria* has been much debated. For some scholars, it is an elusive concept – a myth, a pipe dream – whose content is unknown and its source is uncertain (Drahozal, 2005a; Charrett, 2012; Delaume, 1988; Wilkinson, 1995; Cuniberti, 2008; Mustill, 1988). The elasticity in this concept entails that its content changes according to who the arbitrator is and what he or she thinks the law ought to be (McConnaughay, 1999 in Karton, 2010). On the other hand, some scholars defend the existence of the concept of *lex mercatoria*. However, they agree only on the 'being' but not on the 'nature' of *lex mercatoria*. As such, the supporters of the concept of *lex mercatoria* split into two groups. The first group maintains that *lex mercatoria* is a set of substantive norms. According to this notion, there have been academic attempts (e.g., Mustill, 1988; Lando, 1985; Berger, 1999) and institutional initiatives (e.g., UNIDROIT and the CENTRAL compilations) to compile lists of principles or rules that comprise *lex mercatoria* (Karton, 2014). The second group maintains that *lex mercatoria* is not a codification of substantive rules but rather a method to identify these rules that are deemed applicable for each transaction under specific circumstances and will help to resolve the dispute (Moss, 2004; Gaillard, 1995; Lowenfeld, 1990; Gaillard and Savage, 1999).

The theoretical importance of this concept is indeed evidenced by the volume of publications in print (Drahozal, 2007). Its practical importance is, however, overstated. Whatever the outcome of this academic debate is, it is noteworthy that international arbitrators rarely rely on *lex mercatoria* in their awards. The use of this concept was never significant in the past and is expected to diminish in the years to come (Karton, 2012a; Drahozal, 2005a; Dasser, 2008 cited in Karton, 2014; Bond, 1989).

5.3 Role of transnational norms

As is the case with the debate concerning its existence and nature, the scope of application of transnational law has not been allowed to pass without controversy.

As a starting point, there is no controversy that general principles of international commercial law may be used in international commercial arbitration when the parties elect so or when they fail to agree on national law to govern their contract (Rosengren, 2013; Karton, 2013; Moss, 2004; Gaillard and Savage, 1999).

There are views that even if the contract is governed by national law, arbitrators may nevertheless moderate the effect of the national law to meet the parties' expectations by taking into account the transnational nature of the dispute. One technique to do so is for arbitrators to be receptive and open-minded to legal solutions derived from national laws that are not applicable (Nazzini, 2018). As the devil lies in the detail, the question is to what extent arbitrators should be receptive to such legal solutions.

There is evidence that shows that arbitrators' attitudes and practices vary widely in this area. Although by no means uncontroversial, some arbitrators resort to transnational law to supplement incomplete national laws or complement insufficient legal submissions made by the parties under the governing law (Rosengren, 2013). Likewise, some arbitrators apply what they believe to be a general principle of international commercial law, such as 'good faith', even if the substantive law contains no such duty (e.g., ICC Case No. 6197/1995, ICC Case No. 3267/1979, ICC Case No. 1784/1975) (Karton, 2013). What appears to be more controversial is that some arbitrators believe they can deploy this notion to avoid the application of legal rules in the substantive law that are inconsistent or inadequate to the needs of international commerce (Gaillard, 1995; Lando, 1985; Lowenfeld, 1990; Gélinas, 2016b) or that will lead to commercially unreasonable results (Karton, 2013). In this instance, a reviewing court might find that the tribunal failed to comply with its mandate and, hence, set aside or refuse to enforce an award (Gaillard and Savage, 1999).

In this regard, Karton (2012b) argues, based on evidence from arbitral awards, that international arbitrators may depart from the substantive law and apply transnational legal norms on matters of contract interpretation. The transnational approach appears to require a subjective interpretation of the contract. Thus, even if the governing law might be English law, international arbitrators may accept extrinsic evidence of the parties' intention. He also found evidence of this transnational approach from a series of interviews he undertook with international arbitrators. This preference for a transnational approach to contract interpretation has been encouraged by some scholars. For instance, DiMatteo (2013) maintains that it is preferable in international commercial arbitration to use contextual interpretation that accepts contextual evidence, including customs, trade usages, commercial practice, previous dealings, and prior negotiations and communications, etc. In his opinion, this transnational approach is better capable to reveal the parties' intentions and it also prevents a national law bias in matters of contract interpretation.

On the other hand, the proposition that arbitrators have the power to use transnational rules of law instead of the parties' choice of national law has been rejected by others (Błaszczak and Kolber, 2013; Moss, 2004). According to this viewpoint, arbitrators should not hide behind a transnational approach façade to disregard provisions of the governing law (Nazzini, 2018).

Regardless of the exact scope of the transnational law, which is open to debate, it appears that international arbitration will remain the environment for experimentation on the use of transnational rules of law to determine disputes arising from international commerce. International arbitrators' interest in creating a global legal order is believed to have led to the construction of transnational legal norms, also referred to as *lex mercatoria*, that could be applicable to international commercial contracts (Dezalay and Garth, 1998). However, as the growth of international commercial arbitration leads to distinct types of species of international commercial arbitration (Landolt, 2012), specialised branches of *lex mercatoria* have been argued to exist, such as *lex maritime* in the maritime industry, *lex constructionis* in the international construction industry, and *lex petrolea* in the international oil and gas industry (Gaillard and Savage, 1999). It follows that as international merchants have their merchandise law, international constructors may also have their construction law. The merits of this proposition are discussed in the next sections.

5.4 International construction law: A myth or a reality

Some arbitrators, from common law or civil law backgrounds, maintain that norms of international construction law exist or are at least in development. These norms, in their opinion, come in different forms and can be found in different sources. They referred, more or less, to the same sources that are discussed in the next section.

Conversely, some scholars and practitioners are sceptical about the 'mythical' construct of international construction law. Knutson (2005) asserts that the existence of 'a common construction law' remains speculative. Charrett (2012) argues that the differences between various jurisdictions make it rather difficult to discern even broad principles of common construction law.

Similarly, arbitrators with a common law background were sceptics of the claim that ICL exists. For example, an English arbitrator interviewed by the author answered a question concerning whether ICL exists as follows:

> I have a great caution about that ... that is like lex mercatoria but in construction ... I think the problem with that idea is that what is the authoritative source for that law? I mean in England you can say it is the Parliament and the Supreme Court ... but what is the authoritative source of lex mercatoria ... where can I look for it? ... similarly, what the principles of international construction law are and where they are located or to be found.

An Irish arbitrator interviewed by the author sarcastically stated:

> If I was setting in an exam, and the question was to outline the principles of international construction law, you will get a white sheet paper from me.

Another arbitrator who doubts the existence of these principles justifies this on the grounds that most construction law is contractual and that legal systems have different views on a number of construction-related legal points. Therefore, in his opinion, it is necessary to bridge that gap between civil law and common law jurisdictions before achieving a 'common law of construction'.

In between the two polar ends, there are some arbitrators who think that these principles are coming into existence. In their opinion, a convergence around certain basic principles of construction law is taking place. The following is an exemplary quote from an interview with a Canadian arbitrator:

> It is happening [the development of ICL] ... but it is not here yet ... there is definitely a convergence around certain basic principles of construction law ... I probably will not be around when it jells but it is happening.

The arbitrator suggested that the good faith principle and the enforcement of notice provisions are examples of the 'convergence' that is taking place.

5.5 Sources of international construction law

This section discusses what ICL is, how it has come or is coming into existence, and what effect it has on arbitral decision-making on the substance of international construction disputes. Drawing on data from the author's interviews with international arbitrators and evidence from arbitration awards and other secondary sources, this section reveals that some arbitrators, in fact, use the concept of ICL or similar notions to arrive at, or at least justify, their decisions.

5.5.1 FIDIC

The first source of ICL is international standard forms of construction contract, and FIDIC contracts in particular. FIDIC publishes standard forms of construction contract that have been developed with input from representatives of the international construction community who come from various civil law and common law jurisdictions. As such, FIDIC contracts represent a consensus between various interest groups and are widely accepted as fair and balanced around the world. They are well understood and widely used in many jurisdictions around the world. It can be said with confidence that FIDIC contracts are the world's leading standard forms of construction contract that are used in international construction projects.

In the opinion of the arbitrators interviewed by the author, FIDIC contracts have a two-way relationship to commercial practice in the global construction industry. On the one hand, the widespread familiarity with FIDIC contracts shapes the industry's commercial practice. The repeated use of the same contractual arrangements over a long period of time around the globe allows the emergence of a common understanding of how the contracting parties should behave. On the other hand, FIDIC contracts are affected by changing practices. Since FIDIC published its first standard form of construction contract in 1957, they have been updated and revised several times to reflect and embed the industry's good practice from around the globe.

Given this background, some arbitrators believe that FIDIC contracts constitute a source of international construction law. The following is an excerpt from an interview with an arbitrator, who is also a member of one of FIDIC's committees, which illustrates this belief:

> I think FIDIC conditions of contract are part of international construction law ... I think they are probably the closest we have got to widely accepted principles...but certainly not universally applicable as they have provisions that are in conflict with mandatory laws of various countries ... but overall, they have many provisions that I think reflect what is generally done as international practice ... I cannot think of any other documents that would be persuasive in terms of international usages in construction other than FIDIC contracts.

The arbitrator stated that FIDIC contracts can be used as evidence of 'international construction law principles' and 'international usages in construction'. It is not uncommon to use these two terms or their equivalents interchangeably (see Section 5.2).

Notwithstanding the classification of FIDIC contracts, being used as evidence of either international customary practice or transnational law, what really matters is their potential application in arbitral practice.

The majority view holds the opinion that FIDIC conditions can be used in interpreting international construction contracts. As such, arbitrators may rely on commentaries, courts' judgements, and arbitral awards on FIDIC conditions of contract to interpret international construction contracts that have similarly worded clauses. In this context, an English arbitrator stated:

> I would only use jurisprudence on FIDIC conditions if I find that a term in the parties' contract was written in the same words (i.e., was built on or derived from a FIDIC clause) … if I found that the DNA of a particular term in the parties contract was FIDIC's DNA ... it may help me in the interpretation of the contract … but … I would not say I am going to fill a gap in the parties' contract using FIDIC conditions.

Likewise, a Lebanese arbitrator said:

> If the parties had copied FIDIC clauses to draft their bespoke contract, and the term was recognisable to be a FIDIC term, as often the case is, then I would say this clause was modelled on FIDIC clause X which reads as follows … then I will certainly be interested to look at authorities and commentaries on FIDIC conditions … and use them to explain the meaning of the clause … and starting from there I will assess whether the interpretation is compatible with the substantive law of the contract or not.

This approach might seem problematic as the arbitrator appears to be relying on the intention of the FIDIC drafting committee rather than seeking to find the intention of the parties. The counterargument is that when the parties borrow a clause from FIDIC conditions of contract, then they are assumed to know what the clause means and how it is intended to operate. Further, it is usually the case that construction contracts are drafted by consultants who presumably have knowledge of FIDIC contracts. According to the Lebanese arbitrator, this would be the assumption unless there is evidence to the contrary regarding the parties' intention.

There is also evidence from arbitral awards that arbitrators follow this interpretation technique in practice. For instance, in ICC Case No. 5029/1987, which involved a dispute that arose from a construction contract between a French company and an Egyptian employer, the tribunal interpreted a clause in accordance with the interpretation of its identical original FIDIC clause. The tribunal noted that clause 67 of the contract was identical to clause 67 of the FIDIC conditions (3rd edition, 1977), which was commonly used in international construction contracts. That clause provided for a two-tier system for the settlement of disputes between the parties. From that perspective, the tribunal proceeded to interpret how this clause was intended to work as a time bar.

Another question might arise in connection with a bespoke contract that has a clause that has been recognised or identified by the tribunal as having its origin in a similar or identical FIDIC clause. In this event, what is to prevail in governing the interpretation of this clause: the substantive law or transnational jurisprudence on FIDIC conditions?

The proponents of the transnationalisation of substantive norms suggest that, in matters of interpretation of international standard forms of contracts or even bespoke contracts, a consistent transnational interpretation should be preferred over national interpretation (i.e., based on the national law governing the contract) to further uniformity (Rosengren, 2013; Nazzini, 2018).

A Palestinian arbitrator who is based in Dubai explained in an interview with the author why international arbitrators could be less attached to the substantive law in questions of contract interpretation and more concerned with a transnational approach. The arbitrator, whose experience extends over 30 years in the construction business, stated that he does not feel constrained by the stipulations of the governing law when interpreting international standard forms of construction contracts, especially FIDIC contracts. He justified his approach on the ground that FIDIC's contracts originated from the common law world but are mostly applied in civil law jurisdictions. For instance, the first edition of FIDIC Conditions of Contract for Works of Civil Engineering Construction, published in 1957, was based on the Institution of Civil Engineers (ICE) conditions of contract, which is an English standard form of contract for civil engineering. In recent editions, however, FIDIC conditions of contract have incorporated a mix of legal concepts from common law as well as civil law legal systems.

The fact that FIDIC contracts use mixed-legal terminologies from common law and civil law systems and are intended to be used across different legal systems may give the impression that they are self-sufficient and less dependent on national laws. It follows that some arbitrators might feel detached from or less constrained by any system of national law on matters involving the interpretation of international construction contracts adopting or derived from FIDIC conditions of contract.

This stance is by no means uncontroversial. Some arbitrators interviewed by the author argue that contract interpretation must be primarily governed by substantive law for two reasons. First, when the parties select substantive law, then this represents their objective intention to have their contract interpreted according to the substantive law. Second, the choice of law clause in FIDIC contracts means that they are not designed to be standalone or to float around in the ether without a governing law. FIDIC contracts cannot exist in a legal vacuum. They must be interpreted in accordance with the rules of law or national law chosen by the parties.

However, this should not prevent an arbitral tribunal from considering case law from other jurisdictions. Foreign legal authorities have some weight under many legal systems. Further, given the widespread use of FIDIC contracts around the world, it can be argued that the contracting parties, or a reasonable party in the position of the contracting parties, have or should have understood the meaning of FIDIC clauses to be as explained by the authorities available in different jurisdictions.

Some authors expressed their support for such a transnational approach. For instance, Samuelsson and Iwar (2005) suggest that if the parties enter into a contract based on a FIDIC form, it may be deemed that they also agreed to the interpretation available on it in commentaries and courts' judgements. For instance, they suggest that the role of the engineer in the FIDIC forms should be understood in accordance with its historical context and origin in English law. Knutson (2005) disagrees with this particular proposition because many jurisdictions, in his opinion, have adequate guidance on the role of the engineer. Although Knutson (2005) does not think the role of the engineer merits a universal treatment, he opines that other FIDIC clauses would benefit from a transnational approach to their interpretation. He noted that some of the key phrases in FIDIC forms remain identical to the key phrases in the Institution of Civil Engineers (ICE) form, such as the wordings regarding adverse physical conditions, and, hence, English authorities on what these and similar phrases mean and how they should be interpreted are relevant. Following such a transnational approach does not mean that arbitrators deciding under a different national law will simply import the relevant legal solution from the English law, but they will consider them.

In fact, evidence from available and accessible arbitration awards reveals that some arbitrators prefer to follow a transnational approach to the interpretation of international construction contracts, especially those incorporating or modelled after FIDIC contracts. A manifestation of this preference is the arbitral practice involving citations to international construction arbitration awards, journal articles, textbooks, treatises, or other academic references, as shown in the next section.

Overall, the available evidence suggests that there is a wide acceptance of the idea of using FIDIC contracts as an aid to the interpretation of international construction contracts. This, however, does not seem to extend to gap-filling. The prevailing view is that gaps in the parties' contract must be filled according to the guidance provided under the governing law of the contract. In the very rare situation when both the contract and the governing law are silent on the issue in dispute, a few arbitrators interviewed by the author suggested that FIDIC contracts can be used for supplementing the parties' contract.

For example, an American arbitrator considered that FIDIC contracts could be used as evidence of international construction law principles or could qualify as evidence of international commercial usage in the international construction industry and, hence, can be used for gap-filling in case both the contract and the substantive law are silent on the issue in dispute. He noted that the parties sometimes compare the default allocation of risks in different standard forms of contracts to illustrate that standard forms around the world allocate risks similarly and argue that such a default allocation of risks has become a widespread usage in the industry. The following is an excerpt from his interview:

> If an issue came up which the contract is silent on and the governing law is silent on … then in trying to find what the principles of international construction law are, I think arbitrators could look at those standard forms which have been used in international construction for decades and have stood the test of time and say ok all these forms have this particular clause, so we are going to view that as one of the tenets of international construction law … it is possible to look at a form like FIDIC as one of the customs and trade usages.

Similarly, a Canadian arbitrator said he would consider FIDIC contracts for gap-filling as they represent an internationally recognised contractual practice:

> I think a FIDIC contract is a reflection of what has become an industry's standard, and it did not fall out of the air … it is a standard form of contract that manifests a standard way of doing things … and in a search for a sensible solution, as something had the parties directed their minds to, they might have adopted it. So, if a contract did not deal with something and there is no guidance in the governing law, then looking at how a FIDIC contract deals with it would make sense. I would expect one of the parties at least will be arguing that a FIDIC contract deals with it in this way, and this is a way that is commonly accepted in the construction industry … it is not an automatic supplementation but it is something I would look at.

However, the few arbitrators who showed an inclination to consider arguments supporting the use of FIDIC contracts to fill gaps in international construction contracts were cautious in describing the extent to which FIDIC clauses can be used to fill gaps in the parties' contract. They emphasised that FIDIC contracts cannot be used for automatic gap-filling, but arbitrators may accept a party's argument to look at them to find a solution. In this case, the party arguing for using FIDIC conditions of contract to fill a gap in their contract would argue by analogy and the argument can be strong or weak. In the end, arbitrators need to be comfortable that such supplementation is not contrary to the parties' expectations and does not offend the risk allocation pattern expressed in their contract. The arbitrators suggested that two tests must be satisfied before being able to conclude that the parties must have intended to regulate a matter in a similar way to how it is regulated under a FIDIC contract. First, an arbitrator needs to find that a provision in a FIDIC contract reflects an industry's practice. The arbitrators stated that FIDIC contracts are not to be treated as codifications of international construction usage, but they can be viewed as a reflection of industry practice. As they are commonly used and have been used for a long period of time, then they tend to reflect the industry's practice. Although it is possible that there is a provision in FIDIC contracts that is intended to change the industry's practice for some reason, it is sensible to expect, certainly over time, that industry's practice and FIDIC contracts coincide. Second, an arbitrator needs to find that the parties did not deliberately decide not to use FIDIC conditions of contract. For instance, if the parties' contract includes some FIDIC clauses but leaves out other clauses, then the parties may have intended to avoid the application of these clauses. In this case, arbitrators should respect the parties' intention.

It is noteworthy that few arbitrators stated that it is not uncommon to have one of the parties in international construction arbitration attempting to persuade a tribunal that certain FIDIC clauses have become customary in international construction contracts or at least represent an international consensus. This argument has some merit because FIDIC contracts are not developed and updated in isolation to practice. Those responsible for drafting and updating FIDIC contracts do not impose their own views but seek the opinions of consulting engineers, contractors, and employers on how to regulate different aspects of the contractual relationship.

While this argument has some truth in it, the arbitrators suggested that it is normally difficult to convince tribunals that FIDIC clauses do, in fact, reflect the industry's customs and usages. The issue of whether FIDIC conditions of contract constitute international trade usages is not settled in theory or practice.

On the one hand, some scholars and practitioners hold the opinion that FIDIC conditions of contract could be treated as international construction usage. For instance, Gama (2016) suggests that FIDIC conditions of contract could qualify as transnational 'contractual usages'. This opinion seems to have some support in arbitral practice, as shown in ICC Case No. 14392/2009 summarised below.

ICC CASE NO. 14392/2009

The arbitral tribunal in ICC Case No. 14392/2009 had to decide whether FIDIC conditions of contract quality as usages of the international construction industry. The parties entered into an EPC/Turnkey contract for the construction of oil and gas facilities in 2002. The substantive law was Portuguese law. The dispute concerned, amongst other things, the scope of work under the EPC/Turnkey arrangement and the liability for the delay and additional costs resulting from what the contractor (the claimant) claimed to be additional works that fall outside the scope of work. The dispute was referred to the ICC International Court of Arbitration. Given that the contract was a 'Lump Sum Turnkey' type of contract, the claimant argued that they had unrestrained discretion as to the design, engineering, choice of materials, and construction of the works subject to compliance with the approval procedure set out in the contract. As Portuguese law did not contain specific rules applicable to Lump Sum EPC/Turnkey contracts, the claimant relied on trade usage to support their argument and asserted that pursuant to Article 17(2) of the ICC

Rules, the 'relevant trade usages' should also be taken into account. The claimant asserted that EPC/Turnkey contracts are 'typical' in international construction and are usually negotiated on the basis of standard forms of contract, such as those published by FIDIC. The parties' contract was no exception. Both parties agreed that their contract was based on the FIDIC conditions of contract for EPC/Turnkey projects (known as the Silver Book). The claimant acknowledged that the FIDIC conditions of contract do not qualify as 'usages of international trade' per se, but they still hold an important 'guidance value' that is widely acknowledged. It follows that the rules and principles set out in the FIDIC conditions of contract can and should be used to 'fill gaps' in contracts that were based on or inspired by them, such as the contract at hand. The arbitral tribunal stated that although the FIDIC conditions of contract are not applicable per se, they may be relied on to understand and characterise the nature of the contractual relationship between the parties. The tribunal noted that FIDIC conditions of contract 'are universally known and are tantamount to usages in the international construction industry'. Nevertheless, the tribunal clarified that pursuant to Article 17(2) of the ICC Rules of Arbitration, they must give priority to the actual wording of the contract, which reflects the parties' agreement. They stated that they will refer to international usages when they may assist in interpreting the contract or filing lacunae as long as they are compatible with the substantive law. The arbitral tribunal referred to the wording of the FIDIC Silver Book and commentary on it and concluded that more risks are shifted to the contractor under EPC/Turnkey contracts than under Design and Build contracts. It noted that under the FIDIC Silver Book, the contractor is responsible for the design of the works and for the accuracy of the employer's requirements, with limited exceptions. The tribunal found that, in light of the wording of the parties' contract as confirmed by the international usages (i.e., FIDIC conditions of contract), the contractor was responsible for the design and that it had to comply with the employer's requirements.

Commenting on this ICC case (i.e., ICC Case No. 14392/2009), Jolivet et al. (2016) stated that the tribunal considered the FIDIC standard form to be proof of the existence of usages rather than being a set or a codification of usages in itself. They also noted that the tribunal applied the usages 'without requiring the parties to prove their existence'.

On the other hand, some arbitration cases answered in the negative the question of whether clauses in FIDIC conditions of contract had become widely accepted to qualify as international trade usages that may apply to the parties' contract in the absence of an express agreement by the parties. In ICC Case No. 8873/1997, the tribunal found that FIDIC clauses did not qualify as trade usage for two reasons. First, the party that invoked this argument failed to prove that FIDIC clauses had been constantly used in practice to a sufficient level. Second, the party did not discharge its burden to prove that FIDIC's clauses were applicable to international construction contracts by default even if the parties had not expressly agreed to incorporate them (Seppala, 1998).

Although the argument that FIDIC clauses may reflect the industry's practice has some merit, the counterargument is that many employers change the default risk allocation in FIDIC contracts. This practice, which is by no means limited to FIDIC contracts, has been going on for decades and in all parts of the globe. So can we still claim that FIDIC's default risk allocation reflects what actually happens and how contracting parties actually behave? Or is FIDIC's aspiration from proposing fair and balanced risk allocation meant to change the practice? This question requires empirical investigation to quantify the extent to which contracting parties stick to or deviate from the default risk allocation and, hence, verify the claim that FIDIC contracts reflect what usually happens in the industry. For accurate results, such an analysis or investigation should be undertaken at a specific clause or theme level (i.e., how a particular obligation or risk is dealt with) but not at the whole document level.

5.5.2 Construction arbitration awards and scholarly writings

The second source of ICL is the works of academics and arbitrators (i.e., arbitration awards and scholarly writings), keeping in mind that the line between the two is blurred in international arbitration. This is because many academics are practising arbitrators and many arbitrators are involved in scholarly work and academic publications (Karton, 2013).

International construction arbitration awards could have some precedential value – persuasive and not obligatory – in providing guidance to international arbitrators on matters of contract interpretation especially when such guidance is lacking in the governing law (Weidemaier, 2009). Seppala (2012), in his third commentary on 'ICC arbitral awards dealing with FIDIC contracts', referred to the idea of arbitral precedent. He commented on the tribunal's decision in ICC Case No. 12048/2004 as follows:

> The tribunal's decision to order the payment by an arbitral award of a final and binding decision of the engineer is consistent with established precedent.

In its decision, the arbitral tribunal concluded that it had no authority under clause 67 of the relevant FIDIC contract to open up or review the engineer's decision that had become final and binding because it had not been disputed by either party within the timeframe stipulated under that clause. Seppala (2012) cited a series of ICC arbitral awards (e.g., the joined ICC Cases No. 3790/3902/4050/4051/4054) dealing with the same matter to illustrate how this interpretation has become a precedent followed by several international construction arbitral tribunals.

In their article 'International Arbitrators as Lawmakers', Moloo and King (2014) assert that arbitrators make law in the sense of making decisions that are likely to influence the behaviour of contracting parties and arbitral tribunals in the future. Commenting on arbitral lawmaking in the context of the international construction industry, they pointed out that the ICC routinely publishes excerpts from arbitral awards dealing primarily with FIDIC contracts and that counsel and arbitrators are likely to use the arbitral jurisprudence in these awards to support their arguments as to how contractual provisions in FIDIC contracts should be interpreted. They noted that past arbitral awards tend to have greater persuasive value when there is a gap in the governing law or at least some vagueness.

Seppala (2009) plays down the effect and precedential value that arbitral awards have in international construction arbitration practice. His review of the sparse published construction arbitration awards dealing with FIDIC conditions of contract found that out of the 40 accessible awards, only five awards cited previous arbitral decisions. These decisions are limited to the interpretation of the time bar in clause 67 of the second and third editions of the FIDIC Red Book. As such, he concludes that international construction arbitration has not provided fertile soil for the growth of arbitral precedent.

Although the small number of cases Seppala (2009) reviewed renders such a conclusion tentative, his conclusion agrees with Kaufmann-Kohler (2007)'s observation that citing arbitral awards with respect to matters of substance is rare in the larger field of international commercial arbitration.

In addition to arbitration awards, the academics' works and publications in the form of textbooks, treatises, and scholarly articles in law reviews are a source for transnational construction law jurisprudence. Some arbitrators interviewed by the author referred to the international construction law review (ICLR) as a leading authority in international construction law jurisprudence. The following paragraphs demonstrate that arbitrators consider scholarly opinions published in journals and textbooks when interpreting international construction contracts, especially those based on FIDIC.

ICC Case No. 5428/1988 illustrates how arbitrators may consider textbooks as well as authorities and case law from more developed jurisdictions (see Section 5.5.3). This arbitration case concerns a contract for the construction of a highway between a European contractor (claimant) and the Ministry of Public Works of an Arab country. The contract, which declared the law of the Arab country to be the governing law, incorporated the FIDIC conditions (2nd edition). In this case, the tribunal had to decide whether certain claims were time-barred with respect to clause 67 and some other provisions of the FIDIC conditions. In their submissions regarding the interpretation of these clauses, the parties cited textbooks, such as André Brabant's *Le Contrat International de Construction* (the International Construction Contract) and Duncan Wallace's first *Supplement to the International Civil Engineering Contract* (Wallace, 1980). Further, although the governing law of the contract was the law of an Arab country, the parties cited English cases (e.g., *Tersons Ltd. v. Stevenage Development Corporation* (1965) and *Monmouthshire County Council v. Costelloe & Kemple* (1965)) in support of their arguments. It is uncertain whether the tribunal took into consideration the English authorities. The tribunal noted:

> We do not propose to go into a detailed analysis of these legal submissions. It seems to us that the purpose and intent of the FIDIC scheme is that notice of claims of whatever nature should be made to the Engineer in writing … at the earliest practicable opportunity and when made should be as detailed as possible having regard to the nature of the claim.

In ICC Case No. 15956/2010, a dispute arose from the employer's termination of a construction contract incorporating FIDIC conditions of contract because of the contractor's breach of contract. In the award, the tribunal cited Seppala (2005), which is an article published in the ICLR that explains how the tiered dispute resolution clause is intended to apply (Corbett, 2017).

Seppala (2009) noted that book commentaries on the FIDIC contracts are an important authoritative source that arbitrators use to reach and justify their decisions. However, he did not provide evidence of arbitrators' citations of these books in their awards. Instead, he demonstrated the persuasive value of these books by reviewing English and common law courts' citations to them. In particular, he examined the courts' references to four commentaries on FIDIC contracts (listed below) and found that the courts cited them in hundreds of cases:

- Wallace, I.N.D., (1974). *The International Civil Engineering Contract: A Commentary on the FIDIC International: Standard Form of Civil Engineering and Building Contract.* London: Sweet & Maxwell. (and its 1980 supplement)

- Corbett (1991). *FIDIC 4th – A Practical Legal Guide: A Commentary on the International Construction Contract.* London: Sweet & Maxwell.
- Bunni, N.G. (1991, 1997, 2005). *The FIDIC Forms of Contract.* New Jersey: Blackwell Publishing.
- Glover, J., Hughes, S. & Thomas, C. (2006). *Understanding the FIDIC Red Book: A Clause by Clause Commentary.* London: Sweet & Maxwell.

The following text discusses a sample of arbitral awards in which arbitral tribunals cited ICLR articles, construction law textbooks, and arbitral awards to interpret what used to be one of the most contested and debated clauses in FIDIC's Red Book: Clause 67 of the second and third editions of FIDIC's Red Book.

In ICC Case No. 5277/1987, the tribunal noted that the interpretation of this clause had not been settled. The tribunal cited various articles and books that were divided and suggested different interpretations. This is an excerpt from the award:

> Upon this point we were referred to a number of decisions of arbitrators and textbook articles in which both points of views received support. Thus, the contention of the claimant is supported by an article by Mr. Duncan Wallace, QC in the International Construction Law Review: 'The Time Bar in FIDIC Clause 67'; and the award in ICC cases no. 1896 and 5029, while the contention of the defendant is supported by the award in ICC cases no. 3790 and 4707. We were also referred to certain English decisions but we did not find them to be directly in point. We were not referred to any decisions by the courts of country X [the country of the substantive law].

In ICC Case No. 15282/2010, the tribunal referred to the following sources to determine the meaning of Clause 67 of FIDIC conditions (i.e., the correct procedure to follow to avoid a dispute being time-barred):

- Bunni, N. G. (2005). *The FIDIC Forms of Contract* (3rd ed.). New Jersey: Blackwell Publishing.
- Seppala, C. (1986). The Pre-arbitral Procedure for the Settlement of Disputes in the FIDIC (Civil Engineering) Conditions of Contract. *International Construction Law Review*, V4, pp. 315–337.
- Jaffe, M. & McHugh, R. (2009). *International Construction Disputes in Today's Economy.*

The exact procedure of how Clause 67 under the second and third editions of FIDIC conditions was intended to operate gave rise to many disputes that reached ICC arbitration. The main question was: 'what action was a claimant obliged to do under Clause 67 in order to preserve its right from being time-barred and be able to submit a dispute on it to arbitration?'. To be more specific, was a claimant obliged to 'notify' the other party of its intention to refer the dispute to arbitration or to actually 'submit' an arbitration request to the ICC?

The answer was highly important as a failure to follow the 'correct' procedure could have and, in fact, did have grave consequences for contractors who were barred from being able to litigate or arbitrate disputes involving large sums of money, which is not uncommon in international construction arbitrations (Seppala, 1998). Several arbitral awards held that it was the claimant's obligation to actually 'submit' a request for arbitration to the ICC within the relevant 90-day period, in order not to forfeit its legal rights to arbitrate the relevant disputes (Seppala, 1998). Consequently, many contractors lost their entitlements for what can be seen, in hindsight, as an incorrect interpretation of the clause by several arbitral tribunals. In later arbitrations that took place in the 1990s (e.g., ICC Case No. 7641/1996, and ICC Case No. 5948/1991), arbitral tribunals held that the actual commencement of arbitration was not necessary and it was sufficient for the claimant to notify the other party of its intention to arbitrate in order to preserve its right from being time-barred and to proceed thereafter to arbitration (Seppala, 1998).

It is worth mentioning that the uncertainty of the meaning of this clause and how it was intended to work have been resolved in the fourth edition of the FIDIC Red Book published in 1987 (Seppala, 1998). The fourth edition made it clear that it is sufficient for the claimant to notify the other party of its intentions to commence arbitration in order to protect its right to arbitrate from being time-barred (Seppala, 1998).

The historical account concerning the interpretation of Clause 67 of the FIDIC Red Book's second and third editions illustrates how certain aspects of international construction law evolve. The correct interpretation of the meaning of a key clause in the most widespread international standard form of construction contract was debated in several ICC arbitration awards and ICLR articles until, eventually, its meaning was settled. However, it is not certain whether the debate concerning the meaning of Clause 67 was settled as a result of arbitrators' scholarly discussions and the soft power of arbitral precedent or FIDIC's intervention in releasing an updated edition of its conditions of contract that contains clear wordings on how the clause is intended to operate.

What is certain, at least, is that FIDIC updates its contracts in response to arbitral awards and court decisions that reach conclusions that are contrary to the intentions of FIDIC's drafting committees.

ICC Case No. 11813/2002 provides another example of this practice. In this case, the tribunal concluded that the employer's right to set off under English substantive law is not excluded by the wording of FIDIC's Yellow Book (the test edition published in 1998). Seppala, a member of the FIDIC Update Task Group that drafted the 1999 FIDIC books, stated that the tribunal's construction was contrary to FIDIC's intention. In light of this arbitral award, which appears to be relevant to the 1999 FIDIC books, Seppala advised that FIDIC should modify its conditions of contracts to expressly exclude the employer's right of set-off (Seppala, 2013).

5.5.3 Construction law of developed jurisdictions and the technocrats of construction arbitration

The third source of ICL is the construction law of jurisdictions that have developed and mature legal systems. This construction law is sometimes used by a group of construction arbitration technocrats (e.g., arbitrators, counsel, experts) from these jurisdictions to support their arguments and legal conclusions.

Many large-scale infrastructure projects around the world are financed by multilateral development banks, designed by cosmopolitan engineering firms, and built by multinational construction conglomerates (Venoit, 2009). The contracts are often drafted by lawyers coming from more mature and sophisticated legal jurisdictions using legal terminologies from their legal traditions (Moss, 2004). If a dispute arises from an international construction contract, it is highly likely to find that the arbitrators as well as the counsel and experts appearing before them are from the same developed legal jurisdictions.

The influence of developed legal systems, particularly English law, on the evolution of international construction law is evident from the interviewed arbitrators' accounts, scholarly writings, and arbitral awards, as this section shows.

According to some arbitrators interviewed by the author, English construction law probably sets the gold standard internationally. English law has a significant impact on the development of construction standard forms of contract, including the FIDIC contracts themselves. Therefore, international construction contracts may contain phrases or concepts that have roots in English law. Further, the legal environment in England and Wales, which comprises a specialist court (the Technology and Construction Court), specialist judges, and specialist construction lawyers, has facilitated the development of law in this area.

Likewise, Seppala (2009) opines that English law has a significant impact on international construction law because of its strong influence on the most widespread international standard form of construction contracts that are published by FIDIC. FIDIC contracts were originally modelled on the English Institution of Civil Engineers (ICE) conditions of contract. Also, the periodic updates of FIDIC conditions have always been drafted mainly by English engineers. Further, the main commentaries on FIDIC contracts are authored by English engineers and lawyers. For these reasons, and as the official and authentic text of FIDIC contracts is the English version, English case law is essential for understanding and interpreting FIDIC clauses.

A Dubai-based British lawyer shared with the author an example of how legal concepts from developed legal systems are sometimes relied on to resolve disputes that are governed by less-developed legal systems:

> Typically concepts from more mature legal markets with more developed laws on delay, disruption, concurrency, global claims and so on … will be shoehorned into the local law … these concepts are not dealt with in the laws of the Arab Gulf countries … so, often you find that those concepts will be imported into the case and lawyers will try to find arguments in the civil code that support their position on that particular issue … and there is a risk that a tribunal may decide that there is no such concept of concurrency in the governing law and dismiss it … but a lot of the tribunals that I have appeared before comprised Western lawyers who are comfortable with the concepts of concurrency and disruption, and global claims.

The international arbitrators' preference for a transnational approach to contract interpretation and reliance on guidance from foreign courts' judgements is facilitated by the lack of development of 'construction law' in some countries, such as the Arab Gulf states. The shortage in state-supplied construction law or national interpretation of FIDIC clauses in these states is because construction disputes arising from FIDIC contracts are not submitted to the local courts but are referred to arbitration. As arbitration awards are not published, the main guidance both arbitrators and counsel are left with is from the cases that are dealt with by foreign courts.

Likewise, an Egyptian arbitrator stated that national laws in the region have no or little guidance on how to deal with disputes in relation to concurrent delay. Further, in his experience, this matter is rarely regulated by contract provisions. As contracts and the governing laws are usually silent on how to resolve concurrent delay disputes, the tribunal approach to their resolution is 'up in the air'. The arbitration outcome tends to rely on the composition of the tribunal, the experts before them, and their traditions. The arbitrator observed that delay analysis experts, in international arbitration, tend to come from more sophisticated legal jurisdictions. Many of these experts come from the United Kingdom, and they bring their own standards and good practice to the case. For instance, they refer to the UK Society of Construction Law (SCL)'s Delay and Disruption Protocol or English courts' judgements to support the use of certain delay analysis methodologies. Despite the important 'guidance value' of the SCL's Protocol, it has only a persuasive value and not all tribunals follow its recommended approach. For example, in ICC Case No. 12654/2005 and ICC Case No. 10847/2003, the tribunals took a different position from the SCL's Protocol regarding the contractor's concurrent delay claim (Seppala, 2012).

In this context, it is worth mentioning that Jørgensen (2010) (cited in Klee, 2015) finds that concurrent delays and float ownership are two areas that are not regulated in 12 civil law and common law jurisdictions with England seemingly the sole jurisdiction that deals with them.

The aforementioned arbitral accounts illustrate how international arbitrators, counsel, and experts from mature legal systems work together and contribute to the formation of a global understanding of how to deal with certain construction disputes or how to interpret specific clauses in standard forms of construction contracts, such as the FIDIC form. This process of transformation of national construction laws into transnational or international construction law is undertaken by a cosmopolitan society of construction arbitration technocrats who sometimes find themselves in a situation where they need to find a solution for a particular dispute on which the governing law is silent. The following three international arbitration cases illustrate how this happens in practice.

ICC CASE NO. 5277/1987

This case is related to a dispute that arose from a 280 km canal construction contract between a French contractor and the government of an African country (Seyadi, 2017). The parties' agreement included FIDIC conditions of contract 2nd edition (1969). The governing law of the contract was the law of the African country, which originated from English law. In construing clause 66 in the parties' contract, which reads as 'in the event of the contract being frustrated', the tribunal noted that the concept of 'frustration' is not recognised in the governing law but is familiar in the English law. Accordingly, the tribunal followed the English concept of 'frustration'.

CRCICA CASE NO. 175/2000

An Egyptian tourism company and a European JV contractor entered into a Design and Build Lump Sum construction contract to deliver a five-star tourist resort in 1998. A dispute arose from the employer's (the respondent) termination of the construction contract due to the slow progress and delays in the completion of the works. The contractor (the claimant) started arbitration proceedings at CRCICA.

The claimant did not contest that the project activities were delayed but argued that the delay in progress was largely caused by the respondent's lack of expertise in project management. Further, the claimant asserted that the respondent's termination was wrongful because the project's completion date was a long way into the future and remained achievable. The respondent argued that many project activities were late and did not proceed according to the time schedule, which made it impossible to deliver the project on time. The respondent referred to a provision in the contract that, according to its interpretation, allows the employer to terminate the contract in case the contractor 'fails to fulfil any of its contractual obligations within a maximum period of 60 days from its due date' (Alam Eldin, 2014). To decide whether the termination was correct or not, the tribunal had to interpret the meaning of this contractual provision.

The tribunal, which was composed of two Egyptian arbitrators chaired by a UK arbitrator, noted that 'It is a principle of international construction law, particularly in the case of design and build contracts, that such a time schedule attached to the contract is merely a management tool'. The purpose of the time schedule, the tribunal added, was to enable both parties to manage their work to achieve the contractual completion date(s). It allowed the contractor to manage its resources in the most efficient way and informed the employer that its obligations, such as providing the contractor with access to the site and approving the contractor's submittals, must be achieved at specific times in order not to prevent the contractor from achieving the completion date(s). The tribunal noted that the time schedule was not a contractual document and, hence, did not impose an obligation on the contractor to achieve the start and finish dates of specific activities or work packages. The only contractual dates were those specifically defined by the contract. The tribunal concluded that the respondent and its project manager were mistaken in treating these dates as imposing contractual obligations on the claimant. The tribunal found that the project completion date was still achievable, particularly if an account is taken of the extension of time to which the tribunal found the claimant to be entitled. Hence, in the tribunal's view, the termination was premature and, therefore, unjustified (Alam Eldin, 2014).

In this case, the contract was governed by Egyptian law. Yet, the arbitral tribunal cited a principle of 'international construction law' rather than an authority in Egyptian law, the governing law of the contract, as a premise for their legal conclusion. The arbitration award elaborated neither on the source of this principle of 'international construction law' nor where it was to be found.

CRCICA CASE NO. 310/2002

This arbitration case is rich in content that gives insight into how the notion of international construction law can be used in practice.

This case arose from a construction contract between a Belgian construction company (the claimant) and a Saudi-Egyptian tourism company (the respondent) for the construction of a five-star hotel. The tribunal was composed of a British chairman with two Egyptian co-arbitrators. The governing law of the contract was Egyptian law. The main dispute concerned delays in project completion. The claimant (the contractor) made a claim for an extension of time (EOT) totalling 273 days and the costs associated therewith, which the respondent (employer) denied.

As such, the claimant referred the dispute to arbitration under the auspices of the Cairo Regional Centre for International Commercial Arbitration (CRCICA).

The respondent stated that the contract expressly entitled the contractor to an extension of time for completion in limited circumstances, namely, suspension by the employer, force majeure, and changes to the works ordered by the employer. The respondent asserted that most of the claimant's delay claims did not fall within the aforesaid limited circumstances. In addition, the respondent asserted that there was nothing under the Egyptian Civil Code that allowed a court to extend the time for completion on grounds other than those expressly set out in the contract. They contended that there was no 'law' or 'usage' whereby a term for extension of time should be implied in the contract in addition to those expressly stated therein.

The claimant, on the other hand, argued that whilst the contract expressly provided for an extension of time in three circumstances, it did not exclude other causes of delay. Further, they submitted that the contract has terms implied by the Egyptian Civil Code. They referred to authorities in support of this argument, such as the Court of Cassation judgements and El-Sanhoury writings that provide that the contractor shall not be responsible for delays in completing the works should such delays be attributable to the employer. They also referred to provisions in the Egyptian Civil Code (e.g., Articles 215, 216, 157/2, 272) to prove that it is possible to grant an Extension of Time (EOT) under the law. Accordingly, they submitted that their extension of time claim should be allowed, since Egyptian law entitled the contractor to an extension of time in the case of an owner's default, whether or not a provision has been made in the contract.

The tribunal, in its award, held that an EOT for the completion of the work is possible under Egyptian law. They appear to have arrived at this conclusion of law, or at least reasoned it, by drawing a logical analogy between 'general principles of international construction law' and Egyptian law. The tribunal started its reasoning in describing the English law concepts of 'time is of the essence' and 'time at large' as generally accepted in all international construction contracts (but they did not explicitly state where these concepts come from). They explained 'time is of the essence' as follows:

> In most, if not all, construction contracts the stipulated time for completion of the works is of the essence, which importance is supported by the employer's right to levy liquidated damages against the contractor if such time for completion is not met. Correspondingly, construction contracts typically contain a provision for extension of time so that, if it is the employer/owner who causes a delay … the time for completion is not nullified.

Then, the tribunal explained the English law's implied term concept of 'reasonable time' or 'time at large' that applies in case the EOT clause is absent. They stated:

> Where a contract provides for a date for completion of the works, but the employer through its acts or omissions prevents the contractor from achieving that date and there is no entitlement to an extension of time under the contract in such event, the time for completion in the contract is nullified. This in turn means that the employer loses his right to levy liquidated damages and, whilst the contractor's obligation to complete the works remains, he must do so only within a reasonable time ... On that basis, therefore, and in light of the principle of construction law if … the respondents' delays … have been proven, the arbitral tribunal finds

that the claimants' obligation to complete the works would be within a reasonable time and the respondents would have no entitlement to levy liquidated damages.

Then, the tribunal stated the following two other general principles that allow them to grant an EOT for the contractor in case of delays caused by the employer:

It is accepted in all international construction contracts that:

(a) whereas it is the duty of the contractor to do what the contract requires to be done (as designed and specified by the employer), the employer shall allow the contractor to do that which is to be done without hindrance; and
(b) a party cannot benefit from its breach to the detriment of the injured party.

The first principle matches the English law implied term providing that the employer should not hinder or prevent the contractor from (Knutson, 2005; Chappell, 2011)

a. carrying out its obligations in accordance with the terms of the contract;
b. completing the works in accordance with the contractor's programme.

That is not to say that provisions to similar effects do not exist in Egyptian law or other legal systems. For instance, in French law, the implied duty of good faith in contract performance includes an obligation not to interfere with the contractor's work (Klee, 2015).

The second principle seems to be universally accepted across national laws, including common law and civil law jurisdictions. Under common law jurisdictions, the long-established 'prevention principle' provides that a party may not enforce a contractual obligation against the other party where it has prevented the other party from performing that obligation. Under civil law jurisdictions, a similar principle provides that no party may benefit from its own wrong (or breach of contract) (Klee, 2015). In particular, the Egyptian Civil Code states in Article 124 (Klee, 2015):

> A party who has committed a mistake cannot take advantage of the mistakes in a manner contrary to the principles of good faith.

Having laid the foundation of general principles of international construction law, the tribunal, by logical analogy, found that under Egyptian law a debtor (contractor) who is delayed in his performance for reasons due to the creditor (employer) is entitled to an EOT. After finding the legal basis for granting an EOT, the tribunal needs to determine the extent of the delay. Quantification of a delay period sometimes involves complex questions of legal causation when there is a concurrent delay (Klee, 2015). In this regard, the tribunal also appeared to have relied on the English approach of 'dominant cause' (Burr, 2016). The following is an excerpt from the award:

> Therefore, the arbitral tribunal holds that the late provision of the permanent power utility dominated all other delays to MEP testing and commissioning … and caused a critical delay to practical completion of the Works.… The claimants have claimed that the impact of late availability of the gas utility was to delay completion … However, it is clear that this claimed delay was concurrent with, and dominated by, the critical delay determined by the arbitral tribunal in respect of the provision of the permanent power utility.

This arbitration case is an example of the process of transnationalisation or internationalisation of construction law, which is happening in practice. It is noteworthy that the arbitrator's background might be a factor that at least facilitates the transformation of legal rules from their own legal tradition into transnational rules. It is possible that this is what happened in this case. The legal concepts referred to as principles of international construction law and the legal terminologies used in the arbitration award were mostly derived from the chairman's own legal tradition (i.e., English law). The persuasive effect of foreign authorities in international arbitration seems to depend on the composition of the arbitral tribunal and the legal counsel appearing before them. It is easier to convince an arbitrator to apply a legal solution from their legal tradition than apply a legal solution they are not familiar with. Unfortunately, the sparse arbitral awards that are available do not help to solidify this inference especially because they are normally in redacted form and do not include information about the tribunals' composition. Nevertheless, Chapter 8 provides evidence of the effect of arbitrators' backgrounds, including their legal tradition, on their decisions.

There is evidence from arbitrators' writings that support the author's argument concerning the effect of developed legal jurisdictions on the development of ICL. Seppala (2009) notes from his personal experience that courts' precedents from developed systems of law are often used to fill gaps in the governing law, which is normally the underdeveloped national law of the employer. Drawing on four international construction arbitrations cases he was involved in, Seppala (2009) illustrated the practice whereby the parties submit legal authorities from developed systems of law that belong to a different family of law from that of the governing law, which arbitrators take into account and use to justify their decisions. At the end of his article, he opines the following:

> Where there are gaps in a governing law, that is underdeveloped, the analysis and solutions that courts in developed legal systems can provide should most certainly not be disregarded. On the contrary, to the extent that they are in complete harmony with the governing law and provide good, rational solutions, they should be considered and, where appropriate, applied by international arbitral tribunals. By virtue of their international character and multinational composition (usually), international arbitral tribunals may be better qualified, and should be more receptive, than national courts to look to comparative law for solutions.

One final note regarding the use of developed jurisdictions' construction law is that the parties' counsel are mindful not to turn a blind eye to the substantive law the parties agreed on to govern their contract. They attempt to anchor or 'shoehorn' the legal principles into the governing law. In other words, they strive to explain how legal principles, from a developed system of law, fit and are compatible with the governing law. The arbitrators, in turn, are mindful that they need to justify their reliance on such foreign authorities in order to protect their awards from the risk of challenge or criticism from scholars and practitioners.

Although an international, or transnational, approach to arbitral decision-making in international construction disputes could be helpful and commendable, it is paramount not to put aside the governing law altogether. There could be a fine line between a transnational approach and a neo-colonialist approach. The latter approach, which is sometimes, rightly or wrongly, associated with Lord Asquith's decision in the famous *Petroleum*

Development Ltd v. The Sheikh of Abu Dhabi [1952] case, resulted in significant reputational damage to international arbitration and posed a serious threat to its acceptance. In this case, the English arbitrator considered the law of Abu Dhabi, which draws on Islamic law, as largely non-existent and has no legal principles applicable to the interpretation of modern commercial contracts. Although the English arbitrator acknowledged that English law was inapplicable as such, he applied English law principles to resolve the dispute (Gaillard and Savage, 1999).

A similar approach was followed in the case of *Ruler of Qatar v. International Marine Oil Co. Ltd. [1953]*, whereby the arbitrator stated that the applicable Qatari law had no principles relevant to interpreting the contract at hand. Ten years later, the arbitral tribunal in *Saudi Arabia v. Arab American Oil Co. (ARAMCO) [1963]* made a similar observation and stated that the applicable Saudi Arabian law had to be supplemented by 'general principles of law, by the custom and practice in the oil business and by notions of pure jurisprudence'. What is common between all these cases in the early years of international commercial arbitration is the arbitrators' reliance on the laws of developed Western jurisdictions or 'general principles of law' that are rooted in the laws of these jurisdictions (Stovall, 2009).

5.5.4 International principles of contract law

It is widely accepted that construction law has some distinct aspects from the broader commercial law. However, at the end of the day, a construction contract is a commercial contract (subject to private contract law) (Dyson, 2015) and, in rare instances, an administrative contract (subject to government procurement or administrative law) (Molineaux, 1997; Ismail, 2016). Accordingly, the fourth source of ICL is based on general principles of international commercial contract law.

These principles are now codified in soft law instruments such as UNIDROIT Principles of International Commercial Contracts, first published in 1994 with a third edition published in 2016 (UNIDROIT Principles, 2016). According to a Canadian arbitrator interviewed by the author, if the parties do not wish their contract to be governed by national law, it is safer to select UNIDROIT principles than broad notions, such as general principles of law, *lex mercatoria*, or the like. He added that the concept of 'general principles of law' lacks certainty. The parties will not be able to ascertain their obligations and liabilities with certainty. The arbitrators, on the other hand, will have wide discretion, and, at the end of the day, one party is going to be disappointed with the outcome and stuck with an award that is final and binding.

In addition to this codification of the transnational law (i.e., UNIDROIT Principles), there are systematic collections or compilations of sets of transnational rules or principles, such as the one developed and maintained by the Centre for Transnational Law (CENTRAL) at the University of Cologne (https://www.trans-lex.org/principles). There are also restatements of international contract law. These restatements are not binding, but they have persuasive authority. They provide arbitrators with guidance or inspiration as to what the legal solution could be when the substantive law is vague.

Although rare in practice, transnational rules of law (such as general principles of law or UNIDROIT Principles or the like) apply when contracting parties select them and agree that their contract is to be governed by them (Karton, 2013; Charrett, 2012). They can also be applied by the tribunal when the parties fail to select or agree on any rules of law to govern their contract (Rosengren, 2013; Karton, 2013; Moss, 2004; Gaillard and Savage, 1999; Farnsworth, 1997) or when the governing law provides no guidance on the issue in dispute (i.e., to fill a gap).

Several arbitrators interviewed by the author stated that, upon the parties' submission, they would look at these sources (UNIDROIT Principles, CENTRAL, restatements, etc.) as restatements of what the law should be. They noted that UNIDROIT Principles can be useful to interpret contracts when the governing law has little guidance on the issue in dispute. For example, an Australian arbitrator said:

> If you have nothing else to work with ... if the contract does not contemplate something, and the law does not contemplate something, and say even the customs or trade usages have never dealt with something like this before, then I would expect that one of the parties, at least, to be arguing based on an analogy between UNIDROIT Principles and analogous situation under the applicable law.

Controversially, arbitrators may unilaterally apply transnational rules of law even if the parties have not authorised them to do so and even if they objected to their application (e.g., ICC Case No. 8873/1997) (Karton, 2014; Karton, 2012b). DiMatteo (2013) cited a few international commercial arbitration awards and arbitral opinions to show that 'soft law' (*lex mercatoria*) can be used, and has been used, to trump 'hard law' (the substantive law chosen by the parties)

5.6 A list of international construction law principles

The previous section indicates that ICL does not necessarily exist in the form of a code or an abstract list of grand principles. Rather, it constitutes a body of knowledge from which solutions for disputes can be obtained on a piecemeal basis.

However, to move from abstraction to particularisation, the author asked the international arbitrators who believe in the concept of ICL to mention examples of principles that they consider as a part of ICL. Some arbitrators had a hard time mentioning a single principle without deep thinking. The following is a non-exhaustive list of principles some arbitrators interviewed by the author believe to constitute ICL:

- Time is of the essence: a contractor has to deliver the work on time;
- Extension of time/prevention principle: a contractor is always entitled to EOT if he is delayed by the employer;
- Timely payment: a contractor is entitled to be paid without delay;
- Termination: the employer has a right to terminate the contract for non-performance;
- *Force majeure*: parties are excused from their contractual obligations when certain events that are beyond their control occur;
- Deemed acceptance: practical completion will be deemed as having taken place, depending on factual evidence of the employer's taking over, even if the employer has not issued the practical completion certificate;
- Duty of good faith: parties must act in good faith in performing their contract;
- Duty to mitigate damages: an injured party has a duty to mitigate its damages.

Although these principles may not be unknown to construction disputes and resolution practitioners, the arbitrators who suggested these principles agreed that they are not codified and cannot be found in a single document. Instead, they can be derived from the sources that were identified in the previous section.

In fact, there was an attempt to develop a list of general principles of international construction law that can be used in interpreting international construction contracts particularly when the substantive law is incomplete. Molineaux (1997) coined the term *lex constructionis* (construction *lex mercatoria*) and proposed the following ten principles:

1. *Pacta sunt servanda:* agreements are to be kept;
2. *Rebus sic stantibus:* viewed as the competing or complementary principle, or sometimes the exception, of *pacta sunt servanda*, which means an agreement is binding as long as circumstances do not change. It applies only in extreme situations. Several excuse concepts under different systems of law are linked to this general principle such as *imprévision*, frustration and *force majeure*;
3. The good faith principle is explicit in civil law and embodied in the common law in the form of implied terms of a similar effect;
4. Contract variations or scope changes instructed by the employer do not amount to a breach of contract and they are inherent to construction contracts;
5. Unforeseen physical conditions: additional cost resulting from encountering physical site conditions more onerous than reasonably expected is to be borne by the employer;
6. The decisions regarding the construction schedule/programme (i.e., the sequence of activities) and construction methodology reside with the contractor;
7. Extension of time: a contractor is entitled to an extension of the time for completion in case of delays caused by an event for which the contractor is not responsible. Extension of the time claims must be assessed promptly;
8. Mitigation of damages: an injured party has a duty to mitigate its damages. This principle extends to 'total cost' claims in which causation is difficult to prove;
9. Prompt claims management: the parties must act promptly to submit claims and respond to them;
10. Notice provisions may often be ignored as a procedural technicality when it is found that the employer is aware of the facts and that a claim is en route.

It is noteworthy that it is not necessary for a principle to be recognised by all national laws in order to be considered a principle of ICL. For instance, a Lebanese arbitrator said he would accept an argument by a party to a dispute that 'a duty to mitigate loss' is a universal principle in international construction law and, hence, binding on the parties in international arbitration. According to him, although this principle is not universally recognised by all national laws and it is perhaps unknown to someone from France, as it is non-existing in French law, he would still apply it as an ICL principle.

5.7 The applicability of ICL

It is noteworthy that some of the arbitrators who reject the notion of ICL accept more or less the same practical effect it has in arbitral practice but contest its theoretical status.

They opine that the term 'ICL' might be misleading as it indicates that ICL is codified or universally applicable somehow. Therefore, they prefer to use alternative terminologies such as 'concepts' or 'legal principles' that are 'widely recognised', 'widely accepted', or 'generally accepted'. Nonetheless, these expressions have also been criticised. For instance, the parties to the Channel Tunnel construction contract agreed to govern their contract by 'principles generally acceptable to English law and French law'. According to a Canadian arbitrator interviewed by the author, this looked like a lovely compromise until they tried to make it work when they went to arbitration, but they found nothing much in common between the two legal systems.

Anyhow, it is more sensible and purposive to escape this terminological debate and focus on the effect of such principles. In this regard, most arbitrators interviewed by the author believe that ICL can be helpful if the substantive law is silent or incomplete. It is one of the tools arbitrators might resort to in order to supplement the parties' contract. They can also use it to interpret a term in the contract. To this end, arbitrators put great emphasis on applying ICL by way of analogy with the governing law.

The starting point for all arbitrators is that if the parties did not choose or incorporate ICL principles in their contract, then they would not constitute a source of obligations. Arbitrators could be deemed to be in breach of their duty if they decide on the basis of a rule that is external to the governing law (Karton, 2015). Nevertheless, in a situation in which the parties' contract and the governing law they have chosen are incomplete or do not answer the particular problem, arbitrators would not necessarily start by ruling anything out but equally speaking they might not be persuaded as to why something should come in. To put it simply, ICL is not obligatory but arbitrators may rely on it as a sort of guidance. As such, it seems that ICL does not play a dominant role, but it is a subsidiary source of legal norms concerning international construction contracts.

However, there was an exception to the prevailing view regarding the status and application of ICL. For instance, an Egyptian arbitrator interviewed by the author suggested that ICL might, in limited circumstances, trump a term in the parties' contract. According to him, the more unreasonable the term is, in the opinion of the tribunal, the higher the chance that this could happen. Using the legal principle of deemed acceptance, which originated from the civil law system and evolved into an international principle of construction law in his opinion, he gave an example of how a principle of international construction law might take precedence over a term in the parties' contract as follows:

> If the contract is silent on the concept of handing over... I think it has been established in international construction law that once the employer starts using the works pursuant to their intended purpose and even if the employer has not signed the handing over certificate, then preliminary handing over is deemed to have taken place ... even if the contract states otherwise, let's say the contract says handing over will not be deemed to have taken place unless the employer signs five documents ... but the employer starts using the works, I have not seen a case where the tribunal would say there is no handing over here because the employer has not signed the documents.

5.8 Conclusion

This chapter examines how legal norms that do not belong to the governing law might have an impact on arbitral decision-making. It empirically constructs the concept of

ICL, which is a body of transnational legal rules related to construction contracts. While acknowledging that the objective existence of ICL is deeply contested, and what counts as ICL is unclear, this chapter unpacks its sources, authority, and application in international construction arbitration.

It finds that ICL is the result of the internationalisation and globalisation of construction works and construction dispute resolution. International construction arbitration, as the fundamental method of cross-border construction dispute resolution, provides the perfect environment for bringing transnational rules into existence. The process of transforming national rules into transnational rules is led by construction arbitration technocrats from developed jurisdictions. These transnational rules, or ICL, can be used for contract interpretation as well as supplementation. The arbitral preference of a transnational approach to contract interpretation is further facilitated by the widespread use of international standard forms of construction contracts, particularly the FIDIC standard form.

Although the authority of ICL lacks full consensus, this chapter argues that the prevailing view considers ICL as a 'method' to find a reasonable and sensible solution in case the parties' contract and the governing law do not provide for such a solution.

5.9 References

Berger, K. (1999). *The Creeping Codification of the Lex Mercatoria.* The Hague: Kluwer Law International.

Błaszczak, Ł. & Kolber, J. (2013). General principles of law and equity as a basis for decision-making in arbitration. *Comparative Law Review*, 15, 189–208.

Bond, S. R. (1989). How to draft an arbitration clause. *Journal of International Arbitration*, 6(2), 65.

Bunni, N. G. (1991). *The FIDIC Forms of Contract.* New Jersey: Blackwell Publishing.

Bunni, N. G. (1997). *The FIDIC Forms of Contract.* 2nd ed. New Jersey: Blackwell Publishing.

Bunni, N. G. (2005). *The FIDIC Forms of Contract.* 3rd ed. New Jersey: Blackwell Publishing.

Charrett, D. (2012). A common law of construction contracts: Or vive la différence? *International Construction Law Review*, 29(1), 72–84.

Corbett, E. C. (1991). *FIDIC 4th: A Practical Legal Guide: A Commentary on the International Construction Contract.* London: Sweet & Maxwell.

Corbett, E. C. (2017). FIDIC 1999 books: Commentary on clause 15. *Knowledge Hub: FIDIC 1999 Books Clause Commentaries* [Online]. Available at: http://corbett.co.uk/wp-content/uploads/Clause-15.pdf [Accessed 10 March 2018].

Cuniberti, G. (2008). Beyond contract: The case for default arbitration in international commercial disputes. *Fordham International Law Journal*, 32, 417.

Dasser, F. (2008). Mouse or monster? Some facts and figures on the lex mercatoria. *In*: Zimmermann, R. (ed.) *Globalisierung und Entstaatlichung des Rechts.* Tübingen: Mohr Siebeck.

de Boisséson, M. (2015). Chapter 8: Substantive applicable law in international arbitration: An arbitrator's perspective. *In*: Bortolotti, F. & Maye, P. (eds.) *The Application of Substantive Law by International Arbitrators.* Paris: ICC Publication.

Delaume, G. R. (1988). Comparative analysis as a basis of law in state contracts: The myth of the lex mercatoria. *Tulane Law Review*, 63, 575.

Derains, Y. & Schwartz, E. A. (2005). *A Guide to the ICC Rules of Arbitration.* The Hague: Kluwer Law International.

Dezalay, Y. & Garth, B. G. (1998). *Dealing in Virtue: International Commercial Arbitration and the Construction of a Transnational Legal Order.* Chicago: University of Chicago Press.

DiMatteo, L. A. (2013). Soft law and the principle of fair and equitable decision making in international contract arbitration. *The Chinese Journal of Comparative Law*, 1(2), 221–255.

Drahozal, C. R. (2000). Commercial norms, commercial codes, and international commercial arbitration. *Vanderbilt Journal of Transnational Law*, 33, 79.

Drahozal, C. R. (2005a). Contracting out of national law: An empirical look at the new law merchant. *Notre Dame Law Review*, 80(2), 523.

Drahozal, C. R. (2007). Busting arbitration myths. *Kansas Law Review*, 56(3), 663.

Drahozal, C. R. (2005b). The Making of the Award: Comments on Case Law Developments Under the UNCITRAL Model Law. *International arbitration law review*, 8, 183–190.

Dyson, L. (2015). The contribution of construction cases to the development of the common law. *The Turkish Commercial Law Review*, 1(3), 175.

Farnsworth, E. (1997). An international restatement: The UNIDROIT principles of international commercial contracts. *University of Baltimore Law Review*, 26(3), 1–7.

Gaillard, E. & Savage, J. (1999). *Fouchard, Gaillard, Goldman on International Commercial Arbitration*. The Hague: Kluwer law international.

Gaillard, E. (1995). Thirty years of lex mercatoria: Towards the selective application of transnational rules. *ICSID Review: Foreign Investment Law Journal*, 10(2), 208–231.

Gaillard, E. (2001). Transnational law: A legal system or a method of decision making? *Arbitration International*, 17(1), 59–72.

Gama, L. (2016). Usages and implied obligations under the UNIDROIT principles of international commercial contracts. *In*: Gélinas, F. (ed.) *Trade Usages and Implied Terms in the Age of Arbitration*. Oxford: Oxford University Press.

Gélinas, F. (2016). Trade usages as transnational law. *In*: Gélinas, F. (ed.) *Trade Usages and Implied Terms in the Age of Arbitration*. Oxford: Oxford University Press.

Glover, J., Hughes, S. & Thomas, C. (2006). *Understanding the FIDIC Red Book: A Clause by Clause Commentary*. London: Sweet & Maxwell.

Ismail, M. A. (2016). *Globalization and New International Public Works Agreements in Developing Countries: An Analytical Perspective*. Abingdon: Routledge.

Jaffe, M. & McHugh, R. (2009). International construction disputes in today's economy. Available at http://fidic.org/sites/default/files/2%20jaffe09.pdf [Accessed 25 December 2023].

Jolivet, E., Marchisio, G. & Gélinas, F. (2016). Trade usages in ICC arbitration. *In*: Gélinas, F. (ed.) *Trade Usages and Implied Terms in the Age of Arbitration*. Oxford: Oxford University Press.

Jørgensen, J. C. (2010). *Delay Clauses in International Construction Contracts*. Alphen aan den Rijn: Kluwer Law International.

Karton, J. (2010). *The Culture of International Arbitration and the Evolution of Contract Law*. Doctor of Philosophy, University of Cambridge.

Karton, J. (2012a). A conflict of interests: Seeking a way forward on publication of international arbitral awards. *Arbitration International*, 28(3), 447–486.

Karton, J. (2012b). International commercial arbitrators' approaches to contractual interpretation. *International Business Law Journal*, 383–404.

Karton, J. (2013). *The Culture of International Arbitration and the Evolution of Contract Law*. Oxford: Oxford University Press.

Karton, J. (2014). International arbitration culture and global governance. *In*: Mattli, W. & Dietz, T. (eds.) *International arbitration and global governance: contending theories and evidence*. Oxford: Oxford University Press.

Karton, J. (2015). The arbitral role in contractual interpretation. *Journal of International Dispute Settlement*, 6(1), 4–41.

Kaufmann-Kohler, G. (2007). Arbitral precedent: Dream, necessity or excuse?: The 2006 Freshfields lecture. *Arbitration International*, 23(3), 357–378.

Klee, L. (2015). *International Construction Contract Law*. Chichester: John Wiley & Sons.

Knutson, R. (2005). *FIDIC: An Analysis of International Construction Contracts*. 2nd ed. The Hague: Kluwer Law International.

Lando, O. (1985). The lex mercatoria in international commercial arbitration. *International and Comparative Law Quarterly*, 34, 747–768.

Landolt, P. (2012). Arbitrators' initiatives to obtain factual and legal evidence. *Arbitration International*, 28(2), 173–224.

Lowenfeld, A. (1990). Lex Mercatoria: An arbitrator's view. *Arbitration International*, 6(2), 133–150.

McConnaughay, P. J. (1999). The risks and virtues of lawlessness: A second look at international commercial arbitration. *Northwestern University Law Review*, 93(2), 453.

Molineaux, C. (1997). Moving toward a construction Lex Mecatoria. *Journal of International Arbitration*, 14(1), 55–66.

Moloo, R. & King, B. (2014). International arbitrators as lawmakers. *New York University Journal of International Law and Politics*, 46(3).

Moses, M. L. (2008). *The Principles and Practice of International Commercial Arbitration*. Cambridge: Cambridge University Press.

Moss, G. (2004). Introductory materials on international commercial law. *Transnational Dispute Management*, 1(3), 1–161.

Mustill, M. (1988). The New Lex Mercatoria: The first 25 years. *Arbitration International*, 4, 86.

Nazzini, R. (2018). *Transnational Construction Arbitration: Key Themes in the Resolution of Construction Disputes*. New York: Informa Law from Routledge.

Rosengren, J. (2013). Contract interpretation in international arbitration. *Journal of International Arbitration*, 30(1), 1–16.

Samuelsson, P. & Iwar, L. (2005). Sweden. *In*: Knutson, R. (ed.) *FIDIC: An Analysis of International Construction Contracts*. The Hague: Kluwer Law International.

Seppala, C. (2012). International Construction Contract Disputes: Third Commentary on ICC Awards Dealing Primarily with FIDIC Contracts. *ICC International Court of Arbitration Bulletin*, 23(2).

Seppala, C. R. (1998). International construction contract disputes: Commentary on ICC awards dealing with the FIDIC international conditions of contract. *ICC International Court of Arbitration Bulletin*, 9(2).

Seppala, C. (2013). International construction contract disputes: Fourth commentary on ICC awards dealing primarily with FIDIC contracts. *ICC International Court of Arbitration Bulletin*, 24(2).

Seppala, C. (1986). The pre-arbitral procedure for the settlement of disputes in the FIDIC (civil engineering) conditions of contract. *International Construction Law Review*, V4, 315–337.

Seppala, C. (2005). The Arbitration Clause in FIDIC Contracts for Major Works. *International Construction Law Review*, 22(1), 4–15.

Seppala, C. (2009). The development of a case law in construction disputes relating to FIDIC contracts. *International Construction Law Review*, 26(1), 105–116.

Stovall (2009). Arbitration and the Arab Middle East: Some thoughts from a commercial lawyer. The Chicago International Dispute Resolution Association Meeting on 22nd September 2009. Available at 2019-07-24_17_11_25_arbitration_in_the_arab_middle_east.pdf (stovall-law.com) [Accessed 15 December 2023].

UNIDROIT Principles (2016). Available at https://www.unidroit.org/wp-content/uploads/2021/06/Unidroit-Principles-2016-English-i.pdf [Accessed 10 October 2021].

Venoit, W. K. (2009). *International Construction Law: A Guide for Cross-border Transactions and Legal Disputes*. Chicago: American Bar Association Publishing.

Wallace, I. D. (1980). *The International Civil Engineering Contract: First Supplement: Comprising Commentary on the Third Edition of the Conditions of Contract (International) for Works of Civil Engineering Construction with Forms of Tender and Agreement*. Sweet & Maxwell.

Wallace, I. N. D. (1974). *The International Civil Engineering Contract: A Commentary on the F.I.D.I.C. International: Standard Form of Civil Engineering and Building Contract*. London: Sweet & Maxwell.

Weidemaier, W. M. C. (2009). Toward a theory of precedent in arbitration. *William and Mary Law Review*, 51, 1895.

Wilkinson, V. L. (1995). The New Lex Mercatoria: Reality or academic fantasy? *Journal of International Arbitration*, 12(2), 103–117.

CHAPTER 6

Fairness as a substantive norm

6.1 Introduction

While many arbitration scholars and practitioners believe that arbitration is better than litigation for a variety of procedural aspects, some commentators suggest that arbitration is superior for substantive reasons. They assert that arbitration provides better solutions to the parties' disputes by allowing arbitrators to deviate from legal norms and decide according to their sense of fairness. Aristotle is believed to have expressed his preference for arbitration over litigation because arbitration follows equity while litigation follows the law. The following quote, or similar wordings, are attributed to Aristotle (Kidane, 2017; Sucre, 2013; Blankenship, 2010):

> It is equity to ... prefer arbitration to court litigation, for the arbitrator sees what is equitable, but the judge only looks at the law, and for this an arbitrator was first appointed, in order that equity might prevail.

This chapter endeavours to determine to what extent international arbitrators take into account fairness considerations to reach their decisions on the merits of the parties' claims. This chapter does not intend to engage in fairness discourse and debate. What fairness is constitutes a far-reaching inquiry. There is an extensive theoretical scholarship on this subject (Naimark and Keer, 2002) but among the most remarkable are the works of John Rawls (Kläger, 2011), such as *A Theory of Justice* (Rawls, 1999) and *Justice as Fairness* (Rawls, 2001), and Franck's theory in fairness in international law (Franck, 1998). Nor does this chapter attempt to find a concrete meaning of the word 'fair'. Many scholars have tried and generally failed to do so (Ossman, 2003).

Then, this chapter examines how arbitrators decide under two concepts that have been traditionally associated with equity-based decisions in arbitration settings: *amiable composition* and *ex aequo et bono.*

6.2 Fairness as a normative standard in arbitral decision-making

Notwithstanding that they are inextricably intertwined, or interwoven, the starting point of this inquiry assumes that fairness is a distinct concept from legal justice (Sharma, 1999; Sadurski, 1985; Horwitz, 1974; Błaszczak and Kolber, 2013) or commercial justice (Akehurst, 1976; Trakman, 1980; Błaszczak and Kolber, 2013) because the sources of their substantive norms are different. Legal rules can be found in national law or transnational law, and they need to be pleaded and argued as a point of law. The commercial norms can be derived from customs and commercial practice, and they need to be proven as a point of fact (Gélinas, 2016a). Fairness, on the other hand, is subjective and depends on the normative standard of the decision-maker (Błaszczak and Kolber, 2013). It is an abstract

DOI: 10.4324/b22975-6

concept that is difficult to particularise, formulate in concrete terms, and be reduced into rules. Unlike legal rules that are formulated a priori and are generally known or should have been known by the parties, fairness rules are deduced from the specifics of each case. Accordingly, it may change from context to context, and it largely depends on the specific facts and circumstances (Goldman and Cropanzano, 2015; DiMatteo, 1995).

In this sense, it could be possible that a decision drawing on equity and fairness as perceived by an arbitrator to be different from outcomes that would have been achieved if the normative standards were legal rules (Sharma, 1999) or customary rules (Akehurst, 1976). Also, an inquiry into fairness involves a decision on whether a certain contract rule should be disregarded in order to achieve a fair and equitable result (DiMatteo, 1995).

The conversation concerning the association between arbitration and equity-based decisions is evident in arbitration scholarship and practice, but it is almost entirely related to arbitration in the United States. One of the early arbitration scholars in the United States, Soia Mentschikoff, argued that the basic job of arbitrators was to decide with fairness the merits of the parties' claims (Mentschikoff, 1961). Published more than 60 years ago, the results of her survey soliciting arbitrators' opinions on their adherence to the substantive law show that arbitrators perceived their role to require them to decide disputes in an equitable rather than strictly legal manner. The results show that 80% of the arbitrators surveyed thought that 'they ought to reach their decisions within the context of the principles of substantive rules of law', but almost 90% believed that 'they were free to ignore these rules whenever they thought that more just decisions would be reached by so doing'. This indicates the arbitrators' understanding that they ought to follow the substantive law, but they can depart from it in the interests of fairness (Mentschikoff, 1961).

This understanding is not inconsistent with the US courts' view as to how arbitrators should decide. The courts in the United States acknowledge that arbitrators are under no duty to apply the law, and they may decide according to their perception of fairness. One of the early examples of this view is the court judgement in *Park Construction Co. v. Independent School District [1943]* in which the court pronounced (Casetext, 2018):

> Arbitrators as a rule are unlearned in law. They are expected to decide the matters in dispute according to those principles of equity and good conscience which, in their opinion, will do justice between the parties, untrammeled by the niceties of the law.

A number of US courts made similar pronouncements that arbitrators do not have to follow the law, and they may base their judgements on broad principles of justice, fairness, and equity (Levin, 1997). More recently, in 2016, a New York appellate court stated in its judgement in *Fagan v. Village of Harriman*:

> An arbitrator is not bound by principles of substantive law or rules of evidence, and may do justice and apply his or her own sense of law and equity to the facts as he or she finds them to be.

It is notable that the courts, by and large, have not drawn distinctions between various contexts of arbitration (e.g., construction, commercial, labour and employment etc.) when it comes to the role of the substantive law in arbitration (Levin, 1997). The courts' pronouncements give the impression that arbitration, at least in the United States, is an equity-oriented dispute resolution system. Some authors also noted the association that is often made between US domestic arbitration and equitable or compromise-based decision-making (Carrington and Haagen, 1996; Dezalay and Garth, 1998; Drahozal, 2000). However, this remains an impressionistic and not an empirical account of what arbitrators actually do (Drahozal, 2006).

Consensus is wide amongst scholars and practitioners that international arbitrators may decide according to their perception of fairness only if the parties explicitly authorise them to do so (Park, 2010). However, the lack of explicit authorisation does not necessarily mean that arbitrators may not covertly undertake a fairness inquiry (Akehurst, 1976). In fact, there is empirical evidence that international arbitrators may follow their own sense of equity and fairness, even if the result is contrary to the governing law (Stipanowich and Ulrich, 2014).

In light of this uncertainty, to assess how far arbitrators may fall back on considerations of equity and fairness without being specifically instructed to do so, the author asked the arbitrators interviewed in the study underpinning this book the following question: 'Are you concerned to achieve a fair and just outcome even if it is not in line with the provisions of the contract and the law?'

For most interviewed arbitrators, fairness is not a concept that can be used to overrule the terms of the contract the parties agreed on or the provisions of the law the parties chose. They suggest that fairness is devoid of any substantial or concrete meaning, indeterminate and inherently subjective. They opine that the subjectivity or relativity of the concept of fairness is the reason why different national laws may have different views on what is fair. For this reason, the interviewed arbitrators assert that it is their duty to apply fairness principles as per the substantive law's view. For the same reason, they maintain that it is not their mission to rewrite the parties' contract according to their own notions of fairness. Rather, they consider that their job is to simply apply the contract and the law, with no further inquiry into a fair outcome.

For example, a Scottish arbitrator believed that interpreting contracts in accordance with fairness principles in order to reach a fair decision is wrong and falls outside the arbitral mandate:

> You are not there as an arbitrator to decide what is fair if the parties' contract is unfair ... what I think is fair might be different from what you think is fair and might be different from what somebody else thinks is fair... it is for the parties to the contract themselves to determine what is fair.

A Canadian arbitrator differentiated between fairness and justice. Fairness is inherently subjective and uncertain, whereas justice aspires for objectivity and establishes a benchmark against which a party's conduct is to be measured. From this perspective, she argued that her role as an arbitrator is to administer justice according to the law and not to decide in accordance with fairness:

> Fairness is a difficult concept of course ... my concept of fairness might not be as theirs ... quite often I would have a party saying it is not fair. I would reply it is not fair, it is not designed to be fair, but it is designed to be just, and justice means you get what you are entitled to under the law. So, are we in arbitration to be fair or to be just? Now there are some commercial people who say we want a fair decision, we do not care about the law. The question is which one do you use as a measuring stick, and for us the measuring stick is the law.

Having discounted any consideration of fairness in her arbitral decision-making approach, the Canadian arbitrator maintained that fairness, for her, is an overarching concept that can be used to check the predictability of the decision and to make sure that the decision meets the reasonable expectations of the parties, or at least one of the parties:

> For me, fairness is an overarching concept in terms of … does this produce a result which one might expect to get, which the parties could reasonably expect to happen, or is this going to give them a result which nobody really wanted and ever dreamed would happen … because for me predictability and fairness go hand in hand.

On the other hand, some arbitrators maintained that fairness is something that they are concerned about. It follows that they do not seek a sort of rigid application of the contract and the law. Rather, they seek an interpretation that is fair and just. So, even if there was a contractual clause that was clear but was dealt with unjustly (e.g., unpaid variation or time bar), then some arbitrators said they would be willing to go around the contract to bring justice. Nevertheless, in so doing, they apply general principles of law, such as good faith and abuse of right in civil law or unjust enrichment in common law. In this regard, there seems to be a recognition, particularly amongst civil law arbitrators, that the common law tradition is more restrictive than the civil law tradition.

For example, several arbitrators interviewed by the author stated that some standard forms of construction contracts stipulate that contract variations must be ordered in writing by the employer in order for the contractor to be entitled to payment for the additional works. Despite the clear wording, the arbitrators said that they would not strictly apply such a provision. If the contractor can prove that they have actually performed additional works and that this has been done as instructed by the employer, then they would decide in the contractor's favour (i.e. the contractor would be entitled to payment, even though the instruction for the variation order was not given in writing). This approach does not seem to be uncommon. Knutson (2004) states that in most construction arbitration cases related to unpaid extra works, tribunals do not find difficulty in applying notions of the duty of good faith or unjust enrichment in lieu of a detailed set of contractual pre-conditions to find that additional works need to be paid for. Although the arbitrators' main concern is fairness and justice in this case, they still ground their decisions in the law.

The use of grand principles, such as good faith, reveals a remarkable feature of the contract interpretation process in that it is malleable and flexible enough to accommodate the tribunal's sense of fairness to dictate the outcome. It can be a powerful tool in the hands of arbitrators to justify what they consider to be a fair and just result (Rosengren, 2013). However, the exact scope and function of the good faith principle are often debated, sometimes misunderstood, and vary from one jurisdiction to another. It remains an elusive concept in contract law for some scholars (Rosengren, 2013) or is even inconsistent with a well-established view on the nature of the contract, which will ultimately bring an undesirable level of uncertainty (DiMatteo, 2013). In any case, Karton (2013) asserts that good faith should not be misused and interpreted broadly to allow arbitrators to substitute applicable legal norms with their own notions of fairness. Similarly, Rosengren (2013) asserts that the concept of good faith in contract law should not be understood as an overriding norm of fairness in commercial contracts. It is not a principle that arbitrators can use to impose their views of fairness on the parties without consideration of other legal rules and doctrines under substantive law.

The duty of good faith in contractual relationships is a fundamental principle of contract interpretation in civil law jurisdictions. Most common law legal systems do not recognise such an obligation. They have different tools relevant to contract interpretation, such as implied terms to assist in achieving a fair and just result. Although it can be argued that all legal systems seek fair outcomes, and considerations of fairness and reasonableness underlie their legal rules, they follow different reasoning approaches. For example, English law does not consider it appropriate to follow a top-down approach and start the reasoning process from broad principles of fairness. Instead, English law follows a bottom-up piecemeal approach to address problems of unfairness (Rosengren, 2013).

An Egyptian arbitrator interviewed by the author criticised arbitrators who claim that they are not concerned about fairness and only concerned about 'the law, only the law and nothing but the law'. He described them as hypocrites who perform a sort of legal acrobatics to reach a conclusion that they already had in mind. He also described them as the 'priests of Amun' who convinced ordinary people in ancient Egypt that they had exclusive access to God. The hypocritical arbitrators pretend as if they were the only people who knew how to apply the law. He said that the law, by its nature, is normally broad enough to deliver fairness.

The Egyptian arbitrator said that he is keen to make fair decisions. In his description of how the standard of fairness comes into play in his arbitral decision-making, he stated two interesting points.

First, he affirmed that acting as an arbitrator requires disengagement from the philosophical debate as to the concept of fairness because such philosophical questions, by definition, persist and have no solution. He argued that an arbitrator must take a stand and apply fairness in accordance with his own point of view. Below is a quote from his statement:

> Fairness can differ… You have to make a point of view. If you just want to say philosophically what is fair for this guy is unfair for the other guy, and vice versa, then you should not act as an arbitrator, because then you will not be able to make any judgment in life. But if you are going to make a judgment, you have to decide what fairness is in your view.

Second, he revealed a mysterious aspect of the 'thinking process in arbitral decision-making'. Little is known whether arbitrators use a deductive-rational approach to make legal conclusions or they follow an intuitive process (Madden and Spiecker, 2016; Sussman, 2013) whereby arbitrators make initial judgements in accordance with what they believe is fair and then justify their decisions with legal principles. In this regard, he said:

> Once you have decided what is fair… then you can start finding the legal mechanism to apply this fairly. So, first you look for fairness, and then you look for the legal solution.

This reasoning method, reasoning backwards from a fair result, is not something unheard of. Similar accounts of international arbitrators following this approach were presented by Karton (2015). For instance, a Swiss arbitrator pronounced that he often forms an opinion as to who was right and who was wrong, makes a decision that is fair and just, and then drafts an award that fits the legal rules of the governing law. He bluntly stated that 'lawyers are good at reasoning almost any outcome according to the law' (Karton, 2015). In fact, there is a line of scholarship in the socio-legal field that is dedicated to examining the reasoning process in judicial decision-making. There are two main theories in this field.

The 'formalist' model proposes that judges make their decisions in a logical and deliberative approach, whereas the 'realist' model proposes that judges reach their decisions in an intuitive way and then rationalise and justify their judgements on the basis of the law (Guthrie, Rachlinski, and Wistrich, 2007). On this basis, the realist model makes a subtle distinction between 'reasons' and 'reasoning'.

Nonetheless, the arbitrators who candidly told the author that they take the fairness of the dispute outcome into consideration in their decision-making admitted that sometimes there were constraints on doing so. They recognise that, on certain occasions, arbitrators are confronted with the tension between the decision they would like to reach and the one the law or the contract tells them they should reach. After all, making a sound judgement needs objectivity. Hence, what they feel or what they might like the answer to be is not necessarily relevant.

For example, the Egyptian arbitrator quoted earlier said:

> Fairness is a very important thing of what we do ... it is the overarching object, but it does not always prevail ... there will always be occasions when someone feels that the result he is impelled to is not necessarily the one that he would wish to reach. Sometimes, the contract is very tight and there are no legal solutions in place. You know, you cannot go here, you cannot go there. Then, you feel bad, and have no choice but to apply the agreement of the parties, but if you can find a way around that unjust agreement, you will as an arbitrator. People do that sometimes.

Similarly, a Canadian arbitrator said:

> Sometimes as an arbitrator you have to make a decision that does not accord with what you think is right because that is what the law is ... you will, if you possibly can, reach a construction which you think does fairness. But occasionally, you have to reach a decision which you regret ... I think that does happen ... sometimes you try ... and you come to a result which may not be fair...You never like reaching a judgement which you think is not fair...but as arbitrators, we are bound by the law that there will be times when we cannot deliver fairness.

An American arbitrator expressed a similar sentiment. He stated that a good arbitrator is one who can find justice within the boundaries of the contract and the law. This is because a fair result does go back to the contract. He maintained that arbitrators cannot ignore the contract, at least in an explicit way, even in civil law countries. What arbitrators tend to do is talk about the obligation of good faith and fair dealings to come up with a result that they think conforms to fairness. The following is an excerpt from his interview:

> Civil law judges frequently look at what they regard as fair and just under the duty of good faith and fair dealings ... similarly, in civil law countries, the approach is that arbitrators do justice. In my view, good arbitrators find justice in the contract and in the implied and express obligations.

Based on these arbitrators' accounts, it is safe to conclude that even those arbitrators whose main concern is to achieve a fair and just result will not do so at the expense of the law. This has to be within the confines of the law. At the end of the day, they recognise that their decision needs to be grounded in, reasoned, and justified by law.

In the same vein, Karton (2015) argues that the arbitrators' mission is to deliver justice within the perimeters of the law. Acting otherwise, by detaching fairness from legal norms, would entail a misconception of arbitration (Karton, 2015).

A reliance on fairness to arbitrate disputes is problematic for several reasons that are explained in the following paragraphs.

On a conceptual level, there is hardly an objective content of fairness. It is an inherently subjective notion. It is indeterminate and normatively empty. It provides no normative criteria that allow arbitrators to move from the 'is' to the 'ought'. That is why it is metaphorically said that fairness is like a chameleon: changing colour depending on the background (Park, 2010; Ossman, 2003).

The subjectivity inherent in ad hoc fairness is inconsistent with the contracting parties' interest in the predictability of the dispute outcome and stability of economic relations (Park, 2010). Both a contractor and an employer work hard, negotiate an allocation of risks in their construction contract, agree on the contract terms and governing law, make calculations accordingly, and agree on a price, and thereby arbitrators must respect that. To decide according to fairness *ex-post* leaves the contracting parties with little information on how to price their contracts *ex-ante* (Park, 2010). It is next to impossible to appraise a prospective arbitrator's sense of fairness in advance.

This situation, i.e., deciding according to *ex-post* fairness, is akin to having two sporting teams participating in a game the rules of which are unknown *ex-ante* and the referee will make up the rules of winning the game at the end. As is often said: 'a game without rules is no game at all'. The expectations and satisfaction of the teams are met only when they play within the confines of a set of well-defined rules (Gluck, 2012).

The matter is no different in arbitration. The losing party needs to know why it lost. For that reason, some arbitrators, who were interviewed by the author, stated that they are keen to explain, in the reason section of their awards, to the losing party why they lost. The following quote, from a common law arbitrator, is illustrative of the importance of explaining the decision's reasons:

> An arbitrator has to decide on two issues: who is the winner (in case of several issues, they need to decide on each one), and why he decided so... always distinguish between the two stages ... in the latter stage, an arbitrator should always write the reasons for the loser, the winner will always skip to the last page and will not care what the arbitrator has written ... the arbitrator should always write his decision for the unsuccessful party and make sure that if he was in its shoes, he would be satisfied.

After reading the award, the losing party should be in a position to acknowledge that they should have known and could have known the rules that are applicable to the dispute. The reasons should be within the contemplation of the parties. Otherwise, it will be frustrating to the losing party to be left without explanation based on rules that are objectively ascertainable by themselves.

In this regard, Fuller (1969) outlined in his renowned work *The Morality of Law* eight criteria that a legal or justice system must meet to be moral (Gluck, 2012). The legal system fails to be moral in case one or more criteria are not met. Two of these failures are:

1. A failure to set out rules so that each dispute is to be resolved on an ad hoc basis;
2. A failure to make available for the parties the rules they are expected to observe.

Fuller (1969) asserted that a failure to meet any criterion results in a defective legal system (Gluck, 2012). The same seems to hold true for international arbitration as a global justice system.

In addition to the morality element, a dispute resolution system that denies any measure of certainty and predictability is detrimental to capitalism, which underpins international construction business (Linder, 1994). To achieve the peak of capitalism, Max Weber emphasised that it is necessary to have a rational and legalistic system of law with restrictions and constraints on decision-makers (Trubek, 1972). When decision-makers are confined to a more or less closed system of rules for the source of their 'reasons' and they are required to give reasons for their decisions, then predictability may be achieved (Friedman, 1966 cited in Bonn, 1972).

Further, some scholars and interviewed arbitrators explained that the legal and arbitral procedure requiring a claimant to establish the cause of action (i.e., a breach of a duty or an obligation) makes it difficult to make or justify decisions on the basis of fairness. In this regard, Kläger (2011) asserts that allowing fairness to be an acceptable cause of action would invite the submission of an almost infinite range of claims related to perceived unfairness. In the same vein, an Australian arbitrator interviewed by the author ruled out fairness as a weighty norm that entitles the parties to rights or makes their claims meritorious. The following is an excerpt from her interview:

> You still have to show a source of that obligation and a source of that right. So, your right to claim it against me creates an obligation for me to pay it, but you have to show me where it comes from. It is not just because it is not fair… I do not think you can just make a decision on fairness because where is the fairness in making someone to pay when there is actually no obligation to pay.

According to her, fairness and unfairness appear as opposite sides of the same coin. The party for which a contractual provision or legal rule creates a loss will welcome a softening of that rule. The other party will, of course, insists on the application of a contractual provision or legal rule that gives them a commercial advantage.

6.3 *Amiable composition* and *ex aequo et bono*: In theory

Two concepts that are closely related to arbitral decisions based on equity and fairness and widely discussed in arbitration scholarship are *amiable composition* and *ex aequo et bono*. However, Błaszczak and Kolber (2013) argue that decision-making based on principles of fairness and equity differs from *amiable composition* and *ex aequo et bono*. They maintain that fairness or equity is fully subjective, while decisions based on *amiable composition* and *ex aequo et bono* have some connection with objective criteria as set out in the parties' contract and the substantive law. This section provides a brief review of these two notions.

It is widely accepted in the international arbitration community that it is only permissible for arbitrators to decide according to their perceptions of fairness if the parties explicitly authorise them (Park, 2010). In practice, this might be in the form of a requirement in the arbitration clause or the arbitration rules the parties agreed on to decide in accordance with *amiable composition* or *ex aequo et bono*. For example, the 1998 ICC Rules provide in Article 17(3) that '[t]he Arbitral Tribunal shall assume the powers of an *amiable compositeur* or decide *ex aequo et bono* only if the parties have agreed to give it such powers'. Similarly, the 1985 UNCITRAL Model Law on International Commercial Arbitration amended in 2006 ('Model Law') provides, in Article 28, that [t]he arbitral tribunal shall decide *ex aequo et bono* or as *amiable compositeur* only if the parties have expressly authorized it to do so'.

The authorisation to decide *ex aequo et bono* or as *amiable compositeur* is rare in practice (Karton, 2013; Mistelis and Martin, 2010). Parties to international arbitration authorise tribunals to decide *ex aequo et bono* in only 2%–3% of arbitration cases each year (Born, 2014), and this seems to be in decline (Karton, 2013). The unpopularity of this type of arbitration is probably because of concern amongst parties in international arbitration and their counsel that empowering arbitrators to decide *ex aequo et bono* will lead to unpredictable results and abuse of discretion by arbitrators (Teramura, 2020). The parties' expectations, as discussed in Section 3.7.5, appear to be an arbitral decision based on law and not on indeterminate notions of fairness.

Another evidence of the scepticism towards arbitration decisions based on *amiable composition* or *ex aequo et bono* is found in the *UNCITRAL Legal Guide on Drawing Up International Contracts for the Construction of Industrial Works* published in 1987. The following is an excerpt from this legal guide that shows UNCITRAL's warning to contracting parties about the risks of authorising arbitrators to determine their disputes based on *amiable composition* or *ex aequo et bono*:

> It is advisable for the parties to be cautious about authorizing the arbitral tribunal to decide disputes ex aequo et bono or to act as amiable compositeur ... such authorizations may be interpreted in different ways and lead to legal insecurity. For example, the terms might be interpreted as authorizing the arbitrators to be guided either only by principles of fairness, justice or equity, or, in addition, by those provisions of the law applicable to the contract regarded in the legal system of that law as fundamental. An additional source of uncertainty may be whether the arbitrators, applying the principles mentioned above, may disregard certain terms of the contract.

Teramura (2020) argues that the criticisms of *ex aequo et bono* decisions based on uncertainty and unpredictability of arbitrators' decisions and the abuse of discretion by arbitrators are exaggerated. This is because the Model Law, in Article 28(4), constrains the powers of arbitrators authorised to act *ex aequo et bono* by requiring them to 'decide in accordance with the terms of the contract" and "take into account the usages of the trade' in all cases. In addition, arbitrators deciding *ex aequo et bono* may depart from the substantive law and revert to their subjective perspective of fairness and good conscience only when they find that the law is 'inadequate to deal with the dispute'. The arbitrators' sense of fairness and equity remains a final gap-filler for determining the parties' intentions in exceptional situations. The same applies to court litigation. Over centuries, judges have had recourse to equity principles to fill gaps in the law. Further, the concern that arbitrators may not follow the law is not limited to *ex aequo et bono* arbitration but also to arbitration at law. This is because, in the context of international commercial arbitration, arbitrators' application of the law is virtually immune from judicial review (Teramura, 2020).

To better understand the argument for and against the application of *amiable composition* and *ex aequo et bono*, it is important to first define the two concepts. Historically, the concept of *ex aequo et bono* originated in Roman law, whereas the concept *amiable compositeur* originated in the French Napoleonic Code (Ayoğlu, 2012). Substantively, there is some confusion and incoherence in the use of these concepts in arbitration theory and practice.

According to Park (2010) and Weinberg (1994), many authors use the two concepts interchangeably even though they are not precisely the same. Others distinguish between them based on what deciding according to them entails (with respect to the tribunal's adherence to the contract terms, law provisions, mandatory rules of the governing law, and application of transnational rules or general principles of law) (Gaillard and Savage, 1999) as follows.

Arbitrators deciding *ex aequo et bono* start and finish their reasoning based on a personal sense of fairness and a private view of what is right in the circumstance. They can decide based on what they think is fair and reasonable without being concerned with what the law says (Park, 2010; Weinberg, 1994). On the other hand, arbitrators deciding as *amiables compositeurs* have more restrictions on their decision-making power. They are required to start their reasoning with the rules of law with the permission to moderate or temper the strict application of the contract terms or law only if the results of such an application would be harsh and unfair from the arbitrator's point of view (Weinberg, 1994; Park, 2009; Park, 2010; Błaszczak and Kolber, 2013; Natanson, 2013; Gaillard and Savage, 1999). Of course, arbitrators can reach an equitable result by applying the governing law. In such a case, there is no need to depart from the law and search for a fair and equitable solution outside what the law provides.

Another distinction is that *ex aequo et bono* allows an arbitrator to deviate from the mandatory rules of the governing law, whereas *amiable composition* does not (Weinberg, 1994; Gaillard and Savage, 1999). However, this does not extend to mandatory legal rules of a public nature. Arbitrators are keen to not disregard mandatory rules of national or international public policy because this exposes the award to the risk of setting aside or non-enforcement (see Chapter 7). An award rendered *ex aequo et bono* is subject to the same enforcement regime as an award rendered at law. The criteria that govern the award validity and enforceability are independent of the substantive norms arbitrators apply to decide the parties' dispute (Moss, 2004).

Despite these theoretical attempts to distinguish between *ex aequo et bono* and *amiable composition*, the difference between these two concepts in practice is not clear. The drafters of the UNCITRAL Model Law acknowledged the difficulty of defining in a practical manner the tribunal's mandate to decide *ex aequo et bono* or as *amiable compositeur* (UNCITRAL Working Group on International Contract Practices, 1982).

Some scholars (e.g., Park, 2010) consider the difference between the two concepts to be significant. As there is nothing inherently unfair in the law, arbitrators will have no or little reasons to depart from the law when deciding as *amiables compositeurs* (Park, 2010). Hence, a decision based on *amiable composition* is expected to be derived from the applicable legal rules, whereas a decision based on *ex aequo et bono* is expected to be derived from the arbitrator's view of fairness.

On the other hand, Gaillard and Savage (1999) believe that the distinction between *ex aequo et bono* and *amiable composition* is artificial because arbitrators could make their perceptions of fairness override the law under both systems. This can be facilitated by relying on legal principles, such as good faith, when deciding as *amiable compositeur,* or even when they lack such authorisation by the parties and are required to decide according to the applicable legal rules. This view also finds support in arbitration practice. In ICC Case No. 7986/1999 and ICC Case No. 10728/2001, the arbitral tribunals cast doubt on the distinction between *ex aequo et bono* and *amiable composition* (Teramura, 2020).

Similarly, Teramura (2020) maintains that the distinction between the two concepts is impractical because arbitrators with the power of deciding *ex aequo et bono* can still find a fair solution inside the law. This concurs with Trakman's (2008) view on the distinction between finding fairness inside the law (equitable decisions) or outside the law (*ex aequo et bono* decisions), which is illustrated in the following excerpt:

> The demarcation between equitable discretion in law and discretion unrestrained by law is often difficult to draw ... Those who insist on a strict division between equity within the law and fairness outside the law achieve structural symmetry at the expense of the substantive ends which both conceptions of equity under law and fairness outside law share. Those shared ends include arriving at fair results suited to each case. If ex aequo et bono decisions are directed at redressing injustice, then surely they should embody comparable ends to those sought through the law of equity.

It is worth mentioning that Trakman's (2008) comparison is focused on 'gap-filling' under the law of equity (i.e., those situations where the law is not clear or settled) and decisions *ex aequo et bono* that aim to arrive at a fair result to the parties' specific dispute. He argues that there is no strict divide between the two, and, as a practical matter, the dividing line between discretion in accordance with the law or outside the law is hard to draw.

However, if it is possible to agree, as many arbitrators do, that there is nothing inherently unfair in the law and that legal systems have different tools to assist judges or arbitrators to reach fair results, then it is worth investigating the scope and nature of the fairness inquiry under *ex aequo et bono* or *amiable composition.* This would provide us with a better understanding of how the scope and nature of fairness inquiry under these notions are different from principles of fairness as embedded in the law. It could be argued that while legal rules seek generalisation, consistency, and predictability, fairness considerations require attention to the specifics of each case and allow exceptions to the general rules.

One potential effect could be relaxing some legal precedents or rules that would lead to unfair results. For instance, deciding *ex aequo et bono* or as *amiable compositeur* in a dispute governed by a common law system that has a preference towards a literal interpretation might permit arbitrators to relax these rules and move closer to the civil law approach that requires contextual inquiry into the parties' intention. Whereas a literal and objective approach seeks to achieve predictability of dispute outcomes and efficiency in dispute resolution and case management, a contextual approach is probably more likely to achieve a fair result. This is because it requires a full understanding of the parties' relationship, including their prior business dealings, prior communications and negotiations, conduct, and so on.

The background of an arbitrator is another aspect that is worth considering when comparing decisions based on the law and decisions based on equity and fairness. The influence of arbitrators' backgrounds on their decisions is probably greater when they are deciding *ex aequo et bono* or as *amiable compositeur.* This is because they have less legal constraints on their decisions. Several arbitrators interviewed by the author said that they would do their best to reach a fair result as much as they are allowed to under the governing law. This indicates their belief that at least sometimes legal answers to the parties' disputes may not be fair. Once they are liberated from these legal constraints and given the discretion to decide *ex aequo et bono* or as *amiable compositeur*, they can reach different conclusions.

The next section provides examples, from arbitration practice, of how international construction arbitrators make their decisions when empowered to decide according to *amiable composition* or *ex aequo et bono.*

6.4 *Amiable composition* and *ex aequo et bono*: In practice

This section reviews two construction arbitration awards that were based on *amiable composition.* These are the only relevant construction arbitration cases that were published and accessible by the author at the time of writing the book. This is not surprising given the lack of published international construction arbitration awards and the parties' disinclination to empower arbitrators to decide based on *amiable composition* or *ex aequo et bono.*

The two arbitral awards demonstrate that acting as *amiable compositeur* does not entitle the tribunal to discard the contract or ignore mandatory provisions of the law. An arbitral tribunal acting in this capacity has an obligation to apply the contract and the law, especially mandatory law.

The two arbitral awards also provide some insight into the choice of law questions under *amiable composition.* The principle of party autonomy in international arbitration allows the parties to decide how they want their disputes to be resolved. This includes the choice of the substantive law and whether to empower arbitrators to decide as *amiables compositeurs* or not. It is not uncommon for the parties to combine an *amiable composition* clause with a clause selecting the applicable legal rules (whether these rules are national or translational). Arbitrators deciding as *amiables compositeurs* still need to apply the legal rules selected by the parties. Arbitrators start their reasoning from the applicable legal rules and they may depart from them in case they think their application would lead to an inequitable result (Gaillard and Savage, 1999). When the parties do not agree on the legal rules that should govern the interpretation of their contract, arbitrators must select the applicable legal rules.

There are two approaches that can be used by international arbitrators to determine the law that should be applied to the parties' dispute in case the parties failed to include a choice of law clause in their contract or arbitration agreement. The arbitral tribunal may apply either 'the law which it determines to be appropriate' or 'the law determined by the conflict of laws rules which it considers applicable'. International arbitrators acting as *amiables compositeurs* tend to follow the former approach and apply general principles of commercial contract law, even though they may ultimately depart from those principles (Gaillard and Savage, 1999; Karton, 2013). The two arbitral awards discussed in the next subsections support this assertion.

6.4.1 Role of Amiable Compositeur: ICC Case No. 3267/1984[1]

ICC Case No. 3267/1984 concerns a dispute that arose from a construction contract to deliver a large building in two Saudi Arabian cities. The contract between a Saudi Arabian government entity and a Belgian consortium was entered into in 1976. One of the

1 Note: This award was reported in two different volumes of the *Yearbook Commercial Arbitration.* The partial award was reported in 1982 and the final award was reported in 1987.

consortium members was the defendant. The defendant subcontracted part of the project to the claimant (a Mexican construction company).

The parties granted the tribunal the power to decide as *amiable compositeur*, but they had not agreed on which law was applicable to the contract. The tribunal had to first consider which law should be applied because arbitrators acting as *amiables compositeurs* should start their reasoning from the contract and legal provisions. In this regard, the tribunal noted 'at the outset, the contract has to be analysed from a purely legal standpoint'. In this regard, the claimant asserted that the legal issues raised in the arbitration proceedings may be resolved with reference to general principles of commercial law and that the determination of a specific legal system was not necessary. The defendant neither agreed nor disagreed.

The tribunal stated that when arbitrators are authorised to act as *amiables compositeurs*, they do not need to decide which specific law governs the contractual relationship between the parties. On this basis, the tribunal decided to determine the issues under generally accepted legal principles governing international commercial relations, without specific reference to a particular system of law. This reference to generally accepted or widely accepted principles of international commercial law is tantamount to a reference to *lex mercatoria.*

In this arbitration case, the defendant argued that irrespective of the legal rules governing the contract, arbitrators acting as *amiables compositeurs* are entitled to modify or disregard the provisions of the contract and to depart from *lex mercatoria* when their application constitutes an abuse of right or would lead to results contrary to natural justice or to the principles of fairness.

This contention raises the question of the nature and extent of the power of arbitrators acting as *amiables compositeurs.* The tribunal's view was that when empowered to act as *amiables compositeurs*, ICC arbitrators have a duty to apply the provisions of a contract, but they may disregard a party's legal or contractual rights in limited situations. The tribunal expressed their view on the nature of *amiable compositeur* role as follows:

> Although some legal writers have expressed the opinion that arbitrators sitting as 'amiables compositeurs' may disregard the provisions of the agreement between the parties, this view has not been accepted in international arbitration. On the contrary, it is a generally accepted principle in international arbitration that the paramount duty of the arbitrator, even as 'amiable compositeur', is to apply the contract of the parties, unless it is shown that the provisions relied on are clearly against the true intent of the parties, or violate a basic commonly accepted principle of public policy.

The tribunal emphasised the importance of enforcing the parties' contract as this is a basic requirement for the security of international trade and also a requirement under ICC Arbitration Rules. They noted that Art. 13 (5) of ICC Arbitration Rules imposes a duty on ICC arbitrators to apply the provisions of the contract in any case, even if they have the powers of *amiables compositeurs.* However, the tribunal added a further exception to this rule as follows:

> In addition to the power to decide on the dispute before him on the basis of generally accepted legal principles ... the arbitrator sitting as 'amiable compositeur' is entitled to disregard legal or contractual rights of a party when the insistence on such right amounts to an abuse thereof. This authority is of a particular importance in legal systems that have not developed an extensive theory of 'abuse of right', such as Swiss law under Art. 2 of its Civil Code.

This position is in line with the majority scholarly opinion in international arbitration. According to Gaillard and Savage (1999), the majority of arbitration scholars accept that, without going too far, arbitrators acting as *amiables compositeurs* can modify the contract to avoid or minimise harsh or onerous results.

However, there is a more restrictive opinion that does not permit arbitrators acting as *amiables compositeurs* to modify contract provisions and only allows them to depart from rules in the substantive law if necessary. This opinion was expressed in ICC Case No. 3938/1982 as follows (Gaillard and Savage, 1999):

> The view most widely accepted by authors and international arbitral practice is that an arbitrator acting as amiable compositeur remains bound by the contract ... the considerations which may lead the arbitrator to correct distortions which may result from a strict application of the provisions of the law to the particular circumstances of the case are not valid with regard to the contract, which is a special set of rules resulting from the parties' own intentions.

The suggestion that applying the contract can be separated from applying the law is problematic for the following reasons.

First, the application of the contract requires interpreting its meaning. The contract interpretation exercise draws on guidance provided by the law. Contracts cannot be interpreted in a legal vacuum. The governing law of the contract governs its validity and meaning.

Second, arbitrators can still disapply contract provisions even when they are following the law. For example, some legal principles, such as the doctrine of change in circumstances or the doctrine of good faith, that can be found in some civil law countries, permit arbitrators to adjust or amend the contract conditions in specific exceptional situations (Gaillard and Savage, 1999). So, arbitrators applying the law may not give effect to certain contractual rights in case their application may lead to an unfair result in the arbitrators' opinion. Hence, stating that arbitrators can never depart from the contract is incorrect, whether they are acting as *amiables compositeurs* or not.

Third, the power of arbitrators acting as *amiables compositeurs* to depart from legal rules of contract interpretation, including mandatory rules, means that they can, on the same basis, depart from the rule that contracts are binding in case they consider this would lead to an inequitable result. The outcome of departing from such a legal rule is freeing the tribunal from adhering to the contract (i.e., an opposite result to the opinion that arbitrators acting as *amiables compositeurs* can depart from the law but not from the contract).

Having said that, the distinction between departing from the law and departing from the contract is still useful. The distinction is more related to the nature of arbitration than the nature of *amiable composition* or *ex aequo et bono* decision. The parties usually pay more attention to drafting and negotiating their contract than analysing the law and its effect on the terms they agree on. The parties may not be familiar with the law they selected to govern their contractual relationship. It follows that a strict legal analysis may lead to a result that does not reflect the parties' common intentions. Hence, arbitrators may naturally feel more free to disregard a legal rule that the parties may have not considered or paid little attention to than a contractual provision the parties negotiated and agreed on. Further, arbitrators are the parries' private judges. They have a duty towards the parties to resolve their dispute according to the rules the parties agreed on. Unlike judges, arbitrators do not have a duty towards the state whose law governs the parties' contract to strictly and consistently apply the law. Also, unlike judges, arbitrators do not have to consider the effect of their decision on the wider commercial community, but only on the individual parties' expectations.

Therefore, the idea that arbitrators acting as *amiables compositeurs* should be more attentive to the parties' contract than the governing law seems sensible.

As illustrated in ICC Case No. 3267/1984, as a matter of principle, the arbitral tribunal did not reject the view that an arbitrator acting as *amiable compositeur* may go beyond certain legal solutions derived from the applicable legal rules (whether it is a national law or *lex mercatoria*) and the parties' contract. The question, however, is how far an *amiable compositeur* can go, especially when faced with specific provisions of a contract. This question is probably difficult to answer in the abstract. The lack of certainty and predictability in relation to how far an *amiable compositeur* can go is probably the reason for the parties' disquiet about empowering arbitrators to resolve their disputes in that capacity.

In this arbitration case, ICC Case No. 3267/1984, the arbitral tribunal confirmed in the arbitration award that they did not depart from the terms of the contract. In their view, applying different legal rules or systems of law would not have made a difference to the outcome of the dispute. The tribunal affirmed their satisfaction that their strict adherence to the contract and to the applicable legal rules (widely accepted general principles governing international commercial law) was totally consistent with the principles of fairness.

6.4.2 Role of Amiable Compositeur: ICC Case No. 3540/1980

ICC Case No. 3540/1980, published in the Yearbook Commercial Arbitration in 1982, concerns a dispute that arose from a subcontract between a French company (claimant) and a Yugoslav subcontractor (respondent) to perform construction works in the Soviet Union. The main contract in the project was concluded between the French company and a Soviet client.

The subcontract included an arbitration clause providing for ICC arbitration in Geneva, and empowering arbitrators to decide as *amiables compositeurs*. As the subcontract contained no choice of law clause, the tribunal had to identify the legal system they intended to use to guide their decisions. The parties disagreed on the substantive law that should govern their contract. The claimant demanded the application of Swiss law while the respondent argued for applying French law.

The tribunal stated that international arbitrators facing this question do not have to follow the choice of law process and they can instead follow a 'direct approach' of choosing specific substantive law without applying any choice of law rules. The tribunal decided to apply *lex mercatoria*.

Sitting as *amiable compositeur*, the tribunal noted that they do not need to apply the law. However, they stated that they cannot discard the mandatory provisions of the law. The following is an excerpt from the award that shows the tribunal's understanding of the nature of the role of the *amiable compositeur* especially when there is no choice of law in the parties' contract:

> Considering that, having the power of amiables compositeurs, the arbitrators should look even closer at the circumstances of each specific case, and accompany their partial decision with

> measures to safeguard the legitimate rights of each party, since 'they have been given the opportunity to put the principles of equity above the strictness of law, deciding in accordance with their conscience … the amiable compositeur is thus authorized to set aside the application of the law within the limits set by the mandatory provisions of the applicable legal system.
>
> That, however, the arbitral tribunal, holding it appropriate not to avoid all references to a national law, will examine whether the solution contained in its award based on the lex mercatoria and the application of the maxim pacta sunt servanda – leaving aside the international public policy – would be fundamentally different from that resulting from national law … or, rather, from the two national laws invoked by the parties: Swiss law by Claimant and French law by Defendant.

6.4 Conclusion

There is an idea that an arbitrator does not necessarily have to follow the law to give legal solutions to the parties' dispute but to follow their conscious to reach a fair result. This may have been true in the old times as evidenced by Aristotle's quote at the beginning of this chapter. Today, arbitration is different. In international construction arbitration, the parties expect arbitrators to apply the law. Fairness does not seem to be an acceptable norm in international construction arbitration. The parties are keen to have their disputes determined under certain, ascertainable, and predictable norms. That is why they generally tend to select a specific national law or body of legal rules and require arbitrators to decide in accordance with their contract and the governing law.

However, this does not necessarily mean that arbitrators turn a blind eye to fair and equitable considerations. Some of them still strive to achieve a result that is fair and equitable, but they will do so within the limits of the contract and the law. Different legal systems provide arbitrators with different tools to reach fair results.

In international arbitration practice, the closest we have got to fairness-based arbitral decision-making is when the parties authorise the tribunal to decide *ex eque et bono* or as *amiable compositeur.* Arbitration scholars and practitioners reached no consensus on the specifics of these concepts. This is driven by the difficulty of drawing a dividing line between fairness at law and fairness outside the law. Nevertheless, there is a general acceptance that arbitrators must always endeavour to respect and enforce what the parties agreed on in their contract and that arbitrators can, if needed, depart from legal rules in limited circumstances.

6.5 References

Akehurst, M. (1976). Equity and general principles of law. *The International and Comparative Law Quarterly*, 25(4), 801–825.

Ayoğlu, T. (2012). Application of trade usages in international institutional arbitration: Some reflections. *ASA Bulletin*, 30(3), 539–547.

Blankenship, J. T. (2010). Isomorphism of construction arbitration: The key to its prevention and reversal. *Dispute Resolution Journal*, 65(2), 114–123.

Błaszczak, Ł. & Kolber, J. (2013). General principles of law and equity as a basis for decision-making in arbitration. *Comparative Law Review*, 15, 189–208.

Bonn, R. L. (1972). The predictability of nonlegalistic adjudication. *Law & Society Review*, 6(4), 563–578.

Born, G. (2014). *International Commercial Arbitration.* 2nd ed. The Hague: Kluwer Law International.

Carrington, P. D. & Haagen, P. H. (1996). Contract and jurisdiction. *The Supreme Court Review*, 1996, 331–402. https://www.journals.uchicago.edu/toc/scr/1996/1996.

Casetext. (2018). *Fagan v. Vill. of Harriman [2016]* [Online]. Available at https://casetext.com/case/fagan-v-vill-of-harriman [Accessed 03 January 2023].

Dezalay, Y. & Garth, B. G. (1998). *Dealing in Virtue: International Commercial Arbitration and the Construction of a Transnational Legal Order.* Chicago: University of Chicago Press.

DiMatteo, L. A. (1995). The norms of contract: The fairness inquiry and the law of satisfaction: A nonunified theory. *Hofstra Law Review*, 24, 349–454.

DiMatteo, L. A. (2013). Soft law and the principle of fair and equitable decision making in international contract arbitration. *The Chinese Journal of Comparative Law*, 1(2), 221–255.

Drahozal, C. R. (2000). Commercial norms, commercial codes, and international commercial arbitration. *Vanderbilt Journal of Transnational Law*, 33, 79–146.

Drahozal, C. R. (2006). Is arbitration lawless. *Loyola of Los Angeles Law Review*, 40(1), 187–215.

Franck, T. M. (1998). *Fairness in International Law and Institutions.* Wotton-under-Edge: Clarendon Press.

Friedman, L. M. (1966). On legalistic reasoning: A footnote to weber. *Wisconsin Law Review*, 148.

Fuller, L. L. (1969). *The Morality of Law.* New Haven: Yale University Press.

Gaillard, E. & Savage, J. (1999). *Fouchard, Gaillard, Goldman on International Commercial Arbitration.* The Hague: Kluwer law international.

Gélinas, F. (2016). *Trade Usages and Implied Terms in the Age of Arbitration.* Oxford: Oxford University Press.

Gluck, G. (2012). Great expectations: Meeting the challenge of a new arbitration paradigm. *The American Review of International Arbitration*, 23(2), 231–243.

Goldman, B. & Cropanzano, R. (2015). "Justice" and "fairness" are not the same thing. *Journal of Organizational Behavior*, 36(2), 313–318.

Guthrie, C., Rachlinski, J. J. & Wistrich, A. J. (2007). Blinking on the bench: How judges decide cases. *Cornell Law Review*, 93(1), 1–43.

Horwitz, M. J. (1974). The historical foundations of modern contract law. *Harvard Law Review*, 87(5), 917–956.

Karton, J. (2013). *The Culture of International Arbitration and the Evolution of Contract Law.* Oxford: Oxford University Press.

Karton, J. (2015). The arbitral role in contractual interpretation. *Journal of International Dispute Settlement*, 6(1), 4–41.

Kidane, W. (2017). *The Culture of International Arbitration.* Oxford: Oxford University Press.

Kläger, R. (2011). *'Fair and Equitable Treatment' in International Investment Law.* Cambridge: Cambridge University Press.

Knutson, R. (2004). Recent treatment of construction awards by the ICC international court of arbitration. A paper given to a Meeting of the Society of Construction Law. London

Levin, M. S. (1997). The role of substantive law in business arbitration and the importance of volition. *American Business Law Journal*, 35(1), 105–180.

Linder, M. (1994). *Projecting Capitalism: A History of the Internationalization of the Construction Industry.* Westport: Greenwood Press.

Madden, J. & Spiecker, S. (2016). Are construction arbitrators and jurors really that different? American Bar Association Forum on Construction Law: The 2016 Annual Meeting.

Mentschikoff, S. (1961). Commercial arbitration. *Columbia Law Review*, 61(5), 846–869.

Mistelis, L. & Martin, P. (2010). *2010 International Arbitration Survey: Choices in International Arbitration.* London: Queen Mary School of Law, School of International Arbitration. Available at https://arbitration.qmul.ac.uk/media/arbitration/docs/2010_InternationalArbitrationSurveyReport.pdf [Accessed 12 December 2022].

Moss, G. (2004). Introductory materials on international commercial law. *Transnational Dispute Management*, 1(3), 1–161.

Naimark, R. W. & Keer, S. E. (2002). International private commercial arbitration: Expectations and perceptions of attorneys and business people: A forced-rank analysis. *International Business Lawyer*, 30(5), 203.

Natanson, R. (2013). *The Choice of the Applicable Law as a Strategy in International Commercial Arbitration*. M.Sc., Toulouse Capitole University.

Ossman, G. (2003). *Construction Arbitration Consistency and Reliability: An Empirical Study*. M.Sc., Pepperdine University School of Law.

Park, W. W. (2009). Arbitrator integrity: The transient and the permanent. *San Diego Law Review*, 46, 629–703.

Park, W. W. (2010). Arbitrators and accuracy. *Journal of International Dispute Settlement*, 1(1), 25–53.

Rawls, J. (1999). *A Theory of Justice: Revised Edition*. Cambridge, MA: Harvard University Press.

Rawls, J. (2001). *Justice as Fairness: A Restatement*. Cambridge, MA: Harvard University Press.

Rosengren, J. (2013). Contract interpretation in international arbitration. *Journal of International Arbitration*, 30(1), 1–16.

Sadurski, W. (1985). *Giving Desert Its Due: Social Justice and Legal Theory*. Boston, MA: D. Reidel Publishing Co.

Sharma, K. (1999). From sanctity to fairness: An uneasy transition in the law of contracts. *New York Law School Journal of International & Comparative Law*, 18, 95–179.

Stipanowich, T. & Ulrich, Z. (2014). Arbitration in evolution: Current practices and perspectives of experienced commercial arbitrators. *The American Review of International Arbitration*, 25, 395–480.

Sucre, A. (2013). *Aristotle's Conception of Equity in Context*. M.A: Master of Arts in Philosophy thesis, University of Missouri - St. Louis.

Sussman, E. (2013). Arbitrator decision making: Unconscious psychological influences and what you can do about them. *The American Review of International Arbitration*, 24(3), 487–514.

Teramura, N. (2020). *Ex Aequo et Bono as a Response to the 'Over-Judicialisation' of International Commercial Arbitration*. Alphen aan den Rijn: Kluwer Law International BV.

Trakman, L. E. (1980). The evolution of the law merchant: Our commercial heritage-part I: Ancient and medieval law merchant. *Journal of Maritime Law and Commerce*, 12(1), 1–24.

Trakman, L. (2008). Ex Aequo et Bono: Demystifying an ancient concept. *Chicago Journal of International Law*, 8(2), 621–642.

Trubek, D. M. (1972). Max Weber on law and the rise of capitalism. *Wisconsin Law Review*, 3, 720–753.

UNCITRAL Working Group on International Contract Practices (1982). *Report of the Working Group on International Contract Practices on the Work of Its Third Session*, New York. Available at https://digitallibrary.un.org/record/30077?ln=en. [Accessed 25 December 2022].

Weinberg, K. S. (1994). Equity in international arbitration: How fair is fair: A study of lex mercatoria and amiable composition. *Boston University International Law Journal*, 12, 227–254.

CHAPTER 7

Mandatory rules of foreign law

7.1 Introduction

According to the evidence presented in the preceding chapters, international arbitrators determine the parties' disputes primarily based on the parties' contract and the law governing the contract. In doing so, they normally apply the mandatory provisions of the governing law of the contract as they prevail over contractual terms that are not compatible therewith.

International construction contracts usually involve multiple legal systems that have a connection to the construction project or the resolution of a dispute arising from it. They include the law of the place of performance (i.e., construction), the law of the seat of arbitration, the laws of the places of domicile of the parties to the construction contract, and the law of the place of enforcement.

If the governing law of the contract is different from the law of the place of performance (i.e., the construction site), the law of the seat, the law of the state in which enforcement of an award is likely to be requested, or the law of the domicile of the parties, difficult issues of a legal nature could arise. In this situation, it is sensible to question the status of mandatory rules of law that belong to other jurisdictions that have a connection with an international construction contract. To put it differently, could the mandatory law of a jurisdiction that has a connection to the construction contract but is different from the law governing the contract affect the arbitral decision on the substance of the dispute? If the answer is no, does that mean the parties' choice of law will exclude all mandatory rules that belong to other legal systems that are connected to the dispute?

The parties may assume that the mandatory rules of law in the jurisdictions that are connected to their project are irrelevant. The principle of party autonomy, which is a fundamental tenant of international arbitration, allows contracting parties to choose the substantive law that will govern their contract. Thus, the parties may expect that the interpretation of their contractual obligations will be governed by the substantive law they agree on in their contract, not by rules of law that were not chosen by them. After all, international arbitration tribunals derive their authority from the agreement of the parties. It can be argued that their contractual mandate is bound by the will of the parties and, in turn, by their chosen law, not by a national system of private international law – like the one that exists in court litigation – that would require an arbitrator or a judge to apply mandatory rules of law foreign to the chosen law (Baniassadi, 1992). Although this is largely true, there are some exceptions, as we will see in this chapter.

In fact, the applicability of foreign mandatory rules of law appears to be one of the most contentious issues in international commercial arbitration scholarship and practice. Although the parties may have agreed on a law to govern their contractual obligations, there could be another set of mandatory rules belonging to different jurisdictions that

DOI: 10.4324/b22975-7

affect the validity of the parties' clauses and, hence, the parties' obligations (Moss, 2004; Baniassadi, 1992). There are arguments that arbitrators may apply or consider mandatory rules of law other than those chosen by the parties provided that they are closely connected to the dispute (Gaillard and Savage, 1999).

Warning against this possibility, the UNCITRAL' Legal Guide on Drawing up International Contracts for the Construction of Industrial Works (1988) recommended parties to a construction contract take into account, in addition to the governing law, the mandatory rules of the country or countries where construction works are taking place and the mandatory rules of the parties' home jurisdictions when negotiating contracts (UNCITRAL, 1988).

The dispute over the applicability of foreign mandatory law usually comes to light when the claimant demands damages for non-performance or non-payment, while the defendant responds that the contract is void or some of its terms are unenforceable because they breach mandatory rules of foreign law.

This chapter sheds light on the controversial question of whether arbitrators apply mandatory rules of public law that were not chosen by the contracting parties but are closely connected to their dispute. There is less emphasis in this chapter on what arbitrators should do and more emphasis on what arbitrators actually do.

To simplify the inquiry into this controversial question, this chapter discusses each of the key jurisdictions that are typically associated with the parties' contract in turn. These jurisdictions are the place of performance (Section 7.3), the seat of arbitration (Section 7.4), the domicile of the parties (Section 7.5), and the country in which enforcement of an award is likely to be sought (Section 7.6). Prior to discussing the effect of mandatory rules in these jurisdictions, the next section provides more clarity on the meaning of 'mandatory rules' (Section 7.2).

7.2 The concept of mandatory rules

It is important to recognise the distinction made between 'mandatory rules' and 'overriding mandatory rules' by the Rome Convention (Moss, 2004) and in international arbitration scholarship (Rau, 2008; De Ly et al., 2008). Mandatory rules, in the ordinary meaning, are those rules that belong to the governing law. They govern the obligations of private parties and cannot be derogated from by agreement. These mandatory rules of law and how international arbitrators deal with them when interpreting the parties' contract are discussed in Section 3.5.5. There is another set of mandatory rules that are 'overriding' in the sense that they may prevail over the parties' choice of law stipulations (also known as *lois de police* in French). These 'overriding mandatory rules' relate to the state's public policy. They are a matter of public law not private law.

For example, the rules on the limitation of rights are mandatory and will be applicable according to the governing law. The mandatory rules on limitations of another law that has a connection to the dispute are not overriding and, hence, may not be applicable (Moss, 2004). Even with this distinction, Moss (2004) argues that the general rule remains that foreign mandatory rules should not be applicable.

Mandatory rules reflect the domestic or international public policy of the state that imposes them and can be either procedural or substantive. They are intended to protect the fundamental procedural (requiring the observance of due process) and substantive (related to the merits of the case) legal order in that state (Teramura, 2020). It seems that most controversy surrounding the application of foreign mandatory law concerns substantive mandatory rules (Barraclough and Waincymer, 2005).

Determining whether a mandatory rule has an overriding character is not straightforward, as it might differ from one state to another (Basaran, 2014). Ultimately it depends on the arbitrator's construction, which should be restrictive and narrow. Deeming a mandatory rule overriding should be an exception and is generally not desirable due to the resulting unpredictability of dispute outcomes (Moss, 2004). A non-exhaustive list of mandatory rules that might be deemed overriding includes rules that concern the protection of a national economy (e.g., import-export regulations, foreign exchange regulations, competition regulation) or public interest (e.g., embargo or boycott law) (Gaillard and Savage, 1999; Baniassadi, 1992).

The theory of transnational or international mandatory rules, or overriding mandatory rules (*lois de police*), proposes that arbitrators have the power and duty to consider mandatory rules that belong to a legal system other than that chosen by the parties to govern their dispute. It allows arbitrators to avoid a strict application of the parties' contract and its governing law on the basis of certain national policies (Gaillard and Savage, 1999).

7.3 The law of the place of performance

Typically, the law governing the construction contract will be the law of the place of construction works. This is because most large-scale civil engineering and infrastructure projects are government-sponsored. The government or government agencies set the law of their own jurisdiction as the governing law of the contracts they enter into with their tier 1 contractors and suppliers. The contracts that flow down the supply chain are likely to be on a back-to-back basis. Hence, the obligations and the governing law flow down to subcontractors.

However, this is not always the case. The governing law of the main construction contract may be different from the law of the place of performance. This could be the case in construction contracts between private parties (for example, a construction contract between a private investor and a contractor to build a five-star hotel) or even in a contract concluded with a government that has less bargaining power than a multinational contractor. The governing law of the main construction contract may also be different from the law governing the subcontracts.

As part of the research underpinning this book, the author interviewed international construction arbitrators and asked them whether the law of the place of the construction works influences their decision on the merits.

There is an agreement between arbitrators that certain classes of legal rules and regulations will normally be applicable regardless of the law the parties choose to govern their contract. These include health and safety law, environmental law, building codes and standards, labour law, and so on (UNCITRAL, 1988). Charrett (2012) asserts that it is an 'overarching duty' of all parties working within a given legal jurisdiction to obey its laws and regulations. Notwithstanding the uncertainty surrounding the nature and source of this duty, it is normally the case that compliance with such regulations is not problematic. This is because it is a standard practice in international construction contracts to require compliance with the regulations of the country where the contract is to be performed.

These issues do not seem to be contentious because they would not necessarily be something that arbitrators deal with unless they arise from breach of contract claims. These issues are likely to be dealt with by the local authorities.

However, the mandatory rules at the place of performance are not limited to the technical aspects of construction activities and deliverables. There are rules that relate to the state's public policy in matters concerning economic and public interest, such as customs duties, taxes, import, export, and foreign exchange regulations, etc. These rules are applicable to commercial activities associated with the construction works taking place in the place of performance (UNCITRAL, 1988). A few examples of these overriding mandatory rules are mentioned below.

Some legal systems impose a decennial liability, as an overriding mandatory rule, on the parties to a construction contract. The decennial liability can be found in the civil law codes of some countries, such as France and the Arab countries. Decennial liability is normally considered a matter of public policy of the state (relating to public safety considerations) where construction is taking place. It follows that the parties' choice of foreign law to govern their contract does not necessarily mean a party can escape from a decennial liability (Sakr, 2009). For instance, a European construction company building a hotel in Egypt may not be able to avoid a decennial liability by agreeing to English law to govern the construction contract.

In France, the French subcontracting law (Law 75-1334 of 1975) that aims to provide some financial protection to subcontractors is an overriding mandatory provision or *loi de police* (the French term for overriding mandatory rules). As such, it is applicable to all construction projects in France even if the parties choose a substantive law to govern their contract other than French law (Burr, 2016).

In the United Kingdom, the UK Construction Act (Housing Grants, Construction and Regeneration Act 1996) appears to have an overriding mandatory character. For instance, it says in the introductory provisions of the part devoted to construction contracts: 'This Part applies whether or not the law of England and Wales or Scotland is otherwise the applicable law in relation to the contract' (Burr, 2016). So, even if the parties agree on foreign law to govern their construction contract that is to be performed in the United Kingdom, the UK Construction Act remains applicable.

These kinds of mandatory rules are more controversial than those concerning the technical aspects of construction. The controversial issue here is that certain clauses may be valid under the parties' choice of law but invalid according to the law of the place of performance. How should an arbitrator construe the contract then?

The application of such rules depends primarily on three considerations. The first consideration concerns the parties' submissions. If a party has not elevated the issue, arbitrators seem reluctant to make initiatives to raise the point of applicability by themselves. The second consideration concerns the proper construction of the mandatory rule to examine its intended scope of application. The third, and perhaps the most important consideration, concerns the arbitrators' views on it. If one of the parties raises it, arbitrators must decide on the matter. Based on the author's interviews with international arbitrators, there appear to be two views on how arbitrators may deal with this matter.

The first view is that the law of the place of performance may be considered when determining the parties' dispute. This view arises from the belief of some arbitrators that the parties should have no power to ignore certain mandatory rules of the country they are operating in. Allowing this to happen would be derogatory to the state's sovereignty, and international arbitration would reproduce imperialist practices. However, this view represents the minority view of arbitrators interviewed by the author in the study underpinning this book.

The second view is that the law of the country where construction works were undertaken has no relevance to arbitrators' substantive decisions. The virtue of international arbitration is that an award can be enforced anywhere the losing party has assets. The court recognising and enforcing the award is not going to be interested in what the law of the place of performance requires. Some arbitrators argue that applying a law that the parties have not agreed to subject their obligations to may qualify as an 'excess of power' and, hence, lead to non-enforcement of their award. However, even though their starting position is to consider the law of the place of performance irrelevant, this might change if they think the award recognition and enforcement will be in danger. The question of the applicability of the local law becomes problematic if the country where the project work is located is also the country where award enforcement will be sought (because, for example, it is the only place the losing party has assets). If the enforcement jurisdiction was the same place where the works were carried out, then the court may consider it against public policy to escape from the applicability of its mandatory rules of law and refuse to enforce the award. Ultimately, the main concern that arbitrators have appears to boil down to the issue of award enforcement.

The following excerpt is from an interview with a Canadian arbitrator. She stated that the mandatory law of the place of performance is irrelevant to determining the parties' obligations and that the parties can escape from it. However, she expressed some pragmatism in dealing with this issue because her main concern is to see her award enforced:

> The place of performance for me is probably irrelevant… unless it is also the place of enforcement … as an arbitrator, I am only looking at the contract between the private parties. The fact that it might be illegal or invalid in the place where they are working, for me, is irrelevant. I do not represent the state where construction works are taking place. I am not there to defend its law. That is not my charter as an arbitrator. I am there to look at the contract between those two… but if it is also the place of enforcement … you know, my main concern is the enforceability of the award … So, I will ask the parties what they need from me to make sure that whatever I decide will be enforceable?

This view reflects the views of most arbitrators to enforce clauses that may be valid under the parties' choice of law but invalid according to the law of the place of performance. For example, if the parties' dispute arises from a construction project in a country the law of which considers a pay-when-paid clause void, but according to the governing law of the contract it is legal, arbitrators will be inclined to enforce it. Their inclination would be to start with the idea that they would enforce the pay-when-paid clause because it is permitted under governing law and the parties have agreed to it, even though it is prohibited in the place of performance.

As regards the risk of annulment or non-enforcement when enforcement is sought in the country of performance, some arbitrators opined that this is a risk the winner bears. After all, the winning party may negotiate the award with the losing party, or even the losing party may voluntarily comply with the award.

This view, which represents the prevailing opinion among the arbitrators interviewed by the author, is also reflected in international construction arbitration awards and their courts' enforcement decisions. A brief summary of three cases is provided below to illustrate how arbitrators deal with this issue in practice.

7.3.1 Westacre Investments

Westacre Investments provides an example of the relevance and importance of mandatory law of the place of performance when enforcement is sought somewhere else. This famous case involved a dispute concerning the payment of commissions for government officials to secure contracts. Westacre (the claimant) acted as a consultant to assist a Yugoslavian government agency (the defendant) to win contracts for the sale of military equipment in Kuwait. The place of contract performance was Kuwait. The parties agreed on Swiss law to govern their consultancy agreement and to have the seat of arbitration in Switzerland. A dispute arose and the claimant initiated arbitration proceedings. The defendant alleged that the agreement was void on public policy grounds because it involved paying bribes to win contracts. The tribunal dismissed this argument and made an award in favour of the claimant. Then, the claimant sought to enforce the award in England. The Court of Appeal held that an agreement to pay a commission for lobbying government officials was contrary to the public policy in the place of performance. However, it found no basis for non-enforcement under the public policy ground in the English Arbitration Act 1975. The court concluded that enforcement was permitted because the agreement was not contrary to the public policy of the seat of arbitration (Switzerland) or the governing law (Swiss law) (Rau, 2008).

7.3.2 The Hilmarton case

The famous Hilmarton case is another case that concerns the relevance and importance of the mandatory law of the place of performance when enforcement is sought somewhere else. An English company (Hilmarton) entered into a lobbying agreement with a French company (OTV) to assist it to win a public works contract in Algeria. The agreement, which was governed by Swiss law, provided for arbitration in Switzerland under the rules of the International Chamber of Commerce. A payment-related dispute arose and Hilmarton (the claimant) initiated arbitration proceedings. The claimant argued that payment of commissions was due for helping the French company obtain a public works contract in Algeria. The defendant alleged that the agreement was void on public policy grounds because it violated the law of the contract's place of performance (Algeria), which prohibited the involvement of intermediaries in connection with public contracts. The arbitrator found that the agreement breached the overriding mandatory rules of the place of performance of the contract (Algerian law), but it was not illegal under Swiss law. As such, and as there was no evidence of bribery or corruption, the arbitrator enforced the agreement and decided in the claimant's favour. The arbitral award was enforced in England. The English court noted that the parties' agreement was not contrary to English public policy and that the Algerian mandatory rule of law under contention is a matter of domestic public policy, which is up to the arbitral tribunal to consider (Rau, 2008).

7.3.3 The Mitsubishi case

The famous Mitsubishi case (*Mitsubishi Motors Corp. v. Soler Chrysler–Plymouth Inc.*) is an example of a situation in which the parties attempt to circumvent the application of mandatory rules of public law in the place of performance by subjecting their contract to a substantive law that is different from the law of the place of performance of the contract (Baniassadi, 1992). Mayer (1986) commented that the Mitsubishi case is a perfect illustration that the international nature of a contract makes arbitrators more reluctant to apply mandatory rules of law at the place of performance.

The contract was governed by Swiss law and the seat of arbitration was Tokyo. It seems that the parties' agreement to subject their contract to Swiss law was an attempt to avoid the application of the mandatory rules of the place of performance (US mandatory law in relation to anti-competitive practices).

A dispute arose but the defendant refused to participate in arbitration proceedings. The claimant commenced litigation in the US court to compel arbitration. The defendant argued that the agreement was unlawful as it violated the US antitrust law and the dispute was not arbitrable. It requested a ruling that the US federal court alone was competent to decide disputes involving issues of anti-trust law. The Supreme Court held that the dispute was arbitrable and that arbitrators should have the jurisdiction to decide on it. However, the court warned against the possibility that the arbitral tribunal may construe the choice of law clause to have the effect of excluding the US mandatory law even when it is applicable to the dispute. The court noted that empowering arbitrators to determine anti-trust disputes is conditional on them applying the US law to the merits regardless of the parties' choice of law. Otherwise, US courts may refuse to enforce the arbitral award on public policy grounds.

The court decision generated criticism from those who oppose the arbitrability of anti-trust disputes (because there is no way to guarantee that arbitrators will apply the US anti-trust mandatory law) and those who oppose its extraterritorial application (because those arbitrators do not think it is their duty to apply mandatory rules of law that do not belong to the law governing the contract) (Mayer, 1986).

7.4 The law of the seat of arbitration

One law that is applicable in international arbitration and often viewed to be the most crucial law is the law of the seat of arbitration including both its arbitration law (also known as the curial law or Lex arbitri) and its procedural law. An arbitration law provides the legal framework that governs the conduct of arbitrations proceedings. Subject to mandatory procedural rules of the seat, the rules of civil procedure at the seat are not applicable and the parties are at liberty to design their own procedure to conduct their arbitration. Normally, the parties agree on standard arbitration rules, such as those published by various institutions (e.g., ICC, LCIA, AAA or UNCITRAL, etc.). However, arbitration laws and arbitration rules are generally silent on the exact procedure to be followed, and, hence, they leave arbitrators with wide discretion (Uff, 2008).

It is important for arbitrators to comply with the mandatory rules that are applicable at the place of arbitration. This is because the court at the seat may set aside an award that is contrary to its public policy. An award that is set aside at the seat is largely worthless anywhere in the world. That is why arbitration scholars, such as Mayer (1986), suggest that arbitrators may take into account the law of the country where the arbitral tribunal sits.

All arbitrators interviewed by the author agreed that the law of the seat of arbitration is limited to the conduct of the arbitration itself, and, hence, it has no effect on the tribunal's decision on the merits. Uff (2008) notes that the outcome of arbitration appears to be largely the same no matter what the applicable procedural law or rules are. In his view, different procedures are merely different approaches to reaching the same result.

Having said that, some arbitrators and scholars (Moses, 2008) pointed out that, in a few cases, the dividing line between substance and procedure is not clear and it may differ from country to country. Typical areas that include elements of both procedure and substance are interest on damages (Karton, 2015) and limitations (Uff, 2008).

Some arbitrators state that interest on damages and its assessment method varies from one jurisdiction to another. Under some jurisdictions, it is a procedural right and is prescribed in the arbitration law, while, under others, it is a substantive right and can be found in a different part of the law. Yet, the uncertainty does not stop here. Some scholars (e.g., Karton, 2015; Park, 2010) argue that interest on damages is one of the areas where international arbitrators have the power to depart from the stipulations of the governing law and rely on transnational norms. Although rules on the quantum of damages are a matter of contract law and thus belong to the substantive law (UNCITRAL, 1988), some arbitration laws and arbitration rules of procedure grant arbitrators the power to award either simple or compound interest on damages at a rate and over a period they deem proper (Karton, 2015).

The law on limitation can be considered to belong to the substantive law (i.e., it governs the prescription of rights) or to the procedural law (i.e., it governs the limitation of actions) (UNCITRAL, 1988). Generally speaking, civil law countries characterise the prescription period to be substantive (i.e., part of the law of obligations) and common law countries consider the limitation period to be procedural in nature and this could be problematic in international arbitration (Osing and Neumeier, 2012).

Putting aside these two areas, it seems there is nothing else in the procedural law that may have an impact on the parties' obligations. However, it remains that arbitrators need to take the public policy of the state where arbitration is seated into consideration. This is because, under the New York Convention, the court at the seat of arbitration may set aside an award that violates its public policy. What is a matter of public policy is not clear-cut and it differs from country to country. Nevertheless, what is generally accepted is that it should be invoked in exceptional circumstances when the outcome reached by applying the foreign substantive law would contradict the fundamental principles of the society of the forum. A difference between a legal rule in the substantive law and a mandatory rule of the law of the seat, even if being an overriding mandatory rule, would not qualify as a violation of the public policy of the seat (Moss, 2004).

However, arbitral tribunals might reach surprising results based on a broad interpretation of public policy of the seat of arbitration. In ICC Case No. 5946/1990, the dispute concerned a wrongful termination of a distribution agreement between a French seller of wine and an American buyer. The substantive law was the law of New York, and the arbitration seat was Geneva. The arbitrator denied the buyer's claim for punitive damages on the ground that: 'Damages that go beyond compensatory damages to constitute a punishment of the wrongdoer . . . are considered contrary to Swiss public policy, which must be respected by an arbitral tribunal sitting in Switzerland even if the arbitral tribunal must decide a dispute according to a law that may allow punitive or exemplary damages as such' (Rau, 2008).

An arbitrator's decision on the relevance of overriding mandatory rules of the law of the seat is likely to be influenced by the theory of arbitration they believe in. The jurisdictional theory assumes that arbitrators derive their power from the law of the seat, and, as such, they must apply its mandatory rules. The contractualist theory assumes that arbitrators derive their power from the parties' agreement. It denies the relevance of the seat and, hence, does not require arbitrators to apply its mandatory rules, at least those that are substantive, as opposed to procedural, in nature (Barraclough and Waincymer, 2005; Rau, 2008).

7.5 The laws of the places of domicile of the parties to the construction contract

The laws of the places of domicile of the parties could be relevant to the determination of the parties' dispute. Arbitrators may have to decide whether mandatory rules at the parties' home jurisdictions are applicable to their legal relationship even though they are foreign to the substantive law of the contract chosen by the parties. The purpose of these rules is typically to ensure compliance with the economic and foreign policy of the state. These mandatory rules may relate to legislation on customs duties and taxes on activities connected with the construction project. They may prohibit or restrict exports, imports, the transfer of technology, and the payment of foreign exchange.

Understanding how arbitrators decide on this issue is important to the parties. Arbitrators may refuse to give effect to the mandatory rules of law of the parties' respective countries when such rules are foreign to the substantive law of the contract. Conversely, if arbitrators find them applicable, the mandatory rules may have the effect of rendering terms in the parties' contract invalid. As such, it is important for the parties to understand all sources of their legal obligations to make sure they do not breach a law that may be relevant.

In its publication titled *Legal Guide on Drawing Up International Contracts for the Construction of Industrial Works*, the UNCITRAL noted (UNCITRAL, 1988):

> In addition to legal rules applicable to the contract by virtue of a choice of law by the parties or by virtue of the rules of private international law, certain mandatory rules of an administrative or other public nature in force in the countries of the parties may affect certain aspects of the construction. The parties should take those rules into account in drafting the contract.

This text includes a clear warning to construction parties that certain mandatory rules of law that relate to public policy in the parties' home countries might be relevant to their contractual relationship. As arbitral tribunals may find certain mandatory rules applicable, the parties need to consider these rules when they negotiate and draft their contract.

The following is an excerpt from an interview the author undertook with a Swiss arbitrator. It illustrates the uncertainty surrounding the applicability of foreign mandatory rules of law, including those that belong to the parties' respective countries:

> If you have two European parties that agree on things that are in violation of the EU competition law, and referred their dispute to arbitration in Switzerland, then Swiss law is applicable. So technically, the EU competition law will not be applicable but then you have to think very hard whether you really should do that or whether you consider the public interest behind the mandatory rules, such as these competition rules, to be of higher importance than the will of the parties. I cannot say there's a general rule. I think it depends on the case, it depends on the closeness of the relationship between the mandatory rules in question and the fact pattern that has to be decided.

The Swiss arbitrator highlighted that it is usually the case that one party argues that a foreign mandatory rule is applicable to the dispute because it will be beneficial to that party. Usually, the defendant will raise this point and demands the application of the foreign mandatory rule to escape from its non-performance. The arbitral tribunal will decide based on the evidence before it and may consider the principle of good faith in contract negotiation and performance. In a situation where no party raises the issue of the applicability of foreign mandatory law, it seems arbitrators will be less inclined to raise the issue by themselves. If they do raise the issue and then both parties argue that the foreign mandatory law should not be applied, then it will be easier to go with the parties' submissions. Deciding otherwise puts the arbitrator in a more difficult situation.

The following text provides a summary of three international arbitration cases that illustrate how arbitral tribunals deal with disputes over the applicability of foreign mandatory rules of law of the parties' home jurisdictions. Overall, they demonstrate that this is an issue on which arbitrators are divided.

7.5.1 ICC Case No. 1399/1967

ICC Case No. 1399/1967 involved a contract between a Mexican party and a French party that was governed by French law. It seems the parties agreed to govern their contract by French law in an attempt to evade Mexican customs laws. In this case, the arbitral tribunal refused to consider Mexican customs laws. Although the tribunal found that the Mexican customs law was an overriding mandatory law (*loi de police*), they affirmed that it did not qualify as international public policy and therefore its scope of application should not reach the place of performance of the contract (France). It added that a contract involving bribery and corrupt acts was likely to be declared null and void, but a contract that violated tax laws or import/export law of a foreign country would not necessarily be invalidated (Shehata, 2017). Accordingly, the tribunal concluded that the parties' contract was valid even though it did not comply with foreign mandatory rules relating to customs law.

In this case, the tribunal held the view that a breach of a law other than the governing law has no effect on their decision. Some commentators support the tribunal's decision as in their opinion there is nothing wrong with disregarding a breach of law that is not applicable (Gaillard and Savage, 1999). In their view, it is not illegal to break a law that is not applicable (Gaillard and Savage, 1999). As long as the illegality does not rise to the level of a violation of international public policy, the illegality should not concern arbitrators (Kreindler, 2013).

7.5.2 ICC Case No. 8528/1996

This ICC arbitration case illustrates the potential legal effect of mandatory rules of a foreign country on the parties' obligations. In this case, the arbitral tribunal had to consider the applicability of foreign mandatory law to the parties' dispute. The governing law was Swiss law, and the seat of arbitration was Geneva. The claimant was a US construction company. The defendant was a Turkish construction company. The parties in dispute formed a joint venture and won a construction contract with a Turkish public works authority. The dispute concerned the applicability of Turkish mandatory tax legislation (a foreign mandatory law) in relation to the transferability of tax benefits. The claimant (the US construction company) claimed that the tax benefits that the defendant (the Turkish company) profited from due to tax incentives provided by the Turkish government to Turkish contractors should be shared by the joint venture. The claimant relied on express and implied agreements made with the defendant stipulating that the tax benefits were to be shared by the JV partners. The defendant argued that mandatory provisions of Turkish law supersede the parties' agreement and prohibit a Turkish beneficiary of the tax benefits from sharing them with foreign partners (Arnaldez, Derains, and Hascher, 2003).

The tribunal rejected the claimant's argument that an arbitral tribunal sitting in Switzerland, applying Swiss law, would not be obliged to apply mandatory Turkish law. The tribunal justified its conclusion by reference to the Swiss Private International Law Statute, the Rome Convention on the Law Applicable to Contractual Obligations of 1980, arbitration scholarly material published in journal papers (such as Werner, 1995; Hochstrasser, 1994), and courts' decisions stating that arbitrators may, or even should, apply foreign mandatory rules outside the substantive law that are closely connected to the dispute. The tribunal also cited Art. 26 of the ICC Rules, which provides that 'the Arbitral Tribunal shall make every effort to make sure that the award is enforceable at law' (Arnaldez, Derains, and Hascher, 2003).

The tribunal found that the parties' agreement to share tax benefits would be illegal in Turkey, which is the place of performance and the place of the domicile of one of the parties. As such, the tribunal found that the parties' agreement to share the tax benefits was invalid as it was contrary to a foreign mandatory law that is closely connected to the dispute. The tribunal held that tax benefits were non-transferable privileges between the Turkish government and the defendant (Arnaldez, Derains, and Hascher, 2003).

7.5.3 ICC Case No. 6320/1992

This ICC arbitration case illustrates that arbitral tribunals may rely on a foreign mandatory law (relating to the place of domicile of one of the contracting parties) besides the substantive law chosen by the parties to determine the legality and validity of the terms agreed upon by the parties. Although in this case the tribunal did not apply the foreign mandatory law in dispute, it indicated that a different result might be possible in another case depending on the facts and circumstances of the case.

This arbitration case concerns a dispute arising from a power plant construction project in Brazil. The claimant (a Brazilian company) and the respondent (a US contractor) entered into a contract in 1972. The contract was governed by Brazilian law and the seat of arbitration was Paris. The dispute involved the application of foreign mandatory law. The claimant argued that the US mandatory law in relation to fraud and corrupt practices must be applied to the legal relationship between them notwithstanding the private contractual relationship the parties had between themselves.

The tribunal noted that arbitration scholars and commentators as well as the few published arbitral awards dealing with this issue are divided on whether an international arbitral tribunal should be allowed at all to apply a mandatory law in derogation of the law otherwise chosen by the parties.

In this case, the tribunal stated that a mandatory foreign law (i.e., a law not chosen by the parties) may be applicable if it forms part of transnational or international public policy. The following is an excerpt from the arbitral award:

> This tribunal accepts the premise that there may be situations in which an international arbitral tribunal should admit the application of mandatory rules different from the law that the

> parties have chosen to govern their claims or relationships. The tribunal emphasizes, however, that such an application outside the *lex contractus* is subject to particularly stringent conditions: the tribunal must be satisfied that the mandatory rules different from the law that the parties have chosen to govern their claims or relationship must clearly be a 'loi de police'.

The tribunal acknowledged the importance of the will and autonomy of the parties in international arbitration in relation to substantive and procedural choices, the selection of the forum, and the selection of arbitrators. However, it emphasised that party autonomy must be construed to be subordinate to international public policy.

In the end, the tribunal refused to apply the US mandatory provisions of the RICO Act because it was not satisfied that (1) this particular legislation was intended to have extraterritorial application, and (2) its breach had any substantial anticompetitive effect on the US market (Rau, 2008). The tribunal used a conflict of laws analysis to determine how closely connected the mandatory law in dispute was to the facts of a case. It found that the link was weak (Shehata, 2017).

7.5.4 ICC Case No. 2977/1978, 2978/1978, and 3033/1978

These joint ICC arbitration cases demonstrate that an arbitral tribunal may refuse to give effect to the mandatory rules of law of the parties' countries when such rules are foreign to the substantive law of the contract. This arbitration case concerned a dispute between a Swedish shipyard and a Libyan buyer that arose from a contract for the construction of three oil tankers. The contract was governed by Swedish law and the seat of arbitration was Paris. The defendant (the Libyan buyer) refused to accept the three ships alleging that the claimant (the Swedish shipyard) violated Libyan laws and regulations relating to the boycott of Israel.

The arbitral tribunal refused to apply the mandatory law because the parties selected Swedish law to govern their contract. It stated that this choice of law should be construed to exclude the application of foreign mandatory law including the Libyan boycott law unless there is a special reference for it in the contract (in this case it would be treated as any contractual term) (Baniassadi, 1992).

7.6 The law of the place of enforcement

Another legal jurisdiction that is important in international arbitration is that where the winner seeks to enforce its award. The importance of this legal jurisdiction comes from the fact that under the New York Convention, a court may refuse to enforce an award if it violates the public policy of the country in which the enforcement is sought. The enforcement jurisdiction could be different from the jurisdiction the law of which governs the parties' contract.

In international arbitration practice, there were cases requiring arbitrators to determine the legality and validity of the parties' contract, or a term in the parties' contract, by reference to the law of the place of enforcement and not by reference to the substantive law (Radjai, 2009). One party, usually the defendant who attempts to escape its liability for non-performance, would argue that the contract should be declared illegal and invalid because an award enforcing it would be contrary to the public policy of the country in which the award would be enforced.

For example, in the famous case of *Soleimany v. Soleimany*, a father and son entered into a joint venture agreement to export carpets from Iran, which was in violation of Iranian revenue laws and export controls. A dispute arose between the father and the son, and it was referred to a Jewish tribunal sitting in England and applying Jewish law. The arbitral tribunal found that the contract was illegal in Iran, but this fact was not relevant because the substantive law was Jewish law, under which the contract was valid. The losing party challenged the arbitral award and the English Court of Appeal refused enforcement of the award on the basis that enforcement of an illegal contract would be contrary to English public policy (Rau, 2008).

In light of this background, the author asked the arbitrators he interviewed in the study underpinning this book whether the law of the place of enforcement (i.e., the state where the award might be enforced) is relevant to their decision on the substance of construction disputes.

The answer was generally no. The unanimous view of the interviewed arbitrators is that the mandatory law of the place of enforcement will not affect their decision on the substance of a dispute.

For example, an English arbitrator justified his view that the law of the place of enforcement is irrelevant as follows:

> I would not know where to stop this inquiry … I would not know where a party would have assets in the world, I could not imagine having to worry about that while writing an award … if the parties have some specific concerns about that, I would expect them to be studious enough to shape the award in their submissions … so what you are looking at always is your compliance with the mandatory laws of the seat and your compliance with New York convention.

The English arbitrator eloquently stated that his duty to render an enforceable award does not entail an obligation to make sure the award will be enforced in each and every country:

> I want my award to be enforceable not enforced, and there is a difference between the two … let's take the award of interest for example … if I am setting in London, and the applicable law is English law, but I know there is a party who is going to enforce the award in Saudi Arabia ... it would not be a concern of mine that if I awarded interest properly based on the substantive law and the facts of the case, that the winner would not be able to enforce the award in Saudi Arabia … that is not my problem … as far as I know I am rendering an enforceable award..

What the English arbitrator meant by "rendering an enforceable award" is making sure that the award is not exposed to Model Law challenges. He, like all other arbitrators, keeps the Model Law grounds for refusing recognition or enforcement in the forefront of his mind when drafting an arbitral award.

The unanimous view of the interviewed arbitrators on the irrelevance of the place of enforcement to their decision on the substance of a dispute is in line with the arbitrators' opinions expressed in the literature (Derains and Schwartz, 2005; Moses, 2008). The interviewed arbitrators justify their views based on several reasons that are briefly discussed below.

First and foremost, the arbitral tribunal normally has no idea where the award is going to be enforced. Sometimes there are multiple places of reinforcement, especially for money awards. The place of enforcement depends on, first, who the losing party is, which might not be known until the end, and, second, on the countries where the losing party probably has assets. The tribunal may give an award in Dubai but the winner may seek to enforce it in Paris or London. If the losing party trades in dollars, then the winning party may decide to take the award to Manhattan in the Southern District of New York and ask the court for an attachment to secure payment the next time the losing party has a dollar transaction in the federal reserve.

Second, the arbitral tribunal should not change its view on the right application of the substantive law because of fear of non-enforcement. A contradiction concerning the legality and validity of contractual terms between the substantive law and the law of the enforcing jurisdiction is not a ground for challenge according to the New York convention, and, hence, it should not be a reason to refuse enforcement. Having said that, some arbitrators pointed out flawed practices by courts of some jurisdictions where they do not apply the correct grounds for refusing to enforce awards. Rather, based on a broad interpretation of public policy, they refuse to enforce awards for a variety of reasons, amongst which is the nonconformance to their substantive law, which is improper.

Third, it is the parties and their lawyers' job to ensure that an arbitral award conforms to the requirements of the arbitration law of the country they intend to seek enforcement in. As such, the parties' counsel should inform the tribunal of any specific requirements in drafting the award and give the tribunal submissions on that. A Swiss arbitrator interviewed by the author underlined the parties' responsibility to consider enforcement issues in the early phases of contracting as follows:

> People must do their homework. If someone knows that an award is likely to be enforced in country X, and then they put into the contract something that contravenes the mandatory rule of the law of that country, it is on them. I don't see it is the role of arbitrators to correct parties' mistakes or correct a lack of legal due diligence in the formation of the contract.

Fourth, it is up to the parties to decide what to do when an award is given. After all, the losing party may voluntarily agree to comply with the award. Empirical evidence suggests that there is a relatively high degree of voluntary compliance with arbitral awards. Alternatively, the parties may decide to negotiate a settlement. Only a small number of cases appear to require recognition and enforcement proceedings (Lagerberg and Mistelis, 2008).

Fifth, some arbitrators drew a distinction between ad hoc arbitration and institutional arbitration regarding the activity of searching the content of the law of the place of enforcement. They referred, in particular, to the ICC practice. Under the ICC arbitration, arbitral awards are scrutinised by a team of experts who have specific knowledge and experience of enforcement issues in the jurisdiction where enforcement is sought to make sure the award is in compliance with the arbitration law of that jurisdiction.

These reasons are convincing and there seems to be no controversy concerning the irrelevance of the law of the place of enforcement to the arbitral decision on the merits. Most arbitrators are aware that there might be substantive or procedural mandatory rules that might be viewed as matters of public policy by the court at the intended place of enforcement. However, they assert that it is up to the parties' counsel to inform them of any specific requirements regarding the drafting of the award to make sure it is in compliance with the law of the place they seek enforcement. It is important to emphasise that these mandatory rules will affect only the drafting of the award but not its substance. The following two examples, mentioned by the interviewed arbitrators, show how arbitrators may 'shape' their awards to ensure compliance with procedural and substantive mandatory rules of the place of enforcement.

The first example concerns the UAE and Qatar's famous cases where the courts refused to enforce arbitral awards based on public policy grounds. In the UAE, it is a requirement under the law that all evidence must be sworn. It is a mandatory provision in the civil code that can render an award unenforceable. In Qatar, it is a mandatory rule that every arbitrator must sign every page of the award (not initial but sign). Some arbitrators, who frequently receive appointments on cases related to the Arab Gulf states, spoke of the need to keep such things in mind when drafting an arbitral award. They said that if they envisage that the award will be enforced in the UAE, they will ask witnesses to swear an oath in the same form described by the UAE code.

These issues concerning signature and witness evidence affect the draft of the award but not the decision on the merits. They are procedural and not substantive norms at the place of enforcement. Although they are not binding on an arbitrator, it appears that most arbitrators hold the view that an arbitral tribunal may comply with them when it is not difficult to do so (Waincymer, 2011). This is a matter of pragmatism. Although arbitrators are only bound by the mandatory rules of the seat, they also consider the mandatory rules of the place or places where enforcement of the award is likely to be sought (Karton, 2013). This is because, under Article V(2)(b) of the New York Convention and various national arbitration laws, courts may refuse to recognise or enforce an arbitral award that contravenes the public policy of the state where enforcement is sought (Karton, 2013).

The second example concerns the potential difficulty in enforcing awards containing interest on damages in certain jurisdictions, such as Saudi Arabia. In this case, the interviewed arbitrators asserted that it is the winning party's responsibility to inform the tribunal that in case they find in its favour to draft the award in a specific way that facilitates its enforcement. The winner may ask the tribunal to use phrases that may not be offensive to the public policy of the jurisdiction where enforcement will be sought. For example, they may use the phrase 'damages on late payment' rather than 'interest payments'. Alternatively, as a pragmatic solution, the tribunal can issue two separate awards. The first award will be limited to the main issues in dispute, which will be safe to enforce in Saudi Arabia. The second award concerning interest can be enforced in other jurisdictions where the losing party has assets. This allows the winning party to secure enforcement without changing the outcome.

Although most arbitrators appear to leave enforcement issues to the parties as long as they are satisfied that their award is enforceable according to the Model Law and New York Convention, some arbitrators tend to be willing to assume a slightly more active role to ensure the award is more likely to be enforced. They keep the law of the place of enforcement in the back of their minds when drafting an award. As such, if they know of certain matters that may hinder getting the award recognised and enforced, they might invite the parties to comment on that.

Few arbitrators indicated that they may go one step further. For instance, a Lebanese arbitrator said he may be able to envisage the likely place of enforcement, and, hence, he might do quick research to be confident that his award is compliant with the mandatory law of the place of enforcement. In case the place of enforcement is obvious, and if he finds something relevant that may jeopardize the enforceability of the award, he might raise it and ask the parties to comment on it. Below is an excerpt from his interview:

> Although you do not know where the award is going to be enforced as under New York convention a money award can be enforced anywhere in the world where the money is … but at least in the most obvious cases I think you have an obligation to accommodate this … but without being too zealous as you are not supposed to consider and assess all of the laws of the world … if it is a construction case, the place of enforcement is highly likely to be the same place of the construction project or the place of the incorporation of the losing party because these are where most likely you will find assets … I will be writing my award for these courts besides the court of the seat.

This 'due diligence' aiming to increase the chances of post-award enforcement, while legitimate, should not leave a trace in the award that might indicate a mandatory rule of an enforcement jurisdiction has influenced the tribunal's reasoning (Rau, 2008). Indeed, the Lebanese arbitrator affirmed that he would not refer to the law of the place of enforcement in the award. He would only draft the award in a way that ensures compliance with that law.

A Swiss arbitrator interviewed by the author shared a similar opinion with the Lebanese arbitrator. He cautiously suggested that the law of the place of enforcement may shape his award as follows:

> You are trying to avoid rendering an award that would be unenforceable at the likely place of enforcement. The duty of an arbitrator is not to render a piece of paper. So, I may consider the law of the place of enforcement. I mean to the extent that the place of enforcement can be foreseen, as sometimes it is not so easy to foresee. If one party raises a valid point, I will look at it … For instance, if the case involves the award of interest, and if the likely place of enforcement is a Muslim country where the local laws are not sympathetic to the award of interest, at minimum, I would be receptive to an argument saying I should not award interest because the award is not capable of enforcement.

Although he would keep an open mind, the Swiss arbitrator stressed that it is unlikely to find that the law of the place of enforcement on its own provides sufficient ground for not applying the parties' contract. There must be a stronger connection to the foreign mandatory rule in question.

This view that supports taking the law of the place of enforcement into consideration finds an echo in arbitration practice and literature.

ICC Case No. 15977/2010 provides an example, which is not necessarily representative or generalisable, of how international arbitrators may deal with enforcement concerns in practice. This case dealt with a dispute concerning the application of commercial agency law. The place of arbitration was Germany, and the substantive law was German law. In this case, the sole arbitrator acknowledged his duty to render an enforceable award as required under the ICC rules. However, the arbitrator stated that this duty should not be understood to require arbitrators to search and consider the public policy of all states in which the winning party may seek enforcement of the arbitral award. It is sufficient for the arbitrator to consider the public policy at the most likely enforcement jurisdiction. In this case, the arbitrator inquired whether there was any violation of the public policy of the UAE, and he found none (Shehata, 2017).

Although it is neither possible nor desirable to take into account the mandatory rules and public policy of each and every possible state, some scholars recommend arbitrators consider, while drafting their awards, at least the requirements of the most important international conventions that relate to enforcement of the arbitral award and, in particular, the New York Convention (Moses, 2008).

Some scholars recommend arbitrators consider more than that. Derains (1987) suggests that arbitrators should give some attention to enforcement issues when it is possible to envisage the probable place or places of enforcement. Barraclough and Waincymer (2005) agree and opine that it is sensible to apply a state's mandatory rules if the losing party's assets are only in that state. Some authors suggest that arbitrators must consider the public policy of the most likely enforcement jurisdictions and make sure their awards do not violate their public policy (Baniassadi,1992; Rau, 2008).

Mayer (1986) also underlines the importance of carefully considering the public policy of the country or countries where the parties are likely to seek enforcement of the award. He warned that arbitrators may find themselves in a difficult situation when their award can be enforced only in the country whose mandatory rule of law is in question. The following is a quote from his article:

> Arbitrators should pay heed to the future of their award. They should consider that if they do not apply a mandatory rule of law, the award will in all likelihood be refused enforcement in the country which promulgated that rule. It often turns out that that country is the one, or at least one of several, exercising a de facto control over the situation; it is not reasonable to disregard its attitude.

Baniassadi (1992) suggests that an arbitrator 'must ensure that the enforcement of his award does not violate the national public policy where enforcement is sought'. This wording appears to impose a stricter responsibility on arbitrators to make sure their awards are enforced. There does not seem to be a lot of support for this position.

Overall, as discussed in Sections 7.3 and 7.5, the law of the place of enforcement becomes more relevant when it is the same as the law of the place of performance or the law of the place of domicile of either party. This is because non-compliance with the mandatory rules of the place of performance or the contracting parties' home jurisdictions could be viewed as offensive to the public policy of the state, and, hence, the court of that state may refuse to enforce an arbitral award.

7.7 International public policy

The earlier sections of this chapter indicate that the application of mandatory rules other than those of the governing law remains highly controversial. The arbitral jurisprudence that can be found in arbitral awards and arbitrators' writings appears to be divided on this issue and not yet settled. In some arbitral awards, arbitrators stated that party autonomy is not without limits and that they had the power to apply foreign mandatory rules. In other arbitral awards, arbitrators refused to go this far (Gaillard and Savage, 1999).

In support of a less interventionist role of arbitrators, Mayer (1986) asserts that an arbitrator is not the guardian of the public policy of any state. It follows that an arbitrator does not have a duty towards any state to defend its public interest and apply its overriding mandatory rules. The arbitrator's main duty is towards the parties. Although there is nothing wrong in principle with this argument, some arbitration scholars and practitioners do not accept that party autonomy has no limits. There are two main reasons to impose a limit on the will of the parties.

First, arbitrators should keep in mind the fate of their award. The question of whether to apply overriding mandatory rules has consequences on enforcement. Arbitrators who proceed to apply international mandatory rules beyond the parties' submissions and beyond the limits of their jurisdiction may see their awards refused enforcement on the grounds of 'excess of power' (Rau, 2008). However, it is also possible that if arbitrators refuse to apply mandatory rules that are overriding, they assume the risk that the award would be refused enforcement by at least the state the mandatory law of which is ignored on the ground of public policy (Moses, 2008). If the contract involves issues that violate the public policy (e.g., competition law) of the seat of arbitration or the place of enforcement, then the award is at risk of annulment or non-enforcement (Moses, 2008). The New York Convention enables the court where enforcement is sought to refuse recognition and enforcement of an award when they find that such recognition or enforcement would be contrary to its public policy. Despite this risk, Kuhn (1997) argues that the parties' choice of law must be respected, and any risk of non-enforcement must be accepted by the parties.

Second, arbitrators have a duty to maintain the credibility and preserve the integrity of international arbitration as an institution. If arbitration ends up being used as a conduit to evade the public policy of states that are closely connected to a commercial activity, its reputation may suffer (Baniassadi, 1992; Shehata, 2017). There will be implications for this. Hostility against arbitration may increase. Legal opinions in the states whose laws have been ignored may change regarding the arbitrability of certain disputes. The result of this would be a shrinking of the scope of arbitration and the jurisdiction of arbitrators.

For these reasons, some arbitrators may feel that they have no choice but to apply foreign mandatory rules that have a close connection to the parties. As applying foreign mandatory rules is not without problems, some arbitrators resort to the concept of international public policy. In Section 7.2, a distinction was made between private mandatory law and public mandatory law. Some scholars and arbitrators make a further distinction to assist their decision on whether to apply foreign mandatory law or not. They differentiate between overriding mandatory rules that reflect the national political and economic policies of a state and overriding mandatory rules that relate to transnational public policy (and, hence, reflect a wider consensus amongst the international community) (Shehata, 2017). Arbitrators may use either notion to sanction more or less the same group of conducts widely viewed as unacceptable (such as apartheid, corruption, customs offences, breaches of embargoes, and antitrust violations) (Gaillard and Savage, 1999). However, given that an arbitral award relying on foreign mandatory rules is vulnerable to the risk of setting aside based on the grounds of arbitrators' exceeding their power or mandate, applying the notion of international public policy appears to be safer and more acceptable. Thus, it is advisable, if in need, to base a decision on international public policy ground that sounds more consistent with the source of legitimacy of international arbitration. In practice, the controversy surrounding the application of mandatory rules by arbitrators becomes more significant when the mandatory rules neither belong to the governing law chosen by the parties nor reflect an international public policy (Gaillard and Savage, 1999).

Although it is true that parties to an international contract can opt for arbitration to privately resolve their dispute and are free to choose the law that they wish to govern their contract and to influence the arbitration process and decision-making constraints, it is also true that arbitrators' powers are constrained by international public policy considerations (Gaillard and Savage, 1999). These considerations, derived from international public law, aim to limit contractual and arbitral freedom. If an arbitral tribunal finds that the parties' contract contradicts principles it views as forming part of truly international public policy, it should apply such principles over the will of the parties (Baniassadi, 1992). It follows that contracting parties cannot enter into an agreement to pay bribes or to engage in anti-competitive business practices to secure the award of construction contracts and then expect the international arbitration system to legitimately enforce that agreement (of course in case of full detachment, by the loser voluntary compliance, this can escape from scrutiny) (De Ly, di Brozolo, and Friedman, 2008). In a number of ICC cases (e.g., ICC Case No. 1110/1963, ICC Case No. 3916/1982), arbitrators refused to enforce contracts involving bribery, and they declared them contrary to international public policy and thus void. Nevertheless, evidence from arbitration awards illustrates that some arbitral tribunals applied overriding mandatory rules that were neither part of the substantive law nor part of international public policy (Shehata, 2017).

To sum up, the issue concerning the arbitral duty regarding the applicability of foreign mandatory rules or international public policy has not yet been resolved. The problem is deeply rooted in the classical dilemma concerning the line that needs to be drawn between party autonomy and state(s) interests (Rau, 2008). In fact, most contentious issues in the theory and practice of international arbitration can be traced to the tension between the 'contractualist' and 'jurisdictionalist' theories of international arbitration (Barraclough and Waincymer, 2005; Martin, 2016). Under a contractualist conception of arbitration, which privileges party autonomy, an arbitrator has no power or mandate to apply foreign mandatory law that is closely connected to the dispute in lieu of what the parties' contract and its governing law provide. Under a jurisdictionalist conception of arbitration, the conflict of laws rules of the seat of the arbitration would provide guidance on the relevance and applicability of foreign mandatory rules (Barraclough and Waincymer, 2005). The arbitrator's approach depends on how the nature of arbitration is viewed, and, since that can be legitimately conceptualised in different ways, a universal approach to the applicability of foreign overriding mandatory rules does not exist (Barraclough and Waincymer, 2005). Overall, it seems arbitrators tend to be reluctant to apply mandatory rules other than those of the governing law (i.e., *lex contractus*) (Gaillard and Savage, 1999). In so doing, they stick to their contractual mandate.

7.8 Conclusion

This chapter examines whether mandatory rules of foreign law might be applicable to disputes arising from international construction contracts. It finds that arbitration practice is divided on this issue. In a number of arbitration awards, the tribunals applied mandatory rules of foreign law or declared the possibility of doing so. A small number of the arbitrators interviewed by the author indicated their willingness to keep an open mind on the issue of the applicability of mandatory rules of law that are foreign to the substantive law chosen by the parties. They tend to be receptive to arguments that foreign mandatory law should be considered when that law is closely connected to the dispute. The close connection argument assumes more weight when, for example, the foreign mandatory law is the law of the place of performance or the law of the parties' home countries and at the same time the law of the enforcement jurisdiction. In this case, the risk of non-enforcement leads some arbitrators to follow a pragmatic approach. With the lack of a sound theoretical rationale for applying the mandatory law of a foreign country, this pragmatic stance could be justified. It is more difficult to justify that arbitrators should consider or apply a foreign mandatory law that is not the law of the country of enforcement of an arbitral award without the parties' agreement. Nevertheless, the international arbitration community remains divided on this issue.

Despite the lack of consensus among the arbitration community, this chapter provides evidence that it seems rare for foreign mandatory rules to affect arbitrators' substantive decisions. This largely agrees with the statement of Gaillard and Savage (1999): 'we know of virtually no cases where the arbitrators have relied on the application of a mandatory rule to justify a decision other than that would have resulted [in any event] from the application of the law chosen by the parties'.

Three reasons explain arbitrators' disinclination to apply a foreign mandatory law of public nature (reflecting the state's public policy).

First, when arbitrators decide on whether to apply a foreign mandatory rule, they carefully consider the implications on the enforceability of the arbitration award. There is a non-enforcement risk if arbitrators apply mandatory rules of law that are foreign to the governing law of the contract. The arbitral award may not be enforced on 'excess of power' grounds.

Second, enforcing a foreign mandatory law could have the effect of rendering the parties' contract null and void. This, in turn, would allow one party, usually the non-performing party (defendant), to free itself from the obligations to which it freely agreed. Entering into a contract and later on arguing that the contract is void because it violates a foreign mandatory law the parties were aware of is a breach of the principle of good faith in contract negotiation and performance. The duty of good faith is recognised in civil law countries and is a generally accepted principle of international commercial law (e.g., see UNIDROIT).

Third, arbitrators consider themselves as the private judges of the parties with a mandate to determine their disputes according to their contract and the law they chose to govern their contract. Thus, they are keen to meet the legitimate expectation of the parties. In most cases, a tribunal's decision on whether to apply a foreign mandatory rule will frustrate at least one party. However, in less frequent situations, the tribunal may frustrate the parties' expectations when they raise the issue of the illegality of the contract by their own initiative and determine that the contract is void on the ground that the contract is contrary to international public policy (e.g., a contract involving bribery). Although many arbitrators do not view their role as the guardian of a state's public policy and its interest in having its mandatory law applied, it seems there is a general acceptance of the notion of international public policy that challenges practices that are widely viewed as immoral and unethical. Thus, as long as there is nothing fundamentally immoral and unethical, which otherwise is usually viewed as a violation of international public policy, international arbitrators seem to be reluctant to impose mandatory rules of law foreign to the substantive law the parties selected to govern their commercial relationship.

7.9 References

Arnaldez, J.J., Derains, Y. and Hascher, D. (2003). *Collection of ICC arbitral awards, 1996-2000* (Vol. 4). Alphen aan den Rijn: Kluwer Law International.

Baniassadi, M. R. (1992). Do mandatory rules of public law limit choice of law in international commercial arbitration? *International Tax & Business Lawyer*, 10, 59.

Barraclough, A. & Waincymer, J. (2005). Mandatory rules of law in international commercial arbitration. *Melbourne Journal of International Law*, 6, 205.

Basaran, H. R. (2014). Is International Arbitration Universal. *ILSA Journal of International & Comparative Law*, 21, 497.

Burr, A. (2016). *Delay and Disruption in Construction Contracts.* Oxford: Informa Law from Routledge.

Charrett, D. (2012). A common law of construction contracts: Or vive la différence? *International Construction Law Review*, 29(1), 72–84.

De Ly, F., di Brozolo, L. & Friedman, M. (2008). *Ascertaining the Contents of the Applicable Law in International Commercial Arbitration.* International Commercial Arbitration Committee of the International Law Association. Available at https://www.ila-hq.org/en_GB/committees/international-commercial-arbitration-1989 [Accessed 12 December 2016].

Derains, Y. & Schwartz, E. A. (2005). *A Guide to the ICC Rules of Arbitration.* The Hague: Kluwer Law International.

Gaillard, E. & Savage, J. (1999). *Fouchard, Gaillard, Goldman on International Commercial Arbitration.* The Hague: Kluwer law international.

Karton, J. (2013). *The Culture of International Arbitration and the Evolution of Contract Law.* Oxford: Oxford University Press.

Karton, J. (2015). The arbitral role in contractual interpretation. *Journal of International Dispute Settlement*, 6(1), 4–41.

Kreindler, R. H. (2013). *Competence-Competence in the Face of Illegality in Contracts and Arbitration Agreements.* Leiden: BRILL.

Kuhn, W. (1997). Choice of Substantive Law in the Practice of International Arbitration. *International Business Lawyer*, 25, 148.

Lagerberg, G. & Mistelis, L. (2008). International Arbitration: Corporate Attitudes and Practices. Queen Mary University of London and School of International Arbitration. Available at https://arbitration.qmul.ac.uk/media/arbitration/docs/IAstudy_2008.pdf [Accessed 12 December 2022].

Martin, J.B. (2016). Contractualists Versus Jurisdictionalists: Who is Winning the Mandatory Law Debate in International Commercial Arbitration?. *The American Review of International Arbitration*, 27(4), 475–477.

Mayer, P. (1986). Mandatory rules of law in international arbitration. *Arbitration International*, 2(4), 274–293.

Moses, M. L. (2008). *The Principles and Practice of International Commercial Arbitration.* Cambridge: Cambridge University Press.

Moss, G. (2004). Introductory materials on international commercial law. *Transnational Dispute Management*, 1(3), 1–161.

Osing, S. and Neumeier, F., 2012. Limitation periods in construction law: An international overview and comparison, exemplified by common and the civil law jurisdictions. *Construction Law International*, 7, 35.

Park, W. W. (2010). Arbitrators and accuracy. *Journal of International Dispute Settlement*, 1(1), 25–53.

Radjai, N., (2009). Where there's smoke, there's fire? Proving illegality in international arbitration. *Arbitration Newsletter*, 139–143.

Rau, A. (2008). The arbitrator and mandatory rules of law. *The American Review of International Arbitration*, 18, 51–88.

Sakr, M. (2009). Turnkey contracting under the ICC model contract for major projects: A Middle Eastern law perspective. *International Construction Law Review*, 26(2), 146.

Shehata, I. (2017). Application of overriding mandatory rules in international commercial arbitration: An empirical analysis. *World Arbitration & Mediation Review*, *11*(4), 383–418.

Teramura, N. (2020). *Ex Aequo et Bono as a Response to the 'Over-Judicialisation' of International Commercial Arbitration*. Alphen aan den Rijn: Kluwer Law International.

Uff, J. (2008). Diversity in international construction arbitration: Is it to be avoided or welcomed? The Society of Construction Arbitrators, Budapest. Available at https://www.constructionarbitrators.org/publications [Accessed 18 November 2022].

United Nations Commission on International Trade Law (UNCITRAL) (1988). *Legal Guide on Drawing Up International Contracts for the Construction of Industrial Works*. Vienna, Austria: UNCITRAL.

Waincymer, J. (2011). International Arbitration and the Duty to Know the Law. *Journal of International Arbitration*, 28(3), 201–242.

CHAPTER 8

The arbitrator's background

8.1 Introduction

It is often said in arbitration circles that 'Arbitration is as good as the arbitrator'. The arbitrator has a significant effect on managing the arbitration procedure and making sure it runs smoothly, efficiently, and without committing procedural errors that might affect the enforceability of the award. This saying applies not only to the procedural aspects of arbitration but to the substantive aspects as well. The final decision on the substance of the parties' dispute might depend on who is making the decision. This is the elephant in the room, which probably not many writers in the field talk about. This is not surprising because most writers and commentators tend to be arbitrators themselves, and they may not be keen to reveal all things that influence their decisions. This chapter aims to bring to the forefront the conversation on the relationship between the arbitration outcome and the arbitrator's background.

This chapter examines the factors other than the merits of the case as presented by the parties which may influence arbitrators' decisions and the outcome of the dispute. Specifically, it discusses the potential effect of different forms of unconscious bias, which may originate from the arbitrator's professional or legal background, for instance, on the arbitration outcome. In the context of this book, the professional background relates to the arbitrator's current and past experience in the construction industry. The potential effect of the arbitrator's engineering and construction experience on their decisions is discussed in Section 8.3. The legal background refers to the legal system the arbitrator was trained in. The potential effect of the arbitrator's legal background on their decisions is discussed in Section 8.4. The arbitrator's experience in setting as an arbitrator in international arbitration is another factor. The moderating effect of the arbitrator's experience on their preconceptions is touched on in Section 8.5. Then, the practical implications of the arbitration community's understanding of the bias effects, especially in relation to the selection of arbitrators, are discussed in Section 8.6. This is followed by a discussion of how the party-appointment system in international arbitration may have an influence on arbitrators' decisions.

8.2 Background of the arbitrator

Arbitrators are rational human beings, and they make rational decisions. However, this rationality assumption can be challenged based on psychological theories. The human mind creates an interpretive system to make sense of events in the outside world. This complex system of interpretation and construction of meaning is the central foundation of human psychology. It comes into being as a result of accumulations of knowledge and experiences that are stored and organised in the human mind and called upon in the future

DOI: 10.4324/b22975-8

to interpret and understand certain events, behaviours, and so on (Bruner, 1990 cited in Waites and Lawrence, 2010). As decision-makers, arbitrators do not make decisions without first taking into consideration their worldviews. They use lenses to view and perceive the world around them. These lenses filter everything arbitrators hear and read in accordance with their previous life experiences. If a party's arguments match the arbitrator's worldview, then they are likely to be accepted by the arbitrator. On the other hand, if a party's arguments are inconsistent with the arbitrator's views of what acceptable conduct and contracting behaviour look like, then they are harder to win (Waites and Lawrence, 2010).

So, ultimately, the arbitrator's decisions on the facts (i.e., what they believe to have happened) and on the interpretation of the parties' contract and the law (i.e., what they believe to be wrong and what they believe to be right) are influenced by their own interpretive system (Waites and Lawrence, 2010). Hence, although the factual and legal merits of the case are the strongest predictors of the arbitration's outcome, they are not the only factors affecting the decision. Arbitrators, like judges, are influenced by psychological factors that affect how they view and assess evidence and how they interpret the parties' contract and applicable law (Diamond, 2003).

Arbitrators are human beings. They cannot completely set aside their own knowledge and experiences. They cannot unlearn what they learnt and unsee what they saw. They cannot detach themselves from origins, from environments, or from cultural, religious, and social values (Bedjaqui, 1988).

The arbitrator's background is a multidimensional construct. The arbitrator's formation may come from his or her professional practice, legal tradition, arbitration experience, nationality, culture, beliefs, and value system. This naturally gives rise to some form of bias, such as professional bias, legal tradition bias, cultural bias, subject-matter bias, and also appointment party bias (Diamond, 2003; Sussman, E., 2014). Any discussion of arbitral decision-making without reference to biases is incomplete.

Bias means prejudice or an inclination to prefer somebody or something over another. It can be conscious, deliberate, and apparent or subconscious and, hence, hidden and unrecognised. If bias is apparent then the parties can challenge it. Deliberate bias to favour one party, usually the appointing party, qualifies for misconduct and this can be procedurally challenged. However, this is not the type of bias discussed in this chapter. The exclusion of its discussion is not because it is less important or limited in frequency. In fact, many arbitrators have spoken of horror stories they experienced in arbitration proceedings involving 'hired gun' arbitrators acting as party partisans (Capper, 2014; Mayer, P., 2014; Meyer, B., 2014). However, this form of bias relates to the problem of corruption and unethical practice and is relatively easier to deal with than other types of biases.

Arbitration institutions have published guidance and rules to restrict the appointment of arbitrators who appear to be lacking neutrality and independence. These usually require the application of objective tests to determine whether a prospective arbitrator has a current or previous business or personal connections to the parties in disputes or a specific interest in the outcome of the dispute (e.g., the IBA Guidelines) (Kurkela and Turunen, 2010; Caron, 2015).

Further, the parties can challenge this conduct based on procedural grounds. A key instrument to counter appointing party bias is having a strong chair. Whereas in many arbitrations each party selects an arbitrator, the two party-appointed arbitrators select a third arbitrator acting as the chair of the tribunal. The chair is independent of the parties and tends to be more neutral. Of course, in theory, all tribunal members must be neutral, but, in practice, this is not always the case.

This chapter is not concerned with biases arising from an arbitrator's lack of independence and neutrality which are objective and easier to identify and challenge. It is mainly concerned with cognitive or mental biases or inclinations formed by education and experience (i.e., the partiality of mind problem). These predispositions or predilections (i.e., subconscious biases) are probably more problematic. They are mental inclinations that all people develop, including judges and arbitrators, and appear to be more widespread than deliberate bias in international arbitration. They are unconscious and honest distortions of how something is viewed or interpreted. They are hard to recognise even by the arbitrators affected by them. By definition, these are subconscious biases that arbitrators are not aware of. If they can be identified, they can be controlled and neutralised by the tribunal itself or challenged by the parties.

As they are difficult to prove, subconscious biases are not the concern of the law. Although judges have preconceived notions, a lawyer has no chance to challenge a judge's decision on the ground that the judge is sceptical of a legal theory on which the lawyer bases his case (Paulsson, 1997). The English law position as stated in *Locabail v. Bayfield Properties [2000]* is 'the law does not countenance the questioning of a judge about extraneous influences affecting his mind'.

Similarly, in international arbitration, subconscious biases do not qualify as a valid reason for annulling an award. Arbitration laws and rules have focused only on the deliberate bias. All these reasons make the subconscious or unconscious form of bias the most serious bias in international arbitration.

There is anecdotal evidence of different forms of unconscious bias in international arbitration. This evidence is reported in the next sections. There is also a considerable empirical body of literature on how subconscious bias affects judicial decision-making. The units of analysis are judges, jurors, and arbitrators. The vast majority of these studies come from the US domestic context, and they draw on different fields, such as psychology and economics. The studies specifically dealing with commercial and construction arbitrators are limited, and, in the context of international arbitration, they are scant (Karton, 2014; Waites and Lawrence, 2010; Drahozal, 2003; Karton, 2013). The author is not aware of any study that empirically tests the relationship between one or more international arbitrators' characteristics and their decisions. Hence, the evidence on international arbitrators' proneness to subconscious bias remains anecdotal in nature.

This problem was described by Goodman-Everard (1991), cited in Flood and Caiger (1993), as follows:

> All international lawyers and arbitrators are firmly rooted, sometimes unwittingly so, in a national framework of law, culture, economic and social circumstances, political and/or religious values and convictions, providing them with a cultural baggage which largely colours their way of thinking and reasoning. This rootedness may cause misunderstandings or false understandings, as much between extremes as between neighbours: similarity and dissimilarity of cultures may in equal measure be enemies of a proper understanding of the parties' viewpoints

8.3 Arbitrator's professional background

An arbitrator's professional experience in the construction industry is part of their formation. An arbitrator may be a practising architect, engineer, contract manager, or project manager. However, this profile seems to be rare in international construction arbitration. This is why most writings in this area tend to be focused on domestic construction arbitration and particularly in the United States. These writings are concerned with the question of whether the arbitrator's experience in the construction industry leads to certain preconceptions about certain types of disputes (Ossman, 2003).

Arbitrators may have an inclination or a predisposition to evaluate facts or the disputants' behaviour and conduct according to the area of the industry they have served in. They may use the same lenses they used as practitioners and, hence, be protective of their profession and fellow professionals. It follows that an engineer arbitrator may tend to be protective of the engineering profession and be sympathetic to the arguments of fellow engineers involved in the dispute. Similarly, contractor arbitrators may sympathise with contractors involved in the dispute, recognising similar experiences in their own past (Ossman, 2003). Although the advantage of having an arbitrator who has a background in engineering and construction is that they find it easier to comprehend the technical details and the facts of the dispute, the danger is that they may also have preexisting ideas that make them lean towards one side or the other. They may rely on similar experiences they had to decide whether to believe something and to decide the likelihood or believability that something happened. This cognitive bias is called the 'representativeness heuristic'. It is a mental shortcut that helps people quickly understand events in the social world around them. Therefore, an arbitrator's prior professional experience in the construction industry can be both a strength and a weakness (Coulson, 1990).

This belief has led some writers to recommend disputants select arbitrators who share with them the same profession or experience. In his chapter titled 'How to Win at Arbitration' published by the American Arbitration Association, Madden (1994), cited in Ossman (2003), wrote the following:

> A contractor defending a claim by an owner may believe that a contractor arbitrator would be more sympathetic to his position … a contractor would most certainly favor a lawyer arbitrator if the contractor has a very strong legal case.

This means that arbitrators' predispositions have implications for practice and, specifically, for arbitrator selection. It seems this is something that has been recognised and pursued by the parties and their legal counsel in practice, as will be explained later in this chapter.

Several studies were undertaken in the context of US arbitration to examine the influence of arbitrators' background characteristics on their decisions. Some of these studies focused on the 'affinity effect' or the 'affinity bias'. Affinity effects happen as a result of the decision-makers' influence by their social backgrounds, prior experiences, and professional affiliations when judging the wrongness or rightness of the parties' behaviour. This form of unconscious bias causes decision-makers to favour or share the perspective of those who share with them a similar set of prior experiences or background characteristics (Diamond, 2003).

One of the early studies on decision-making bias in commercial arbitration was undertaken by Haggard and Mentschikoff (1977). Twenty panels of arbitrators on the American

Arbitration Association list of arbitrators had to decide on a distribution dispute. Half of the arbitrators who participated in the study were brokers, while the remaining half were manufacturers. The results of their study indicated that brokers acting as arbitrators were far more likely to favour the broker defendant than arbitrators from the manufacturers' group.

However, not everyone agrees with this hypothesis of ingroup favouritism (i.e., an arbitrator favours the disputing party with a similar industry experience). Two similar 'theories' that may provide an alternative explanation of the effect of an arbitrator being an affiliate of a professional or industry group are 'similarity breeds contempt' and the 'black sheep effect' (Ossman, 2003). The 'similarity breeds contempt' theory suggests that decision-makers may disassociate themselves from the wrongdoer who belongs to their group by imposing a heavier penalty than what they would impose on a member of a different group misbehaving in the same manner. The 'black sheep effect' theory suggests that judgements about in-group members, whether in favour or against, are more extreme than judgements about out-group members. In other words, judgements about in-group members may be more positive or more negative than judgements about out-group members. The 'black sheep effect' theory is derived from the 'social identity' theory. It suggests that decision-makers will protect the group's identity and reputation by favouring norm-compliant members and heavily penalising deviant members (Marques, Yzerby, and Leyens, 1988).

Ossman (2003) examined the question of subconscious bias in US construction arbitration. He used quantitative research in a study in which 429 construction arbitrators participated that required them to decide on a hypothetical construction dispute scenario. He found no evidence of ingroup favouritism. Quite the opposite – he suggested that the 'similarity breeds contempt' theory better explained the results of his study. He concluded: 'A contractor with a shaky claim foundation or questionable history should not engage another contractor to judge the claim'.

The author undertook a qualitative study into how construction arbitrators make their decisions in Palestine. Drawing on 12 semi-structured interviews with engineers, contractors, and lawyers who sat as arbitrators in domestic disputes, there was evidence, but inconclusive, of in-group favouritism. A few arbitrators from the contractors' group expressed their distaste or hostility towards certain contractual clauses that exist in some standard forms of contract. They stated that these contracts are drafted or amended by the employer and, thus, are biased towards the employer. They are usually offered on the basis of 'take it or leave it'. Although they stated that their starting point is to enforce the contract, they suggested they may not enforce such 'onerous contractual clauses' when they sit as arbitrators. On the other hand, the arbitrators from the engineers' group, and also the lawyer group, appeared more likely to adhere to the contract even if its terms are unfair or onerous (Besaiso, 2017).

Most of the literature concerned with the effect of arbitrators' professional affiliation on their decision focuses on US commercial arbitration and, to a lesser degree, construction arbitration. Although useful, it is important to note that the environment of domestic construction arbitration in the United States is different from international construction arbitration. The overwhelming majority of international construction arbitrators come from the legal profession (lawyers, barristers, retired judges, etc.). Hence, the applicability of the foregoing assertions to international construction arbitrators is almost null.

Nevertheless, the author managed to interview a few international construction arbitrators who had previous technical and/or commercial experience in the construction industry before qualifying as lawyers or sitting as international arbitrators. The interviews with them shed some light on the potential influence of professional formation on the decisions of international construction arbitrators.

One aspect of arbitral decision-making that seems to be affected by an arbitrator's background is their approach to contract interpretation. Having a professional background seems to lead arbitrators to give more weight to commercial practice than legal theory. A few arbitrators interviewed by the author believe that their professional backgrounds and their detailed knowledge of how a particular industry works make them better able to understand the facts, evaluate the expert opinion, and construe the contract in a manner that leads to 'the right' result that is fair and just and meets the parties' commercial expectations and intentions.

The author's interview with the Palestinian construction arbitrator who is based in Dubai (see Section 4.3.3) shows how his background in the construction business influenced his interpretation approach. He said he might not enforce certain contractual clauses and specification requirements that are typically used in all construction contracts but that no one pays attention to them. This is because the parties' real intention, in some situations, is more likely to be that which is understood from the norms and customs of the industry. Accordingly, he said that strong customs may trump express terms in the parties' contract.

A Scottish arbitrator, who was interviewed by the author, defended the importance of having experience in the relevant industry or commercial understanding of how it operates when sitting as an arbitrator. He started his career in the construction industry and, specifically, in the construction of large oil production platforms and oil rigs before practising arbitration. He referred to an arbitration case concerning the operation of an offshore oil well and asserted that the tribunal, which was composed of lawyers with no previous exposure to oil and gas contracts, reached a wrong decision on a matter of contract interpretation. In his opinion, the tribunal's lack of familiarity with the customary practice in the oil and gas industry was the main reason for the incorrect result that was based on a black letter law analysis and did not meet the parties' expectations. As a commercial man and lawyer in the oil and gas sector, he said he would have arrived at a different conclusion that makes commercial sense. This view demonstrates that even though the contract and the governing law are the fundamental grounds for finding a solution, different arbitrators may reach different conclusions based on their backgrounds.

Similarly, an interview the author conducted with an Egyptian arbitrator illustrates how an arbitrator's professional background may affect his or her contract interpretation approach. The arbitrator stated that he follows a business common-sense interpretation and criticised those who reach conclusions that do not make commercial sense and hide behind claims that the result was in accordance with the law. The arbitrator underlined the importance of the applicable law in determining disputes under international arbitration, but he asserted that the result must be commercially sensible. He explained the rationale for his commercial approach to contract interpretation by referring to his previous experience in the business world prior to embarking on his legal career. In the early years of his professional life, he worked as an engineer at a multinational technology company and, then, following receiving a law degree he worked as an in-house counsel at a multinational law firm. This allowed him to develop a good understanding of the business side of things. Throughout the rest of his professional life, he practised law and arbitration. Given this background, as an arbitrator, he always tries to follow a commercially reasonable interpretation. In his view, the law should serve commerce, and judges and arbitrators should be the wheels of commerce by upholding the commercial expectations of the parties. He was critical of the argument that businesses prefer the predictability of dispute outcomes and that is why businesspeople expect arbitrators to apply the law. He described this argument as 'academic' and one that does not reflect the commercial expectations of businesspeople, who focus on the 'commercial deal' rather than the 'law of contract'. The Egyptian arbitrator was critical of those who claim they follow the law and justify their non-commercially reasonable decisions by strict adherence to the law. In his experience, such claims are sometimes used by arbitrators who are biased and intend to reach conclusions that favour the party that appointed them even if the conclusions are not sensible from a commercial point of view. The following is an excerpt from his interview:

> Talking about the predictability of the law is one of those claims that are used by people who are narrow-minded, captivated by the text without having the common sense and commercial approach to interpretation, or biased; looking to find a way out for the person who nominated them. In another case, you can see him or her saying a completely different thing. That is what I call hypocrisy because you should have one approach.

The professional background of arbitrators might affect how arbitrators assess evidence and decide whether to believe it or not. It is difficult to find international arbitrators who are or were engineering and construction professionals (e.g., engineers, contract managers, commercial managers, project managers, and the like) because the international arbitration landscape is dominated by legal professionals. However, the author interviewed a few arbitrators who had significant commercial experience in the engineering and construction industry. They had significant experience in dispute resolution, but their participation in international arbitration was limited. They believe that their commercial experience gives them an advantage, over arbitrators with no similar credentials, in assessing evidence and finding the facts. At the end of the day, the assessment of evidence is a subjective exercise. The result depends on the person and his or her set of experiences in life. Although arbitrators can use the procedure to let people tell them the facts, they can rely on their own knowledge and experience to give weight to the evidence the parties provide. That is why it is important for an arbitrator to have the right characteristics, including relevant industry knowledge and experience. Reflecting this viewpoint, an English arbitrator interviewed by the author stated:

> In a dispute I arbitrated … I questioned the commercial director for the contractor … I am myself a commercial director and lawyer… and I found that I just did not believe him because I know how I would deal with a particular problem, and he was saying something I knew I would never have done and therefore I thought that he was either a complete fool or he was not telling the truth … I did not believe he was a fool, therefore, he was not telling the truth … you know, my experience told me not to believe his evidence.

Although arbitrators refer to their relevant industry knowledge and experience as an advantage to get to the 'truth', the psychology literature warns that this may lead to 'expectations bias' or 'confirmation bias'. Decision-makers in all settings, including arbitrators, tend to give more scrutiny and possibly reject information or evidence that is inconsistent with their expectations. People tend to give more attention to and better remember information that is consistent with their experience (Diamond, 2003).

An Irish arbitrator, with significant domestic and international adjudication experience but limited participation in international arbitration, revealed how he relies on his experience in the construction industry to determine the credibility and believability of factual evidence. The construction industry has an infamous reputation for adversarial employer-contractor relationships and prevailing claim culture. Some contractors prepare the ground for claims in an early stage. They plan their claims even before the contract award and implement their plans in a way that may give neutral observers the impression that they were not aware of certain facts and problems leading to the claim. It is like a theatrical performance where some contractors quietly construct the factual matrix of the dispute, without employers taking notice, to give them a contractual and legal advantage when it comes to adjudication or arbitration. Having been exposed to this practice and contracting behaviour, the arbitrator said he would be able to detect it.

The few arbitrators with relevant industry experience interviewed for this work were critical of the dominance and control of the legal profession in international construction arbitrations. The criticism is based on two assertions. The first assertion is that construction professionals, such as engineers and project managers, are better able to reach decisions that make commercial sense. Familiarity with commercial practice, trade customs, and usages is important to understand the parties' expectations and reach decisions that are commercially sensible. The second assertion is that construction professionals are better able to assess factual and expert evidence. In their opinion, tribunals that are entirely composed of legal professionals are likely to make incorrect or unfair judgements. They referred to arbitration cases they are familiar with in which tribunals reached wrong decisions in their opinion. They attributed the 'wrong result' to the tribunal's lack of familiarity and experience in the relevant industry. Therefore, they argue that a more balanced composition of arbitral tribunals is needed. In their opinion, a balanced tribunal includes construction professionals who are good at assessing the evidence and finding the facts and understanding commercial practice, without excluding legal professionals who are the masters of procedure and naturally better at interpreting and applying the law to the facts. They maintain that construction professionals should be more represented because the resolution of construction disputes largely depends on finding the facts.

The competition between legal professionals and engineering and construction professionals on who makes a better construction arbitrator is not new. More than 100 years ago, Wright (1913) argued against the involvement of legal professionals in construction arbitration in the United States. He asserted that construction professionals are better at arbitrating construction disputes than their legal counterparts. He wrote:

> Technical arbitrators have a way of getting down to the facts. They go at once to the very essence of the dispute, and are not hampered by precedent, cases, or court rules. In short, they quickly get to the truth, the whole truth, and nothing but the truth, without formality or hindrance, and are then able to render judgment according to the testimony coupled with their own technical knowledge in a common-sense, business-like manner, and their decisions are usually accepted in good grace by the disputants.

In his view, most construction disputes concerned factual questions, which still hold true today, and technical arbitrators are better able than legal professionals to understand the construction contract, including its drawings, specifications, and trade customs.

Similar sentiments were expressed in the United Kingdom. In the early 20th century, construction arbitration was less legalistic as lawyers were hardly involved. However, this gradually changed after World War II. The court's dissatisfaction with errors in law in arbitration awards rendered by non-lawyer arbitrators was the main driver for this change. Non-lawyer construction arbitrators were deciding cases with no reference to legal principles. The struggle between construction professionals and legal professionals over the legitimacy to preside over construction arbitration has raged for decades. A manifestation of this struggle was a debate on whether lawyers were killing arbitration at the Chartered Institute of Arbitrators in 1991 (Flood and Caiger, 1993).

Flood and Caiger (1993) undertook interview-based sociological research on the perceptions of UK construction arbitrators on the struggle between lawyers and non-lawyers over the control of arbitration. One architect arbitrator who started his arbitration career in the 1940s insisted that:

> An arbitrator must know the trade otherwise he cannot decide what is right or wrong. He must know some law: some evidence and contract, not too much. And he must have the ability to weigh evidence. This can be learned.

In fact, the idea that merchants or 'commercial men' are the best judges of their own disputes has existed since at least the Middle Ages. Merchants selected merchants to determine their disputes based on the customs and trade usages (alternatively known as merchant law).

Nowadays, the international construction arbitration environment is dominated by legal professionals. There are two reasons for the dominance of the legal profession. First, the procedural aspects of arbitrators' decisions are more critical than their substantive aspects. This is because procedural errors can lead to an annulment or non-enforcement of an arbitral award, whereas erroneous fact-finding or legal conclusions do not normally constitute grounds for challenge. Second, the parties expect their disputes to be resolved in accordance with their contract and the governing law. They want a legal solution to their dispute, and this is the reason for their choice of a specific national law to govern the interpretation of their contract and the choice of arbitrators with legal backgrounds. If the parties want a different result to their dispute that is not necessarily based on the law, then they should select construction professionals, not legal professionals, as was suggested by some arbitrators with legal backgrounds in their interviews with the author.

Although the formalist view of arbitral decision-making assumes that the outcome is independent of the arbitrator and it depends solely on the wording of the contract and the governing law, arbitrators may reach different conclusions due to their different backgrounds. Construction professionals are likely to give more attention to the facts of the dispute and interpret the contract based on what makes commercial sense with little attention being given to the law. This is because they will have more difficulty applying the law than legally qualified arbitrators. On the other hand, legal professionals with little or no knowledge of the industry are likely to give more attention to the law and legal interpretation of the parties' contract with little attention being given to commercial practice.

This view, however, is not shared by everyone in the international arbitration community. Unsurprisingly, legally qualified arbitrators did not think they are inferior at finding the facts. This is especially the case for legal professionals with significant experience in the construction industry (i.e., specialists, not generalists). For example, construction lawyers are used to preparing cases as counsel, dealing with factual evidence, quantum experts, and large contract documents, such as specifications, drawings, contract conditions, etc. The same thing applies to specialist judges, such as those sitting in the Technology and Construction court in England and Wales. However, this may not extend to law professors. Arbitration lawyers have differing opinions on whether law professors make good arbitrators. In general, civil law lawyers tend to think professors make good arbitrators, while common law lawyers tend to think otherwise. The main concern of common law lawyers is that law professors tend to lack sufficient practical commercial experience and focus on legal analysis (Moses, 2008).

Although legally trained arbitrators did not agree with the proposition that construction professionals are better at assessing evidence of fact, they acknowledged that they need more assistance and guidance with the technical and engineering aspects of disputes. However, they played down the effect of this as they can seek expert opinion. Experts can be appointed by the tribunal or by the parties to provide opinions on technical matters in relation to engineering, construction, and project management (e.g., causes of defects, delays, quantum).

As stated earlier, the international construction arbitration environment is dominated by legal professionals. As a result, unconscious bias regarding the construction parties' professional affiliations tends to be of minimal effect. The most serious bias affecting international arbitrators is probably that related to their legal tradition. The next section provides a brief discussion of the effect of bias arising from the legal tradition of international arbitrators.

8.4 Arbitrator's legal background

> The most serious bias in our world of international arbitration is the one we are least aware of. The most serious bias confronting this group of people in this room or any discussion of international arbitration is that unspoken, often unrecognised legal cultural bias; that we bring our formation into the room with us and do not even realise it is there. I have been horrified especially by my co-English arbitrators who have not realised that the English solution is simply an English solution. They may think it is universal, perfect, objective and to be admired and they are wrong on all counts in some cases ... It is this unspoken, unrealised type of bias which seems to me to be the most significant.
>
> *(Capper, 2014, p. 46)*

In addition to the professional background, the legal background of an arbitrator may influence their approach to contract interpretation and their understanding of the legal principles that would apply to interpretation. This was explicit in the interviews the author conducted with international arbitrators in which some of them expressed their inclination towards the legal approach of the jurisdiction they trained in.

A Danish arbitrator stated that his decision would be based on the substantive law selected by the parties, but he was candid that his legal tradition would influence his decision. The following is an excerpt from the interview:

> I have to apply the substantive law because that is the choice of law in the contract, but ... the interpretation will of course be influenced by my experience and my tradition ... the decision is always influenced by the person making the decision and the tradition that this person comes from.

A Canadian arbitrator who was first trained in common law but later studied law in France said that she would interpret the contract according to the governing law chosen by the parties, but evidence of the possible effect of her legal background on her approach to contract interpretation emerged at various points throughout the conversation with the author. Drawing on her dual formation in common law and civil law legal systems, she stated:

> My feeling is that if you compare me to an English barrister I will be much less a black-letter lawyer … my civil law experience I think let me seek a practical and commercial decision and try to fit that within the four corners of the contract.

The perception that civil law lawyers tend to be closer to commerce and the realities of commercial practice resonates in international arbitration literature. The civil law arbitrators interviewed for this work expressed similar sentiments, but the common law arbitrators, unsurprisingly, did not agree with this.

The Canadian arbitrator referred to an arbitration case she was involved in as a legal counsel. Her account of the case illustrates her belief that the legal background of the arbitrator matters. The following is an excerpt from her interview:

> I had arbitration a few years ago, and the moment I heard the name of the arbitrator, I thought game over … because I knew that we would be relying on the circumstances surrounding the contract in order to interpret the responsibilities of my client under that contract… but the arbitrator was an English barrister…and I knew I would never be able to convince him to take a civil law approach and that was what we needed in order to win this arbitration … So, had we had a French lawyer or somebody from the area who understood the situation there, we probably would have had a completely different result.

The argument that an arbitrator's legal background has an influence on the arbitration outcome has significant implications for practice. The significance of this cannot be overstated especially because not many arbitrators acknowledge their biases and preconceptions, at least in public. The Canadian arbitrator elaborated on this theme and shared her experience and observations regarding legal tradition bias. The following is an excerpt from her interview:

> When I teach arbitration I always tell my students that once they have been appointed as arbitrators, they do not represent any one legal tradition and they do not have home jurisdiction anymore except the seat of arbitration. They should leave their bags at the door. That is what I teach. That is the theory. The reality is many arbitrators do not do that. They consciously do not do that. They say this is how I decide, this is how I was trained, this is what I think is right, this is how it should be done and I am going to do it that way. You get that a lot ... So what I am saying, is when you choose an arbitrator ... you know they say arbitration is as good as the arbitrator.

The observation made by the experienced arbitrator here is that while arbitrators are supposed to not bring their preconceptions to the case (i.e., leave the bags at the door), the reality is that some arbitrators do not do so. They do not bring a 'blank canvas' to decision-making. While unconscious bias can be understood and is probably acknowledged by most if not all arbitrators to varying degrees, conscious bias is difficult to justify. The full extent of conscious bias is unknown. It is important to clarify here that conscious bias is not the same as corruption or deliberate bias to decide in favour of the party-appointed arbitrator. Conscious bias is used here to refer to the bias in thinking that comes into being as a result of the arbitrator's education and experience in a particular legal system. Sometimes, the legal culture bias can be subtle and less recognised, and, hence, it can subconsciously affect the arbitrator's reasoning. On the other hand, the legal culture bias can be pronounced as some arbitrators feel legal concepts and principles from their home jurisdiction are superior to others found in other jurisdictions. Although there is evidence that this form of bias exists, and it was reported in some arbitration stories (Capper, 2014), the full extent and effect of it are still unknown.

An Egyptian arbitrator interviewed by the author criticised the legal-tradition deliberate bias. According to him, some European arbitrators do not pay full attention to the substantive local law and tend to, at least sometimes, bring legal solutions from their own home jurisdictions. The following quote illustrates the problem of legal tradition bias that is sometimes combined with appointing-party bias:

> In most arbitration cases in our part of the world, the governing law would be the national law of an Arab country … some European arbitrators who don't speak Arabic and don't understand the law, unfortunately, I hate to say that, they have an inherent bias, they don't respect the legal system of these countries and so you feel that they're paying lip service to the local law and jurisprudence, and at the end of the day they will apply the law as they feel it should be from their countries' perspective.

The legal tradition bias is sometimes coupled with appointing-party bias because normally the parties will select arbitrators who share with them the same nationality or culture. For example, in construction disputes involving an Arab employer and a European contractor, the Arab party tends to choose an Arab arbitrator while the European contractor tends to choose a European arbitrator.

Although some arbitrators acknowledged that they bring their own preconceptions with them, whether consciously or not, the constraints imposed on their decision-making by the contract and the law moderate their initial predispositions. For example, an interview with another Canadian arbitrator revealed how his background may influence his approach to contract interpretation. This is an excerpt from his interview:

> My view on interest is that it should compensate a party its losses. It is really a form of damages, it makes its time value of money. So, my inclination would be, left to my own devices, to want to award interest that puts the injured party in the position it would have been ... But if the parties have chosen a law that does not allow you to do that, for instance, a Sharia law, you might bend over backwards to see if there is a way around it. If it is clear that you cannot award interest, then that's it. You are stuck.

The aforementioned arbitral accounts show evidence that an arbitrator's background is part of the decision-making framework whether we like it or not. Realistically, at least some arbitrators have preexisting attitudes and opinions about some of the topics that frequently arise in arbitration. As a result, they may hold non-neutral positions across these topics. If a party's argument conveniently fits in with an arbitrator's preconceptions, it will be easier to convince the arbitrator to accept its argument. On the other hand, if a party's argument is against the arbitrator's preconceptions, the party's task of persuading the arbitrator to accept its argument will be more challenging.

While some arbitrators acknowledge the background's effect, whether in bringing conscious or subconscious bias to the case, others maintain that their background has an insignificant effect. They said that they attempt to identify their biases or preconceptions, and that self-awareness should nullify their effect. For instance, an English arbitrator who has significant experience in international arbitration in different parts of the world maintained that his decision will depend on the parties' contract and the governing law and that his legal background is irrelevant. The following is an extract from his interview:

> Approaching the case from my legal tradition's viewpoint would be completely wrong because then you would be bringing preconceptions to a case which would be outside the parameters of the decision-making process ... you must decide each case according to how the parties have structured the dispute resolution process in which they have agreed on applicable law to the substance of the case ... and although sometimes what the parties do or have agreed is not what I would have agreed but it is not to me to decide, it is to them to decide between themselves.

Although it is rare to find people who are totally free of predispositions in an absolute sense, some arbitrators appear to be relatively more detached from their legal tradition than others. A Canadian arbitrator interviewed by the author rejected the idea that his legal background might influence his decision on a dispute governed by a different system of law. He maintained that he controls his legal orientation bias, listens carefully to the parties, and decides based on the legal merit of their arguments. He said:

> I bring no preconceptions to the case ... I come with an expectation that legal counsel will inform me of the applicable legal principles and I carefully look at the facts as proven by the parties and I find the path based on that ... I do not come with preconceptions at all ... I do not have this sort of inhibitions ... or sympathy ... this is the reason why the statue of justice is blindfolded.

Having found evidence of bias in international arbitration, it is sensible to investigate the effect of arbitrators' experience in international arbitration on the extent to which their decisions are affected by their preconceptions. This relationship is difficult to determine in a qualitative inquiry such as the one underpinning this book. A quantitative approach drawing on valid data and a large sample is needed. Therefore, the author's findings and observations shared in the next section are only tentative

8.5 Arbitrator's experience

Another element of the arbitrator's background is their experience in international arbitration (measured in terms of the number of arbitration cases and diversity of applicable laws). Upon comparing the interviewed arbitrators' accounts of their approaches in contract interpretation and how they apply certain clauses, a specific pattern relating to experience can be noticed. The more experienced arbitrators tended to be more open-minded and clearly stated that they would wait for the parties' submissions before making up their minds. They suggested that it is for the parties themselves to argue their cases and propose a solution to the dispute. The less experienced arbitrators tended to describe how they would resolve certain disputes in accordance with their own legal tradition or professional experience. However, no arbitrator said, at least bluntly, that they would ignore the governing law and impose legal solutions that concur with their legal tradition or experience.

The fact that most international arbitrators interviewed for this work have significant experience in international arbitration makes it difficult to ascertain the effect of experience on moderating conscious and subconscious biases. However, it is possible to tentatively conclude that the more experienced arbitrators are better able to control their biases. Similar propositions can be found in the arbitration literature. For instance, Mulcahy (2015) noted that:

> It is sometimes difficult to leave all cultural baggage at the door of the arbitration room, and less experienced practitioners may struggle with their cultural predisposition.

8.6 Implications of bias on selection of arbitrators

The selection of arbitrators is probably one of the most important decisions the parties to a dispute need to make (Moses, 2008). This is because the risks in international arbitration are higher than in national litigation. Unlike national judges, arbitrators' decisions cannot be overturned on the basis of errors in fact or law. The international arbitration system provides no assurances that the arbitration award will be 'legally correct'. Therefore, it is up to the parties to do what they can to manage this risk properly. Selecting 'the right' arbitrator is a key method to mitigate the risk of getting a result that does not meet the parties' expectations (Moses, 2008).

Some arbitration reports, surveys, and publications (e.g., Lagerberg and Mistelis, 2006) limit the factors affecting the parties' choice of arbitrators to their reputation, expertise, knowledge of the substantive law and of relevant languages, knowledge and familiarity with the industry, and the like. These arbitrator competencies have a significant impact on the quality of the process and the award. However, there is another important factor that the parties and their in-house counsel are aware of, and that is an arbitrator's predisposition. There is no shortage of evidence that the parties and their in-house counsel attempt to find and select arbitrators that are inclined to agree with their arguments. This section presents some of this evidence.

Arbitration regimes, whether domestic or international, allow the parties to select their own arbitrators. This freedom of choice, which is rooted in party autonomy, has limited constraints. Parties in disputes are free to select arbitrators who appear to be predisposed to the legal or factual bases of their cases (Craig, Park, and Paulsson, 2001, cited in Karton, 2013). Indeed, there is evidence from the literature that arbitrators' predispositions are certainly a factor that affects the appointment decisions made by the parties and their counsel (e.g., Capper, 2014; Craig, Park, and Paulsson, 2001).

For instance, Professor William Park, an arbitration scholar and practitioner from the United States, stated (Park, 2014, p. 6):

> Publicly, lawyers talk about the proverbial good arbitrator who will be honest and intelligent. Yet in evaluating candidates to sit in their own cases, they doubtlessly hope for someone well-disposed to their arguments.

Almost three decades earlier, Martin Hunter, an arbitration scholar and practitioner from the United Kingdom, stated (Hunter, 1987, p. 223):

> When I am representing a client in an arbitration, what I am really looking for in a party-nominated arbitrator is someone with the maximum predisposition towards my client, but with the minimum appearance of bias.

As long as arbitrators are independent and neutral, arbitration rules and laws do not prevent the appointment of partial arbitrators. This is because, as Paulsson (1997, p. 2) put it:

'Doctrinal sympathies or antipathies are not disqualifying'. Likewise, Bishop and Reed (1998) concur that 'partiality of mind' cannot be used as a basis for disqualifying an international arbitrator, and it is sensible to expect that the parties will naturally look for an arbitrator who is sympathetic to their cause. On the first page of their article, they noted that:

> A party will strive to select an arbitrator who has some inclination or predisposition to favour that party's side of the case such as by sharing the appointing party's legal or cultural background or by holding doctrinal views that, fortuitously, coincide with a party's case ... this need carry no suggestion of disqualifying partiality.

Bishop and Reed (1998) opined that it is understandable for parties in international arbitration to select arbitrators who share their commercial, legal, and cultural background and/or hold views that may be helpful to resolving the dispute in their favour. Carter (2000), cited in Karton (2013), went even further by considering arbitrators' preconceptions to be one of the advantages of arbitration that allows the parties to 'legitimately shop for arbitrators with specific backgrounds and experience'. Indeed, it is widely accepted in international arbitration scholarship that the party-selection process contributes to the legitimacy of the arbitration process and outcome. The parties are more likely to perceive the arbitration process as fair and self-enforce the award that it produces (Rau, 1998).

A British lawyer, with significant experience as legal counsel in international arbitrations in the Arab Gulf countries, shared similar sentiments on the importance of considering an arbitrator's background when selecting them. In an interview with the author, he shared his observation that the background of an arbitrator might affect their interpretation approach to contract provisions, such as time-bar provisions. The validity and enforceability of time-bar clauses in Arab countries is a controversial matter. There are competing legal principles on whether notice provisions intended to act as a condition precedent are effective or not. Given that legal jurisprudence is divided on the matter, the arbitrator's legal tradition may be an important factor to consider when choosing an arbitrator or estimating the strength of a case. For example, an English arbitrator's starting view is likely to be unsympathetic to arguments against the enforcement of time-bar clauses. This is simply because English law is clear on notice provisions and the consequence of not giving timely notice. There is a commonly held view amongst lawyers that if somebody spends every hour of every working day practising a specific national law, then their starting position is likely to be in accordance with what they are used to. Then, it is up to the parties to try to convince the arbitrator to move away from their initial position. Unless an applicable law has clear and settled jurisprudence on the legal question, then an arbitrator is likely to accept arguments that concur with their own views.

Of course, the proposition regarding the likely relationship between an arbitrator's background and their interpretation of notice provisions can be extended to other legal issues. For example, if the case's success hinges on following a contextual approach to contract interpretation, then choosing an arbitrator from a civil law jurisdiction could be helpful. If lawyers' assessment of their client's case suggests it is strong on law, then recommending the selection of an arbitrator with a legal background and reputation of a strict application of the law could be a good strategy. If the case has some commercial merit but is weak in law, then choosing an arbitrator with a commercial background could lead to a more favourable outcome compared to lawyers or retired judges.

Similar views can be found in the arbitration literature. At the Swiss Arbitration Association (ASA) annual conference held in Zurich in 2013 on the topic "Inside the Black Box: How Arbitral Tribunals Operate and Reach Their Decisions", Capper (2014) stated the following:

> We as counsel, especially in the larger law firms ..., spend an enormous amount of effort thinking about the selection of the right arbitrators and I know all other practitioners do the same ... I do not mean for one moment that they intend any kind of bias but they clearly think they are selecting something distinctive. They must believe that there are characteristics in these people selected which are more than expeditious, fair-minded, intelligent, well qualified available skill sets ... What is it that parties and their counsel are seeking? ... there must be some expectation in selecting and appointing arbitrators, that there is some characteristic present ... one person's characteristic is another person's bias.

This arbitrator's 'characteristic' or 'bias' may help one of the parties in dispute by favouring its argument or sympathising with its 'cause'. For example, arbitrators may have a view on a given issue or may have expressed their dislike of a legal proposition that gives an advantage to one of the parties (Paulsson, 1997). They may have shared their opinions, which clearly show their bias towards certain issues, in talks and seminars or in their writings. It would be wise for a disputant to select an arbitrator who shares their worldview.

Craig, Park, and Paulsson (2001) made a similar observation. They stated that when the parties select an arbitrator, they make the selection in part based on 'the normative standards' they want to be applied to the dispute. This observation in the arbitration community led some arbitration scholars and practitioners, such as Park (2003), to assert that the choice of arbitrator is such an important decision as this may have a more significant impact than the applicable law on the dispute outcome.

8.7 Appointing-party bias

One of the fundamental characteristics of arbitration, as a private forum for dispute resolution, is the parties' power to select their arbitrators. Typically, each party in dispute selects a co-arbitrator, and the two co-arbitrators selected by the parties agree on a chair (Brekoulakis, 2013). The party-appointment regime is the most dominant method used to select arbitrators in international arbitration (Diamond, 2003; Karton, 2013; Brekoulakis, 2013). Given that international arbitration lacks many of the safeguards of a national litigation system, especially on substantive grounds, the party-led selection process naturally gives rise to one of the most obvious concerns participants in international arbitration may have. The concern relates to an arbitrator's lack of neutrality, independence, and impartiality or, to put differently, 'an appointing-party bias'.

Appointing-party bias is a deliberate bias and refers to the arbitrator's inclination to favour the argument of the party that selected them. Although in theory a party-appointed arbitrator is not supposed to have any biases in favour of that party, in practice this may not be the case. This problem has serious repercussions on the legitimacy of international arbitration. A party-appointed arbitrator may feel inclined to decide in favour of the party appointing them. They may feel that they owe them something in return for choosing them. This inclination might be motivated by a desire to be reappointed in future arbitrations. Some arbitrators depend fully or to a large extent on their income from arbitral appointments. This financial dependence and pressure might lead some arbitrators to be supportive or at least sympathetic to the party appointing them (Karton, 2013). However, not everyone agrees with this line of argument. Many arbitrators truly believe that the key to success in their careers is integrity. They want to be seen as honest and honourable arbitrators who make their decisions based on a careful assessment and analysis of the facts, the contract, and the law.

In recognition of the fact that not all arbitrators maintain their integrity, some arbitration institutions came up with a formula to control repeat appointments. This might help but it is not a panacea to malpractices and that is why the appointment of a chairman is very important. There is a recognition amongst the arbitration community that a chairman plays a key role in countering any potential appointing-party bias.

Two related but different concepts are relevant to the discussion of appointing-party bias: independence and impartiality. All arbitration rules and laws require arbitrators to be 'independent' and/or 'impartial' (some of them add that arbitrators must be 'neutral' or 'objective') (Cuniberti, 2008; Gaillard and Savage, 1999; Bishop and Reed, 1998). This is fundamental for the administration of justice. These closely related concepts may be given different meanings in the context of international arbitration.

Independence refers to the absence of a prior or current personal or business relationship between the arbitrator and the parties that may influence the arbitrator's decision. The test of independence is objective. It examines the nature of the relationship between prospective arbitrators and the parties and aims to determine whether this relationship creates emotional or financial pressure that might affect their decision. Impartiality, on the other hand, is different from independence. It refers to the absence of predisposition and prejudice in relation to the parties or the subject matter. This is what some arbitrators may refer to as maintaining an 'open mind' that is free of predisposition or prejudice. Partiality refers to unconscious bias in the mind of arbitrators towards certain matters. It is a mental state. It is subjective, difficult to prove, and often not recognised by the arbitrators themselves (Bishop and Reed, 1998; Gaillard and Savage, 1999). In one sense, it is irrelevant to challenging arbitrators' appointments but relevant to selecting them.

While some national arbitration laws and institutional arbitration rules require arbitrators to be merely independent (e.g., ICC rules), others require them to be both independent and impartial (e.g., UNCITRAL Model Law, UNCITRAL, LCIA and AAA rules, and the IBA Ethics) (Bishop and Reed, 1998; Gaillard and Savage, 1999). It is not clear whether arbitration laws, institutional rules, or guidelines omitting the requirements of 'impartiality' implies a recognition that it is not required in international arbitration or indicates a different view of what the term means (for example, used as a synonym to independence). Gaillard and Savage (1999) opine that, as it is practically difficult to prove impartiality or lack thereof, arbitrators should at least be required to be independent.

Some arbitrators interviewed by the author stated that they were involved in arbitrations where co-arbitrators appeared to be defending the party that appointed them. Sometimes this bias is obvious but, in other cases, it is subtle and more difficult to deal with in the tribunal deliberation. This is because a biased co-arbitrator attempts to be viewed during the deliberations as someone who is carefully assessing evidence, interpreting the contract, and applying the law.

Similar horror stories of co-arbitrators adopting the position of their appointing party and acting as their advocate were reported by arbitration practitioners (Berger and Schneider, 2014; Giovannini, 2003). In some situations, the deliberate bias of one of the co-arbitrators cannot be contained by the chair and the other co-arbitrator. The deliberations would seem to be going nowhere, and the biased co-arbitrator may end up writing a dissenting opinion (Berger and Schneider, 2014).

The available anecdotal evidence suggests that this form of bias seems to be an infrequent issue in international arbitration (Lowenfeld, 2005 cited in Cuniberti, 2008). There are limited scholarly attempts to quantify the scale of the problem. The author is aware of only one empirical study that was conducted by Stipanowich and Ulrich (2014) in the United States. The study used a survey to solicit arbitrators' opinions on arbitration practices to which 134 arbitrators with experience in US domestic and international commercial arbitration responded. They found that almost nine out of ten respondents believe that at least sometimes, party-appointed arbitrators "are predisposed toward the party that appointed them" and "decide close questions in favour of the party that appointed them" even when the arbitration rules and law require them to be independent and impartial.

An Egyptian arbitrator interviewed by the author noted that it is important to differentiate between acting as a chairman and acting as a party-appointed co-arbitrator. The party-appointed arbitrator should make certain that the chairperson and the other party-appointed arbitrator fully understand the perspective of the party that appointed him or her. In his opinion, a party-appointed arbitrator has a duty to clarify and explain the appointing party's position to the other arbitrators in the tribunal. This duty does not allow the arbitrator to act as an advocate or argue the case on behalf of that party, as might be the case in US arbitration, because this is wrong in principle. Although the US arbitration community are perceived to accept a partisan role of party-appointed arbitrators, this view is not shared by almost all other domestic and international arbitration contexts. The duty of the party-appointed co-arbitrator is to provide assurance that the tribunal members pay attention to the arguments of the party that appointed him or her. Of course, an arbitrator shall pay attention to the arguments of both parties in dispute. However, a party in dispute selects a specific arbitrator because they want to make sure that their 'case is heard'. This could be because the arbitrator is familiar with the region, the local culture, the industry's practices, and substantive law. This shared background allows the party-appointed co-arbitrator to make sure the party's case is understood by the rest of the tribunal even if the arbitrator is not convinced themselves.

This stance has support in the arbitration literature. It is accepted in the arbitration community that a party-appointed co-arbitrator has a duty to make sure that the arguments presented by the appointing party are understood and fully considered by the tribunal (Moses, 2008; Kapeliuk, 2010). The chair arbitrator can rely on the party-appointed arbitrators to explain to him or her pertinent issues in the governing law or the factual background of the case. In fact, this role of party-appointed arbitrators as translators of the parties' different legal or professional cultures is a celebrated feature of international arbitration as it can lead to fair and balanced decisions (Kapeliuk, D., 2010; Lowenfeld, 1995; Rau,1997; Bishop and Reed, 1998). A party-appointed co-arbitrator may perform this role but decide at the end to reject the arguments of the party that appointed them.

This role of a party-appointed co-arbitrator is not controversial but there is an interesting part of it which is rarely revealed and largely unacknowledged in arbitrators' writings and talks. The Egyptian arbitrator stated that he will decide in favour of the party that appointed him when the law is not settled on the issue in dispute. The following is an excerpt from his interview:

> In my view, if something is black and white in law, which is rare, I must make the correct decision even if this results in deciding against the party that appointed me. However, the law is grey in many areas and can be interpreted in different ways. If the question of law is a grey area, there are a number of authorities going that way, and a number of authorities going that way, and both points of view hold merits, then, in that case, I will put forward the point of view of the party that appointed me because I'm not there to create a new law in an area that lacks settled legal jurisprudence.

When the law is silent or has no settled jurisprudence on the issue in dispute, the outcome of the dispute is highly uncertain (see Section 3.6). In this case, as suggested by the Egyptian arbitrator, a party-appointed co-arbitrator may lean towards the argument of the party that appointed him or her. In any case, an arbitrator is likely to accept arguments that coincide with their background or beliefs. This proposition finds empirical support in the literature on judicial decision-making that comes predominantly from the United States. This body of literature reveals that when the evidence of fact or law is somewhat vague, there is room for non-evidentiary and extra-legal factors (such as the judge's social background) to influence judicial decisions (Diamond, 2003).

To conclude, this section suggests that appointing-party bias is a reality that should not be ignored. Some international arbitrators follow a hidden agenda of clientelism and are willing to favour the position of the party that appointed them. The extent and effect of this problem are not yet known, but it seems sensible for the parties and their counsel to be prepared for this eventuality. It is safe to conclude that, overall, a party-appointed arbitrator is more likely to be less impartial than an arbitrator selected jointly by the parties or by a neutral arbitration institution (Paulsson, 1997).

8.8 Conclusion

This chapter argues that an arbitrator's background is certainly a factor that affects their decision. It may play a greater or lesser role depending on the circumstances, but rarely if ever does it play no role at all. The assumption that the arbitration result will be a function of the contract and the governing law but nothing else seems very idealistic to accept. This mechanistic view is challenged in this book. Arbitrators' backgrounds, whether they know it or not, consciously or subconsciously affect their decisions to varying degrees.

It is hard to argue against the proposition that interpretation is influenced by the interpreter. Interpretation is not a mechanical exercise that is independent of the interpreter. Such notions of 'perfect objectivity' are elusive. 'We see things not as they are but as we are'. People see things differently as a result of their different sets of experiences, the circumstances they found themselves in, and their values. Hence, how arbitrators perceive the world or the lens through which they perceive the world is important.

In the context of dispute resolution settings such as international arbitration, contract interpretation is influenced by the arbitrator. Usually, a number of competing legal rules and principles can be applied to a commercial dispute. When deciding a dispute, international arbitrators seem to be rarely fully constrained by the law, just as they are rarely totally free to decide as they wish. The effect of arbitrators' biases appears to be stronger when the contract has no clear solution to the dispute and the governing law is silent or vague on the issue in dispute.

This margin of indeterminacy that is left by the law will ultimately be filled by the unconscious. This subconscious bias has been recognised in arbitration scholarship and acknowledged by arbitrators.

It seems that the arbitrator's experience in international arbitration moderates the effect of conscious and unconscious biases but the latter is very difficult to completely eradicate. As the saying goes 'Once you see it, you can't unsee it', or once you learn something, it is difficult to unlearn it.

The implication of these findings is that the selection of an arbitrator is very important if not the most important decision a party in international construction arbitration needs to make. This is particularly true because international arbitration allows limited grounds for challenging arbitrators' decisions on the substance of disputes, which gives arbitrators some leeway in their decisions. While selecting arbitrators with potential preconceived ideas is considered legitimate by many practitioners and commentators, deliberate bias in favour of the appointing party threatens the administration of justice and the legitimacy of international arbitration.

This chapter concludes with the same opening statement: 'arbitration is only as good as the arbitrator'.

8.9 References

Bedjaqui, M. (1988). Arbitrator: One man-three roles-some independent comments on the ethical and legal obligations of an arbitrator. *Journal of International Arbitration*, 5, 7.

Berger, B. & Schneider, M. E. (2014). *Inside the Black Box: How Arbitral Tribunals Operate and Reach Their Decisions*. New York: JurisNet, LLC.

Besaiso, H. (2017). *How do Construction Arbitrators Make Their Decisions? A Perspective from Palestine*. The Society of Construction Arbitrators' Publications. Available at Norman_Roye_Prize_paper_2017.pdf (constructionarbitrators.org)

Bishop, D. & Reed, L. (1998). Practical guidelines for interviewing, selecting and challenging party-appointed arbitrators in international commercial arbitration. *Arbitration International*, 14(4), 395–430.

Brekoulakis, S. (2013). Systemic bias and the institution of international arbitration: A new approach to arbitral decision-making. *Journal of International Dispute Settlement*, 4(3), 553–585.

Bruner, J. (1990). *Acts of Meaning*. Cambridge, MA: Harvard University Press.

Capper, P. (2014). Dealing with bias and obstruction. *In*: Berger, B. & Schneider, M. E. (eds.) *Inside the Black Box: How Arbitral Tribunals Operate and Reach Their Decisions* (pp. 43–58). New York: JurisNet, LLC.

Caron, D. (2015). Regulating opacity: Shaping how tribunals think. *King's College London Dickson Poon School of Law Legal Studies Research Paper Series*, Paper No. 2015-07.

Carter, J. H. (2000). Improving life with the party-appointed arbitrator: Clearer conduct guidelines for "nonneutrals". *The American Review of International Arbitration*, 11, 295–298.

Coulson, R. (1990). The Decisionmaking Process in Arbitration. *Arbitration Journal*, 45(3), 37–41.

Craig, W. L., Park, W. W. & Paulsson, J. (2001). *International Chamber of Commerce Arbitration*. New York: Oceana Publications.

Cuniberti, G. (2008). Beyond contract - The case for default arbitration in international commercial disputes. *Fordham International Law Journal*, 32, 417.

Diamond, S. S. (2003). Psychological aspects of dispute resolution: Issues for international arbitration. *In*: van den Berg, A. J. (ed.) *International Commercial Arbitration: Important Contemporary Questions* (pp. 327–342). The Hague: Kluwer Law International.

Drahozal, C. R. (2003). Of rabbits and Rhinoceri: A survey of empirical research on international commercial arbitration. *Journal of International Arbitration*, 20(1), 23–34.

Flood, J. & Caiger, A. (1993). Lawyers and arbitration: The juridification of construction disputes. *The Modern Law Review*, 56(3), 412–440.

Gaillard, E. & Savage, J. (1999). *Fouchard, Gaillard, Goldman on International Commercial Arbitration*. The Hague: Kluwer law international.

Giovannini, T. (2003). The psychological aspects of dispute resolution commentary. *In*: A. J. van den Berg (ed.) *International Commercial Arbitration: Important Contemporary Questions, ICCA Congress Series, Volume 11* (pp. 348–352). The Hague: Kluwer Law International.

Goodman-Everard, R. E. (1991). Cultural diversity in international arbitration: A challenge for decision-makers and decision-making. *Arbitration International*, 7(2), 155–164.

Haggard, H. & Mentschikoff, S. (1977). Responsible decision making in dispute settlement. *In*: Tapp, J. L. & Levine, F. J. (eds.) *Law, Justice, and the Individual in Society: Psychological and Legal Issues*. New York: Holt, Rinehart and Winston.

Hunter, M. (1987). Ethics of the international arbitrator. *Arbitration*, 53, 219.

Kapeliuk, D. (2010). The repeat appointment factor: Exploring decision patterns of elite investment arbitrators. *Cornell L. Rev.*, 96, 47.

Karton, J. (2013). *The Culture of International Arbitration and the Evolution of Contract Law*. Oxford: Oxford University Press.

Karton, J. (2014). International arbitration culture and global governance. *In*: Mattli, W. & Dietz, T. (eds.) *International Arbitration and Global Governance: Contending Theories and Evidence* (pp. 74–116). Oxford: Oxford University Press.

Kurkela, M. & Turunen, S. (2010). *Due Process in International Commercial Arbitration* (2nd ed.). New York: Oxford University Press.

Lagerberg, G. & Mistelis, L. (2006). International arbitration: Corporate attitudes and practices. Queen Mary University of London and School of International Arbitration. Available at https://arbitration.qmul.ac.uk/media/arbitration/docs/IAstudy_2006.pdf [Accessed 12 December 2022].

Lowenfeld, A. F. (1995). The party-appointed arbitrator in international controversies: Some reflections. *Texas International Law Journal*, 30, 59.

Lowenfeld, A. F. (2005). Lowenfeld on international arbitration: Collected essays over three decades. Juris Publishing, Inc.

Madden, J. P. (1994). *How to Win at Arbitration, Chapter 12 of ADR A Practical Guide to Resolve Construction Disputes, American Arbitration Association*. Dubuque: Kendall Hunt Publishing Co.

Marques, J. M., Yzerbyt, V. Y. & Leyens, J. P. (1988). The "black sheep effect": Extremity of judgments towards ingroup members as a function of group identification. *European Journal of Social Psychology*, 18(1), 1–16.

Mayer, P. (2014). Dealing with dissenting opinions. *In*: Berger, B. & Schneider, M. E. (eds). *Inside the Black Box: How Arbitral Tribunals Operate and Reach Their Decisions* (pp. 67–72). New York: JurisNet, LLC.

Meyer, B. (2014). Structuring a bargaining process. *In*: Berger, B. & Schneider, M. E. (eds.) *Inside the Black Box: How Arbitral Tribunals Operate and Reach Their Decisions* (pp. 59–66). New York: JurisNet, LLC.

Moses, M. L. (2008). *The Principles and Practice of International Commercial Arbitration*. Cambridge: Cambridge University Press.

Mulcahy, C. (2015). What does it mean-contractual interpretation in international commercial arbitration. *Dispute Resolution International*, 9, 15.

Ossman, G. (2003). *Construction Arbitration Consistency and Reliability: An Empirical Study*. M.Sc., Pepperdine University School of Law.

Park, W. W. (2003). The specificity of international arbitration: The case for FAA reform. *The Vanderbilt Journal of Transnational Law*, 36, 1241.

Park, W. W. (2014). A fair fight: Professional guidelines in international arbitration. *Arbitration International*, 30(3), 409–428.

Paulsson, J. (1997). Ethics, elitism, eligibility. *Journal of International Arbitration*, 14(4), 13–22.

Rau, A. S. (1997). Integrity in private judging. *South Texas Law Review*, 38, 485.

Rau, A. S. (1998). On integrity in private judging. *Arbitration International*, 14(2), 115–156.

Stipanowich, T. & Ulrich, Z. (2014). Arbitration in evolution: Current practices and perspectives of experienced commercial arbitrators. *The American Review of International Arbitration*, 25, 395–480.

Sussman, E., 2014. Arbitrator deliberations: The impact of the unconscious on decision making. *New York Dispute Resolution Lawyer*, 7(2), 8–12.

Waites, R. C. & Lawrence, J. E. (2010). Psychological dynamics in international arbitration advocacy. In: Bishop, R. D. and Kehoe, E. G. (eds), *The Art of Advocacy in International Arbitration*, 2nd edn. New York: Juris Publishing, Inc.

Wright, G. A. (1913). *Wright on Building Arbitrations: A Manual for Architects, Students, Contractors and Construction Engineers*. San Francisco: Wale Printing Co.

CHAPTER 9

Conclusion

9.1 Introduction

This book inquires into how international arbitrators decide on the substance of construction disputes arising from international construction contracts. In particular, it aims to construct an arbitral decision-making conceptual framework that identifies the substantive norms international arbitrators apply, assesses their effects on arbitrators' decisions on the merits of international construction claims, and explains the reasons for the determined effects. This aim has been achieved. This book provides a comprehensive descriptive and explanatory empirical account of how arbitrators decide and why they decide in the way they do. Section 9.2 summarises how arbitrators decide and why they decide in the way they do. Section 9.3 provides a theoretical explanation based on Bourdieu's theory of the social field. Section 9.4 summarises the book's contribution to theory and practice. Section 9.5 acknowledges the methodological limitations of the research underpinning this work.

9.2 Summary findings on the impact of certain substantive norms on arbitrators' decisions on the substance of international construction disputes

The arbitral decision-making process requires arbitrators to consider competing norms. This section describes to what extent arbitrators use these norms to determine the outcome of a dispute and explains the rationale for this.

9.2.1 Substantive law

The first question posed in this book is: to what extent do substantive law norms influence arbitral decision-making, and what is the rationale for this?

This book argues that international construction arbitrators follow the law unless the parties specify otherwise, which is rare in practice. In most cases, the parties designate a national law to govern the interpretation of their construction contracts. Arbitrators normally follow the provisions and stipulations of the governing law to determine the parties' rights and obligations. It is highly unlikely for international arbitrators to depart from or twist the wording of the contract or disregard the stipulations of the substantive law in favour of rival norms drawing upon commercial practice, international construction law, or their subjective views of what is fair and equitable.

This book finds nine reasons for the dominance of the legal model in international construction arbitration decision-making (see Section 3.7). Overall, the legal model seems to

DOI: 10.4324/b22975-9

be a result of the power struggle encompassing the social construction of the international construction arbitration field (see Section 9.3).

However, there is an important unique characteristic of this 'legal model' of arbitral decision-making. Acknowledging that arbitrators follow a legal model in their decision-making by no means entails that they apply the law in an identical manner to national judges. There are several procedural and institutional differences between national litigation and international arbitration that affect the dispute outcome. They are discussed in the following paragraphs.

9.2.2 Party autonomy

The first difference concerns the sources of power of the decision-makers. Whereas national judges derive their power from the state, arbitrators derive their mandate from the parties. As a result, party autonomy – a core principle underpinning international arbitration – has a large influence on arbitral decision-making. International arbitrators rely on the parties to a great extent to determine the content of the law due to certain considerations (see Section 3.4). If arbitrators are aware that the parties have not pleaded certain parts of the law they believe to be relevant, they may or may not raise it by themselves. Even if arbitrators believe that certain legal rules are applicable, but the parties contested their application, many arbitrators seem to respect the parties' wishes. Further, if the parties demand the disapplication of mandatory rules of the governing law that render their clauses void or give them a different effect, some arbitrators will be receptive to the parties' desire. Arbitrators are keen to apply the law but are also keen to meet the parties' legitimate expectations. Judges, on the other hand, are less concerned with the parties' expectations and the specificities of their dispute and commercial relationship, and they are more concerned with the implications of their judgement on the commercial community and wider society. Judges are responsible for the law of the land and have a duty towards the state to apply the entirety of the law in the hierarchical way prescribed by the law. Therefore, the scope and the 'standard of accuracy' of legal decisions are not the same in international arbitration and national litigation.

9.2.3 The absence of an appeal mechanism in international arbitration

The legal systems of almost all nations allow the parties to appeal judges' decisions in case they believe they were erroneous. The appeal process is viewed as a means of error correction. A judge setting in a lower court always has at the forefront of their mind that in case they get it wrong, then the losing or dissatisfied party will appeal and seek reconsideration before a higher court. No judge likes to see their decision overturned. This may harm their reputation and lead to professional embarrassment. Thus, the existence of the appeal process is in itself an incentive for judges to do their best to reach correct legal conclusions. It is a powerful mechanism to enhance the quality of judicial judgements. The existence of appeal courts provides a form of insurance against legal error. In essence, the appeal process is not only a means of error correction but also error prevention. The absence of an appeal mechanism in international arbitration may lead arbitrators to be less concerned about making decisions that are perfectly aligned with what judges would decide in similar circumstances.

9.2.4 Commercial practice

Another institutional difference concerns the origin and original purpose of arbitration. Courts are an integral part of state governance. Judges have to apply the national law equally to all citizens. Arbitration, on the other hand, originated in commerce, and its key purpose was to resolve commercial disputes between merchants. This might lead people to believe that arbitration justice is an alternative to court justice in that the purpose of arbitration is to achieve commercial justice as opposed to legal justice. It follows that commercial practice and customs of the trade might be perceived to have a privileged status in arbitration and play a more significant role in arbitrators' decisions than in judges' decisions.

The second question posed in this book is: to what extent do commercial norms influence arbitral decision-making, and what is the rationale for this?

Unlike trade and exchange of goods, which has been going on since early civilisations, construction is a relatively young industry. International construction, in particular, is a modern commercial activity. It can be traced to the second half of the 19th century but the significant leap dates back to the 1970s and afterwards.

As such, international construction customs and usages are of relatively recent origin. It follows that the application of customs is limited, in most cases, to the local custom and commercial practice in the place where construction takes place that international construction companies are bound to observe.

By and large, international arbitrators accord customs and usages the authority they entertain under the governing law. However, this book argues that there are limited exceptions to this prevailing view depending on how the parties configure and structure their dispute resolution method.

The majority of international arbitration rules and national arbitration laws explicitly require arbitrators to take into consideration customs and usages relevant to the commercial activity. They do not leave it to the governing law to specify the proper authority of customs. This requirement expressed in similar wordings in various arbitration rules and laws is opaque and open to different interpretations. It appears to have been intentionally drafted in vague terms or could be the result of a compromise between the two polar models of arbitration: the legal model and the commercial model. While this vagueness ensures adaptability and flexibility of arbitral decision-making, it also entails a certain degree of uncertainty and even vacuity. It seems that some arbitrators construe this requirement as an authorisation to alter or moderate the hierarchy between different sources of law as designated in the governing law, or even to make a customary rule supersede a contractual provision or a legal rule. Overall, the real intent of the architects of the arbitration rules requiring arbitrators to take trade usages into account remains unknown. What is known, however, is that this requirement obscures the classification of custom in international arbitration (i.e., is it part of the law or an external norm?) and intensifies the tension between the legal model and commercial model. It indicates that arbitration still keeps some traits from its origin and roots.

In addition, if the parties, when structuring their dispute resolution process, select construction arbitrators from the industry, then this will probably have practical implications on the outcome of their dispute. This is because construction practitioners have a different approach from legal professionals and are closer to construction commercial practice. This book finds elements of truth that construction practitioners, when acting as arbitrators, might give more weight to arguments based on commercial practice and even make a custom or usage overtake a contractual clause or legal provision. Arbitrators' different attitudes towards commercial practice do not only originate from their professional background (i.e., legal vs. non-legal), but they are also rooted in the civil law and common law divide. There is a perception amongst both scholars and practitioners that civil law arbitrators tend to be more receptive to arguments based on commercial practice.

9.2.5 International construction law (ICL)

Another element of the institutional structure of the international arbitration system that makes it different from national court litigation is that the former operates in an international environment. This environment brings transnational legal norms, or, in the context of the construction arbitration international construction law principles, to the arbitral decision-making box.

The third question posed in this book is: to what extent do international construction law norms influence arbitral decision-making?

The notion of ICL is conceptually challenging on two levels. First, the arbitral opinion is divided on the mere existence of a body of transnational legal norms related to international construction. Second, arbitrators who defend the existence of these norms do not agree on their nature (i.e., are they codified in a list of rules and principles or are they uncodified rules and principles that are derived from a number of sources and devised at the time of decision-making on a case-by-case basis?).

This book argues that ICL is, in essence, comprised of unwritten norms of wide-ranging character that are derived from a multiplicity of sources. These norms are concretised at the time of arbitrating the parties' dispute.

ICL stands on two pillars. First, ICL hinges on the proliferation of FIDIC standard forms of construction contracts along with its commentaries and courts' decisions. Second, ICL depends on the construction law of developed and mature jurisdictions. Legal concepts that are rooted in sophisticated national laws are made transferable to the international context of international arbitration by a group of cosmopolitan construction arbitration technocrats (arbitrators, counsel, experts). These concepts, however, must be anchored in the governing law in order to contribute to an increased legitimacy and acceptance of ICL norms.

Generally, ICL has two application areas. The first concerns contract interpretation. Arbitrators who lean towards a transnational approach to the interpretation of international construction contracts, especially if they incorporate FIDIC or FIDIC-modelled conditions of contract, feel less constrained by the interpretation rules of the national law governing the contract. A transnational approach to contract interpretation is also manifested in some arbitrators' inclination towards a subjective approach even if the governing law provides otherwise. As these arbitrators do not strictly adhere to the governing law of the contract, they may justify their conclusions by referring to general principles of international construction law or the like. The second concerns gap-filling in the contract and its governing law. ICL norms are deemed residuary norms in the sense that they may govern only when the governing law provides no specific regulation. The difficulty is that the challenge of indeterminacy of ICL, as substantive norms, is not much different from the problem of gaps in national laws.

Although seem to be rare, the generally accepted use of ICL in contract interpretation and supplementation may be subject to an exception. It is not impossible for an arbitrator to invoke the notion of ICL to supersede an express term in the parties' contract that they deem to be unfair and unreasonable.

9.2.6 Fairness

Although fairness is generally viewed as a virtue and many decision-makers seek to make fair decisions, state judges are constrained by the law and legal precedent (*stare decisis*). Arbitrators, as private judges hired by the parties to resolve their own dispute, might be perceived to be less constrained by the law and legal precedent. Hence, assuming they have the incentive, they will be more able to 'inject fairness' into their decisions.

The fourth question posed in this book is: to what extent do international arbitrators follow their own sense of fairness to arrive at their decisions, and what is the rationale for this?

This book argues that arbitrators do not resort to the notion of fairness and equity as a substantive norm to determine the parties' dispute. It shows that it is difficult to reduce fairness to a norm that is self-contained. Also, the users of international construction arbitration seemingly prefer predictability and certainty, which are almost non-existent in a discretionary decision-making system that depends on what the decision-maker views as fair and equitable.

Yet, some arbitrators are keen to find a fair outcome. However, they do not decide disputes solely on the basis of what they feel is fair. They distil their feelings of what constitutes a fair outcome through the filter of legal rationality as provided for under the governing law. They recognise that it is an imperative function of legal reasoning, which underpins arbitral reasoning, to reclassify these feelings and exhibit them in traceable legal concepts in order to make them rationally revisable.

Even when arbitrators are authorised by the parties to act as *amiables compositeurs*, they do not have a free hand to decide on the grounds of fairness and good conscience. Respecting the parties' choice of law and the terms they agreed to is viewed as the foundation of fairness. The doctrine of *amiable composition* allows arbitrators to deviate from the law as a last resort to amend legal answers that are against the reasonable commercial expectations of the parties.

9.2.7 Mandatory rules of foreign law

Whereas judges normally resolve disputes between parties who belong to the same country and are subject to the same legal rules, international arbitrators deal with more complicated situations due to the international nature of the disputes they are called to resolve. International construction contracts could involve multiple legal systems that have a connection to the construction project or to the resolution of a dispute arising from it. One of the controversial issues international arbitrators must decide in some cases is the applicability of mandatory rules of foreign law and whether they may override the parties' agreement.

The fifth question posed in this book is: to what extent do foreign mandatory rules of law influence arbitral decision-making, and what is the rationale for this?

This book finds that the arbitration community seem to be undecided on this issue. Nevertheless, in practice, foreign mandatory rules of law seem to have no or negligible effect on arbitrators' decisions on the substance of the parties' disputes. Unless arbitrators find that the parties breached international public policy that challenges practices that are fundamentally wrong, it is highly likely that they will not consider mandatory rules of law that are foreign to the governing law of the contract. The arbitrators' motivation in doing so is to avoid or minimise the risk of award non-enforcement on the ground of exceeding their power and to not allow the parties to act in bad faith by entering into an agreement and then attempting to escape their obligations on the ground that the agreement was in breach of a mandatory rule of foreign law. In addition, arbitrators do not consider themselves as the guardians of a state's public policy and its interest in having its mandatory law applied. Their mandate is to resolve the parties' private disputes according to the parties' contract and the rules of law selected by the parties.

9.2.8 The arbitrator's background

All decision-makers, including judges and arbitrators, are subject to bias. However, the international arbitration environment makes the issue of arbitral bias more serious than judicial bias. Parties cannot choose their court judges, but they can appoint their arbitrators and they often do. This arbitrator selection method and the fact that international arbitrators come from more diverse backgrounds than judges may introduce bias into the decision-making process.

The sixth and last question posed in this book is: to what extent do the background characteristics of international arbitrators influence their substantive decision-making?

This book argues that an arbitrator's background is certainly a factor that affects their decision. Arbitrators' backgrounds consciously or subconsciously affect their decisions to varying degrees. It is difficult to quantify the effect of arbitrators' backgrounds on their decisions but the effect seems to be stronger when the contract and the substantive law provide an uncertain answer to the issue in disputes. The belief in the arbitration community that arbitrators' decisions are influenced by their background has led parties and their legal advisors to take advantage of and capitalise on this opportunity when selecting their arbitrators.

9.3 Theoretical reflection

In national litigation settings, judicial decision-making follows a structured process whereby the norms to be applied are specified and their authorities are regulated in the law. To ensure compliance with the prescribed methodology of decision-making, there are normally one or two levels of appeal. This appeal mechanism functions as an assurance that judges will not deviate from the methodology dictated by the higher authorities responsible for making the law and applying it.

The international arbitration setting is different. A quality management system to supervise and correct international arbitrators' decisions is non-existent. A social context that is not rule-based (i.e., lacking a centralised legislator to set out the rules and enforcer to enforce them), will be governed by the interaction between the social actors themselves.

In reaching this conclusion, the author finds that one of the main influential theories that explains social behaviour in this kind of environment is Bourdieu's theory of the social field. It provides an adequate explanation for arbitral decision-making, which is a complex product of social construction. As such, although this book does not draw on the work of Bourdieu, the theoretical statements put forward in this section borrow some of his vocabularies, especially in relation to the social struggle and competition in the field, which seemingly plays a major role in shaping arbitral decision-making in international construction arbitration.

According to Bourdieu, a field's habitus is a social setting where the rules of the game are never set and are subject to challenge (Bourdieu, 1977). A field is a dynamic space characterised by forces of competition and change. In this field, there are agents and institutions that constantly interact within the rules and struggle over the rules of the game (Bourdieu and Wacquant, 1992; Bourdieu, 1986). The positions of agents in the field are determined by the level of the 'symbolic capital' they possess. Symbolic capital refers to an agent's prestige and accumulated characteristics that are considered important in the field. The size of symbolic capital each agent possesses determines its degree of influence in the field and its capability to bring a change to the rules of the game (Dezalay and Garth, 1998; Bourdieu and Wacquant, 1992).

Hereunder, the book's arguments are revisited using the vocabulary of Bourdieu's social field theory. This book argues that decision-making in international construction arbitration is a social construct. The attributes of this social construct have come into existence throughout a process of social interaction that took place over a long period of time (and is still ongoing). The rules of decision-making are not set out by a central authority in the field. As such, the rules are undergoing a process of social construction. This social construction, which is taking place in the field of international construction arbitration, involves a number of social actors: arbitrators, the parties and their lawyers, arbitration institutions, and national states.

Arbitrators compete amongst themselves to build their reputation and symbolic capital. The key elements to do this are through building a reputation that they respect the parties' contract terms and their choice of law, they do not substitute the parties' objective choices by their own subjective views of fairness, and they are competent in applying the law and rendering enforceable awards.

The parties themselves demonstrate great support for this legal model. They tend to choose legal professionals (as opposed to engineers or construction professionals) to arbitrate their disputes as well as to represent them and select national laws (as opposed to commercial, transnational law or fairness norms) to govern their disputes. The emphasis the parties put on legally qualified arbitrators and counsel has assisted in creating an image that the symbolic capital in the field is to be derived from professionalism in the law. As such, to meet the parties' expectations, arbitrators, whether veterans or newcomers, strive to build their symbolic capital by gaining qualifications in law and arbitration and publishing scholarly articles and textbooks related to international arbitration, commercial law, and construction law.

International arbitration institutions (e.g., ICC, LCIA) also play a role in underpinning the legal model of arbitral decision-making through their own arbitration rules. Similarly,

UNCITRAL publishes arbitration rules and the Model Law, which has inspired a large number of national arbitration legislations. These arbitration rules and laws, which appear to have a significant impact on arbitration practice and scholarship, are intended to govern the arbitration process, including the decision-making on the substance of disputes. Although these arbitration rules and laws do not require arbitrators to have legal training or qualification, they prescribe that arbitrators shall apply the rules of law designated by the parties.

However, the international arbitration system has one important caveat that renders these prescribed rules of arbitral decision-making vulnerable to neglect and subjects 'arbitral decision-making' to the social forces in the field. When arbitrators give their award, the winning party may need to enforce the award in a jurisdiction where the losing party has assets. At the award enforcement stage, the role of national courts in influencing arbitral decision-making comes into play. Almost all national courts relinquish their control of arbitrators' decisions on the merits. They do not review or scrutinise arbitrators' judgements to make sure that they comply with the decision-making rules prescribed in the arbitration rules and laws. This loophole makes international arbitration an 'open loop' system that is incapable of systemically controlling the decision-making process.

Two implications flow from this 'defect' in the international arbitration system. First, the lack of a supervisory regime of arbitrators' adherence to the rules of decision-making renders the seriousness or effectiveness of these rules questionable. The gap in the system (although admittedly is in itself a deliberate choice as a result of a necessary compromise between two incompatible goals: finality and accuracy) indicates that legal accuracy is not the top priority of the international arbitration system. At least, what is certain is that accuracy is inferior to finality. Second, the gap in the system exposes arbitral decision-making, as a product of social construction, to the social forces in the field.

Three social forces have caused, and still cause, a considerable modification to the legal model that would otherwise be similar to the one generally applied in the context of national judiciaries.

First, the tension between arbitrators and parties over the extent of influence of party autonomy comprises an ongoing struggle between two diametrically opposite ideologies. The tension concerns, amongst other things, the arbitrators' power to apply the law, including mandatory rules of the substantive law, regardless of contrary submissions by the parties. The outcome of this struggle will determine the shape of the legal model applied in international arbitration and how far it can get from the judicial decision-making legal model applied in national courts.

Second, there are social forces pushing for a commercial modification of the legal model. The arbitration rules and laws themselves direct arbitrators to take a leap forward towards the commercial model of arbitral decision-making by requiring them to take customs and usages into consideration. Arbitrators, including those from the legal profession, show varying degrees of enthusiasm towards the commercial model. Arbitrators who are construction practitioners are by nature disposed towards construction commercial practice and common-sense rather than legal analysis. These arbitrators, however, are relatively few in number and appear to have less social capital and leverage to significantly influence the 'rules of the game'.

Third, a significant constituent of the entire social struggle in the field concerns the process of transformation of the legal model from its national origin to a transnational version. A group of construction arbitration technocrats, including arbitrators, counsel, and experts from developed legal jurisdictions, are leading this process of transformation, which primarily draws on the developed jurisdictions' construction law and is assisted by the widespread application of FIDIC conditions of contract in international construction projects. Although the 'objective' existence of ICL and the scope of its application remain unsettled, the 'transnationalists' appear to have succeeded in modifying the legal model by sometimes relying on principles of ICL rather than substantive law in matters of contract interpretation and supplementation.

In recognition of the effect of these social forces, this book argues that arbitrators tend to follow a 'transnational legal' model of arbitral decision-making rather than a pure 'legal' model. The choice of this terminology delineates the two main characteristics or pillars of arbitral decision-making in international construction disputes (i.e., a legal model but modified for transnational application). It also emphasises the important difference between the legal model of decision-making followed by judges and the transnational legal model followed by international arbitrators in order to avoid any confusion or misconception that both are identical.

Nevertheless, it is worth noting that the social struggle and competition in the field are unfinished. The social reality of arbitral decision-making constructed in this book is not static or timeless. Rather, it is dynamic and may change from one era to another. As such, there is no guarantee or assurance that the balance of social forces may not shift towards a commercial model according to which the parties prefer construction professionals to arbitrate their disputes on the basis of commercial norms: something similar to commercial arbitration in mediaeval times. Although this statement might sound inconceivable or even radical now, it is possible.

9.4 The book's contribution to theory and practice

9.4.1 Implications for theory and contribution to knowledge

This book starts with documenting the lack of knowledge concerning how international arbitrators reach their decisions and cites a number of scholars and practitioners who voiced the pressing need to provide empirical insight into the secretive and opaque process of arbitral decision-making. Then, it demonstrates that little theoretical progress has been made to respond to this intellectual and practical need.

This book is a timely response to the increasing demand for such empirical knowledge. It presents the first empirical account of decision-making in international construction arbitration. As such, hopefully, this work can bring about a paradigm shift in an area that until now has relied on a non-empirical approximation of reality.

Also, this book draws on a methodological solution that has received little attention in the empirical literature. It contributes to an empirical understanding of arbitral decision-making from a social constructionist perspective. This study finds that the handful of research studies undertaken to investigate arbitral decision-making, whether in the domestic or in the international context, significantly depend on positivistic quantitative approaches. These quantitative studies appear overly simplistic and thereby unable to cope with the inherently complex nature of arbitral decision-making. In addition, they suffer from methodological flaws.

The experimental studies, for instance, examine a single variable, such as the consistency of arbitrators' decisions or the relationship between arbitrators' decisions and their backgrounds. Also, these studies depend on simple dispute scenarios that do not reflect the real-world complexity of construction disputes.

The questionnaire surveys are also inadequate to address the intellectual desire to understand the complex phenomenon of arbitral decision-making. They lack deep descriptions and explanations. They do not give respondents an opportunity to express their own views. Rather, they rely on simple data collection questions in the form of Yes/No closed questions or the Likert scale, which force respondents to choose from predetermined fixed answers. The utility of reducing arbitral decision-making into a simple check-the-box exercise or rating exercise is deeply questioned. In fact, empirical data from the interviews undertaken in the research underpinning this book illustrate that the positivist approach is unable to provide plausible descriptions and explanations of arbitral decision-making.

The main theoretical contributions of this book are outlined below:

1. This book provides the first review that synthesises both theoretical and empirical literature related to decision-making in international construction arbitration. The review demonstrates that arbitral decision-making in international construction disputes lacks theoretical and empirical foundations.
2. This book provides fresh insight into the tension between the principle of party autonomy and competing principles, such as arbitrators' perceived duties and self-interest in properly applying the law, including its mandatory provisions, in a manner that is at least similar, if not identical, to that of a judge.
3. This book sheds some light on how arbitrators decide when the law is silent or incomplete: a topic that is largely ignored in arbitration scholarship.
4. The extant literature generally makes a simplistic either-or representation of arbitral decision-making. According to this dichotomous conceptualisation, commercial interpretation and legal interpretation are mutually exclusive. This book challenges this dichotomy and puts forward an alternative construction that does not necessarily consider commercial reasonableness to be the antithesis of the law.
5. This book contributes to the debate concerning the role of customs and trade usages in arbitral decision-making. It provides an empirical insight into how arbitrators construe the requirement expressed in various arbitration rules and laws to take trade usages into consideration and how arbitrators apply customs and usages in international construction arbitration practice.
6. This book constructs the notion of international construction law. There is one theoretical attempt that conceptualises ICL as an objective and codified list of principles and, accordingly, proposes a number of principles constituting ICL. This book argues that ICL is a 'method' to find a reasonable and sensible solution in case the parties' contract and the governing law do not provide for such a solution.
7. This book challenges views expressed in both the non-empirical and the thin empirical literature that arbitrators at least sometimes decide according to what they believe is fair and equitable in the circumstance regardless of the contract and law provisions.
8. This book provides new insight into the effect of foreign mandatory law on international arbitrators' decisions on the substance of the parties' dispute. This area is

dominated by theoretical work and legal analyses. There is little attempt to unearth how international arbitrators deal with this issue in practice.

9. This book offers rare insight into the effect of arbitrators' backgrounds on introducing bias into their decisions. The problem of bias in international construction or commercial arbitration is not fully understood. There are only a few attempts, mostly quantitative, that focus on psychological factors. Arbitrators rarely, if ever, admit in public that they are affected by preconceptions or predispositions. This book illustrates, using arbitrators' accounts, that some international arbitrators, to varying degrees, are influenced by their professional affiliation and legal tradition, and they may lean towards the party that appointed them in certain cases.

Overall, this book has contributed to a better understanding of how arbitrators make their decisions on the substance of international construction disputes. It provides the first comprehensive descriptive and explanatory framework on decision-making in international construction arbitration from a social constructionist perspective. It emphasises the nature of arbitral decision-making as a socially constructed reality that is progressive and dynamic and dependable on time and space.

9.4.2 Implications for practice

Exploring the decision-making process of international construction arbitrators is not just an academic exercise. A better understanding of this phenomenon may well have practical implications for a number of stakeholders, including the parties and their lawyers, arbitrators, policymakers, and academics.

A deeper understanding of how arbitrators make their decisions may have practical implications for parties to international construction contracts in informing the design of their dispute-resolution strategy. A greater understanding of arbitral decision-making also helps the parties and their lawyers to form a better assessment of the strength of a case and a more realistic expectation of the outcome of the dispute. If the parties knew, or could reasonably predict, the result of the dispute, then the parties would resolve the dispute to the predictable resolution. Typically, when the parties believe the dispute is unpredictable and uncertain, they will seek a third party to provide the resolution. Thus, an informed assessment of the merits of the parties' claims affects their *ex-post* choice of whether to pursue arbitration or to opt for other channels of dispute resolution. This choice is important because, amongst other things, construction arbitration is an adversarial and confrontational dispute resolution technique, and, thereby, a decision to arbitrate holds recognition of the potential negative consequences on the commercial or business relationship between the parties to the dispute. In addition, understanding the decision-making patterns of construction arbitrators and the subtle relations between arbitrators' backgrounds and their decisions may affect the disputants' choice of prospective arbitrators.

Further, an empirical understanding of arbitral decision-making is useful for the arbitrators themselves. Although they are insiders, arbitrators' knowledge is normally limited to anecdotes from their inner circle or their own individual experiences. Their experiences could be atypical or typical but certainly non-representative of the holistic practice. For example, while discussing some aspects of arbitral decision-making with a Canadian international arbitrator interviewed by the author, he stated: 'the big problem of arbitration is that there is no appeal except in some limited grounds and hence it is hard to know what really is going on'. Therefore, arbitrators will benefit from a broader understanding of the general picture that pieces together the scattered individual experiences and their position in it. Also, it encourages more discussion that promotes consistency between individual approaches.

Furthermore, better knowledge is beneficial for policymakers at the national and international levels who can draft rules and statutes on better information.

Academics can benefit from this work by undertaking further research for the purpose of refining, extending, or testing its findings and using them for educational purposes.

9.5 Limitations

This book draws on the author's research during and after his doctorate. Each research undertaking has its own limitations. This research has a number of limitations that merit discussion.

This book largely relies on semi-structured interview data. The interview method is the best choice for collecting the data required to answer the questions that this book aims to answer because, unlike arbitral awards, it gives the author direct access to arbitrators' minds and provides an opportunity to explore a wide range of situations. However, the interview method has limitations. First, it provides access to parts of the reality that the interviewees desire to reveal. Second, what the interviewees reveal is processed through an interpretive process, involving both the interviewee and the interviewer, that could lead to alterations of meanings. Third, eliciting data depends on the interviewees' recall, which is subject to memory distortion and recall bias. Fourth, some accounts were low on specifics due to the nature of arbitral decision-making being fact sensitive. Accordingly, the result of relying on interview data is a social construction that is at best an approximation of reality.

This book also made use of arbitral awards. Unlike interviews, arbitration awards give evidence of what arbitrators actually do as opposed to what they say they do. Arbitration awards, however, are largely unpublished and inaccessible. The small number of published awards tends to be, in most, in a summarised form. Therefore, any conclusions or inferences drawn on this incomplete evidence base will be tentative at best.

Another limitation concerns the generalisability of the book's findings and arguments. This book does not purport to be representative of the entirety of international construction arbitration practice. The generalisation from a sample to the entire population is neither possible nor important in interpretive research. Instead, the object here is to capture a deeper understanding of arbitral decision-making rather than seek generalisable findings.

In addition, this book does not provide quantification or probability statements, but mere possibilities. Its approach is qualitative and not quantitative in nature. If follows that it falls short in measuring the actual or approximate impact or effect of different norms on the arbitration outcomes or how often arbitrators resort to these norms. As such, this book does not provide knowledge regarding, for example, how often arbitrators apply commercial norms in preference to norms of the substantive law. Similarly, this book gives no account of how often arbitrators resort to transnational norms in matters of contract interpretation or gap-filling.

It is highly doubtful that any study, even quantitative surveys, can provide representative results or statistics on the frequency of certain arbitral decisions. Leaving aside the cost and time restraints to undertake such an ambitious worldwide enquiry, the impossibility to generate representative statistics is simply a result of the arbitration's privacy. The actual number of arbitration cases (institutional as well as ad hoc arbitration cases) or active arbitrators is unknown, making it impossible to claim statistically representative results. This gets more complicated with the confidential nature of arbitration that prevents the publication of awards.

The sample of 28 international arbitrators interviewed by the author is not large. However, the governing criterion in qualitative research is reaching theoretical saturation and not reaching a predetermined sample size as is the case in quantitative research.

9.6 References

Bourdieu, P. (1977). *Outline of a Theory of Practice*. Cambridge: Cambridge University Press.

Bourdieu, P. (1986). The force of law: Toward a sociology of the juridical field. *Hastings Law Journal*, 38(5), 805.

Bourdieu, P. & Wacquant, L. J. (1992). *An Invitation to Reflexive Sociology*. Chicago: University of Chicago Press.

Dezalay, Y. & Garth, B. G. (1998). *Dealing in Virtue: International Commercial Arbitration and the Construction of a Transnational Legal Order*. Chicago: University of Chicago Press.

APPENDIX A

Semi-structured interview template

This is a template that was used for each interview. It is only a template; not all of these questions were necessarily asked, nor phrased the same way or asked in the same order in every interview. Further questions emerged during the conduct of the interviews.

General questions

1. Tell me about yourself: your main professional education and experience and particularly that related to construction arbitration.
2. What are the main types of disputes you encounter in construction arbitration?

Arbitration philosophy

How do you see your role as an arbitrator? Do you see your role in deciding the merits of construction disputes as roughly the same or different from the role or practice of national courts?

Construction arbitration decision-making

1. How do construction arbitrators decide on construction disputes? Based on what? What are the factors that influence or shape their decisions?
2. Does the applicable/substantive/governing law influence the outcome of the arbitral award? Do you apply the law in a strict/formalist way or in a liberal way that seeks a commercially reasonable/equitable/fair outcome?
3. While making decisions, do you have any hierarchy in mind between the applicable law, contract, customs/norms, and equity/fairness?
4. How do instructions to follow equity, contract or law, just and equitable, commercially reasonable, standards of fairness, *amiable compositeur/Ex aequo et bono* influence the award? What is your definition of those?
5. Do you apply the contract strictly? What about time-bar clauses/notice provisions, liquidated damages, and limitation/exclusion liability clauses?
6. How do you ascertain the content of the applicable law, how do you find the facts, and how do you determine liability?
7. How do you describe and visualise your role: passive or active, adversarial or inquisitorial?

8. How do you determine the admissibility and relevance of factual evidence? How do you assess and give weight to factual evidence (oral/documentary) and expert evidence? Do you have any rules of thumb?
9. What is the most difficult part of decision-making?
10. Do you think there will be a difference between engineer/contractor/lawyer arbitrators in decision-making (facts, laws, damages)? Is there a difference in their approach? How does your professional background assist you in viewing the evidence/facts and in making decisions on liabilities? Does the arbitrator's background (engineer vs. contractor vs. lawyer) influence their award according to their perception of fairness?

Approach to incomplete contracts

1. What is your approach in the interpretation of contract, i.e., objective vs. subjective interpretation?
2. How do construction arbitrators decide on disputes related to deficient contracts, i.e., the contract is silent on the substance of the dispute? In a similar vein, what do you do when the applicable law is silent on the substance of the dispute?

APPENDIX B

The profiles of the international arbitrators interviewed in this book

No.	Nationality	Experience in dispute resolution	Experience in litigation and/or business	Education (Academic Background)	Age	Titles and memberships
1	Canada	He sits as an arbitrator, adjudicator, and mediator. He has been involved as counsel and arbitrator in around 80 domestic and international construction arbitrations under various institutional rules (ICC, UNCITRAL) in addition to ad hoc arbitrations	He has 40 years of experience in the legal field as an advocate and senior partner. His practice is focused on construction, infrastructure and energy disputes	Law degrees from Canada	65	• Chartered Arbitrator • Fellow, International Academy of Construction Lawyers • Professor of law • Author and co-author of several books and articles on construction law and dispute resolution
2	United Kingdom	He sits as an arbitrator, adjudicator, mediator, and expert witness. He has participated in a handful of construction arbitrations	Although legally qualified, he has not practised law as a barrister or a solicitor. He has more than 40 years of experience in the engineering and construction industry in various roles, including commercial lawyer, claims consultant, commercial manager, and commercial director	Law degree from England	70	• Visiting lecturer on contracts and law • An author of one of the United Kingdom's widespread standard forms of engineering contract

(Continued)

No.	Nationality	Experience in dispute resolution	Experience in litigation and/or business	Education (Academic Background)	Age	Titles and memberships
3	United Kingdom	He has been involved as counsel and arbitrator (chairman, party-appointed arbitrator, and sole arbitrator) in almost 100 international arbitrations, mostly related to construction, infrastructure, and energy sectors and under various jurisdictions and arbitration rules (ICC, LCIA, DIAC, and UNCITRAL)	He has 40 years of experience as an international lawyer specialised in offshore litigation and international arbitration of commercial disputes, particularly construction and energy disputes	Law degree from England	65	• Queen Counsel • Chartered Arbitrator • Deputy Judge of Technology and Construction Court • Visiting lecturer on construction law • Co-authors of chapters on construction law and arbitration • Draughtsman of arbitration rules of three arbitral institutions and arbitration law of one legal jurisdiction
4	United Kingdom	He sits as an arbitrator, mediator, and expert determiner. He has arbitrated around 10 international commercial and construction disputes	He has more than 35 years of experience in the oil and gas industry, including the construction of extremely large oil production platforms. Amongst the various posts he had, he worked as an international consultant, general manager, commercial manager, legal advisor, project manager, and cost engineer	Diploma in International Commercial Arbitration	65	• Chartered Arbitrator • Author of numerous articles and books on arbitration and dispute resolution • Contributor to the drafting of an arbitration act of a European jurisdiction • Visiting lecturer
5	Canada	He sits as mediator and arbitrator. He acted as counsel and arbitrator in several national arbitrations, and only a handful of international arbitrations	He has extensive experience extending over four decades in court litigation as counsel in Canada. His practice is focused on commercial and construction disputes.	Law degrees from Canada and England	65	• Queen Counsel • Fellow, CIArb • Visiting lecturer • Author of construction law treaty and articles
6	Canada	He has participated mainly as a counsel in a handful of construction arbitrations	He has 12 years of experience in construction litigation and construction arbitration	Law degree from Canada	38	• Managing partner at a law firm • Author of a number of articles on construction law • Lecturer at a Canadian LLM course on construction law

7	Ireland	He sits as an arbitrator, adjudicator, mediator, and expert witness. He arbitrated five international construction arbitrations under UK and European jurisdictions	He has significant experience as an engineer and a contractor/business owner in the UK construction industry	B.Sc. in building engineering and a postgraduate diploma in international commercial arbitration	60	• Chartered Arbitrator • Mechanical Engineer • Building Services Engineer • Author of a book and articles on construction dispute resolution
8	United Kingdom	He has been primarily involved as counsel in a handful of construction arbitrations under ICC, DIAC, and QICCA arbitration rules besides ad hoc arbitrations	He has 15 years of experience in litigation and arbitration as a commercial litigator and counsel in Ireland and the Arab Gulf region	Law degrees from Ireland	36	• A managing associate of a multinational law firm practice
9	Lebanon	He has been involved as counsel, expert, arbitrator (co-arbitrator and sole arbitrator) in almost 45 international arbitrations, half of them relate to construction, under various jurisdictions (European and Arab jurisdictions) and arbitration rules (ICC, CRCICA, QICCA, and UNCITRAL). He also sits as a domestic arbitrator in Lebanon	Senior partner and commercial litigator in Paris, Beirut, and Dubai (DIFC), specialised in commercial cases including construction and infrastructure	Law degrees from Lebanon, France, and England	50	• Charted arbitrator • Lecturer on several legal areas, including construction law, commercial law, and contract law. • Author of several books' chapters and journal articles
10	United Kingdom	He has been involved as counsel or arbitrator in 30 international construction arbitrations, under various arbitration rules including ICC and LCIA. In addition, he acts as an adjudicator and mediator	Barrister specialised in domestic and international litigation and arbitration in construction, engineering, and technology	Law degrees from England	60	• Queen Counsel • Chartered Arbitrator • Author of books' chapters and articles
11	Denmark	He has been involved in 100+ construction arbitrations, mostly domestic and nearly all applying Danish law	A lawyer specialised in domestic and international litigation and arbitration in construction	Law degrees from Denmark	50	• Fellow, CIArb • Senior partner • Lecture on construction law • Author of a number of books and articles on construction law

(Continued)

No.	Nationality	Experience in dispute resolution	Experience in litigation and/or business	Education (Academic Background)	Age	Titles and memberships
12	Australia	He acts as expert witness, expert determiner, adjudicator and arbitrator. He had several adjudications, domestic arbitrations, and expert determinations. He has been involved in a handful of international construction arbitrations and adjudications (DAB). His experience is limited to construction, not general commercial, and to common law jurisdictions	Qualified as a lawyer after 30 years of engineering career, with a focus on construction law. He worked as a design engineer and consultant for over 30 years, with no construction site experience	Engineering and law degrees from Australia	70	• Fellow, CIArb • Accredited FIDIC Trainer • Author of books on construction contracts and law, and numerous articles
13	Canada	He sits as an arbitrator and mediator in commercial, technology, and construction disputes. He has acted as a counsel and arbitrator (chair, sole arbitrator, co-arbitrator) in 15+ international arbitrations, all applied common law	His experience, as a counsel and a partner of a law firm, extends to more than 40 years of experience in various sectors, including technology and construction. He is also a Commercial Court Judge in the Supreme Court of a common law jurisdiction	Law and business degrees from Canada. Diploma in International Arbitration	70	• Fellow, CIArb
14	Canada	She sits as an arbitrator (chair, co-arbitrator, sole arbitrator) and mediator in commercial, technology, and construction disputes. She has arbitrated 100+ disputes extending over many common law and civil law jurisdictions under ICC, UNCITRAL, DIAC, and HKIAC rules	Her practice is limited to arbitration and ADR. Recently joined the business world as a business owner	Law degrees from Canada and France	66	• Chartered arbitrator • Lecturer on international, commercial, and construction law in many countries e.g., UK, USA, Canada • Author of many articles on international arbitration

15	Australia	She sits as an arbitrator and mediator in commercial and construction disputes. She has acted as a counsel and arbitrator in 100+ international construction arbitrations in a number of jurisdictions, including England, Europe, Australia, Singapore, Hong Kong, Malaysia, and the Asia-Pacific region	She is a commercial and construction lawyer with more than 25 years of experience.	Law degrees from England and Australia, Diploma in International Commercial Arbitration	50	• Fellow, CIArb • Accredited Mediator • Lecturer on international commercial and construction arbitration • Author of many articles on international arbitration
16	United States	He sits as an arbitrator and mediator in national and international construction disputes. He has acted as a counsel and arbitrator in 20+ international construction arbitrations in a number of jurisdictions, including Europe, Korea, Guam, Afghanistan, and South America	He worked as a contracts officer, litigator, and counsel for 40 years	Law degrees from the United States	65	• Construction lawyer • Lecturer on construction contracts and law • Author of a number of articles and books on construction law
17	Egypt	He acted as an arbitrator (co-arbitrator and presiding arbitrator) in 5+ international construction arbitrations in Arab jurisdictions	He has more than 35 years of experience in the legal field as a judge at the Court of Appeal and a legal advisor to a number of states' entities and multinational corporations	Law degrees from Egypt and England	55	• Fellow CIArb • Lecturer on international commercial contracts and arbitration • Author of many articles on international arbitration
18	Egypt	He has been involved in 80+ international arbitrations, including 20+ international construction arbitrations in four different capacities; counsel, expert witness, and arbitrator	He has more than 60 years of experience in the legal field as a senior partner and legal advisor for a number of multilateral development banks, UN bodies, and state entities	Law degrees from Egypt and France	85	• Professor of international law at a number of universities • Former Judge at the International Court of Justice • Vice president of the ICC's Court of Arbitration • Author of several publications on international law and arbitration

(*Continued*)

No.	Nationality	Experience in dispute resolution	Experience in litigation and/or business	Education (Academic Background)	Age	Titles and memberships
19	Egypt	He is specialised in commercial, technology, and construction disputes. He has acted as a counsel and arbitrator (chair, sole arbitrator, co-arbitrator) in around 100 international commercial arbitrations, including 30+ international construction arbitrations	He has 35 years of experience in the legal field as a lawyer, in-house counsel, and managing partner of a law firm	Law degrees from England and Canada as well as engineering and business degrees from Egypt	60	• Fellow CIArb • Author of a number of articles on international arbitration
20	United Kingdom (based in UAE)	He has been involved as counsel, expert, and arbitrator in almost 45 international construction arbitrations, under various jurisdictions (England and Arab jurisdictions) and arbitration rules (ICC, DIAC, DIFC-LCIA, QICCA, and UNCITRAL)	He has 25 years of experience in construction law as an in-house counsel, barrister, and arbitrator	Quantity surveying and law degrees from England	55	• Fellow CIArb • Fellow Architects and Surveyors Institute
21	United States	He is a full-time arbitrator and mediator of engineering and construction disputes. He acted as an arbitrator or counsel in 100+ construction arbitrations in a number of jurisdictions including the United States, the Middle East, Iraq, Afghanistan, and China	He has 40 years of experience in the private practice of law as an associate, partner, and senior partner. He is specialised in construction law	Law and business degrees from the USA	80	• Chartered Arbitrator • Fellow of the International Academy of Construction Lawyers • Fellow of the College of Commercial Arbitrators • Fellow of the National Contract Management Association • Author of several publications on construction dispute resolution • Lecturer on construction law and international construction arbitration at various universities

22	Palestine (based in UAE)	He sits as an arbitrator, adjudicator, and mediator and gives expert opinions. He has arbitrated (as chairman, co-arbitrator, and sole arbitrator) around 55 national and international construction disputes under DIAC, ADCCAC, and UNCITRAL arbitration rules	He has more than 40 years of experience in the UAE construction industry's contracting and consultancy. He worked in different positions, such as site/project engineer, technical manager, contracts manager, and claims consultant	BSc, Civil and Structural Engineering, UK	65	• MCIArb • • Lecturer and trainer on construction contracts, construction law, and dispute resolution
23	United States/ Greece	He has been involved as counsel in several construction arbitrations under ICC, ICSID, UNCITRAL, and SCC arbitration rules besides ad-hoc arbitrations	He has 15 years of experience in commercial, investment, and maritime arbitrations	Law degrees from the United States	36	• Lecturer on international commercial contracts and arbitration • Author of many articles on international arbitration
24	Switzerland	He has acted as counsel and arbitrator (chairman, party-appointed arbitrator, and sole arbitrator) in over 200 international arbitrations and under various jurisdictions mostly related to telecommunications, construction, infrastructure and energy sectors, and arbitration rules (ICC, LCIA, SIAC, AAA/ICDR, and UNCITRAL)	He has 30 years of experience in the legal field as a senior partner at a leading Swiss law firm, counsel, and international arbitrator. His practice is focused on telecommunications, construction, infrastructure, and energy disputes	Law degrees from Switzerland and the United States	54	• Lecturer on international commercial contracts and arbitration • Former president of the Swiss Arbitration Centre • Former court member of the ICC International Court of Arbitration
25	Switzerland	He has acted as counsel and arbitrator (chairman, party-appointed arbitrator, and sole arbitrator) in over 100 international arbitrations and under various jurisdictions mostly related to construction, infrastructure and pharmaceutical sectors and arbitration rules (ICC, LCIA, and UNCITRAL).	He has 35 years of experience in international arbitration and litigation.	Law degrees from Switzerland and the United States	60	• Lecturer on international commercial contracts and arbitration • Vice President of the ICC Court of Arbitration

(Continued)

No.	Nationality	Experience in dispute resolution	Experience in litigation and/or business	Education (Academic Background)	Age	Titles and memberships
26	Switzerland	He has acted as counsel and arbitrator (chairman, party-appointed arbitrator, and sole arbitrator) in over 250 international arbitrations involving the national law of 30+ countries, mostly related to construction and pharmaceutical sectors and under various arbitration rules (ICC, DIAC, ICSID, Swiss Rules, SIAC, SCC etc.)	He has 45 years of experience in the legal field as a senior partner at a leading Swiss law firm, counsel, and international arbitrator	Law degrees from Switzerland and England	70	• PhD in law • Lecturer on international commercial contracts and arbitration • Author of numerous books, book chapters, and articles on international commercial contracts and arbitration
27	Switzerland	He has acted as counsel and arbitrator (chairman, party-appointed arbitrator, and sole arbitrator) in over 120 international arbitrations under various arbitration rules	He has 25 years of experience in the legal field as a partner at a leading Swiss law firm, counsel and international arbitrator. His practice is focused on construction, engineering, consultancy, energy and joint venture agreement disputes	Law degrees from Switzerland	48	• Former President of the Swiss Arbitration Association • Author of several publications on international arbitration and private international law
28	Germany	He has acted as counsel and arbitrator (chairman, party-appointed arbitrator, and sole arbitrator) in several international commercial and investment arbitrations under various arbitration rules (ICC, DIS, SCC, UNCITRAL, ICSID, etc.)	He has 15 years of experience in the legal field. His practice is focused on international litigation and arbitration of construction, engineering, energy, joint venture, distribution, and insurance disputes	Law degrees from Germany	37	• PhD in law

APPENDIX C: LIST OF ARBITRATION CASES

A list of the international construction and commercial arbitration awards cited in this book

ICC	Reference	Chapter
ICC Case No. 4629/1989	ICCA Yearbook Commercial Arbitration (1993)	3
ICC Case No. 6230/1990	ICCA Yearbook Commercial Arbitration (1992)	3
ICC Case No. 7528/1993	ICCA Yearbook Commercial Arbitration (1997)	3
ICC Case No 12745/2010	Karton (2013); ICCA Yearbook Commercial Arbitration (2010)	3
ICC Case No. 6257	Gaillard and Savage (1999)	3
ICC Case No. 6136	Gaillard and Savage (1999)	3
ICC Case No. 9443/1998	Karton (2013)	4
ICC Case No. 7063/1993	Karton (2013); ICCA Yearbook Commercial Arbitration (1997)	4
ICC Case No. 3820/1981	Karton (2013); ICCA Yearbook Commercial Arbitration (1982)	4
ICC Case No. 5713/1989	Teramura (2020); ICCA Yearbook Commercial Arbitration (1990)	4
ICC Case No. 7710/1995	Teramura (2020)	4
ICC Case No. 8502/1996	Teramura (2020); ICC International Court of Arbitration Bulletin, Vol. 10, No. 2 (1999)	4
ICC Case No. 11320/2001	Teramura (2020)	4
ICC Case No. 10022/2001	Teramura (2020); ICC International Court of Arbitration Bulletin Vol. 12 No. 2 (2001)	4
ICC Case No. 12226/2004	Teramura (2020)	4
ICC Case No. 13919/2007	Teramura (2020)	4
ICC Case No. 9029/1999	Teramura (2020); ICC International Court of Arbitration Bulletin Vol. 10 No. 2 (1999)	4
ICC Case No. 11256/2003	Teramura (2020)	4
ICC Case No. 6197/1995	Karton (2013); ICCA Yearbook Commercial Arbitration (1998)	5
ICC Case No. 3267/1984	Karton (2013); ICCA Yearbook Commercial Arbitration (1987)	5, 6
ICC Case No. 1784/1975	Karton (2013); ICCA Yearbook Commercial Arbitration (1977)	5
ICC Case No. 5029/1986	ICCA Yearbook Commercial Arbitration (1987)	5

(*Continued*)

ICC	Reference	Chapter
ICC Case No. 14392/2009	Jolivet et al., 2016 (Unpublished)	5
ICC Case No. 8873/1997	Seppala (1998)	5
ICC Case No. 12048/2004	Seppala (2012)	5
ICC Cases No. 3790/3902/4050/4051/4054 (joined cases)	Seppala (2012)	5
ICC Case No. 5277/1987	ICCA Yearbook Commercial Arbitration (1988)	5
ICC Case No. 5428/1988	ICCA Yearbook Commercial Arbitration (1989)	5
ICC Case No. 15956/2010	Corbett (2017)	5
ICC Case No. 15282 /2010	ICC International Court of Arbitration Bulletin Vol. 24 No. 2. (2010)	5
ICC Case No. 7641/1996	Seppala (1998)	5
ICC Case No. 5948/1991	Seppala (1998)	5
ICC Case No. 11813/2002	Seppala (2013)	5
ICC Case No. 12654/2005	Seppala (2012)	5
ICC Case No. 10847/2003	Seppala (2012)	5
ICC Case No. 8873/1997	Karton (2013)	5
CRCICA Case No. 175/2000	Alam Eldin (2014)	5
CRCICA Case No. 310/2002	Alam Eldin (2010)	5
ICC Case No. 7986/1999	Teramura (2020)	6
ICC Case No. 10728/2001	Teramura (2020)	6
ICC Case No. 3938/1982	Gaillard and Savage (1999)	6
ICC Case No. 3540/1980	ICCA Yearbook Commercial Arbitration (1982)	6
ICC Case No. 5946/1990	ICCA Yearbook Commercial Arbitration (1991)	7
ICC Case No. 1399/1967	Shehata (2017)	7
ICC Case No. 8528/1996	ICCA Yearbook Commercial Arbitration (2000)	7
ICC Case No. 6320/1992	ICCA Yearbook Commercial Arbitration (1995)	7
ICC Case No. 2977/1978, 2978/1978, and 3033/1978 (joint cases)	ICCA Yearbook Commercial Arbitration (1981)	7
ICC Case No. 15977/2010	Shehata (2017); ICC Dispute Resolution Bulletin 2016, No. 1	7
ICC Case No. 1110/1963	Shehata (2017)	7
ICC Case No. 3916/1982	Shehata (2017)	7

INDEX